America's Wealth

America's Wealth

the economic history of an open society

BY PETER d'A. JONES

The Macmillan Company, New York
Collier-Macmillan Ltd., London

To *"Alf and Madge"*

First Printing

The Macmillan Company, New York
Collier-Macmillan Canada Ltd., Galt, Ontario
Divisions of The Crowell-Collier Publishing Company

Printed in the United States of America

Library of Congress catalogue card number: 63-10662

DESIGNED BY AMJAD N. QURESHI

Contents

Preface

To "explain" America's wealth is not easy. If Providential explanations were still the vogue, as in less secular ages, one could say that God chose the environment, and then chose the people to fill it; national growth came from the creative interaction of these two elements. William Stoughton, for instance, a later Lieutenant Governor of Massachusetts and chief justice of the Salem witch trials of 1692, announced with conviction in 1668, "God hath sifted a nation, that he might send choice grain into this wilderness." Stoughton's view of migration has certain charm, though its acceptance as a theory would not lead to a condition of full employment among economists.

Modern curiosity seeks the satisfaction of mechanistic explanations, the "underlying structure" of a story, the principles of historical growth. Of all the types of historical writing, the economic variety, with its hard core of workable economic theory, should be in a position to meet this modern taste. In fact, however, until recent years historians of the United States have tended to ignore the findings of economics, and in the interim the economists themselves have been contributing historical insights of great value through the application of more or less elementary theory to history. It would be a shame if economic history became a minor subdivision of economic science (called perhaps "institutionalism"?), for the discipline has a quality and a character of its own. What the economist seeks in history he may legitimately take, and few if any economists would deny that "economic growth" is not the whole of economic history. On the other hand the economic historian is less a technician or grand theorist concerned with the scientific structure of economics than a humanistic scholar interested in the economic machinery of the American people as a foundation for and an expression of the civilization of the United States.

In this interpretation of the history of America's wealth, I have used the vocabulary and adopted the attitude of the economist wherever it seemed appropriate. But I hope the reader will find in these pages, among whatever shortcomings there may be, a sustained sense that the book's ultimate concern lies in the American people, and not merely in the glamour of their wealth.

Acknowledgments

Like most authors, I owe a great deal to colleagues and to friends inside and outside the academic profession. The influences upon a person's thinking are hard to define, and I hope that people unmentioned will accept my collective thanks.

More specifically, I want to thank my Smith College colleagues for intellectual sustenance that has carried me further along the road toward what I hope is a better understanding of the United States. The manuscript was read and criticized by: Daniel Aaron, Stanley Elkins, Seymour Goodman, Arthur Mann, Ramón Eduardo Ruiz, and Massimo Salvadori. Others who read parts of the book in an earlier stage include Marcus Cunliffe and Donald Sheehan. I am grateful for the advice and opinions of readers but of course remain responsible for all that the book contains.

For having first introduced me to the United States by way of New Orleans in 1959, my thanks are due to Tulane University, especially the members of its Department of Economics, among whom Clarence Danhof (now of the Brookings Institution), steered me to useful reading matter and Seymour Goodman made me more aware of economic theory. Two Smith students gave valuable secretarial help: Miss Hiroko Watanabe of Japan and Miss Lile Rasmuson of Alaska, and a third, Miss Florence Bryan, of Virginia, helped with the index.

July, 1962
Northampton
Massachusetts

1 COLONY AND NATION
to 1790

Colonial America:
The Economics of Dependency

Few nations on the face of the earth have been exposed to such continuous, searching, and relentless analysis by foreign opinion as has the United States. The American people, whether praised or condemned, feared or trusted, have been consistently anatomized. Almost two centuries of independence following on almost two centuries of colonial status have failed to diminish the enthusiasm or soften the rigors of this never-ending scrutiny. And somewhere in the background of this examination lies El Dorado, the glittering prize of the New World, the "economy of abundance," America's wealth.

Even when that wealth was only potential, its pull was magnetic. Looking backward in 1835 at precolonial America, Alexis de Tocqueville was stunned by the "inexhaustible fertility" of the great Mississippi Valley, that "most magnificent dwelling-place prepared by God for man's abode." In fact, the entire American continent "seemed prepared to be the abode of a great nation yet unborn." How that potentiality came to be realized is the subject matter of this book.

Economics of colonial America

To describe and explain how America's potential came to be realized, we have to abstract the "economic" forces from the social

totality of American civilization. The need to do this becomes obvious once we reconsider America's colonial origins. Colonial culture reveals at the briefest glance a highly complex fusion of religious faith, political conviction, economic interest, and social idealism. Yet there may be some truth in the often-made claim that the nation was "founded as a business enterprise" and that the early history of American society can be explained in terms of the given relationships among the economist's "factors of production" (physical resources, labor, and capital). Without pretending, therefore, to trace colonial historical development, let us sketch a profile of the economy before 1790.

Private business enterprise played a large part in the settlement of the Atlantic seaboard of North America in the seventeenth century, and the British government played only a small part—smaller even than that played by the governments of continental Europe in the earlier settlement of New Spain, Brazil, and New France. Virginia's colonization, for instance, was conceived in business terms —was in fact planned and executed by a joint-stock company, organized rationally as an economic enterprise for profit, a capital investment by a private corporation. Richard Hakluyt, an associate of Raleigh in the luckless Roanoke Island ventures of 1584–1587, gave his countrymen a rudimentary economic theory of colonization and had even capped this with a fairly elaborate plan of campaign. His program faced up to and calculated the heavy risks to be borne by such a large and long-term investment of men and materials. Of the two expeditions authorized by royal charter in 1606, the men who went to Jamestown succeeded where the men who tried the Maine coast failed largely because the former had superior economic organization and the financial backing of the City of London capitalists. All this is not to claim that economic motivation and organization is a full and ample "explanation" or even most of what there is to say about the early settlement of North America. Venture capital and the technique of joint-stock business enterprise take the historian only so far. What about the inspiration of Sir Thomas More's *Utopia*, for example, and the beauty of John Donne's sermons, in which England becomes a bridge or gallery joining the New and the Old World to each other and to the everlasting Kingdom of Heaven? Moreover, the whole colonial movement could take place only within a framework of expanding physical possibilities, created by the new world picture of Galileo and Copernicus and by innovations like the compass, improved cartography, and the Portuguese caravel. From the point of view of the historical evolution of America's wealth, however, the role of joint-stock business in colonial settlement is of prime significance.

A complex of forces drove men to New England's rocky shores in the 1620's; but here too their formal organization, like that of the Virginia settlers, was corporate. In the "middle colonies" even the "proprietors" of Maryland, the Carolinas, New Jersey, and Pennsylvania acted more like free-enterprising land speculators than like feudal aristocrats. In truth, colonial society rapidly developed an ethos of its own, distinct from that of the mother country—more open and flexible, favorable to swifter social change; not yet, perhaps, a business spirit, but one that did not deny individual access to strategic or desired social roles on spurious grounds of pedigree. Personal and political inclination, the Calvinist ethic, and economic necessity combined to dignify manual labor and to make commerce an honorable profession.

It was a happy combination, since the colonial economy lived through overseas trade. The pattern of this trade emerged only after trial and error, when the original high hopes of a quick profit by the discovery of precious metals had faded. Virginia colonists did send home a yellow ore, but on arrival it was analyzed as iron pyrites ("fools' gold"). The real wealth of the seaboard lay in its fertile soil, and would not yield itself up quite so readily. Experimentation revealed the true nature of the comparative advantage[1] that the colonies possessed: the economy was to be agricultural and extractive. The relationship among the factors of production was such that physical resources ("land," in the terminology of classical economics) were abundant, while the other factors in the productive process, labor and capital, were very scarce. Colonial America was short of people, short of specie (currency), and short of capital goods and consumer goods. Not only did the colonies begin as a profit-seeking investment of men and capital by Europeans in the New World; they also remained for many decades entirely dependent on the outside world for further men and women and further supplies of capital. The home government was always reluctant to export specie to the colonists; as a result there was a chronic shortage of currency throughout colonial history, and several local assemblies resorted to the great innovation of printing paper money for them-selves. The general effect of this was inflationary, but it suited the needs of debtors (frontier farmers, for instance), who would be paying back their loans in the future in a depreciated paper cur-rency. Their creditors on the seaboard—rich merchants and the like —would be losing money, and would therefore strongly oppose the issue of paper, or, indeed, any other monetary measure deemed to be inflationary.

Here we see the roots of a great economic conflict that was to continue throughout American history, and reach its climax in the 1890's, with the Bryan free-silver campaign. As for the scarcity of capital goods (and consumer goods), colonial status under mercan-tilism, whatever benefits it brought, precluded the building up of any level of native American production beyond the primary extrac-tive process, for which only elementary kinds of equipment were necessary. Even here, the better hand tools, saw blades, cutting and digging tools for clearing the wilderness, for timber conversion, and for building, would be British imports—many of them from Sheffield.

However desperate was the lack of capital, among the factors of production it was the labor shortage that presented the worst ob-stacle to colonial growth. The reason for this is fairly clear: the early stages of colonization, clearing and settlement, are very highly labor-intensive. One must think of colonial America as an "undeveloped" rather than as an "underdeveloped" economy. An underdeveloped economy (depending on its type) may or may not respond to an influx of capital; but an undeveloped area needs an initial "input" of hard labor before it is ready for capital investment.[2] This was the case, certainly, with the Atlantic-seaboard settlements: the need for labor was greater even than the need for capital. From the outset, therefore, it was the pressure of economic necessity that nurtured what the world has come to call "American ingenuity." If the United States is the home of the labor-saving device and the applied sci-ences, this is surely no accident. An important part of the colonial heritage is that (in Geoffrey Gorer's words) the American dominates his material.

The relationship among the factors of production did not operate entirely against the accumulation of wealth in the colonies. There is still the third factor to consider—physical resources. America's high living standards, in painful contrast with some less fortunate, highly populated nations, have often been attributed to the concept of a high "land-man ratio"—plentiful physical resources per head of population. (Let us say that labor must not be so scarce as to impede economic growth, but not so plentiful as to depress basic living standards.) However, in the seventeenth and eighteenth centuries, the likelihood is that abundance of land and resources retarded the growth of American towns, and ultimately delayed rather than advanced the economic development of the colonies.

This is not only because labor was scarce precisely when it was most needed. There is a more far-reaching explanation. Economic growth depends upon the degree of specialization attained by the productive members of the community ("division of labor"). But specialization, in turn, depends upon the size of the market.[3] In colonial America, domestic markets were restricted, through poor communications, great geographical distances, and lack of urbanization. (Fortunately, an ingenious pattern of international trade was invented by seafaring Yankees, which did allow some native capital to be accumulated in the colonies, as we shall examine later.) In other words the colonies could not develop the highly organized, complex society needed to support a constantly rising standard of life without a great increase in the subdivision of tasks, specialization of function—whatever one chooses to call the process. Those who specialize in order to attain higher levels of achievement must be sure of economic support—market demand. No society can support such an intricate, interdependent economic structure until it has markets of some size and dependability, which the American colonies did not possess.[4]

So the colonial land-man ratio was favorable to a system of fairly widespread property ownership (there was plenty to go around), but at first not too favorable to general economic expansion. And in any event a high land-man ratio is not an actual guarantee that economic growth and high living standards will follow. In Canada, for instance, the ratio was for many decades too high; manpower shortage delayed economic development for a much longer period than in the United States. Economic resources, however abundant they may be, have to be introduced into the market economy—as they were in the United States during the early national period—in order to produce economic growth. There was also, in the American experience, the added stimulus of a war or two. How those physical

resources were brought into full play is the real core of the answer
to the riddle of American prosperity.

Exports and the growth of American wealth

In Richard Pares's fine book *Yankees and Creoles*,[5] we see the
emergence of colonial trade by trial and error, as businessmen
sought for the English market the products of a warm climate:
sugar, silks, oils, wines. An attempt to grow tobacco in Barbados was
abandoned in favor of sugar, and the West Indies soon proved able
to produce other warm-weather staples. The southern colonies began to yield some semitropical goods; New England, none. As late
as the Treaty of Utrecht (1713), most Englishmen prized the West
Indies far more highly than the whole of British North America for
this very reason.

On the subject of America, the English ruling class showed very
little foresight. West Indian hegemony was not destined for a long
life, and the perceptive observer could have discerned the growth
of wealth among the North American colonies through area specialization—the basis of the economic sectionalism that made the Civil
War possible, but also the foundation of American economic development. A degree of specialization seems to have emerged in the
1640's: the West Indies exploited their advantage by changing over
to sugar production, precisely when a lull in New England immigration left that area with excess products and a heavy trade debt to
the home country. Logically, a pattern of intercolonial trade took
shape.

This pattern is worth examining in some detail, because its existence was of profound economic significance. Relatively poor soil
in New England supported only subsistence farming of local importance, apart from some commercial production of sheep and
cattle around Narragansett. Luxury pelts (beaver, mink, fox) traded
from the Iroquois and marketed at Albany or Philadelphia became
available for export. But the foundation of the northern economy
was pine and cod.

In an age of timber construction and timber fuel, when every
backwoods community was dominated by the whir of its picturesque
waterpowered sawmill, the large white softwood "pumpkin" pine of

Maine and New Hampshire provided a material basis of civilization. Lumber conversion as an industry also suited the needs of the colonists in a special economic way, because it took little initial outlay of capital—simply very hard work. (The importance of the reciprocating gangsaw in speeding up this strenuous, highly labor-intensive work cannot be overemphasized.) The same condition of modest capital needs was true, though to a lesser extent, of the cod fisheries organized from the ports of Boston, Salem, and Gloucester: small New England towns penetrated by country and sea, bristling with masts and spires and smelling of rum, tar, country air, and fish. In Nantucket and New Bedford, no less romantic and tangy, the whaling industry grew up a little later in the eighteenth century to supply a market for whalebone stays, perfume base, and fuel oil. The demand for whale oil for domestic lighting was certain to grow with population expansion and urbanization; but *Moby Dick* notwithstanding, the whaling industry never attained the economic significance of the cod fisheries in the regional growth of New England.

Along the middle Atlantic coast from the Hudson to the Potomac, Dutch and German immigrant farmers introduced to the relatively unsophisticated colonies an advanced European form of commercial agriculture, based on individual homestead farms, carved out of the wilderness and worked with free or indentured labor (unlike the larger slave plantations farther south, which owed their existence partly to an all-year-round working climate). These wheat farmers of New Jersey and Pennsylvania kept alive the growing communities of Philadelphia, Baltimore, and New York, and by the mid-seventeenth century could export foodstuffs to the West Indies and elsewhere.

Accordingly, the northern and middle Atlantic colonists traded foodstuffs (flour, fish, meat), cloth, and lumber to the West Indies, and received in return sugar bills of exchange that West Indian planters had earned from London or Bristol. The bills helped to pay for the manufactured goods the Americans had to import from Britain. There was also direct exportation to Britain of fish, lumber, and naval stores, although production of the latter (pitch, tar, and resin) was successfully adopted, using Negro slave labor in North Carolina. The Royal Navy was fortunate enough to be able to buy the finest ships' masts from Portsmouth, New Hampshire, and then from Portland (Maine). Indirectly, the colonists managed to add to their trade with the home country, by sailing their square-rigged, two-masted brigantines across the ocean to southern Europe, to sell high-grade fish to the Catholic nations (and the inferior sort to the West Indies for slave food), along with other foodstuffs, lumber, and furs—in return for salt, spices, citrus fruits, wines, and luxury items generally, which were then resold in Britain. So, in the absence (or in defiance) of mercantilist restrictions on freedom of colonial trade, the balance-of-payments problems of the northern and middle colonies could be to some extent solved.

This was not the sum total of colonial merchant adventuring, for there was a sizable and important trade with Africa, by way of the West Indies, whereby the North imported specie, gold, and molasses from the islands, processed the last into rum,[6] and sold it, together with certain amounts of iron and a quantity of trinkets, in West Africa in return for slaves. The human cargo then took the frightful "Middle Passage" to the West Indies.

Yankee ingenuity was less needed in the richer southern colonies, with their more favorable trading position. The tobacco cultivated in Virginia and later in North Carolina had an absolute advantage in both quality and price over all other tobacco, and as a cash crop, shipped raw to England for handling and resale at a profit, it fitted the mercantilist scheme of things perfectly. Pocahontas' husband, John Rolfe, shipped the weed home in 1614, and began a tobacco craze that led people to grow it in the very streets of Jamestown. Cheap to transport on the numerous waterways of the Chesapeake Bay country because of its high cash value in relation to its bulk, tobacco established a virtual kingdom, a one-crop system of agriculture, and supported an entire way of life. At least, a temporary pattern of life, for the monoculture of tobacco depletes the soil of its natural wealth after about seven years, and encourages constant crop migration. "Soil mining" of this sort would eventually destroy the South's comparative advantage in rich land. The five years preceding the Revolution saw the height of eighteenth century tobacco production.

Later staples to appear on the southern scene were indigo and rice. The dye indigo, introduced into Charleston, South Carolina, from Antigua in 1742, and encouraged six years later by a British government bounty, was a high-ground crop that could be cultivated in association with rice, a low-ground crop. Rice came to the same southern port, according to the legend, from Madagascar in 1694. All three staples, tobacco, indigo, and rice, used slave labor eventually. It is therefore not surprising that by about 1763, at least half the population of Virginia and two-thirds of the population of South Carolina were Negro. Dutch-German homesteads, paddy fields, tobacco plantations, sawmills, fishing ports, slave auctions, southern grandees, Yankee merchant capitalists, frontiersmen—already American society and the American landscape were beginning to reveal that rich heterogeneity, that fascinating complexity that was to be their distinctive character for many years to come.

Colonial merchants

Clearly, the southern economy had evolved along mercantilist lines to serve the mother country by providing semitropical agricultural staples and raw materials. This arrangement was not entirely to the disadvantage of the young southern colonies. In the North, the triangular trading patterns served to meet debt payments to Britain, as we have seen, and also to meet intercolonial payments arising from the complex transactions, arbitrages, and exchanges that took place among the colonists themselves. The trade was organized by an enterprising class of merchants, who performed a whole series of economic functions that, in these preindustrial days, had not yet become specialized or separated. In modest offices and with minimal clerical or accounting aids, colonial merchants handled real-estate deals; engaged in international financing, investment broking, banking, and insurance underwriting; managed rum distilleries; made loans; bought, used, and sold oceangoing vessels; bartered, stored, and bought and sold both wholesale and retail all types of products. Forever in debt to London and Bristol, and forever extending "book credit" for routine transactions at home, they circumvented the chronic shortage of capital and specie, and made it possible for the wheels of colonial economic life to turn.

Even at this early stage the businessman was already casting a dual image to the American public: envied and feared as a man of property and power, admired and imitated as an enterprising creator of wealth. Yet, in point of fact, the large mercantile houses leaned so heavily on British creditors that it was perhaps the smaller West

Indies traders who made the real independent contribution to native American capital formation. At all events, the external trade of both North and South led to a degree of capital accumulation without which there would have been no sustained later development.[7] The wealth of the American people was beginning to grow.

Homemade America

While mercantile capital was being steadily and shrewdly accrued by adventurous Yankee traders, homemade manufacturing was limited by the spirit of the self-sufficient homestead, and usufacture persisted. The industrial situation in the colonies was hardly promising at a time when Britain herself was, in W. W. Rostow's words, "taking off" into self-sustained economic growth through her eighteenth century Industrial Revolution. Apart from shipbuilding and the iron industry, most colonial needs were met by production in the home, on a part-time, unspecialized basis, and there was a widespread dependence on Europe for a whole range of consumer goods. Hard-wearing, everyday cloths were homemade (fustians and jeans—mixtures of cotton and linen or cotton and wool). Finer materials were imported. In food production, families were as independent as possible.

Town and countryside presented no sharp antithesis in this prefactory age. Townsfolk owned farms and tilled the land; no one was very far from the soil. Even the unusually advanced iron industry was rural in character. In the seventeenth century bog-ore furnaces were to be found anywhere from Massachusetts down the seaboard to New Jersey.[8] After about 1720, fairly rapid expansion took place and the industry tended to migrate, taking advantage of the Appalachian ores from New York to Virginia. Coal was not used by the American iron industry in the eighteenth century, since the abundance of timber made charcoal very cheap. Having a decided cost advantage in this respect, the colonial ironmasters multiplied their output almost fourfold between 1771 and 1775, and—very symbolically—achieved a production figure of 30,000 tons in the year of Lexington Green. Britain herself had fewer forges and furnaces at that time.[9]

Boston men had built ships as early as 1631, and the industry thrived so well, the estimate is that the Royal Navy in the War of Independence owed about one-third of its vessels to their craftsmanship. New England's shipbuilding trade was not rural, of course, but it had many rural affiliations through the lumber trade, and was hardly an "industry" in the modern sense of that word; its members were craftsmen, not "hands." The impersonal age of the machine had not yet arrived. One could still be merciful for

> Landscape plotted and pieced—fold, fallow and plough;
>   And all trades, their gear and tackle and trim.

Market towns in the North and the large plantations and "courthouse towns" of the South were able to support a variety of special skills. Forges, furnaces, grinding and slitting mills, sawmills, tanneries, shipyards, artisans' workshops—all gave pungency and flavor to colonial town life.

Carl Bridenbaugh's *The Colonial Craftsman*,[10] portrays the men who created the functional and attractive artifacts of colonial life. Like his British counterpart, the colonial craftsman represented much that is admirable in human society. In Revolutionary America and in England, particularly in the early nineteenth century, the skilled artisan, self-educated, liberal-minded, and rationalist, provided a type of sound, undoctrinaire, radical leadership fitted to the needs of the day. In the colonies the craftsman was even more a disciple of the Calvinist gospel of hard work than was the independent farmer. Could he not see, in a world of scarce labor and wide opportunity, the essential justification of the doctrine? The author of the Bible of self-help, *Poor Richard's Almanack,* was himself a craftsman printer, one of the three artisans to sign the Declaration of Independence. It seems inescapable that Franklin's *Almanack* was a best-seller because real opportunity did exist in the British colonies of the New World, and was buttressed by public opinion, religion, law, and economics.[11] American workers earned real wages from 30 percent to 100 percent higher than those in Britain. Poverty was the exception rather than the rule. Even the indenture system opened the gates of opportunity to the penniless and the unrecognized, by an exchange of labor (albeit irksome) in return for craft training and future status. In any case there was always plenty of land, and an open frontier.

Speaking of property and wealth in early America, Tocqueville claimed: ". . . wealth circulates with inconceivable rapidity, and experience shows that it is rare to find two succeeding generations in the full enjoyment of it." This failure of wealth to establish dynasties and turn class differences into caste distinctions helps to explain the novel attitude of propertied Americans toward their unpropertied brethren.[12] They lacked that inclination of the European upper class to think in rigid categories about "the working classes," "the lower orders"—"the poor" (so terribly permanent!). The British term "servant" very rapidly fell out of use in the New World.

Workingmen were especially fortunate in the northern colonies, where there were no slaves to compete with free labor and depress its value and status. Skilled carpenters, silversmiths (like Paul Revere, Senior, a Huguenot refugee apprentice from the Channel Island of Guernsey), and the like faced no insurmountable social barriers to self-advancement except merit and hard work. Desperate labor shortage forced the colonial authorities to reduce the normal apprenticeship period from seven years to as low as three. Women of all ages, as well as young prentices, found greater relative freedom, more elbowroom, in the new environment. Widows took over their husbands' inns, smithies, workshops, businesses—without much qualm. The European social code gave way slowly before the unrelenting pressure of economic circumstance. In sum, the poor man who came or was sent to the colonies received there nearly everything he had been denied at home: immediate or fairly rapid independence, training, the chance to make a living—even to own land and a house, and above all, an ever-widening horizon of expectations. Massachusetts and Connecticut would go so far as to offer a measure of public basic education for his children. Erratic but on the whole continuous economic expansion and rising property values seemed to guarantee their future.

A *property-owning democracy?*

Tocqueville felt that the democratic impulse in history worked with inexorable power, and turned everything to its own particular use: geography, invention, religion, law, what we have called the factors of production, "the taste for luxury, the love of war, the sway of fashion." The force of this observation cannot easily be denied, even if we are unable to share the feeling of "religious dread" that it generated in Tocqueville's aristocratic breast. But all was not perfect or even democratic in this preindustrial age. The workman's *political* rights did not always match his economic and social opportunity, and the new political framework that was to be established after the Revolution would not in itself guarantee political equality.[13] Moreover, when the economy failed from time to time to make its supposedly automatic self-adjustments (when Adam Smith's "invisible hand" was tightly closed), and the hard times came, it was the colonial artisan who felt the shock. The merchant could retreat; the farmer had his crop. Economic depression would fill the debtors' jails with small men, while the large merchant felt the pinch slightly and curtailed his style of life. After about 1763 the "mechanics" became a radical political force in colonial town life, demanding free public education, rotation in public office, abolition of debtors' jails, and the vote for all taxpayers.

Furthermore, if New England was imperfectly democratic, the South was imperfectly aristocratic.[14] The rice and tobacco gentry of the southern colonies were far more forceful than the status-conscious merchants in Newport, Boston, and Philadelphia, rich speculating landlords in upcountry New York, or prosperous lawyers anywhere. Northern upper-class leaders failed to implant the "aristocratic code" that became the hallmark of the "southern way of life," based ultimately on caste and rural values. Great tobacco planters were the undisputed ruling class of Virginia, as they were of Tidewater Maryland—though in the latter colony the port of Baltimore, dependent more on the backcountry yeoman-type farmer, was already beginning to show signs of its future greatness some time before the Revolution.

South Carolina was a virtual city-state based on Charleston and governed by Charleston "society." Southern leaders, whatever may be the truth about their social origins, did their utmost to reproduce English "county" life, but they could not afford to despise "trade," and were compelled to devote long hours to arduous labor, however much they worshiped the alleged "huntin', shootin', and fishin'" ideal of the English squirearchy.[15] The great Virginian, William Byrd I, sold hardware to the Indians and felt no pangs of class-conscious remorse. His even greater son, the diarist William Byrd II (1674–1744), member of the Royal Society, intimate of Congreve,

Wycherley, and the Duke of Argyll, graduate of the Middle Temple, and owner of a beautiful mansion (Westover), with a 3,800-volume library, made his daily bread dealing in crops and minerals, and by all kinds of promoting—something like a semifeudal capitalist, an American Stroganoff. This great capacity for commerce and this no-nonsense attitude to work are hardly surprising: it has been estimated that at least half of the white migrants to the southern and middle colonies were indentured laborers, and most of Virginia's "First Families" (the "F.F.V.'s") were of English and Scots merchant stock.[16] Even in the South, apparently, with slavery on the increase in the late seventeenth century, society could offer far more opportunity for hardworking artisans and farmers to "get ahead," gain material comfort and economic and spiritual independence, than was available in the Old World.

Sectional discord

"Equality of opportunity," or rather, the equalizing pressure exerted by broad economic opportunities, did not produce a stable society. Rivalries of all sorts split the colonists, and it is worth looking at these differences, if only because some American historians, suspicious of "economic interpretation," feel that sectional dispute and class antagonism have been exaggerated, thus obscuring the genuine integrity of the fabric of colonial life. But economic history is not synonymous with the economic interpretation of history, and to gloss over economic struggles is to do violence to the facts and misrepresent the multiplicity of colonial experience.

Besides the basic North-South distinction produced by American economic geography, there were feuds within sections and within colonies. Boundary quarrels, recurrent outbreaks of hostility between the developed, commercial, creditor area of the seaboard and the underdeveloped (or undeveloped), frontier, debtor areas of the West—a constant strife between the so-called "tidewater aristocracy" and the "yeoman backcountry." Resorts to violence, rebellion, even a kind of civil war, were not infrequent. Americans rapidly earned the reputation of being factious, ill-tempered, and incapable of submitting to regular government.[17] Frontier discontent in Virginia caused by falling tobacco prices and Indian raids gave rise in 1676 to the civil war known as Nathaniel Bacon's Rebellion. Bacon was content to wreak his vengeance on the unfortunate Indians, but some of his crowd had ideas about improving white society by tax and franchise reforms, and not all of them were poor backwoodsmen.[18] In North Carolina almost one hundred years later a similar kind of problem arose when frontiersmen (the "Regulators") won the lower house of the assembly and were eventually defeated in a civil war in 1771. The Quaker colony in 1763–1764 saw frontier frustration once more turn against the Indians; irritation over traditional grievances—taxes, roads, debts—led to the march of the "Paxton Boys" to Philadelphia.

Even when the United States was already eleven years old and Alexander Hamilton was struggling to create the institutions of a national economy, the western counties of Pennsylvania refused to pay excise taxes on domestic spirits. They went so far as to tar and feather the tax collectors, and this "Whiskey Rebellion" had to be subdued with a force of 13,000 militiamen (1794).

Discord and division were not the entire story. In a country the size of the original thirteen colonies, sectional animosities were unavoidable. Here was a dependent colonial society of farmers, laboring under immense hardships and scattered over a wide area, together with a handful of small, isolated towns dotted along a rugged coastline and kept alive by a group of adventurous, speculative merchants. Yet the seeds of future political unity were there, in such worldly things as the spread of internal highways, the improved postal network, the growth of a vigorous newspaper press, and in that vaguer feeling for colonial history expressed in the rise of native American learned societies and professional associations. Somehow, despite their many internal differences, Americans became sufficiently irritated with the vagaries of royal policy in the late eighteenth century, and sufficiently determined to put an end forever to their dependent colonial status, to wage a major war against one of the world's greatest powers.

The Revolution—Americans reject colonialism

With this profile of colonial economic life, we may now make a brief commentary on the American Revolution in its economic aspects. School history texts apparently continue to emphasize the role of American opposition to the Navigation Acts, which in theory, at least, restricted colonial trade according to mercantilist principles. But we have seen that mercantilism was not entirely inimical to the economic growth of the colonies. As a matter of fact, Americans did not openly oppose the navigation laws, even though the system when it operated was very uneven and imposed a disproportionate burden on particular colonies and groups.

Southern producers of tobacco, rice, indigo, and naval stores had everything to gain from government bounties and from a government-protected virtually monopolistic market. They were little affected by the theoretical restrictions on domestic manufacturing embodied in legislation like the Wool Act (1699), the Hat Act (1732), and the Iron Act of 1750. Northerners were less fortunate; their economy did not easily complement that of the home country. On the other hand, the challenge of this problem was readily met, and gave colonial businessmen valuable experience. At least, our previous consideration of colonial trade seems to suggest this.

Meanwhile, all colonists could in theory sell their primary products in a protected market and buy their manufactured and consumer goods from the world's best and cheapest producer. The trouble was, colonial buyers had little safeguard against deliberately inflated prices, fraud, and the delivery of shoddy goods from Europe. They had their backs against the wall. If the royal government should choose to administer the system with civil servants who were venal and grasping, what could be done about it? In his book on the navigation laws, Professor Dickerson castigates the Board of Customs Commissioners, established at Boston in 1767, as "customs racketeers," who by fraud, arrogance, bumbling stupidity, and heavy-handed red tape, managed to alienate wealthy merchants and plain townsfolk alike. If we have learned anything from the later history of colonial relationships, this situation would seem in varying degrees to be almost inevitable. Perhaps the American history schoolbooks accidentally come to the right conclusions for the wrong reasons: for all its benefits, the colonial system was a continual source of irritation. Evidently, the mother country could not in the long run control the economic growth of her colonies whether she wanted to or not, and painstaking inquiry into her true motives seems not of great relevance to this outcome.[19]

From 1775 to 1783 a state of war existed between Britain and America. The impact of independence on American society and on the American economy cannot easily be distinguished from the impact of that war. The overall result of both these forces was to push the newly united states forward a good deal further into the industrial age, the age of iron, coal, and steam. But it was a businessman's world long before 1775. Colonial legislatures were quite prepared to follow the mercantilist lead of England, and stimulate economic enterprise by land grants, bounties, subsidies, tax remissions, prizes, and premiums for quality output and initial investment—even by outright grants of monopoly powers. At this stage in the history of American capitalism the cry "Paternalism!" (raised so often in later years against such schemes as aid to the underprivileged) was rarely heard. The businessman accepted with alacrity a far-reaching colonial program of state aid, with scarcely a murmur of "government interference." And colonial society in turn accepted the businessman (with reservations), rejected the social restrictions of residual feudalism, refused to stigmatize the life of trade, and set its course firmly toward the pursuit of happiness and the creation of wealth.

T W O

Toward a National Market

Colonial society was businesslike, but the great potentiality of its wealth could never be realized within the cramping framework of dependency known as mercantilism. Even so, the coming of national independence did not bring a sudden release of energy, whether economic, political, or spiritual—at least, not immediately. Revolutions are accomplished more readily than nations can be constructed. In 1783 the apron strings of colonialism were severed; now Americans had to hammer out a new self-image and fulfill new, unaccustomed roles. One statesman, Alexander Hamilton, had a remarkably clear image of the new America, and his role in the construction of a national economy was nothing short of amazing. Other leaders, like Jefferson, sought to keep alive in a period of tremendous change the original hopes and ideals of colonial Americans —the agrarian tradition. The interplay of these two forces provides a central theme of United States history down to the Civil War and even beyond; in particular, their mutual antagonism dominates the so-called "Critical Period" between independence and the federal Constitution, in which America was governed by the Articles of Confederation.

The impact of war

The true nature of this "Critical Period"—the 1780's—has long been disputed by historians. Today it is hard to see why past writers ever thought that the eighties were any more turbulent and disturbed politically than the boisterous and uncertain decade that followed the acceptance of the federal Constitution—the 1790's. Economically and socially too it makes little sense to regard the eighties as a distinct decade. In economic history the year 1790 is convenient to choose as a vantage point to glance backward at colonial society and forward to the national market economy that was to emerge. All three decades, the seventies, eighties, and nineties, were molded by the forces of war and independence, forces between which it is hard to distinguish.

Like all prenuclear military conflicts, the Revolutionary War (1775–1783) managed to create as well as to destroy. One economic sector might be totally disabled, but another sector would be stimulated. In the South, certain rice, indigo, and tobacco plantations were badly hit; it has even been said that Tidewater Virginia never fully recovered from the ravages of this conflict. British forces, in spasmodic raids during the years 1778–1781, commandeered crops and Negro slaves in both Virginia and the Carolinas. On the other hand, overall tobacco output actually increased in the war years, cotton made gains, and the nonimportation agreement encouraged native wool production.[1] Increased food demands in the battle zones of the middle colonies, together with a free flow of British and French money, raised prices of agricultural products for most farmers and produced a wartime prosperity for everyone whose land was not overrun. Industry was not so happy in these same areas —British military strategy had aimed to disable or destroy the manufacturing centers. In this respect, Georgia, Virginia, the Carolinas, and New Jersey suffered economic losses; but manufacturers remote from the field of battle were stimulated by the special demands of war, as well as by the pressing need for colonial self-sufficiency in the absence of European supplies. The challenge of war threw Americans onto their own resources, and Congress responded as best it could. Ironworkers were exempted from military service. Centers in Pennsylvania, Connecticut, and Massachusetts (Springfield Arsenal, 1778) were established to equip the Revolution with munitions. The glass, leather, pottery, and paper industries also prospered. Toward the end of the war this industrial progress slackened.

Unlike some other wars, the struggle for American independence was not particularly favorable to the larger manufacturers or farmers. The two world wars of the twentieth century have left "big business" stronger than ever; the Revolutionary War was unfortunate for the big merchants, few of whom escaped losses. This is not to deny that huge fortunes were amassed out of war profits by privateers and by able contractors with useful social connections and credit, like Robert Morris. But for the most part these fortunes were fairly new, and trading houses that were several generations old in contrast suffered badly. Large southern plantations were also adversely affected, while the smaller farmers, whose income was raised by the inflation, the unusual demand, and the labor shortage (caused by the military drain of farm manpower), were better off than before the war broke out. Tocqueville's image of the inevitable, all-encompassing character of the democratic impulse in history seems once more to be sustained by events in the New World. War was made the instrument of democracy.

The two most intractable economic problems during the struggle were the labor shortage (unassuaged by the impressment of Hessian prisoners of war) and the scarcity of currency. Both of these deficiencies proved to be beneficial to the small man. Though labor shortage helped to keep up wage levels, currency shortage led to the issue of floods of paper money, in a desperate attempt to meet outstanding public payments, and the effect was inflationary and highly advantageous to debtors and to small men in business or farming everywhere.

Apart from these economic results, the war—and the status of national independence won for Americans by the war—had an even greater effect on the total social climate. The American merchant, entrepreneur, and farmer were now released from dependency, liberated from the patronizing control of arrogant and bungling civil servants who owed their allegiance to a far-distant government that was ignorant of local conditions and needs. Throughout the eighties Americans were building canals, turnpike highways, and bridges. The first cotton "manufactory" appeared in Massachusetts in 1787.

Loss of the British credit, which, as we have seen, had financed prewar trade, led the more enterprising American merchants to establish native banks. This move was now legally possible: free of imperial restrictions and regulations, the individual states were able to offer charters to businessmen who wished to establish banking institutions. Philadelphians led the movement, with the Bank of Pennsylvania (1780), which became one year later the wide-reaching Bank of North America. By 1784, Boston and New York both had their own banks. The American entrepreneur could now begin to feel free of London and Bristol creditors, free to develop rich western lands and bring new outlying resources into the market economy without fear of breaking any colonial fiat, free to trade in international waters, free to encourage home industries and to diversify the products of his native land—free to conceive a different kind of society.

The impact of independence

An "Americanization" process had in fact already been in operation for some years, and the men of the revolutionary period sought to differentiate their society still further from the European model. Widespread pressure was exerted to abolish the class-conscious colonial inheritance laws. Primogeniture and entail (legal regulations of European origin imposed to perpetuate a landed aristocracy by impeding division or transfer of large estates upon the owner's death) had no part to play in the type of social order that was becoming slowly recognized as "American." By 1790 no such laws existed. Seven years earlier, independence had automatically wiped out the feudal-type payments to landed proprietors known as "quit-rents." As for civil and religious rights, church and state were to be separated for ever. The Anglican Church was rapidly disestablished during the Revolution, though Congregationalism, being a majority faith, maintained its official status in the northeast rather longer. Massachusetts finally cut the Congregational political link in 1833 and brought to an end the formal history of religious establishment in the United States. American penal laws and prison conditions were also greatly improved under Jefferson's leadership.[2] The blight of Negro slavery remained—almost one person in every four was colored in 1790[3]—though even here the Revolution did bring some improvements. For instance six colonies forbade Negro slave trading in the seventies and eighties, and most northern assemblies abolished the institution of slavery itself. In the South emancipation was encouraged by permissive laws, and several thousand slaves were voluntarily released from bondage. But these were precotton days in Dixie.

The Revolution struck deep at the heart of residual feudalism in its land policy. Loyalist estates were confiscated; large holdings were split up and sold by real-estate speculators in more manageable sizes—thus ensuring the maintenance of widespread property-ownership in America. New York state loyalists lost about $2,500,000 worth of property through this (unintentionally) democratic procedure; farther South the Penn family were deprived of about 1,000,000 £ sterling.[4] More than this, the land policy of the "Critical Period" strengthened the American political system. Despite the weaknesses of the much-maligned Articles of Confederation, Congress was able to build up its power through the "public domain" —ownership and control by the national government of unsettled western lands. In 1784 Virginia had decided to cede its western territorial claims to the central government. Other states followed her example, the last being Georgia (1802). How was the government supposed to administer this newly acquired land? There were no precedents except the mercantilist model of colonialism, and it did not occur to American congressmen to "colonize" or subordinate these undeveloped areas in any sense. Quite the contrary; an approach was evolved that was characteristically American, and so highly successful that it formed the basis of United States territorial expansion until much of the continent had been assimilated by the Republic.

This approach was embodied in the Land Ordinance of 1785, which established as the norm a six-mile-square "township" division, divided into thirty-six 640-acre lots. Congress was badly in need of money, and anxious to sell its landholdings without delay, either wholesale or retail. Several private joint-stock company interests combined with some state governments to squash the idea of federal retail sales, and Congress deferred to their pressure. The ordinance required that the basic unit of sale be the square-mile lot, at a price of $1 an acre ($640). Both the price and the lot size were too great for most individual small farmers to handle, and initial sales disappointed Congress in being very slow. It was therefore decided to release huge parcels of land—in areas of up to 5,000,000 acres each —to the privately organized joint-stock "land companies." The companies profited handsomely out of the whole process, but more than private profit was involved. As big purchasers, the land companies were able to demand from the government certain requirements to protect their investment: namely, that Congress should provide orderly government in these territories to attract settlers and speed up resale of the land by the companies. In this way, agitation by the Ohio Company led in 1787 to the passing of the statesmanlike Northwest Ordinance.[5]

So the western lands were hastily carved up and settled by ambitious and impatient Americans, and the history of the wider national economy was to reflect in many ways the history of those western lands: a rapid exploitation of natural riches, in character speculative, erratic, prodigal—and "democratic." The timely interaction of private profit seeking and great political vision that generated this growth was (in the old cliché) "typically American."

Stability, political and economic: the federal Constitution

Under the Articles of Confederation the young American nation had achieved great things. In spite of diplomatic disappointments that could scarcely have been avoided, the war was won and a favorable peace treaty concluded; the economy was encouraged to respond to the needs created by national independence; the social structure was adapted to an emerging concept of Americanism; a technique for developing the West was formulated; population and wealth continued to build up. Structural impediments to economic growth still remained: interstate tariff barriers, the shortage of currency, the lack of a real federal executive, and the political uncertainty that such a deficiency produced. After a four-month-long debate throughout the summer of 1787 in Philadelphia's Independence Hall, the federal Constitution of the United States was finally drafted as an answer to some of these structural problems.

Individual states had constructed tariff walls between themselves partly out of sectional jealousies and the desire of each to protect its own trade. However, the most telling political pressure for state tariffs came from the farmers of the backcountry, from men who saw the need for more state revenue but were bitterly opposed to any further taxation. Whether justifiable on social grounds or not, their attitude and their support for internal tariffs were ultimately inimical to the creation of American wealth. Internal trade barriers kept the American market split up; so long as they existed the United States was a nation with no true national market. Backwoodsmen did not always recognize the basic economic principle that increasing specialization and growth depend upon the extent of the market. On the other hand, opposition to state tariffs was often self-seeking. Merchants of the eastern ports had good reason to prefer a nationwide market, protected by federal tariffs. With federal tariff revenue, Congress could afford to settle its war debts by repaying the Continental bondholders; but the bonds had long since been used as a form of money, and they had gradually passed into the hands of merchants in payment for bills in the normal course of trade. Some merchants had even gone further and bought bonds very cheaply in hope of their future redemption by the government at face value. In fact Gouverneur Morris (whose financial foresight was not a jot inferior to that of his rich cousin Robert) had himself done precisely this. The federal Constitution he helped to draft in 1787 did not fail to empower Congress to regulate interstate trade and to impose federal import duties. Article I, Section 9, abolished internal tariffs.

While the ratification of the Constitution would relieve the tariff problem, the currency question proved to be more intractable. An even greater need for currency and credit had been created by the war, which burdened the Treasury with a public debt amounting to almost $8,000,000. In the five years 1781–1786 only $500,000 was in fact paid into the national coffers—barely enough to cover administrative expenses. What was true of the central government was also true of the state and local authorities; public revenue at all levels was limited, and yet Americans everywhere objected to taxation. Therefore, for the same reason that they erected tariff barriers— revenue—the state governments printed millions of dollars' worth of paper money. Massachusetts had been the first to issue paper money in 1690, and in the following century others copied her example, until there were several kinds of paper in circulation, bills of credit, public-loan bank notes, and land bank notes, all with varying real values. Widespread and panic resort to the printing press was in the long run self-defeating, since the paper money depreciated drastically, giving windfall profits to debtors but deterring creditors from making further loans. Confusion was confounded by the extreme variety of specie in circulation—Spanish silver dollars, Brazilian gold johannes and moidores, French, British, and other coins. Under the colonial system English regulations had forbidden a native American mint, and in any case the colonies lacked the necessary gold and silver.[6] Nevertheless, all calculations were made in terms of "coin of the realm" (British pounds, shillings, and pence), which the colonists themselves rarely even saw. The basic economic act of exchange was thus made unbelievably complex and hazardous; every sale or purchase involved great uncertainty, financial risk, slippery mathematics, and a considerable waste of time. The volume of business was restricted, and the free flow of a major factor of production—capital—was blocked.

Even more disastrous results were to follow. The currency system, or lack of it, meant that at various times first creditors and then debtors in turn would be subjected to sudden profit or sudden loss. Each class or group felt itself to be the victim of the other, while both were simply victimized by the economic situation. A kind of "class violence" flared up on several startling occasions, though never in the classical Marxist terms.[7] Shays' Rebellion is the perfect example.

In 1786 Captain Daniel Shays, a veteran of the Revolutionary War, emerged as leader of the dissident and frustrated farmers of central and western Massachusetts, people who were prepared to face a civil war rather than continue to suffer the slings and arrows of outrageous economic fortune, unheeded by the Commonwealth government. Shays himself was especially ready to take arms against the authorities, who seemed more keen to tax him than to pay for his long years of military service. Wartime agricultural prosperity had by now long since vanished in the chill wind of depression. Caught by falling farm incomes, rising taxes, pressure from wartime creditors, and increasing demands on all sides for payments to be made in specie (rather than in depreciated paper), the small farmer demanded swift action to meet this reversal of his fortunes. Shays' men had one idea: put a stop to the flood of foreclosures for debt, by the simple expedient of closing the courthouses, even if it took force. Violent action did not end here. To prevent the conviction of brother rioters it was soon necessary to close the criminal courts too. Open warfare broke out between rebels and state troops in January, 1787, and did not cease for a month and a half. Shays failed to capture the Springfield Arsenal, and his forces were finally scattered into the hills during heavy snows. Bloody and bitter, Shays' Rebellion passed like a shock wave through American society. What was happening to the ideals of the Revolution?

Two or three months later, the rebellion must still have troubled the minds of the men who gathered in Philadelphia to "render the federal constitution adequate to the exigencies of government and the preservation of the Union." The steps they took to strengthen the federal authority and put an end to political uncertainty also served to remove some of the most basic inhibitions on economic growth. By destroying internal tariffs the federal Constitution secured internal free trade and created a large, unified domestic market that was to be one of the secrets of American material success. Moreover the market was "extended" or deepened by the provision of federal post offices and post roads. As for the foreign market—so important to colonial growth—America's chances to compete within it were much enhanced when the new government assumed, under the Constitution, all responsibility for debts accrued by the Confederation. Federal credit could now be made good, as Congress was given the power to levy national taxes. The control of both domestic and foreign trade was entrusted to the federal government. What is more, the Constitution created a single national currency by giving Congress the sole right to coin and regulate the value of specie.[8]

The men of 1787, whatever their motives were, safeguarded the rights of private property with a hedge of provisions, some useful for immediate economic expansion but fraught with various dangers for the future of American society. Fugitive slaves, for instance, were to be returned to their owners at all costs, and no state was to pass legislation that might impair the obligation of contracts. But talent was encouraged by protecting the private property rights of inventors, men of letters, and scientists in their creations, through patent and copyright laws.

Obviously the Constitution of the United States represented a complex and subtle amalgam of private profit and public concern, of political leverage and open-minded debate, of local interest and national vision. The document has been regarded as a great conspiracy to protect one class against another—despite the fundamental compromises it embodies. The historian Charles Beard's famous thesis was that the Constitution guarded the privileges and property rights of a decided minority of wealthy men, who formed well-organized and strategically placed pressure groups concentrated in urban areas on or near the coast, and represented in every state; in a trading and agrarian society it was relatively easy for them to foist their wishes onto the proletarian majority. Beard's *An Economic Interpretation of the Constitution,* published in 1913 when the spirit of Progressivism and the fear of dangerous private empires of wealth invaded the thoughts of most Americans, tells us more about the author's reactions to late Victorian capitalism than it tells about Revolutionary America. A weakness of his thesis is that recent historical research seems to reveal in the 1780's not a proletarian mass supporting a small wealthy elite, but, on the contrary, a property-owning majority, willing to submit to compromise.[9]

The true worth of the federal Constitution is that it gave political stability to an emergent democracy. The English Revolution gave birth to a military dictatorship under Cromwell; the French Revolution ended in the plebiscitary dictatorship of Napoleon I; the Russian Revolution was betrayed—whether or not permanently— and produced the semitheocratic totalitarian state. The American Revolution resulted in the American Constitution. Only in this light can the real value of that Constitution be judged. Within its framework the "American dream" was nurtured, and the labor of the American people brought forth the riches that in 1790 were still only an exciting possibility.

2 LAND AND LABOR
1790 to 1860

The Extension of the Pre–Civil War Market

The United States of 1790 had emerged from about 180 years of colonialism. Today we are about 180 years away from the men of 1790. Within the time span of American history, the major social and economic transformations have taken place in the years since 1790. The opening chapters of this book were therefore concerned not so much with giving an organic account of colonial historical development as with isolating the strategic factors in colonial society that were to govern later American growth. It was in the holds of Yankee merchantmen that America's wealth was generated.

In our brief examination of colonial America we touched upon the relationship among the factors of production (land, labor, and capital), the pattern of geographical resources and the regional division of labor among the colonies that pattern supported, the land-man ratio and the political foundations that American statesmen laid for future territorial expansion, the social structure as it was emerging, with a degree of upward mobility and wide property ownership (the "open society"), and the great enterprise and way of life that was colonial commerce. We saw that the impact of war and the needs of independent nationhood produced a desire for greater political and economic stability. This desire manifested itself in a federal Constitution and created a nationwide marketing area free of internal tariff restraints. But of all these dynamic variables, the controlling factor in American growth was trade.

For this reason, Part Two opens with a consideration of pre–Civil War foreign and domestic trade, and—let us maintain our link with the great Adam Smith—the "extent" of the market. Since the size and depth of the market depend upon population density, factor mobility, and the ease of communications, this is also the logical place to take a look at the evolution of transportation in pre–Civil War days. What antebellum Americans called "internal improvements" have been thought so important in economic development that a leading historian, George R. Taylor, has entitled his treatment of the prewar years as a whole, *The Transportation Revolution*. Innovations in transportation—new highways, canals, steamships, railroads, and the like—which were themselves initially a response to trade expansion, brought disproportionately high and increasing returns in terms of growing specialization and a great extension of the market, both internal and external.

1. GROWTH OF THE OVERSEAS MARKET

The United States as a neutral power

Before the Civil War, however, the chief source of economic growth was not home but overseas demand. An expansion of the American foreign trade market came about through a series of historical accidents: the more or less continuous military conflicts among the European powers from 1793 onward, in the Revolutionary and Napoleonic wars. Playing the role of chief neutral trader, the United States took quick advantage of the war whenever it could, to trade with both sides. Down to the peace of 1815, the foreign trade sector sustained the rest of the United States economy. Americans captured the carrying trade and the re-export business of the Western world. Once the era of European wars was over (in fact, from Waterloo down to Fort Sumter), the overseas trade sector continued to function as the main expansive force within the economy; but now it functioned through the direct export of southern cotton—the entrepôt and carrying trades having declined in relative significance after 1815.[1]

In the 1790's the same enterprising spirit of commercial adventure that sent Yankee brigantines across the seas in colonial days was still to be found at work, creating American wealth. Export totals were pushed up fivefold, bringing about great national prosperity in the years 1793 to 1807, when the real income per head of Americans reached levels not later regained until the mid-nineteenth century. Perhaps this expansion was "artificial." Did it not depend almost entirely on the fact that Britain, France, and the rest were totally preoccupied with the urgent military task of wiping each other out? The eighteen-month European Peace of Amiens (1801) brought a disastrous fall in United States trading profits; prosperity returned immediately when the war was resumed. Each threat of peace brought economic setback.

Not only this, but American merchants were heavily dependent on the commercial policies and whims of European governments. The Royal Navy drove most Dutch and French competition from the high seas. Yankee sea captains chiefly had to face their old adversaries the British. Nevertheless, there was trouble with the French too: an early agreement had thrown open former French trading routes (from Martinique and Haiti to Nantes and Bordeaux) to American shipping, and in the nineties these privileges were gravely endangered by French suspicion of United States willingness to negotiate on trade matters with Britain. A new pact with the French government in 1800 managed to protect American trading rights and stave off an open war between the two republics. The British were even more of a menace. Quite naturally, after the War of Independence they sought to exclude the new nation from its former rights and protection within the imperial system. Pitt's desire to come to generous trade terms with the United States was ignored, and in 1785 the country followed Lord John Sheffield's advice[2] by rejecting American overtures for a commercial treaty. In fact, the United States was cut off from the triangular trade and debarred from the rich sugar islands of the British West Indies. In May, 1794, the federal government sent John Jay to the Court of St. James's to negotiate over Royal Navy interference with American merchantmen. He managed to secure the Jay Treaty, which gave Americans recognition as legitimate neutral traders and allowed them to traffic (in vessels of up to seventy tons) in the West Indies. On the other hand, when Yankee trading expansion was reaching its height and the commercial clauses of the Jay Treaty lapsed, the British did not renew them; instead they reverted to enforcing the so-called "Rule of 1756," by which trade not open to neutrals in peacetime was closed to them in war.

Meanwhile the French were again proving troublesome to American traders. Napoleon tried to establish his "Continental System"— a "paper" blockade of European ports—through the Berlin and Milan decrees of 1806 and 1807. All trade with British ports or with ships sailing to and from British territory was forbidden by the Emperor of the French. The decrees were to operate throughout Europe. Immediately Britain retaliated with the Orders-in-Council prohibiting all trade with France and her allies *except* through British ports. Theoretically, all neutral trade was wiped out. Caught between the two powers, President Jefferson pushed the situation one stage further in 1807 with his *quid pro quo*, the Embargo Act, which forbade all American sailings to foreign ports. The act boomeranged: its effects were worse for the United States than for Europe, and opposition to the measure at home caused its modification in 1809 and repeal in 1810. The United States then offered to place an embargo on trade with either of the two great warring powers if the other would waive its restrictions against American merchants. Napoleon accordingly repealed his decrees, and the United States passed a Non-Intercourse Act against Britain in March, 1811.

The cumulative effects of all this were very destructive for United States trade. Between 1807 and the outbreak of war with England in 1812, about 750 American merchant vessels were seized or destroyed during the course of neutral trading. Within a year of the Embargo, United States imports were cut to under a half and exports slashed to one-fifth. In 1807 United States merchants had sold in foreign markets about $5,000,000 worth of tobacco and about $14,000,000 worth of raw cotton; in the following year they managed by devious means to market only $1,000,000 worth of tobacco and $2,000,000 of cotton—and even this was a real achievement. Although native American exports did recover, relative losses in the re-export and carrying trades were never regained. Idle ships, deserted quays, unemployment, and financial ruin, these were the human terms. Empty coffeehouses stood in silent contrast with the crowded debtors' jails that contained, in New York alone, thirteen hundred men in 1809.

These were the social costs of rapid economic growth based on a chance factor such as war, and they were very high. But there was also a positive gain: the capital accumulated in the years of prosperity before the Embargo, laid a solid foundation for future economic expansion of a more "real" nature. For instance, the capital market was made more efficient through the extension of banking and insurance facilities; increasing urbanization—the ports of Boston, New York, Philadelphia, and Baltimore—extended the domestic market and led to the growth of supporting industries. Turnpike highways were constructed to meet the urgent need to reduce the cost of transporting foodstuffs from the hinterland to feed the growing ports. And of course the shipbuilding and allied industries were related directly to the expansion of foreign trade, as that expansion was expressed in rising freight rates and growing profit margins.

Most of these gains from trade accrued to the Northeast, especially to Massachusetts and New York. Meanwhile, in the South, Eli Whitney had already invented his cotton "gin" (to separate the fiber from the seed), but the emergence of cotton as the great commercial export crop of Dixie was not to come until after the War of 1812.

The War of 1812

That Anglo-American war, sometimes called the "Second War of Independence," had profound effects on the United States economy, and marked the end of America's international role as a neutral trader. The British Navy blockaded the Atlantic ports south of New London, and very effectively reduced United States imports, causing severe depression and hardship in the West. Smuggling from Canada was probably extensive, but the only genuine hope was for Americans to be free of dependence on foreign imports, to develop their own manufacturing industries. War did help to overcome many of the old agrarian and seafaring prejudices against investment in native industry. There was some surplus capital too, lying idle for want of investment opportunities—Yankee merchant capital, denied its normal outlet in foreign trade by the naval blockade. Industrial development was a long-term affair, however, and in the meantime New Englanders stood to lose a great deal. They tried to prevent the outbreak of war with Britain. It is true that much fuss had been made by the seaboard states about "maritime rights" and a series of cold-war incidents between British and American sailors. It is also true that the Royal Navy thought nothing of violating the three-mile limit, and "arresting" American sailors on the high seas, practically in full view of the United States coast. But northeastern merchants had strong British connections and were highly suspicious of the French, whether in Canada or in Europe. . . . Was not the Anglo-American disagreement a product of Napoleon's machinations? What is more, trade was New England's lifeblood: war with Britain could prove even more crippling than the disastrous Embargo of 1807.

The war came, brought on by radical pressure from a group of "frontier nationalists" in Congress led by John C. Calhoun and Henry Clay—the "Warhawks." Their special vision of an entirely North American Republic was blocked by two elements: the "foreign"-held areas on the continent (such as British Canada), and the Indians. Territorial expansion and a "tough" Indian policy were chief elements in western politics. Unsatisfied even by the doubling of United States territory in 1803 (the Louisiana Purchase), land-hungry expansionist politicians in the Southwest hoped to assimilate Spanish Florida and then go on to Mexico. Farther north, their eyes were on the rich fur trade and the Canadian forests. As John Randolph declared in 1812:

Agrarian cupidity, not maritime rights, urges the war. Ever since the report of the Committee on Foreign Relations entered the House, we have heard but one word—like the whip-poor-will, but one eternal monotonous tone —Canada! Canada! Canada!

The Indians were also a source for anti-British sentiment among the Warhawks: English aid to resurgent Indian tribes was more than a suspicion; in the famous Battle of Tippecanoe (November 6, 1811), when Governor Harrison of Indiana Territory led 1,100 men against Chief Tecumseh's federation, the Indians used British rifles.

An American invasion of Canada and a British invasion of the United States both failed; in 1813 American forces destroyed York (Toronto) and in 1814 the British burned Washington. Eventually representatives of the two nations met in the Flemish medieval town of Ghent and drew up a peace treaty concerning political boundaries and fishing privileges, which made no mention of maritime rights. This was on Christmas Eve, 1814; two weeks later (January 8, 1815) General Jackson won a shattering victory over British land forces at New Orleans, and still a month later, news of the peace treaty reached New York (February 11th). The Battle of New Orleans could not affect the treaty terms in America's favor, but it did create a national hero and a legend out of Andrew Jackson. Politically it helped to assure his later success in the presidential campaign of 1828. Moreover, Jackson's Tennessee militiamen had already destroyed the alliance of Creek and Cherokee Indians at the Battle of Horseshoe Bend (March 27, 1814) on the Tallapoosa River, and forced them to clear out of the western and southern Alabama country.[3] The War of 1812 did not lead to United States annexation of Canada or Mexico, but Jackson's Indian victory had now opened the way for further massive migration of Americans into the rich "black belt" lands of the Mississippi flood plains. In rapid succession the states of Louisiana (1812), Mississippi (1817), and Alabama (1819) entered the Union, and in the 1820's the Southwest became the very heart of the Cotton Kingdom.

A great psychic victory for the frontier nationalists, the War of 1812 also saw a temporary growth of native industry. Two years of blockade and warfare, with imports closed off again, threw Americans onto their own resources. Capital, released from shipping and foreign trade, was set to work drawing native raw materials into the market economy to be processed for home demand—iron and non-ferrous metals, cottons and woolens. But America's wealth was not yet to be in manufacturing. The war impetus was something of a false start, because domestic industrialists were well-nigh ruined altogether after the Treaty of Ghent: an enormous inflood occurred of imported European goods, made with cheaper labor and a more advanced British technology. United States imports multiplied overnight as British manufacturers, starved of markets during the long war and the Continental System, exploited their comparative advantage with heavy exports of finished goods (especially textiles from Lancashire) to American ports. Thriving import houses in New York, Philadelphia, and Baltimore handled about $113 million worth of products in 1815—twice the prewar figure of 1811, and many

times the wartime low of 1814 ($13 million). The exports of 1815 ($53 million) were somewhat lower in value than those of 1811, but were greatly in excess of the wartime low of 1814 ($7 million). This great and rapid expansion of American trade, although it set back the emergence of native industry, was nevertheless the chief source of American wealth in the first half of the nineteenth century.

Cotton exports and the Atlantic Economy

The main component of United States exports from the War of 1812 to the Civil War was cotton. The southern crop represented over a third of total exports in value down to the crash of 1819, rose to two-thirds in the late 1830's, and remained well over half the total until the outbreak of hostilities in 1861. In contrast, America's traditional exports—tobacco, rice, naval goods, lumber, and fish—declined as a percentage of total exports. The sale of American manufactures abroad remained very small and even declined in the 1830's before beginning a gradual rise. Wheat and flour were exported by the middle Atlantic states and made up an unsteady one-tenth of total exports down to 1820, declining afterward. It was rising cotton prices in foreign markets that underlay the economic expansion of the immediate postwar years and of the 1830's, and even in the boom of the 1850's in which many other factors are to be seen—the westward push of the frontier, the Industrial Revolution in the Northeast, gold discoveries in California, waves of immigration—the rising figures of cotton production and cotton exports are still a good guide to the general health of the economy.

Almost half of America's total exports before the Civil War went to help sustain the economy of Britain during its first and greatest period of revolutionary change. France, being slower to industrialize, took on average up to one-sixth of United States exports; the West Indies, no longer a major American customer, bought a steadily declining percentage. Since the export trade was dominated by southern cotton, the chief American consumer was the North of England textile industry.[4] In fact, Eli Whitney's cotton gin, patented in 1794, became available to increase the productivity of southern plantations at a time when the demand for cotton in Britain was increasing voraciously. Of all the economic changes that made up the classical Industrial Revolution in Britain in the late eighteenth and early nineteenth centuries, none were swifter or more powerful than those in the cotton textile trades of Lancashire. The key industry of the British economic revolution and the key export staple in United States economic growth were very heavily interdependent. Justifiably, economists have called the international system that emerged the "Atlantic Economy."

There was more to the Atlantic Economy than the cotton trade, as we shall see later.[5] But that trade itself is comprehensible only in an international setting. After the boom of the 1830's, conditions were changing, and with the coming of a more permanent native American industrialism, internal improvements such as canals and railroads, and an extension of the home market, the United States economy would in time become less dependent. After the Civil War the source of American wealth was a vast and growing domestic demand for industrial products. However, even in that stage of its economic history, in the last quarter of the nineteenth century and long after its "take-off" into self-sustaining growth, the American economy remained a functional part of the wider Atlantic Economy, with the export of foodstuffs (grain and meat) and the "new immigration" from eastern and southern Europe playing rather similar roles (on a larger scale) to those played previously by cotton and the northwest European immigration.

America's merchant navy

In the 1820's transatlantic trade was cut into very heavily by the post-1819 depression. America's chief wealth-producing changes took place internally rather than externally. The river steamboat was perfected, for instance, and in 1825 the magnificent Erie Canal was completed—boosting the growth of the two great ports, New Orleans and New York. External recovery was very slow up to about 1830. Then came a seven-year foreign trade boom, the result of a fundamental general increase in population and productivity, as well as of such specific factors as tariff reductions, international trading agreements, a growing American domestic surplus of foodstuffs, and innovations in ocean transportation.

This new expansive surge of the 1830's was brought to an end by the panic of 1837, which was international in scope, a faltering of the Atlantic Economy. But just before news of the crash broke

upon the market, United States imports were worth $129 million and
United States exports $190 million. Only three years later, America
was already on the road to recovery, though trade fluctuated continually down to 1846. In that year American foodstuffs were
urgently demanded by the British government to save the unhappy
Irish peasant population from total famine and death through disastrous failure of the potato crop. The Prime Minister, Sir Robert
Peel, climaxed his great series of free-trade budgets by abolishing at
last the import duty on imported foreign grain, the infamous "Corn
Law" (originally imposed in 1815 by a Parliament of landlords).
Britain was now free to import American grain to help ease the
Irish situation. Events in other parts of the world gave American
commerce a further fillip—gold discoveries in Australia, Colorado,
and California coinciding with falling United States tariffs.

So the 1840's witnessed an abnormal production of American
shipping to meet trade demands. Regular oceangoing steamship
services brought New York nearer to Liverpool and northern Europe. But the most dramatic development was the brief flowering
of the beautiful three-masted Yankee "clipper ship"—narrow-
beamed, six times as long as it was broad, with concave sides, a
prodigious height and spread of canvas and a sharp, streamlined
prow—the most graceful and the fastest sailing ship afloat. Donald
McKay's *Flying Cloud* plowed through the ocean from Boston to
San Francisco in 89 days and 8 hours[6]—a speed not equaled even
by steamships for many years to come. This speeding up of economic transfers between the east and west coasts of the continent
was by far the most significant service the Yankee clipper made to
United States economic growth.

But it was trade with the Orient that first stimulated the building
of clipper ships before 1848. Americans had long taken the lead in
opening up the Far East to Western trade and culture, and as early
as 1784 the United States *Empress of China* had sailed from New
York to Canton. In 1836 Siam gave special trading rights to Yankee
merchants; in the forties and fifties Anglo-Chinese wars threw part
of the China trade out of British and into American hands, especially since China's ports were more open to all comers after 1844.
In addition, in 1849 Britain relaxed her Navigation Laws, and fast
New England clippers were allowed to compete in carrying tea to
the London market, where the first delivery of the season's tea crop
brought a fabulous price. Five years later (1854) Commodore Perry

broke through the self-spun cocoon of Japanese cultural isolation and dragged that nation out into world trade.

The mid-nineteenth century shipbuilding boom gave the United States a merchant-marine gross tonnage not much below that of Britain herself, the high point of 1861 (5½ million tons) not being equaled again until 1901. A cost advantage in cheap timber underlay the extraordinary growth of the American shipbuilding industry, but as forests near the Atlantic seaboard were steadily depleted of pine and oak, timber prices rose and formerly marginal timber was drawn into use. Yankee builders turned to the less suitable chestnut and birch, and British consumers turned toward Scandinavian and Russian suppliers as the advantageous price differential between the United States and Europe fell drastically. The clipper ship in any case was always expensive to build, and with limited hold space was profitable only for cargo of low bulk and high value or perishability. Circumstances had favored the ship: gold discoveries in California (1849) and in Australia (1851), war (in the Crimea as well as in China), and the European revolutions of 1848. But its days were numbered. Circumstances would soon destroy it—the decline of old trade routes (Brazilian coffee capturing the United States market at the expense of Oriental tea, for instance); the perfection of the steamship in the bulky transatlantic trade markets and the cheap mass-migration passenger field; the Civil War and the preceding Panic of 1857 which was a foretaste of general decline in a shipbuilding industry that lost the initiative and was unprepared for the changeover to steel ship production. Americans lost out to better British clipper designers even before the Civil War, and Britain, since it possessed the world's most highly developed iron industry, used its cost advantage to take the lead in the increasing use of metal ships. United States capital sought new outlets in manufacturing industry and in railroad construction. America turned away from her merchant marine and foreign commerce to the subjugation and internal development of her native wealth.

2. GROWTH OF THE HOME MARKET

Although United States foreign trade increased noticeably down to 1860 and the export sector played a strategic role in general economic growth, the home market expanded enormously and far more dramatically. The "extent" of the market depends on density of population (absolute size and degree of urbanization) and on the efficiency of economic transfers (movement of the factors of production: resources, men, and capital). Both these forces were at work in the United States during the first sixty years of the nineteenth century. Population grew by natural increase and by immigration, with greater urbanization; a network of trails, turnpike highways, canals, and railroads linked the sections and facilitated factor mobility. Moreover, by 1853 United States territorial expansion on the North American continent was almost complete.[7] The purchase of Alaska from Russia after the Civil War (1867) brought the continental United States up to well over three million square miles in area—three or four times the size of the young Republic of 1790. Population was nine times greater: 36 million when the war ended (1865) as opposed to under 4 million in 1790. As the federal Constitution guaranteed there were to be no internal tariffs or artificial barriers to trade among the states, the United States became a huge free-trade domestic market.

The web of sectionalism: interregional economic flows

The size and geographical variety of this market, and its three great sections (Northeast, South, and West) with their differences in "comparative advantage," led to area specialization based on a clearly patterned though changing interregional flow of economic activity. The South devoted itself to plantation staples for the export trade and for the growing textile manufacturing industry of New England, buying much of its food supply from western farmers by way of that great river artery the Mississippi, and obtaining its manufactured goods from the Northeast by sea. The West came to specialize in grain and cattle production to feed the South and the Northeast. The Northeast (New England and the middle Atlantic states) performed a function similar to that of Britain a hundred years earlier for the thirteen colonies: it supplied finished goods, tools and equipment, commercial and building know-how, foreign imports and capital.

It was after the 1812-1814 War that a regional pattern of mutual interdependency became clear. The river steamboat, by accelerating and making rather more certain the tricky passage of the Mississippi River both downstream and upstream, had much to do with this. The flow of domestic trading established before the 1830's depended heavily on the great river flowing north-south from the interior of the continent to the Gulf, which bound the West to the South with the umbilical cord of economic need. Western products floated down the wide, muddy stream through Arkansas, Tennessee, Mississippi, and Louisiana, and very often never reached the port of New Orleans, being landed informally and sold on the way. Cotton, sugar, rice, tobacco—the southern staples—were shipped from New Orleans by coastal vessels to the northern states. In turn the latter provided for southern farmers banking, insurance, transportation, and brokerage services, and manufactured articles. As for the West before 1830, the most valuable eastern manufactured goods could afford to be sent there by the expensive wagon routes, but bulkier products of necessity went first by sea to New Orleans and then by river upstream.

Drastic changes took place after 1830 or so when this web of economic relationships was struck sideways by the "transportation revolution." Internal improvements like the Cumberland Turnpike, the Erie and Ohio canals, and the great railroad systems such as the New York Central, the Erie, the Baltimore and Ohio, and the Pennsylvania linked the industrial, commercial Northeast with the agrarian and frontier West. Major economic flows changed direction; the alliance between West and South was badly weakened at a crucial period in the history of American sectionalism.

After about 1835 western lumber, cattle, and grain reached Buffalo and was transshipped to eastern consumers and exporters. Since 1825 the Erie Canal had served mainly to bring the output of western New York State to the tables of eastern families. Now the completion of the Ohio Canal (1832) brought products from much farther west, and the railway networks of the early fifties completed this transition.

Western trade with the South continued to rise absolutely. Indeed, the antebellum decade was a buoyant era in the economic history of the Mississippi Valley. New Orleans remained America's principal export center as late as 1860, with the port of New York running second, followed by three southern ports—Mobile, Charleston, and Savannah—involved in the heavy coastal traffic, shipping raw staples from Dixie to the eastern states. But New Orleans was

increasingly dependent on these regional staples of its immediate
hinterland. In 1843 Buffalo had the very first grain elevator, and
three years later was transshipping more wheat and flour from western states to eastern markets by way of the Erie and canals farther
west than New Orleans could receive from upstream. The river was
simply inadequate for ever-growing western needs. In the fifties
Ohio's farmers sent the vast bulk of their grain eastward by way of
canals, using the southern route only for whiskey and meat products.
Buffalo's receipts tell a forceful story, with a moral for the South:
in 1836 she received from the West 139,000 barrels of flour and
500,000 bushels of grain; in 1860, well over 1,000,000 barrels of flour
and over 31,000,000 bushels of grain. Consequently the volume of
trade at St. Louis (destined for New Orleans) declined steadily
after the boom of the 1850's. The transportation revolution had
assured the future of New York and sealed the fate of New Orleans.

The mechanism of trade and the growth of cities

American domestic trade, like manufacturing industry in later
years, was not only subject to sudden and revolutionary change but
also revealed a wide variety of conditions. Sharply contrasting marketing systems existed simultaneously, from frontier barter in, say,
the southern Appalachians, to the complexities of international transfers in Philadelphia or New York. Well-nigh self-sufficient backwoodsmen could transport low bulk and high value products (furs,
whiskey, potash) to market by horse; in areas of more settled agriculture the sale of bulk farm surpluses was dependent on river and
lake navigations before the canal and railroad era. At the local level
in all parts of the country the essential mechanism of trade was the
ubiquitous "country store" with its useful extension of "book credit"
to individual farmers.[8] From the 1830's onward, manufacturers and
wholesalers in the cities began a great American tradition by sending out traveling salesmen. And of course the "Yankee peddler" was
encountered everywhere, in the North, the East, the South, and
the West, bearing his load of clocks, "notions," and Connecticut
hardware.
    Large-scale grain, cattle, and cotton marketing on a national and
international basis called for more sophisticated and elaborate sales
organization, with a hierarchy of middlemen and specialists—all of

which usually implied some ultimate degree of control from New York. That city developed the greatest amount of marketing specialization: brokers, jobbers, commission houses, wholesalers, public auctioneers, and even embryo department stores. A. T. Stewart helped to introduce departmental organization into the retail dry-goods business, using the so-called "one price system" that eliminated the haggling of the marketplace—all prices being plainly marked on goods. (Macy's, opened in the city in 1858, followed the same policy, and such famous firms as Arnold Constable and Lord & Taylor were already established, with buyers combing Europe and their stores offering a wide variety of dry goods to the fortunate city dweller). New Yorkers controlled the export of southern raw cotton and the distribution of New England cotton textiles alike, as Boston directed in no more seemly fashion the wool trade and boots and shoes.

Meanwhile the Ohio Valley economy gave birth to Cincinnati, Pittsburgh, and Louisville, and the commerce of Lake Erie nurtured Detroit, Toledo, and Cleveland. All these growing communities were strategically located on nodal points in the western river and lake navigation systems. Farther west, St. Louis sprang into being where the Missouri, still untamed after flowing hundreds of miles east and south from the Rockies across the Great Plains, pours into the Mississippi. St. Louis commanded the very heart of a 4,000-mile-long river system and was the natural place of transshipment where cargo from the major steamboats serving New Orleans and Memphis was transferred to smaller vessels for distribution up far-distant streams. But the coming of the railroad gave Chicago greater advantage. Much better located for control of westward railway traffic, and enjoying a wonderful stretch of navigable lakes and canals eastward, Chicago after midcentury rapidly outrivaled both St. Louis and New Orleans. To about 1850, however, western trade was dominated in fact by Cincinnati,[9] the great meat-packing center on the Ohio, linked in 1845 to Lake Erie (Toledo) by many miles of state-owned canal.

The transportation revolution

The great cities that fought for control of America's growing wealth in the early century owed their existence, many of them, to the transportation revolution. For in United States history transportation innovation was not only a "linking factor" that articulated the whole process of economic development, but very often the essential precondition of the opening up and subjugation of the continental interior. Turnpike highways reached their greatest growth period between about 1790 and the 1812-1814 War. Meanwhile, from about 1807, the river steamboat came on the national scene; its heyday was the 1850's. Canal building was most significant between 1817 and 1850, and railroad construction from the 1830's onward.

Revolutionary changes such as these were not accepted with complete approval by Americans. When internal improvements were encouraged and aided by federal and state authorities at public expense, they became the object of heated sectional and group politics; rarely were they considered as necessary "social overhead capital," except when private and public interest combined. Generally western farmers in dire need of communication with eastern markets supported the enterprises, as did northeastern coastal communities with growing industrial populations demanding cheaper foodstuffs. Land speculation was mixed up with transport history through the federal and state land-grant policy and the soaring land values in turnpike, canal, and railway development areas. But leaving aside politics and finance, the creative force of the transportation revolution is undeniable, not merely supporting but locating and creating human settlements and drawing human and natural resources into the growing market economy. Railway construction in particular often preceded settlement; after about 1850 the companies themselves organized migration from the East and from Europe to the areas flanking their lines. And the political benefits of economic integration were equally obvious, especially with the advent of the transcontinentals and increased use of the telegraph once the Civil War was over. Never was Adam Smith's dictum on the extent of the market illustrated so spectacularly.

Turnpike highways

Pioneer Americans were limited to waterways and crude trails before the turnpike came. The interior was penetrated slowly and painfully along the lines of navigable streams and the safest and most-frequented overland routes. Longer "traces" or "trails" were beaten out by the legendary figures of early American history, like Daniel Boone whose daring Wilderness Road journey of 1775 took him from North Carolina through the Cumberland Gap to the lush bluegrass of Kentucky. Another Cumberland Gap trail led to the Mississippi at Memphis, the "bluff city," by way of Nashville, Tennessee. From St. Augustine, Florida, the Spanish trail to the old seventeenth century settlement Santa Fe (New Mexico) led westward and crossed the "Father of the Waters"; from Independence, Missouri, the United States Army surveyed another Santa Fe trail in 1825, going west through Kansas Territory across the Great Plains to the picturesque Spanish town just beyond the Sangre de Cristo range of the Rocky Mountains. The Santa Fe trail for all its fame bore little traffic, but eventually it was extended to California and was traveled by stagecoaches in the 1850's. To the north and northwest, trails led from the Hudson to Lake Erie, or to Lake George and Lake Champlain (used by the American Revolutionaries who invaded Canada) and by way of the Hudson and Mohawk valleys by stream and portage to Lake Oneida and Lake Ontario.

A network of rural roads built up by about 1815 were of greater local significance than the exceptional long-distance trails. Though atrociously surfaced and barely passable because of snow and floods in winter and lack of permanent bridges, these rural tracks nevertheless formed, linked together, a fairly continuous "highway" from Maine to Georgia, and without them eastern economic life could not have functioned.

Like Britain, the United States experienced a period of highway building financed and built by "turnpike trusts"—private joint-stock companies organized for the purpose, and convinced of the profit potentialities by the hopeless highway inadequacies, revealed during attempts to move troops and supplies in the War of 1812. An improvement on the trails, turnpikes were meant to connect the larger urban communities and lead westward over the mountain barrier. The first American example, the sixty-two-mile-long Philadelphia-Lancaster Turnpike in Pennsylvania was built in 1792-1794 and cost $465,000. Well constructed on a firm stone foundation with a gravel surface, and wisely located in a populous and growing area, the Lancaster Pike was financially an encouraging success. A flurry of similar toll-road building followed immediately in the northeastern states, and during the thirty years that followed, state governments issued hundreds of charters to joint-stock companies, projecting the construction of thousands of miles of roads. By 1811 in New York State alone 135 such companies had managed to complete 1,500 miles of highway, and in Pennsylvania 86 chartered firms built 2,200 miles. Logically, turnpike road construction led to the design of turnpike bridges and other side achievements. Out of this spate of creative activity emerged at least one major feat: the "National Pike" or Cumberland Road, first planned to link the town of Cumberland in Maryland with St. Louis. Despite the passage of thirty or more acts of Congress and the federal expenditure of almost $7,000,000 between 1806 and 1838, the National Road was never extended the short remaining distance beyond Vandalia, Illinois. The idea of nationally subsidized highways did not come except after vigorous debate and disagreement among lawyers and politicians on the subject of "strict construction" (a narrow interpretation of the federal Constitution by those who wished to exclude federal intervention and enterprise) versus "broad construction" (a wider interpretation of the Constitution by those who supported a stronger federal government). Behind the long-winded constitutional exegesis that paralyzed so many congressional debates over this matter lay meaningful economic and political hopes and fears, as we shall see later. Despite opposition, when the labor gangs finally ceased work on the National Road in 1838 it constituted the principal highway to the West. Traveling time from Baltimore to the Ohio River (at Wheeling, West Virginia) was slashed from eight to three days, and surface freight charges were halved. Along the length of its 834 miles of all-weather surface, the Cumberland Pike brought local prosperity and economic growth.

Whether private, federal, or state, toll-road building was most evident in the Northeast. New England's turnpike craze came to an end about 1806, though building continued into the twenties. Pennsylvania and New York—where most activity came after 1812—had the greatest mileage. Road fever hit the Old Northwest in the twenties and thirties, but few roads were completed except in Ohio. In the upper South, Maryland was the progressive leader, having built about 300 miles of toll highways by 1830. No important roads appeared in Virginia, in spite of the permissive Turnpike Act of 1817, until the thirties; as for South Carolina, the turnpike era stopped dead in 1829 when state appropriations were cut off. Previous building in that state had produced several short and two fairly long toll roads under direct state auspices at a cost of $120,000. In the deepest South, building was desultory or nonexistent—a reflection of plantation structure and a low degree of urbanization. As late as 1835 Harriet Martineau's severe strictures on southern travel can be favorably compared to Arthur Young's comments on the state of English roads of half a century earlier.

Turnpikes declined, and the turnpike idea did not achieve real fulfillment until the use of federal aid in the 1920's and again in the 1950's and 1960's with their superb parkways, throughways, and federal defense highways. Canal and railway competition was only a partial reason for their early demise, since the decline had set in before such competition became effective. Few roads were as financially successful as the Lancaster Pike, and on the whole they failed to provide a cheap enough mode of long-distance transport for the bulky or perishable products that were beginning to dominate the economy. For the entrepreneurs of the turnpike trusts, the roads failed to prove a sound investment, if they could even make ends meet at all. Similarly, the ephemeral boom in timber-surfaced roads was brought to a close by the crisis of 1857. These "plank roads" first appeared in New York State (coming by way of Russia and Canada) in 1844, and they spread rapidly for short-distance uses all over the settled areas. Timber being plentiful, initial costs were very much cheaper than the stone and gravel turnpikes, but maintenance and replacement costs were high. As with the turnpikes there was also much evasion of toll payment, "shun-pikes" or roads around toll points being quite common.

Canal mania

The most outstanding technical and economic achievement in American transport history before about 1840 was clearly the creation of the Erie Canal. Proposals were made as early as 1777 to link the Hudson to the Great Lakes by water, but despite the example of the Industrial Revolution and the canal mania in Britain in the 1790's, nothing was done until 1817 when the New York state legislature sanctioned the plan for a Hudson-Erie canal to be financed chiefly by loans from British investors. The work cost over $7 million, covered a distance of 360 miles, and was finally completed in 1825—the tolls collected having already exceeded interest charges on the original loan. About $120 million was taken in tolls before they were abolished in 1882. H. V. Poor's *Railroad Manual* for 1868, looking back to the twenties, claimed that the Erie Canal reduced traveling time from New York to Buffalo from 20 to 6 days and reduced freight charges from $100 to $5 per ton. "The success of the Erie Canal," it stated, "had an electric effect upon the whole country, and similar works were everywhere projected. The states of Pennsylvania, Maryland, Ohio, Indiana and Illinois at once embarked upon elaborate systems. . . ." Certainly, farmland in New York State doubled in value, and New York City doubled its population (1820–1830), while establishing its leadership over Philadelphia and the entire Atlantic seaboard. The new canal linked the Old Northwest more securely to the Northeast than it had ever been linked by the Mississippi or St. Lawrence to the South or to Canada. Ten years after the canal was finished, the state legislature ordered a vast enlargement, brought about in 1862. In spite of railroad competition the Erie Canal's tonnage continued to increase up to its peak carrying year, 1880. Altogether this was a handsome return on a daring and courageous state government investment that had faced great political opposition and severe geographical and engineering hazards.

"Clinton's Big Ditch," as the Erie was called, was an American success story. Unfortunately, the canal mania that followed could scarcely be called the story of the Erie writ large. The speculative mania blew itself out in the crash of 1837. City and state rivalry in the East played a large part in this expansion. Pennsylvania, Massachusetts, and Maryland, fearful for the prestige and trade of their major ports, Philadelphia, Boston, and Baltimore, tried desperately to compete with New York and the Erie by building trunk-line canals. The waterway from Philadelphia to Pittsburgh (1806–1834) cost the Quaker State a full $10 million. Massachusetts, on the other hand, failed to build a canal from Boston to the Hudson, and no New York trade was diverted into the hands of Bostonians. Maryland allied with her sister Virginia to build a canal along the Potomac connecting the Atlantic coast and the Ohio River; they managed to spend $11 million between 1828 and 1850 but never got over the mountains beyond Cumberland. In any case the Baltimore and Ohio Railroad, the first rail contact with the West, had already been begun with official help in 1828: the State of Maryland was competing with itself.

America's largest canal, the Wabash and Erie (1832–1843), was midwestern. Over 450 miles long, it connected the southwestern corner of Indiana (Evansville, on the Ohio) with Lake Erie (Toledo) by crossing the entire state almost diagonally before entering Ohio. Similarly, the Illinois River was joined to Lake Michigan (and even to the upper Mississippi on the Iowa-Illinois border).

America's canals were built predominately as public schemes, not as private enterprise in any real sense, and most of them were not too profitable. Canals were subject to ice, snow, and weather conditions, and they were slow and cumbersome; the railroads came close on their heels. Only the forceful demands of a dynamically expanding economy kept canal mileage on the increase—from nothing to 1,270 miles (1830), doubling to 3,320 miles (1840), and slackening off to 3,700 miles (1850). Though of no use to passenger traffic, canals were infinitely superior to the mule-train and wagon, especially for bulky, heavy goods like grain, flour, ore. The Miami-Erie state-owned canal (already mentioned) that linked Cincinnati to Toledo was opened in 1845; a year later 2 million bushels of grain and 125,000 barrels of pork were exported through it, although neither grain nor pork had previously been exported from the section of northwest Ohio through which it passed. Canals did overextend themselves, did bring financial failure, and certainly stimulated the 1837 crash. Many state governments sold out to private firms and disavowed all further public investment. Others were forced simply to repudiate their debts. But whether or not canals could have been a profit-making immediate investment, they opened up former wildernesses, forests, and mines, stimulated production, diverted existing trade into fresh channels, and created new markets.

The steamboat age

The river steamboat and the railroad both underwent great expansion after 1837. Though the fifties were the "golden age" of the steamboat, it was in 1807 that Robert Fulton first took his "back-

woods sawmill mounted on a scow and set on fire"—the *Clermont*—
up the Hudson River. Its first voyage, New York to Albany, was a
distance of 150 miles covered in 32 hours. The sidepaddle wheels
on this 133-foot-long craft were driven by a British steam engine
made by Boulton and Watt. Invented "with a view to the navigation
of the Mississippi from New Orleans *upward*," the *Clermont* combined several elements of earlier inventions attempted by people
like John Fitch (whose *Thornton* ran a regular packet service on the
Delaware River for some time after 1790). By the end of the 1812
War, steamboats were no longer uncommon on the Delaware and
Hudson, and in 1811–1812 the *New Orleans* had steamed from Pittsburgh to New Orleans in eleven days' running time (and faced
Indian canoes, flood waters, and a minor earth tremor). In the
spring of 1815 Brownsville, Pennsylvania, was reached by a steamboat traveling upstream from New Orleans, the journey taking one
month. From that date progress was very rapid, especially when in
1824 Fulton's monopoly was set aside. The trip from New Orleans to
Louisville took less than five days by fast steamer in the fifties, and
in 1870, in a famous race, the *Robert E. Lee* beat the *Natchez* by
steaming from New Orleans to St. Louis in three days, eighteen and
a half hours. Passenger fares were at first very expensive, but fell
rapidly. In 1818 the New Orleans-Louisville trip cost up to $125, in
the 1830's up to $30. Steamers were mainly used on the Mississippi-
Missouri-Ohio system serving midwestern cities. Almost 600 steamboats were in commission in 1850, many of them more than 300 feet
in length, and made to carry 400 passengers, not including cabin
class. Steam navigation of rivers in California and Oregon developed quickly in the fifties after the gold discoveries, some of these
incredible-looking, topheavy boats actually rounding Cape Horn in
the process.

State and federal aid to steamboat navigation was small and
indirect. Unlike the turnpikes, canals, and railways, steamboat companies received no direct money or land grants from the government, and none of their stocks or bonds were purchased by
governmental bodies, except in Georgia. Attempts were made,
though, to improve river navigation, widen and deepen streams,
and remove "snags" and obstructions. Such work was undertaken
directly by state governments or *ad hoc* chartered companies, and
received some additional federal aid. The first congressional steps

to regulate steamboats were unsuccessful, but a more wisely framed and effective Steamboat Act was passed in 1852. At first the railways stimulated a greater development of steamboat navigation: this was especially true where water navigation was essential to connect railway lines, for instance across lakes Erie and Michigan and on Long Island Sound. Once *through* rail routes were completed, however, the steamboats were doomed. They shared the physical and economic disadvantages of the canals, and were outpaced, if not actually outpriced, by the railroads. The latter combined greater speed, more direct routes, an all-year-round timetable mainly unaffected by weather and temperature, and regularity of service.

Coming of the railroad

If the United States was rather slow to take the British example in the matter of canal construction, she certainly made it up in the adoption of railroads. T. P. Kettell, the southern publicist, said of these years:

The excitement in relation to canals and steamboats was yet at its zenith, when the air began to be filled with rumors of the new application of steam to land carriages and to railroads. . . . In 1825 descriptions came across the water of the great success of the Darlington railroad, which was opened to supply London with coal, and which had passenger cars moved by steam at the rate of seven miles per hour.

Before the Stockton-Darlington line was built in Britain, there had been several native American experiments, but this foreign achievement and the later Rainhill Trials of 1829 were an enormous stimulus to Americans. "The most animated controversy sprang up," wrote Kettell, ". . . [and] with the national energy of character, the idea had no sooner become disseminated than it was acted upon."

A British engine, the *Stourbridge Lion*, was the first locomotive to operate on a commercial track in the United States, but like most British engines imported in this early period it was, strange as it may seem, too heavy for American needs. So the Baltimore and Ohio used on its thirteen miles of track in 1830 a much lighter United States engine, Peter Cooper's *Tom Thumb*, while still experimenting with horse traction and sails. The second commercial railroad in the United States was built in "the agrarian South"—the Charleston and

Hamburg, connecting the major port of South Carolina with the Savannah River in the hope of diverting some of the rich cotton trade from the Georgia port of Savannah at that river's mouth. The Charleston and Hamburg had a regular passenger service from 1831, and claimed in 1833 to be the longest existing railroad in the world (136 miles).

In the Northeast the seaboard states followed a pattern of rivalry similar to that of canals. The Massachusetts Legislature chartered three railroad companies to build outward from Boston in 1831, and ten years later had a through connection to the Hudson—making good her failure to do the same by canal. Pennsylvania rapidly gained ground with four lines in the 1830's going out in all directions from Philadelphia to nearby towns like Columbia, Trenton, Reading, and, farther out, to Baltimore. In fact, by 1840 all the larger eastern states except Maine had significant mileage. Though the Appalachian barrier remained to be conquered, total United States railroad mileage in 1840 equaled that of canals. Ten years later it was almost three times greater (9,000 miles), and the problems were of a different order. The question now was: How soon to the Pacific coast? A through connection to the Great Lakes was made by the New York Central in 1850. In 1853 Chicago and in 1855 St. Louis were joined to New York City, and a year thereafter a railroad bridged the Mississippi. The same decade saw New Orleans linked to Chicago and Memphis, Tennessee with a through connection to the Atlantic coast of Virginia.

No transcontinental railroad could be built until Congress was able to agree. The idea had been in the air since the twenties, but politicians split on sectional lines, and the cities of Chicago, St. Louis, and Memphis were keen rivals in the congressional struggle, each claiming prior right to a transcontinental connection. A line was built across Nicaragua in 1855, but nothing more. Southern secession and Civil War resolved the issue a few years later. By that time several lines stretched to the very cutting edge of the western frontier, and total United States mileage of road actually being operated was well over 30,000 miles.

Public aid to America's railroads

This immense network was built within the space of three decades, 1830–1860. How was such an immense program financed?

Obviously, private enterprise capital alone could not handle such a feat of economic development.[10] It is true that in the thirties private funds were used and foreign loans at high rates were much supported in London by British capitalists and investors. But however locally important this foreign investment was, it proved ultimately inadequate, especially after the debt-repudiation fiascoes of 1837; its function was to help initiate economic developments that would eventually have occurred in any case, if somewhat more slowly. Government stepped into the breach—first state and local authorities and, later on, more massively, federal authority.

Almost all the initial state charters gave wide privileges to the railroad companies, and few, if any, placed restrictions on fares or securities. Professor Milton Heath, a most distinguished student of the South, has shown that the bulk of railroad investment in that section came from government agencies and not from private enterprise. Yet some states went so far as to grant monopoly rights to railroad companies—as did Georgia, South Carolina, Kentucky, Louisiana, New Jersey, and Massachusetts—sweeping aside normal American fears of monopolistic privilege in the scramble for riches. Between New York and Philadelphia the Camden and Amboy Railroad was given the exclusive rights to provide rail transportation. Such relaxations, spurred on by city and state rivalries, were accompanied by tax exemptions, free grants of rights-of-way and permission to establish railroad banks.

This was not all. Huge amounts of outright financial aid were given by state and local governments to private railroad companies. Countries, towns, cities, and states bought railroad securities directly with public money. State debts attributable to railroads totaled $43 million in 1838, and local aid probably exceeded this figure. In the East and West, as well as in the South, tax money was lavished on railroad loans and investments. In the antebellum South this amounted to $144 million by 1861, over 95 per cent of which came from local and state governments; the State of Virginia had supplied $21 million, Missouri over $25 million. State authorities did not stint in doling out public land either; Texas alone gave away five million acres to stimulate railroad construction.

Meanwhile, the federal government was not exactly idle in this field. Army engineers surveyed and even directed the building of some lines, free of charge. Tariffs on imported British rails and other necessities were canceled (1830–1843) by a thoughtful Congress.

But it was from 1850 onward that federal aid became massive, and took the form of Gallatin's proposal of 1808: land grants. A temporary alliance of southern and western states pushed through Congress a demand for land to support a north-south railroad from northern Illinois to Mobile, Alabama. The Act of 1850 gave the states of Illinois, Alabama, and Mississippi alternate sections of land in a strip six miles wide on each side of the proposed line. The states were then to give the land to the railroad companies, who either sold it or sold bonds secured by a mortgage on it. In this way constitutional difficulties over the role of the federal government were neatly sidestepped. The land—almost four million acres— eventually made up parts of the Illinois Central and the Mobile and Ohio railroads. In return the companies promised to convey federal troops and property without charge, and Congress was to fix the rates for mail. Having established a precedent, Congress acted upon it in the years that followed, and by 1857 had handed out to 45 railroad companies (through the intermediary of 10 states) about 18 million acres of the public domain. And this was nothing compared with the enormous land grants to the transcontinental lines after the Civil War. One could perhaps twist an old phrase around and call the American system of railroad financing one of "public enterprise for private profit," without being too far from the truth.

The railroad and the United States market

The railroads did everything to extend the American market that the turnpikes and canals did, only more so. The *Preliminary Report* of the Eighth Census (1860) declared that

. . . our railroads transport in the aggregate at least 850 tons of merchandise per annum to the mile of road in operation. Such a rate would give 26,000,000 tons as the total annual tonnage. . . . At $150 per ton, the aggregate value of the whole would be $3,900 million. Vast as this commerce is, more than three-quarters of it has been created since 1850.

A mere decade of growth! Railroads in the United States had much more to give, and their impetus was not exhausted so soon as in Britain, for the westward movement brought various repeat performances of the original impact, with the lateral extension and sequential growth of the economy. The roads that became part of the northwestern empire of James J. Hill did for Minnesota, North Dakota, and Montana in the eighties and nineties what the Chicago, Burlington and Quincy consolidation (1855) did earlier for the Midwest, and what the pioneer lines did for the Atlantic seaboard in the thirties.

More than any other single force, the rate of public and private investment in the railroads drew unused natural resources into the market economy on a large scale, and within the physical framework of a favorable land-man ratio, created high living standards for the American worker. As a geographically widespread form of social capital, the railroads created jobs all over the nation and even found the labor to fill them. By deliberate "colonizing" and by building in anticipation of traffic, the companies drew into the productive process human as well as physical resources. In any case the very building and maintenance of the network was in itself a major industry with insatiable demands for iron rails, timber, coal (eventually), engines and rolling stock, bridge and tunneling materials, and a wide range of human skills, to say nothing of huge aggregations of mobile capital. A large part of all foreign investment in nineteenth century America was tied up in railroads. New financial techniques and institutions had to be evolved, and in the process agriculture became commercialized, growing urbanization became a structural factor in American social history, the domestic market and foreign trade were metamorphosed. Externally, United States exports were cheapened and latent foreign demand for foodstuffs allowed its full expression; internally, division of labor on a continental scale became a reality—the regional specialization that has already been discussed.

In sum, the railroad created unprecedented demands for all the factors of production, and the economic, political, and psychological disturbance it caused brought successive waves of social change for years to come.

FOUR

The Productive Wealth
of the Market

Capital was accumulated through foreign trade, and the market was extended by population increase, territorial expansion, and transportation improvements. What kind of material wealth was produced, and how, as a result of these sweeping changes? The principal answer is of course agricultural wealth: cotton (and the older southern staples), grain, cattle, and hogs. The United States of 1860 was still a nation of farmers and merchants, if not so distinctly as in 1790.

The 1840's and 1850's, however, experienced steeply rising export prices, the shipping boom, immigration, an influx of foreign capital, native gold discoveries, and the build-up of social overhead capital —all of which interacted magically, bringing to the Northeast nothing less than the Industrial Revolution. New England's economic revolution was a regional and partial affair, but with the railroad drive into the Midwest in the fifties it produced the miracle of "self-sustaining growth" thereafter. In Walt Rostow's now indispensable phrase, the United States had made its "take-off."

Despite this miracle of social change, manufacturing production did not by any means characterize the United States economy in the first half of the nineteenth century. Americans in those years were avidly absorbed in exploiting to the full their most abundant factor of production—the soil. Without the farmers' successes of the pre-war years there could have been no regional specialization, no "interregional flows," and no Industrial Revolution.

1. THE RICHES OF THE SOIL

American agriculture felt the impact of two fundamental changes in the early century: first, the enormous and rapid expansion of the cultivable land area, and, second, the beginnings of scientific farming. Ups and downs came, but the era generally was well-to-do, buoyant, wide open with opportunity for the hardworking farmer who was prepared to make the most of rising prices and of markets at home and abroad that seemed bottomless. In the Old Northwest land values rose and rose, and after about 1830 the price of southern slaves mounted too. Though the populace managed to double itself each decade, labor remained scarce and wages much higher than in the Old World. The United States was destined to have a favorable land-man ratio, it seemed, for perpetuity. Additions to American territory more or less kept up with additions to the population. Six people per square mile in 1800 became only eleven per square mile by 1860.[1]

Labor scarcity and land abundance not only encouraged but dictated a form of cultivation that was extensive rather than intensive. The owner of the average family-size American farm was not a rich man; he lacked capital and equipment as well as labor. He tended to "use up" the soil quickly with primitive agricultural methods that "mined out" all the fertility. Having little knowledge of fertilization and conservation, and no means to pay for it anyway, he promptly moved on to the abundant and cheap virgin lands farther west. This was from our viewpoint "wasteful" of course; we now live in a world of dwindling natural resources. The antebellum farmer and planter sacrificed long-term national interests to short-term private profits. Yet the system made economic sense to the average American of the day: there was plenty of one productive factor and a dearth of the other two; he manipulated his resources to maximize chances of survival and success. Looking backward, some of us would still criticize the restless, speculative spirit of one frontier type—the man who was only secondly a farmer, whose primary desire was to buy land cheaply, hold it in a rising market, then sell out and move on. Private fortunes were built and public resources prodigally wasted. But given the physical framework of possibilities, and in view of the fact that federal land policy both facilitated and encouraged speculation, it is perhaps not so easy to adopt a clear ethical position about the actions of individual speculators and farmers.

The westward-moving frontier

The physical framework of possibilities and federal land policy alike were conditioned by the one central phenomenon of United States agricultural history: the westward movement. In the words of F. J. Turner, creator of the classical "frontier thesis" in American historiography:

American history has been to large degree the history of the Great West. The existence of an area of free land, its continuous recession, and the advance of American settlement Westward, explain American development.

Whether or not the westward movement can be said to "explain American development," there is no doubt that for three centuries the subjugation and exploitation of vast western resources were decisive factors in American economic life and a subject of great political disagreement. Throughout its irregular stages of development—colonial fur trappers and missionaries giving way later to cattlemen, miners, and farmers and eventually to capitalists bent on larger-scale conversion of the natural resources—the "frontier" affected agriculture, industry, labor, and transportation, and the Civil War was in part its outcome.

The Land Act of 1785 and the two ordinances (Northwest, 1787, Southwest, 1790) had established the rectangular survey of townships and the "Territorial" system of government for newly settled areas.[2] As western representatives entered the national government, they brought reductions in the price of land (from $2 to $1.25 in 1796) and in the size of the basic unit of sale (from 640 acres in 1785 down to 80 acres in 1820). Meanwhile the purchase of Louisiana Territory in 1803 for $15 million as an assurance of controlled river outlets for western farm produce doubled the size of the United States. Western pressure was still unrelenting, and two further concessions were granted after 1820: the right of preemption[3] (legalized in 1841) and the actual giving away of the public domain by the federal government to bona-fide settlers (the Homestead Act, 1862).

Under this body of legislation two principal new areas of settlement were opened up: the so-called Old Northwest and Old Southwest. The Old Northwest lay north of the Ohio and east of the Mississippi, and comprised what is now Ohio, Indiana, Illinois, Michigan, and Wisconsin (the "East North Central" states); the Old Southwest covered Kentucky, Tennessee, Mississippi, Alabama (the present "East South Central" zone), and Louisiana.

Agricultural revolution in the Old Northwest

The Old Northwest was rapidly settled by southern backwoodsmen driven northward across the Ohio to escape the overwhelming competition of rich planters, by pioneers from the middle Atlantic and New England states and later by German, Swiss, and British migrants fleeing from intolerable conditions in Europe. As soon as 1803 Ohio was sufficiently settled for admittance to the Union, and Indiana (1816), Illinois (1818), Michigan (1837), and Wisconsin (1848) followed suit. Population multiplied and by 1860 totaled seven million.

The immense potential wealth of the Old Northwest was more fully realized when the Erie and Ohio canals and the railroads opened up the area to wider markets in the East and in Europe, a process of change we have already examined. The terrain into which lines of transportation began to extend was geographically the northeastern part of the Central Basin, one of the world's richest farming areas, created about 25,000 years ago when the glaciers of the great ice cap gouged out the Great Lakes and pushed soil off huge sections of Canada into the United States, laying it sometimes 300 feet thick. For two hundred years of American history new farms were carved out of eastern forest lands in the classic pioneer image, but the frontiersmen of the early nineteenth century, when they reached the Indiana-Illinois border country, emerged from the forest onto an immense, almost treeless plain covered with tall grass of shoulder height, undulating to the distant horizon. Here was a perplexing new experience: the eastern tongue of the American prairie.[4] They hesitated for about a generation at the forest's edge, convinced that treeless soil was barren. In addition, they were unable, with existing plows, to break the thick, heavily matted prairie sod. Therefore it was livestock that assumed immediate importance in the Old Northwest, and since the eastern sections of the newly settled area (Ohio, southern Michigan, and Indiana) had a geographic character not unlike familiar New England, the basic economic unit was the relatively small family farm. Once men overcame their superstitions and improved their technology, they soon discovered that the prairie soil was in fact rich, fertile, and deep—ideal for heavy cereal crops. Indiana, Illinois, and Wisconsin began to replace Kentucky and Tennessee as America's granary. Almost half the nation's crop was coming from the five states of the former Northwest Territory by 1860.

One innovation that made this possible was a new plow. The wooden and cast-iron plows of the eighteenth and early nineteenth centuries were scarcely adequate to break the tough prairie sod despite various improvements such as Jethrow Wood's cast-iron three-piece plow made of standardized, interchangeable parts (1819). In Europe, of course, iron plows had been at work for many centuries, but the prairie needed a heavy plow with a long, sloping moldboard to turn the sod. Labor shortage and growing markets stimulated many Americans like Thomas Jefferson and Daniel Webster to make experiments. Heavy, clinging western soil stuck to pitted iron plowshares; sharp, smoothly polished steel was the answer. In 1833 John Lane of Illinois made a steel plowshare out of strips from an old saw blade; but the first successful all-steel plow was made by John Deere, a leading pioneer in United States farm machinery, in 1847. Despite its higher cost (in pre-Bessemer steel days) the Deere plow and models like it were in widespread use within a decade.

The American farmer's keen interest in all kinds of labor-saving devices brought about the basic mechanization of many hand processes before the Civil War. Patents were taken out for mowers, reapers, threshers, drills, horse rakes, feed grinders, and a host of other inventions in iron and steel. Obed Hussey (1833) and Cyrus McCormick (patent of 1834) independently designed similar machines for reaping. McCormick's machines became the most popular after 1855. About 100,000 mechanical reapers were being worked by 1860, but their greatest application came in the postwar years. Simultaneously the threshing machine replaced the centuries-old European hand flail and threshing floor, Hiram and John Pitts of Maine having introduced a thresher farming mill in 1837. As mechanical threshing spread, much of it was done by itinerant crews traveling about the countryside at harvesttime. A workshop was set up in Racine, Wisconsin, in 1844 to manufacture mechanical threshers representing a labor-saving of two-thirds over the old hand methods.

In Jefferson's words:

In Europe the object is to make the most of their land, labor being abundant; here it is to make the most of our labor, land being abundant.

For this very reason Americans were far less interested in scientific planning and conservation than in mechanization. Few farmers were interested in the ideas of scientific agriculture disseminated in earlier eighteenth century Britain by Arthur Young, Robert Bakewell, Thomas Coke of Holkham, and Charles Townshend. Some idealists and progressive farmers like Washington, Jefferson, and Livingston, acting under the influence of the French prerevolutionary economists (the "physiocrats"), used European methods of fertilization, crop rotation, and breeding. That great political compromiser Henry Clay introduced the first Herefords into the United States in 1817. Beef cattle quality was further improved by importing British shorthorns and Devons, and dairy herds benefited from the introduction of Ayrshires, Jerseys, and Guernseys. English breeds of hogs and sheep (for pork, mutton or lamb), and Spanish merino sheep (for their fine wool) also came to the United States. The slow ox was replaced gradually by the horse, among the popular heavy draft breeds being the tremendously strong Percheron (first imported from France in 1839) and the English Clydesdale, and a lighter general-purpose breed of the famous Morgan family—uniquely descended from a bay stallion called "Justin Morgan" (Vermont, 1795–1821) of unknown ancestry.[5] Some attempt was also made to improve agricultural education with societies, schools, farm journals, county fairs, and the small beginnings of government aid. But busy public men like Washington sadly neglected their model farms for the calls of duty. Mount Vernon was described only twenty-five years after Washington's death as a "widespread and perfect agricultural ruin"; and though Jefferson's son-in-law was the first to introduce contour plowing technique to the Piedmont at Monticello, the place was worth a bare $2,500 at his demise. Improvements in United States agriculture before 1865 were little compared to the changes still to come; but at least the foundations of mechanized farming had been laid down, and according to a specialist, Professor Clarence Danhof, the farm tools and machinery of 1860 would enable a man with a two-horse team to perform ten times the work he could have done by hand.

Western farm products streamed eastward by canal and rail and southward by river steamboat and rail after about 1825. No longer was it necessary to drive cattle and hogs to eastern markets "on the hoof." "Agricultural industries" such as meat-packing and flour milling sprang up quickly at transportation nodal centers, and once the Ohio Valley was settled, Cincinnati ("Porkopolis") emerged—as we have seen—as the key packing and distributing center. After the 1850's Chicago, Kansas City, and Omaha built themselves up as meat-packing cities, and the industry is still today a major midwestern activity, together with the processing of countless by-products: leather goods, glue, fertilizers, soaps and fats. Meanwhile, the second major "agricultural industry," flour milling, flourished before the war in urban centers situated on the great river systems: Cincinnati, Louisville, St. Louis.

Agricultural adjustment in the East

Agricultural revolution and extensive migration to the Old Northwest and the cotton boom in the Old Southwest contrasted sharply with farming conditions in the East at this time. In the middle Atlantic states the pressure of competition from western farm produce could be eased by the growth of local foodstuff demands brought about by urbanization and the gradual industrialization of parts of the Delaware and Hudson valleys. In addition, soil here was more fertile and agriculture more advanced and scientific than farther north.

New England farmers most of all felt the chill wind of competition that blew out of the Old Northwest. They faced the greatest readjustments caused by the completion of western through routes and specialized techniques of bulk transportation. Rapid urbanization and the coming of industry alone saved the most adaptable New Englanders by creating a market for dairy produce, fruit and perishables. "Truck farming" (which the British with equal justification call "market gardening") was developed, entirely dependent on local population centers. After the war Yankee farmers turned even more to specialized types of farming of an intensive sort, one tied to guaranteed urban markets with hopes of continuous growth.[6]

On the southern Atlantic coast, Tidewater lands were abandoned in the early nineteenth century by farmers who migrated to the Piedmont and left behind them scenes of agricultural desolation and soil erosion. Economic depression in the upper South forced Virginia planters into the dubious business of trading slaves to their more fortunate southwestern cousins. Meanwhile, in contrast, the Cotton Kingdom waxed strong on both sides of the Mississippi.

Dixie: the Cotton Kingdom

Although Kentucky and Tennessee were admitted to the Union in 1792 and 1796, respectively, after being settled by backwoodsmen from the upcountry hills of Virginia and the Carolinas in the earlier eighteenth century, for the most part the Old Southwest was occupied at a later date than the Old Northwest. Chief factors in the drive to the Southwest were the invention of the cotton gin and the expansionist spirit that produced the War of 1812.[7] "Land hunger" sent planters from the eroded Tidewater lands westward to the floodplains of the Mississippi and its many tributaries, like the river Yazoo, rich in black, waxy loams. Here the newer states—Louisiana (1812), Mississippi (1817), Alabama (1819), and Arkansas (1836) —tried to reproduce as faithfully as possible the plantation culture of the Southeast as some sections of the Old Northwest aped New England.

Before the moving tide of successful middle-class planters, the "poor white" element was pushed still farther west. This class, composed heavily of northern pioneers and yeomen who abandoned marginal farms to trek south in the hope of doing better with one or two slaves, found that the wealthier whites monopolized the fertile "bottom" lands of the valleys and forced them out onto inferior soils, or westward across the Mississippi and northward back beyond the Ohio. The genuine poor whites, however, the so-called "hillbillies" and "crackers," probably never exceeded a few thousand in number, while the majority of those planters who migrated to the Old Southwest and built the Cotton Kingdom were not themselves large slaveowners.

In colonial days the larger planters depended on tobacco, indigo, and rice; but Whitney's cotton gin, the "take-off" of the British textile industry in the 1790's, and the growth later of United States textile manufacturing in New England soon made cotton the dominant economic consideration of the 7 million whites and 4 million colored slaves who inhabited the southern states in 1860. By 1820 the annual cotton crop (under 350,000 bales) was already the most valuable southern interest, and from thenceforward cotton output doubled every ten years, to a total of nearly 4 million bales (1860). By that time King Cotton involved about two-thirds of all American slaves in its production, and constituted two-thirds of the total value of all United States exports.

Both long- and short-staple cotton were grown in Dixie. Long-staple, fine fabric cotton was restricted mainly to the sea islands off the Georgia and South Carolina coasts and had been introduced from the Bahamas by Loyalist refugees in about 1786. By the 1820's, the peak of long-staple cotton export production, an average 11 million pounds a year, were sold abroad. Small per-acre yield (about 150 pounds) and the need for highly skilled pickers were two serious disadvantages of this good quality "sea island cotton," and it was not this type but the hardy short-staple variety, cultivable in upland and interior regions, that managed to succeed the declining indigo industry. The succession was made possible when Eli Whitney managed to solve the technical difficulties of separating seed and fiber.

Whitney, a Connecticut Yankee and graduate of Yale who migrated south to become a tutor, devised his crude but workable cotton gin on a plantation near Savannah, Georgia, in 1793. His device replaced the labor of ten slaves if hand operated and fifty slaves if horse operated. In March, 1794, he took out a United States patent and expected to make a handsome fortune from his monopoly rights. Other inventors stole and perfected his ideas, and neither planters, entrepreneurs, nor judges would entertain his claims seriously. The field was therefore wide open for rapid exploitation, and the perfection of the sewing machine by I. M. Singer in 1851 added to the voracious demand for cotton. The improved cotton gin enabled a man to work 350 pounds of cotton a day—as opposed to about one pound. But cotton bolls ripen unevenly at different times, and the problem of cotton picking was not solved mechanically until 1925 (the Rust brothers' machine); meanwhile, the slave could cultivate much more than he could pick. Labor shortages were severe at cotton-picking time.

The economics of plantation slavery

Cotton cultivation was intimately bound up with the plantation system and slavery as a social, economic, and racial-caste institution. Since cotton played an essential role in the interregional and international structure that was creating greater American wealth, it is necessary to understand the economic nature of American Negro slavery.

Like the manors of feudal Britain, southern cotton plantations differed widely in character and size, and hasty generalizations about them may well cause distress to the empirically-minded historian.[8] First, we must agree immediately with those writers who have successfully demolished by research the myth of an aristocratic "cavalier" South dominated by huge plantations. At least half the total cotton crop was grown by men who could afford to employ no more than five or six slaves and who worked alongside them in the fields. The yeomen planters, men "on the make," who moved bag and baggage to the Southwest in search of opportunity, sometimes had slaves and sometimes did not. Some large planters migrated, but few of them could rebuild their traditional homes in the Southwest, outside the aristocratic Sugar Bowl area of Louisiana. The Old Southwest, in fact, shared some of the buoyant, aggressive character of the Old Northwest—western qualities on a southern base. As for the South as a whole, less than 3 percent of the white population lived in families owning 20 or more slaves. This latter top 3 percent owned well over half of all southern slaves, although about 2 million whites lived in slaveowning households. Since a minimum of at least 20 slaves was needed to make the employment of a white overseer an economic proposition, and the average Negro field hand of the fifties could tend about 10 acres of corn and 10 of cotton, the minimum economic size of a large plantation would be (including living space, uncultivable wasteland, and so on) about 400 or 500 acres. The truth was that under 3 percent of all southern farm units were bigger than 500 acres.

Of course, statistics can conceal great diversity, like the 2,000-acre cane-sugar plantations of the southeast Louisiana delta that employed large numbers of slaves and were capital-intensive too, demanding in the 1830's steam-powered sugar machinery that could cost up to $14,000. Furthermore, the thousands of modest yeomen farmers who made up the majority of southern whites gave way to the strategic economic and political pressure exerted by the large slaveholding planter, and copied his way of life and thought. Competing socially with colored slave labor on the one hand and great landed wealth on the other, the middle-class white succumbed to strong leadership and came to identify with the white aristocracy of the Cotton Kingdom.

The first American Negroes were brought to Virginia by a Dutch sea captain in 1619, just twelve years after the first successful English settlement was established at Jamestown. There was no precedent in English law for outright slavery, but the first Negroes and those who followed were absorbed into a growing system of servitude based on apprenticeship and vagrancy laws, a system that spread throughout the colonies and provided an important supply of colonial labor for over a century. From 1670 onward, Virginia and the other colonies fixed the legal status of the Negro as a slave, and labor scarcity as much as distinctive coloring seemed to provide whatever sanctions were called for in treating him quite separately.

Slavery in the North did not develop on a large scale, through accident of geography: under colonial rule the contrast was already evident between the northern family farms carved out of deciduous forests and the southern plantation economy. Most northern slaves were in domestic service and were gradually liberated. As late as the Missouri Compromise (1820), however, slave trading persisted in the North, in New York and New Jersey, and Yankees helped to supply slaves to the southern market for many decades. The slave traffic continued illegally after 1808 and was made possible only by northern capital and northern ships. Even after the Civil War, Yankee merchantmen made their fortunes trading slaves to Brazil and elsewhere. The guilt of slavery rests on many shoulders.

It seems likely that for a few years after the War of Independence slavery was in full decline as a labor system; economic depression in the South appeared to indicate future liberation for the Negro. But unfortunately, from the humanitarian viewpoint, the economic crisis passed, and in the boom that followed cotton was crowned, the question of plantation slavery being left over to be fought out, if not finally solved, by bloody civil conflict.

Slave conditions on the southern plantations varied. In larger establishments of a capitalistic nature where productivity overshadowed the social aspect, the Negro was reduced to the status of a mere tool, slave trading was common, and brutal treatment less restrained by peculiar customs and traditions. This "industrial slavery" was less likely to appear on the smaller plantations where the lives of slaves and owners would become of necessity more closely involved in a web of social relationships. Even on the large plantations the house servants who lived and worked closer to whites would be better off; they copied white customs, received a minimum household education, and indeed considered themselves socially superior to the field hands whose principal daily contact was with the white overseer, often an embittered recruit from the small farmer or even "poor white" class. But the number of house servants was negligible, and swamped by the mass of field hands.

Economic necessity and common sense clearly dictated that slaves should be housed, fed, and clothed adequately (according to the general standards of the day, which in the South, as the traveler F. L. Olmsted discovered, were not very high). Slaves normally worked fixed hours or by "stints" (set tasks). Perhaps the frontier farmers of Canada or the factory workers of newly industrialized Britain had somewhat better returns for their labor; but the peasants of Ireland lived more uncertain and precarious lives at a lower level of material well-being. The food of the Negro slave was generally coarse and lacked variety, but no more so than the daily diet of countless country folk in twentieth century Spain and Italy. Material

living standards for the ordinary white farmer in Dixie were probably only a degree or so better than those of the Negro. Slaves, poor
whites, overseers, and yeomen farmers alike wore coarse homespun
cotton and cowhide, and ate corn bread, hominy grits,[9] salt pork,
and milk, with vegetables only in season. They lived in log cabins
usually windowless. Negro slaves worked no longer hours than the
northern "wage slaves" in the textile mills or those who tilled the
soil of Iowa. (Again, sugar plantations are the exception here, slaves
being worked sometimes eighteen hours a day. But conditions for
the Negro generally in Louisiana—with its Spanish and French
inheritance of easier racial attitudes—were better than elsewhere in
the South.) Throughout the year, in and out of season, whether the
crop were good or bad, the southern slave was housed, fed, and
clothed, together with his family. Southerners strenuously defended
their "peculiar institution" against the industrial wage slavery of the
North on these telling grounds: the factory "hand" was subjected
to impersonal cyclical and technological market forces that discarded
him whenever it was profitable to do so.

The worst features of slavery were the domestic slave trade, the
legal discriminations practiced universally against Negroes, and the
personal degradations involved in the system. The economic origins
of the domestic slave trade lay in the decline of the upper South
and the simultaneous growth of the cotton states. Inevitably a trade
in slaves arose from Virginia, Maryland, and North Carolina to states
of the deep South with an increasingly bad labor shortage: Alabama, Mississippi, Texas, and Louisiana. Evidence about outright
slave breeding is hard to evaluate, but there are grounds for sus-
pecting that it took place in Maryland, Kentucky, and Virginia
where the sale of slaves became a principal source of profit to many
planters and farmers. Incentives to breeding could include donation
of land, separate cabins, cash bonuses, clothes, rest—even ultimate
freedom. However, women of both races in the South tended to
begin families very early in life. At any rate the upper South "exported" about 180,000 slaves in the 1840's, and another 230,000 in
the 1850's. With a rough average price of $800 or so, this represented
an enormous traffic for traders, speculators, and auctioneers. Social
stigma was attached to the slave-trading profession, of course, but
it gave rise nevertheless to a class of *nouveaux riches* like the Gads-
dens, Ryans, and De Saussures of South Carolina. Centers of the

traffic were Charleston, Savannah, Memphis, New Orleans, and the federal District of Columbia.

Legal discriminations against Negroes as slaves rapidly became racist in character; even free Negroes had scant protection under the law, and there were few or no laws against assaulting a slave or to guarantee personal property and marriage rights of colored people. As for personal degradation and lack of spiritual freedom, Stanley Elkins has given us the most systematic analysis: the utter dependence of colored slave on white master, the destruction of family structure, and, what was especially crushing, the denial to the Negro man of his normal male role as father, husband, and head of household. Probably this paternalism of the master class, however benevolent at times, was the most pernicious and corrosive feature of American Negro slavery.

Trying to defend slavery, southern spokesmen used arguments culled from Greek democracy, from the Bible, and from pseudo-biology, John C. Calhoun eventually bringing himself to the point where he could declare slavery to be a "positive good." Economically, apart from the important wage-slavery argument, it was claimed that cotton production—the basis of the American economy—needed Negro labor, which was well adapted to subtropical plantation agriculture. Slavery was the best administrative system to control Negroes in large numbers, and it facilitated division of labor and various internal economies. Slaves were less oppressed and poverty-stricken than northern proletarians, and in the South a spirit of cooperation and social conscience was said to replace bitter industrial strife and the class struggle. Lines of defense of this sort ignored the fact that whites did work successfully in the southern fields, as in other subtropical parts of the world, that free labor was very likely much more efficient and easily managed in the long run than slaves, and that despite the alleged social equilibrium and harmonious relations produced by slavery there was a pervading fear of "slave revolt" throughout the southern states.

More recent scholarship has thrown up a different kind of question, though: Was slavery "profitable"? Could you make money as a plantation slaveowner? To combat earlier claims, based on plantation account books, that slavery was in decline before the Civil War broke out and was no longer a viable economic institution, Conrad and Meyers reexamined slave operations in terms of modern capital

theory. Considered as a capital investment, and in view of his initial
cost, life expectancy, annual maintenance costs, and variations in
productivity per head, they concluded that the slave was a profitable
proposition compared with the average returns then available on
securities in the New York Stock Exchange.

In the upper South, given a complex cost structure in a period
of rising prices and falling soil fertility, the investment return on
Negro slaves for plantation work was less certain. Here the central
factors that sustained the slave system as a going concern were
slave breeding and slave trading to meet the unrelenting demand
from the Old Southwest for colored labor. Prime field hands rose in
market price from about $250 (1790) to $1,800 and above (1860).
Highest profits realized on investment in slaves came from plantation units of optimum size, situated on fertile soils, as in Mississippi
during the 1850's. To some degree profits would depend on the skill
and judgment shown by the planter when he originally bought the
slave. Heavy capital gains could also be made by smart speculative
buyers, though naturally bad financial loss could be suffered if
erratic cotton prices fell immediately after slaves had been purchased on a rising market. Mounting slave prices cannot be regarded
as a rough guide to the profitability of slavery as a labor system;
southern planters themselves were never pushed sufficiently by
economic circumstances to consider other economic alternatives,
such as free labor;[10] and perhaps this is some indication that slavery
was not on the point of collapse.

The economics of slavery cannot reasonably be studied on such
narrow grounds as "profitability" alone. Apart from the fact that
Negroes could grow more cotton than they could pick and that all
unfree labor is notoriously inefficient, high cost of slave labor impeded the accumulation of normal regional capital and therefore
slowed down mechanization of agriculture as well as investment by
Southerners themselves in local industries. There was no comparison
at all between the impact of the agricultural revolution in the North
and in the South. F. L. Olmsted (one-time experimental farmer
and the pioneer American landscape architect who designed New
York's Central Park in 1858) reported after three extensive southern
tours that some plantations were so short of capital equipment that
they lacked a plow. Plantation slavery, moreover, was a rigid structure not adaptable to economic production under market conditions

of unstable demand and experimental technology. Its narrowly trained, uneducated, and unadaptable slave-labor force almost dictated monoculture, whether of rice, tobacco, sugar, or cotton. It supported in the South a hierarchical agrarian society dominated by a leisured aristocratic elite and a more generalized "country gentleman" ethos, that opposed itself to social and economic change.

The health of the dependent agrarian economy of the South fluctuated with conditions in world markets and unstable international demand for raw staples. Its transportation and commercial system was relatively undeveloped through a low rate of urbanization caused by the plantation pattern of settlement and the reluctance of Europeans to immigrate. Chiefly through plantation slavery the very population of Dixie failed to grow at anything like the northern rate. Potential immigration was discouraged by lack of opportunity, a more highly stratified social situation, unusual climate, and the need to compete with cheap slave labor. Only 3.4 percent of Southerners were foreign-born in 1860, falling to just over 2 percent by 1900; in New England 15 percent came from Europe in 1860, almost 26 percent in 1900. Both North and South were evenly divided as to total population in 1790, having slightly under 2 million each. By 1860 the North had something under 20 million and the South 11 million. Southerners were "fighting against the census returns," and the institution of plantation slavery had much to answer for.

Traditional southern crops

Cotton was not the only southern crop depending on plantation slavery: sugar cane and rice were also best managed on a large scale. In contrast, tobacco, hemp, corn, wheat, and livestock did not justify the expense of a large slave-labor force. Three slaves could till about fifty acres of hemp. Consequently, in the border states of Kentucky, Maryland, and Missouri the very word "plantation" was almost obsolete by the 1850's.

Rice cultivation in Georgia and the Carolinas was a capital-intensive business with concentrated slaveholdings in some places amounting to 700 Negroes. Peak production was reached on the Atlantic coast in mid-century, after which the area never fully recovered from the ravages of civil war and the competition of rice lands in Louisiana, Arkansas, and Texas. A series of disastrous storms culminated in the tropical holocaust of 1906 and destroyed most of the remaining seaboard plantations, which were eventually turned into game preserves for wealthy Northerners.

Sugar-cane plantations were also highly capitalistic concerns, as we have seen, involving use of expensive equipment that came to be run by steam power. Cane was first brought to Louisiana by Jesuits from Santo Domingo. The island's slave uprisings of 1791–1795 made Louisiana a refuge of French planters. Among their number, one soldier, Jean Étienne Boré, discovered how to granulate sugar from cane juice in 1795, pocketing a profit of $12,000 on his first crop. A typical antebellum sugar plantation of which the records are preserved was Magnolia, about fifty miles south of New Orleans on the rich delta soil. Over 2,200 acres in extent, it stretched a goodly two miles along the Mississippi, absorbed a labor force well over a hundred strong, and produced a gross income of $148,-000 in 1861. Yellow fever, unstable prices, climatic hazards, and international competition faced Louisiana sugar planters. They survived the rivalry of the West Indies only by means of federal intervention—a highly protective tariff imposed in 1821.

Hemp was of local significance chiefly in Kentucky, though always prized as a frontier crop because it supplied a coarse cloth in universal use. In central Tennessee, Missouri, and the bluegrass region of Kentucky hemp growers flourished in the late 1820's, favored, like the sugar planters, by a federal tariff. Henry Clay could scarcely help making federal protection an important plank in his political platform, the "American System," since he had taken good care to marry a hemp heiress.

As for that traditional staple, John Rolfe's weed, its economic history is rather uncertain after the War of 1812. Jefferson's embargo, the war itself, and foreign competition hit the tobacco market adversely for United States planters. After 1840 or so, new species of leaf and new curing methods were used on new lands. The planters migrated to the Piedmont and over the mountains to Tennessee, Kentucky, and Ohio. However, despite the anxiety this caused Virginia and North Carolina, tobacco production doubled and trebled in these states in the 1850's. At the outbreak of war the United States formed the world's greatest tobacco-growing area.

Cotton, sugar, rice, and tobacco were the South's chief commercial crops grown for cash; but in acreage, total weight, and total value none of these staples matched corn (maize). Grown by slaves on cotton plantations and by white yeomen farmers all over, corn was the essential food product that kept the South alive—to say nothing of the whiskey. The upper South "exported" corn to the Old Southwest, but apart from this internal movement, it was rarely marketed.

Despite the considerable variety of southern farm wealth, its commercial agriculture involved dangerous soil-mining and monoculture of the staples in one-crop regions. And the plantation slavery system kept a large percentage of the white population in poverty, supported a caste hierarchy, and gave the South a false unity or cultural identity that its true diversity belied.

2. THE WEALTH OF THE FACTORY

We have looked at the principal kind of productive wealth that the American people created before the Civil War—the riches of the soil. These riches supported contrasting labor systems and social structures in the Northwest and the South. Meanwhile, events were taking place in the northeastern sector that would totally transform the nature of the entire economy when given full rein by public policy and private opinion after the war. Historical forces from various sources were converging in the 1840's and 1850's to produce the kind of social change that Britain had already undergone a few decades before: the transmutation, irrevocable once made, from a farming to a manufacturing society, from merchant to industrial capitalism. This "take-off" impelled Americans willy-nilly toward a world in which the wealth of the factory would far overshadow the riches of the soil.

Between the Treaty of Ghent (1814) and Lee's surrender to Grant at Appomattox Courthouse (1865), the population of the United States multiplied by more than four, the volume of manufacturing output by twelve, the value of manufactured goods by eight. Absolute increases of this magnitude were accompanied by changes in the scale and technique of industrial organization, increased factor mobility through a revolutionized transportation system, increased specialization and deeper local concentration of industry. The Industrial Revolution came to America.

"Take-off" in textiles

Cotton textiles spearheaded the revolution; New England was the chief section and Massachusetts the leading state. Woolen textiles followed cotton's lead only after some delay. The same pattern had occurred in the original Industrial Revolution of northern England, where would-be woolen manufacturers faced greater technical difficulties, craft conservatism (woolens were very old, cottons very new), inelastic raw-material supplies and inelastic demand. American factory woolens not only had all this to contend with; they also had to meet the heavy competition of finer British wool and cheaper British cotton manufactures. Early attempts to manufacture woolens under the factory system—like the Hartford experiment of 1788, mentioned in Alexander Hamilton's *Report on Manufactures* (1791) —dissolved pretty quickly. Americans continued to import finer cloths and make the coarser homespuns on the farm. Expanded home demand caused by the Anglo-American War of 1812–1814 and the introduction of hardy merino sheep with their long, silky wool solved some of the problems of woolen manufacturers. The number of factories rose from 100 (1820) to about 2,000 (1860) —though farmhouse handlooms persisted in the United States, as in Britain, until the later nineteenth century. Overall increase in production of woolen textiles was 51 percent in the 1850's and the value of the year's output in 1860 was about $40 million. Cotton textiles were worth three times as much ($115 million), and their output had increased 76 percent over the decade.

Early attempts to copy and adapt English cotton spinning and carding machinery in the 1780's received a great incentive from the increased output of raw cotton in Dixie made possible by Whitney's gin from 1793. The growth of spinning mills now seemed a necessity. Three years earlier a clever British immigrant, Sam Slater, had designed a mill in Pawtucket, Rhode Island, from memory—in defiance of English laws passed to protect home manufactures by prohibiting export of technical innovations. Slater constructed a twenty-four-spindle waterpowered frame of an English (Arkwright) model, and two carding machines. Though Slater was financed by a rich Quaker merchant, Moses Brown, many mills like his failed, mainly through lack of capital and inexperienced management. Bankers and merchants used to the moderate complexities of commercial organization and management had to learn new tricks—win over consumers, instill factory discipline in masses of rural workpeople, find skilled mechanics to build and maintain machinery, train foremen and superintendents, schedule production in some regular fashion, analyze costs, and learn to keep strict accounts with double-entry bookkeeping. Small rural spinning mills with little capital failed by the dozen. Large, heavily capitalized urban mills, supported by leading merchants in the community, made large profits.

Most famous was the Boston Manufacturing Company sponsored by the big local names, the Jacksons and Appletons, and led by Francis Cabot Lowell. Lowell's "Boston Associates" invested $600,- 000 over a six-year period in an experimental factory at Waltham, Massachusetts, opened in 1813. The "Waltham Plan" meant a unified management governing all the main processes of production from spinning to dyeing in a single plant, a single marketing agency, and the use (up to the mid-1840's) of young female labor drawn from farms far and wide throughout New England and housed in special corporation dormitories. Large capital and a tractable labor force brought spectacular success for Waltham; the company made profits even during the bad years of British competition after the 1812–1814 War. The Boston Associates were able to compete with Lancashire cottons because they turned out a coarse-weave, cheap, standardized, hard-wearing fabric (cotton shirtings and sheetings), easy to mass-produce with unskilled workers, and in great demand everywhere in a society of rural folk. Similarly, the Merrimack Manufacturing Company at Lowell, Massachusetts, concentrated successfully on calicoes, and by the 1820's was in a position to pioneer the truly large-scale use of waterpower through improved dams and machinery (leather transmission belts and metal gears replaced clumsy timber cogs and shafts).

The encouraging example of the Waltham experiment produced a crop of cotton-mill towns succored by the waterpower of New England's streams: Lowell, Lawrence, Manchester, Nashua, and the rest. Almost simultaneously New England emigrants spread the new industrialism into the Mohawk and Hudson valleys. By 1830 the United States had about 800 cotton mills; by 1860, 1,100. Most of these mills were located in Massachusetts, and they devoured 423 million pounds of southern raw cotton in 1860. Why did manufacturers not locate in the South, close to the raw material supply? Some attempt was made to root the textile industry in Georgia and the Carolinas, but without much result until the 1880's. Apparently the New England setting had certain distinct advantages over the South. Opposed to the cumulative disadvantages the South suffered through plantation slavery, social rigidity, and economic dependency, New England could offer the labor of free men and women (added to in the 1840's by immigration), accumulated capital, considerable existing social overhead investment (port installations, transportation facilities, banks and financial institutions), and an elite or leadership group alive to the needs of industry and commerce. In any case cotton is not like a metallic ore or fuel; as a raw material it does not lose weight or get consumed during the manufacturing process, otherwise it would have been more economic to site the mills in the South from the outset. If this location had occurred, the major function of the South would still have been to export raw cotton; even though the number of United States cotton spindles leaped from 20,000 or so (1800) to over 5 million (1860), the British mid-century number stood at about 21 million.

Once the early technical problems were solved, the role of New England textiles was crucial in the spread of revolutionary industrial methods and the factory system through the northeastern states. The region as a whole enjoyed a happy "factor endowment"—river waterpower in New England, coal and iron ore in Pennsylvania, a reservoir of labor skills. In the 1850's the cotton and woolen textile industries became highly localized, and the size of individual firms grew rapidly, tied to nationwide rather than to merely local markets. The business experience and technical know-how learned in this prototype industry reacted on the rich factor endowment, and from the textile sector industrialism spread outward to other crafts.

In the chain reaction of economic growth there are certain strategic interconnections—"backward and forward linkages" (to borrow a phrase used by several economists, including Professor Douglass North). The textile industry was well suited to make these creative connections, forward toward transforming the clothing industry, for example, and backward in the economic process, creating a demand for factory machinery, machine tools, and ultimately a demand for timber, leather, iron, and coal. In this way the manufacture of cloth became for a time America's greatest industry, and in turn made the manufacture of textile machinery America's greatest heavy industry. In addition, innovations made in response to the technical or economic bottlenecks in one industry can often be applied to other areas. Elias Howe's sewing machine (patented 1846) was the product of two influences: his apprenticeship in a cotton textile machinery factory in Lowell and his later training as an instrument maker in Cambridge. The sewing machine he invented, improved by Singer, first revolutionized the clothing industry and after 1860 was rapidly applied to the boot-and-shoe industry in turn (Lyman Blake's sole-stitching patent of 1858). Like textile manufactures, boot-and-shoe production was heavily concentrated in Massachusetts.

The iron roots of heavy industry

The classical Industrial Revolution, although ushered in by the cotton textile industry, was based essentially on coal, iron, and steam power. Formerly-great world powers that lacked coal and iron—like the Netherlands—fell back in the race for hegemony. Countries like Britain and the United States, which possessed great natural resources of coal and iron in proximity, rose to economic wealth.

From the 1830's to the Civil War, United States coal consumption and iron output multiplied at least twentyfold. The iron industry was in 1860 second in importance only to textiles. Yet this fact must not be taken at face value: the industry occupied an inferior position in a predominantly agrarian economy, and its greatness was yet to come. Steam power would herald the age of iron and steel after the war; at present, in spite of the triumph of steam in the transportation system, it had not yet supplanted manual or animal labor and the waterwheel in factory production. America's total pig-, bar-, and rolled-iron output was worth about $42 million in the census of 1860, and cotton-mill products were worth $115 million; but flour and grist mills created a value of over $223 million. Most of the gross national product of 1860 was taken up by the output of flour mills, tanneries, meat-packing plants, and breweries—all of them processing farm products. For all that, in this waterpowered and farm-dominated economy the foundations of United States heavy industry were well laid in the 1840's and 1850's.

From the British viewpoint the transformation of the American iron industry took place backward. A first step in the revolutionizing of the British iron industry was the changeover from charcoal to coal in the primary smelting of the ore; Abraham Darby managed to do this as early as 1709, and after a time lag the move to coal smelting was complete. In the United States the changeover was delayed until the mid-nineteenth century, since there was no timber shortage anyway. Furthermore, eastern coal deposits were anthracite, and therefore did not make a suitable coke. In urban areas (like Pittsburgh) coal was used in earlier years in the secondary stage of refining pig iron, but the first step in the stream of United States innovations was not the abandonment of charcoal smelting but rather the introduction from Britain of Henry Cort's "puddling and rolling" method (1783–1784) of producing bar iron in a continuous process. Cort's technique was adopted in western Pennsylvania in 1817, but even this innovation—so suited to American needs— spread quite slowly. It was made clear that Cort's process saved labor and used coal (which was available and cheap) and that a coal mine in a six-foot seam covering half an acre could replace the timber fuel ordinarily supplied for the ironmasters by up to five thousand acres of forest. The trouble was twofold: keen competition from a well-established British iron industry and the (temporary) superiority in quality of hand manipulated charcoal-refined iron over the product of the crude reverberatory puddling furnaces of the day. These two stumbling blocks vanished in the 1840's with new technical changes that improved the quality of puddled iron and with the huge domestic iron demand that sprang up for the railroads. America's first great rolling mills were built in the late 1840's and 1850's, all adopting Cort's process with coal-burning blast furnaces. Heavy iron rails were first rolled successfully in the United States in 1845 —a foretaste of trouble for British exporters who had up to then monopolized the American market.

Low demand for coal (because of the availability of abundant timber stands) kept the more western coal deposits undeveloped even though they were bituminous and suitable for the Cort method. In the early 1830's an American, F. W. Geisenheimer, experimented with the use of eastern anthracite coal in smelting iron ore by way of a hot blast. When this technique was perfected in 1840 by David Thomas (Lehigh Crane Ironworks, Pennsylvania), anthracite output was quadrupled. By 1856 about 120 iron furnaces were burning anthracite coal. In the same year Henry Bessemer produced his famous converter for making cheap steel in Sheffield, England. The Bessemer process revolutionized the world's steel industry, but its central principle (to decarbonize molten iron into molten steel by forcing air through it and thus burning out the "impurities") had been independently developed five years before by a Kentucky iron-master, William Kelly. In the 1850's and 1860's anthracite smelting surpassed charcoal smelting and was in turn surpassed by bituminous coal smelting after about 1875.

Use of coal brought heavy concentration of the iron industry on the coalfields, and United States iron manufacturing lost forever its rural character. Pennsylvania, with the largest and finest anthracite deposits in the country, was in 1860 producing over half of the United States' pig and manufactured iron, followed in order by Ohio and New Jersey. Total United States tonnage of pig iron was almost 20 times the estimated output of 1810 (nearly a million tons), and was used to make farm implements, machinery, steam engines, heavy rails, small arms (subsidized by the federal government since 1792), and a mass of domestic hardware of which the most successful example was the kitchen stove. Around 400,000 stoves a year were being placed on the domestic market in 1850, a million a year in 1860.[11]

The "American system of manufacture"

The growing United States iron industry released railroad builders from depending on British imports; the flourishing textile industry went further, and began exporting its fabrics. Foreign nations in the 1850's took more than sidelong glances at America's emerging manufactures, especially after the Great Exhibition of 1851 in London where the United States exhibits included a McCormick reaper and Colt's revolver (patented 1835). British eyes were opened, and *The Times* of London forgot to be supercilious for once in its appraisal of something American: "Their reaping machine has carried conviction to the heart of the British agriculturist. Their revolvers threaten to revolutionize military tactics." In 1853 and again in 1854 the British sent investigators to the United States to prepare parliamentary reports on American industry. British experts were impressed not only by the size of the domestic market and population growth but also by the high average wealth of American consumers. Admiring the standardized mass-production methods of American factories and the mechanical ingenuity of native artisans, British reporters attributed these successes to the excellence of the American public schools:

Bringing a mind prepared by thorough school discipline and educated up to a far higher standard than those of a much superior social grade in society in the Old World, the American working boy develops rapidly into the skilled artisan, and having once mastered one part of his business, he is never content until he has mastered all.

As for factory organization the British described with respect the rudimentary form of time-and-motion study and rational shop layout that was already in evidence even in the 1850's:

. . . In the adaptation of special apparatus to a single operation in almost all branches of industry, the Americans display an amount of ingenuity combined with undaunted energy which as a nation we would do well to imitate if we mean to hold our present position in the great market of the world.

The Committee also observed that everything that could be done to reduce labor in the movement of materials from one point to another was adopted. This includes mechanical arrangements for lifting material etc., from one floor to another, carriages for conveying material on the same floor, and such like.

The essential feature of what Europeans began to call the "American system of manufacture" was the principle of interchangeable standardized parts. Interchangeability was introduced in the United States in 1800 by Eli Whitney, who returned to New Haven from his labors on the cotton gin in the South, to enter the small-arms industry. Winning a federal contract (1798) to supply 10,000 muskets, he designed a gun made up of interchangeable precision parts that could be assembled by fairly unskilled workers. Simeon North, a Connecticut gunsmith, had worked out a similar scheme in 1799 for manufacturing pistols, and many ideas could be taken from earlier experiments with automatic processes in the nail-making and woodworking industries. After Whitney's great success, interchangeability and quantity production spread to other light industries, especially clockmaking, which, as a highly skilled craft involving knowledge of various kinds of mechanical motion, had itself long been an invaluable source for new technical ideas. Experiment with automatic machinery had also been stimulated in the flour-milling industry in the late 1780's, with Oliver Evans's brilliant use of a conveyor belt, mill elevator, and gravity grinding process.

Oliver Evans pioneered in the American manufacture of machinery, too, having begun to produce steam engines at the Mars Iron Works as early as 1803. By the 1830's machine shops were fairly widespread in New England, and twenty years later they had grown up elsewhere, manufacturing for home and foreign buyers such articles as reapers, mowers, plows, revolvers, clocks, locomotives, textile machinery, printing presses, and sewing machines. Although United States export totals of machinery were not very great, "Americanization"—with heavy overtones of "mechanization" —was an established concept in 1860.

FIVE

The Nature of the Market

A national market economy emerged in the United States before
the Civil War, and we have examined its growth and its content.
But what kind of market was it? How can we characterize it? A
brief review of national economic policy and public reactions might
give us some clues to answer this question.

1. ECONOMIC THOUGHT AND POLICY

The dialogue of public policy

What role should government play in the national economy?
That question has been the central theme of United States economic
policy for almost two centuries. Of course, the question is ambiguous, like the answers it has received.

For instance, colonial Americans took up arms against royal intervention and regulation of their economic life. They demanded
local participation, an American voice in the making of economic
policy, and fought a republican revolution to win it. But they did

not reject the idea of government intervention itself. To overthrow external economic authority is one thing. But what are the true functions of a popularly created home government? Americans were not sure. The "conventional wisdom" of the late eighteenth century was mercantilism—a belief in strict state regulation of economic life (often down to the smallest details, as in seventeenth century France under Colbert), high tariff barriers against rival nations, favorable trade balances, and dependent colonies. The overall purpose of this bureaucratic economic machine was to build national power and more specifically to bolster the existing dynasty. Against this "received doctrine" was opposed the sweeping, radical ideas of the French physiocrats and the Scots economist Adam Smith (*Wealth of Nations*, 1776). Smith rejected the state authority and centralism of mercantile theory, and his classic statement became the foundation of laissez-faire free-enterprise capitalism: no government "interference" in the private pursuit of individual profits. As the Industrial Revolution spread in Britain and elsewhere, Smith's radical rejection of authoritarianism rapidly became the new conservative orthodoxy and a rationalization or excuse for all kinds of social excesses, like harsh child and female labor, railroad corruption, slum housing. Modern economists can see in many of Adam Smith's statements the true roots of welfare economics; but his Victorian disciples and vulgarizers chose to ignore all but the negative aspects, and failed to recognize that Smith's rejection of government intervention in economic affairs arose under a monarchical, aristocratic, and unrepresentative government that intervened on behalf of its own class interests.

In the United States the negative laissez-faire dogma was enthusiastically adopted for use in political rhetoric. As a party plank, laissez-faire was admirably suited to excite two deeply rooted American popular beliefs conditioned by colonial, frontier, and agrarian history: individual self-sufficiency and natural rights. But in actual practice laissez-faire was Americanized. Like everything else of European origin, Smith's doctrine was employed in the United States, put to use. American conditions produced an ambiguous mixture of laissez-faire and mercantilist principles. Labor and capital scarcity, land abundance, local rivalries between geographical sectors, a federal political structure, immigration, a relatively unstructured social framework, the need to grow from scratch, from an initially low level of social overhead investment—all these demanded, as we have seen, a system not characterized by laissez faire in any real sense but by active government economic promotion, especially at the local and state level. This was the American practice.

Opinions in the 1790's were polarized by the division between two great statesmen, Jefferson and Hamilton. Jeffersonian democracy was a move away from the center in government; an agrarian, republican ideal; a minimum of law and regulation; international free trade. But Jefferson's faith in minimal government was not unmixed. A supporter of "states' rights" against federal authority, he obviously feared local power less than he feared central power; but as the states'-rights argument developed over the years the issue seemed to become one not of the power to intervene but of who should wield that power. Furthermore, Jefferson supported what he judged to be the national interest above all other considerations. The tough federal intervention of 1807 (Embargo Act) was his step, as was the earlier and more far-reaching Louisiana Purchase. On the other hand, Hamiltonianism was the explicit doctrine of a future America, not the idealization of an agrarian image of the past. Hamilton would diversify economic life, encourage the merchant marine, create and protect home industries by tariffs, and build up a powerful central government able to maintain public credit and the prestige abroad of a growing industrial and mercantile nation. Behind the two men lay entrenched American sectional interests: planting-slaveholding groups behind Jefferson, merchant-financial-shipping groups behind Hamilton.

Men have regarded Hamilton as "conservative" and Jefferson as "liberal." Yet today the "liberals" usually stand for more government and the "conservatives" for less government. This paradox is inherent in the mixed United States attitude to the role of government in economic life. Let us make a distinction here between the two great aims of government intervention. A positive social policy of government action can aim at economic efficiency or at social justice. Hamilton said and did many things of which modern "liberals" would approve, but he stood mainly for economic efficiency. Twentieth century Americans support his idea of positive action but widen his aims, to promote public welfare as well as economic growth—full employment, civilized living standards and health conditions, civil rights. Economic efficiency and social justice can be construed in different ways, and often seem incompatible to the economist; in democratic communities their respective roles are delineated in the changing, shaping dialogue of free politics. American public opinion in the nineteenth century was ready to tolerate great divergence from laissez-faire orthodoxy in order to promote growth where capital was scarce. Henry Clay, like Albert Gallatin before him, used all his dialectical skill and considerable understanding of economic development to prove that government intervention and national greatness were synonymous terms. "In old countries where there is a great accumulation of surplus capital and a consequent low rate of interest, they [internal improvements] will be made. But in a new country," Clay pointed out to his suspicious, rural-minded colleagues in Congress, "the condition of society may be ripe for public works long before there is, in the hands of individuals, the necessary accumulation of capital to effect them." On social overhead capital Clay declared directly:

Of all the modes in which a government can employ its surplus revenues, none is more permanently beneficial than that of internal improvement. Fixed to the soil, it becomes a durable part of the land itself, diffusing comfort, and activity, and animation on all sides.

So, despite the prevailing orthodoxy, government intervention in economic life was supported by leading political figures, and public policy took the form of local, state, and federal subsidization of the transportation revolution, federal creation of two national banks, and manipulation of the economy through Treasury fiscal operations, the deliberate use of tariffs to divert the allocation of resources into desired lines of development, and government subsidies to certain industries (fishing, small arms, and, at a state level, agricultural bounties on grain and silk production).

One could say that all this public enterprise and government intervention is of one kind—developmental. But intervention for public welfare also has roots deep in American history: even before the Civil War some Atlantic seaboard states legislated conditions of labor in the new factories, and a host of regulations governed the purity of foodstuffs, railroad and turnpike rates and services, the quality of export goods. This welfare legislation had to fight the negativism of men like Andrew Jackson and his man Van Buren, who believed, probably sincerely, that "all communities are apt to look to Government for too much" and that on democratic grounds the state should not make some men rich at the expense of others, or seek to help businessmen at times of "sudden embarrassment and distress." Intervention for welfare did not lack its theorist, however: Daniel Raymond, the pioneer United States economist whose *Thoughts on Political Economy* was published in Baltimore in 1820, was an emphatic supporter of both development and welfare. Raymond attacked the Jeffersonian-Jacksonian position as a tacit defense of an unjust *status quo*. A negative government merely helps to entrench the rich in their existing status at the expense of the poor, he argued:

A government should be like a good shepherd who supports and nourishes the weak and feeble ones in his flock. . . . The powerful ones in society however are not those who are so by nature, but those who have been made so by art—by the inheritance or acquisition of enormous wealth. . . . These call themselves the nation. . . . It is a prevailing vice in all governments, of extending their patronage and protection to the rich and powerful, to the almost total neglect of the poor and the weak.

The question was: What role should government play in the national economy? It is clear that the prewar United States found no single ideological answer to this question, that the confusion was even greater in actual policy than in thought, and that it all depends on who is intervening in the economy and for what purpose.

The "Hamiltonian system"

The economic revolution that molded the United States in the nineteenth century was Hamiltonian. In fact, Hamilton had laid the keel of American capitalism before George Washington retired from office. Even Jefferson's election in 1800 had very little impact on the economic system that was already firmly founded. The new United States Government had a national Mint, a national Bank, well-established foreign credit, a sinking fund, and the right to draw tariff and excise tax revenues. Hamilton built his system on the *Report on Public Credit* and the Funding Act (1790), the *Report on Manufactures* (1791), the Tariff Acts of 1789 and 1792, and the Mint Act of 1792; and the keystone of the Hamiltonian arch was the United States Bank (1791).

In his role as Secretary of State, Jefferson was deeply opposed to a national bank, and he wrote to President Washington:

The incorporation of a bank and the powers assumed by this bill [July, 1791] have not, in my opinion, been delegated to the United States by the Constitution.

Hamilton tried to meet this "strict-construction" argument with the doctrine of "implied powers." He said: "It is unquestionably incident to sovereign powers to erect corporations." The federal Constitution gave Congress authority to establish any medium to help the government execute its constitutionally ordained functions. A United States Bank would act as the government's fiscal agent. Through it, the United States could collect taxes, regulate coinage, borrow money, and spend funds. Hamilton strongly denied opposition fears that a nationally chartered bank would bring usury, drain off scarce specie (through the competition of bank notes), or divert capital from agriculture into sterile speculative activities. But when the chartering act was passed (February, 1791) only three Southerners supported the law and only one Northerner opposed it. Sectional interests outweighed objective economic arguments.

The act gave the United States Bank a twenty-year charter and allowed it a capital fund of $10 million of which 20 percent was to be subscribed by the federal government. The Bank could issue notes up to the total value of its capitalization. The rate of interest on loans and discounts was not to exceed 6 percent. United States Bank notes were to be accepted in payment of government dues, a step that gave added encouragement to the use of bank notes generally. Until the growth of deposit banking and the check system after the Civil War, the conduct of American economic life rested very heavily on the flow of bank notes.

For the first ten years of its life the United States Bank was quite successful. Opposition forces began to gain support from those who feared foreign ownership (almost 75 percent of the Bank's stock was in foreign hands, though aliens held no voting rights), and from the numerous rival banks chartered by individual state governments. So in 1811 when the United States Bank's charter came up for renewal, it was simply allowed to lapse. Hamilton did not live to see this; he was shot to death by Aaron Burr in 1804. His long-

term ideal—the consolidation of the Union—was far from realization, but he had determined its ultimate shape.

Tariffs and economic growth

Hamilton believed in protective tariffs, and thought them an
essential part of American public policy for native economic growth.
History does not prove that he was right. In all justice it must be
said that neither free trade nor tariff protection can be shown to
be "right" or "wrong" for economic growth in any given period; the
historical evidence is inconclusive. Large-scale manufacturing would
have come to the United States in any case during the nineteenth
century with or without the artificial protection of tariffs on foreign
goods. We have already described the extension of the market
economy, the manufacturing "take-off" of the 1840's and 1850's, and
the build-up of America's wealth, without much reference to tariff
protection. At the very most, all that one could reasonably claim is
that tariffs probably accelerated industrial evolution to some extent,
influenced the cost of living, and helped—politically rather than
economically—to accentuate sectional distinctions.

Up to 1816 United States tariffs were imposed mainly to obtain
revenue to pay the expenses of government. The growth of factories
in the 1812-1814 War and their collapse during the depression that
followed persuaded many Americans, including the "Warhawks,"
that the government should take some measure to protect American
workers and employers from the competition of cheaper foreign
imports. In 1816 duties were imposed at the average rate of about
20 percent, with extra special protection for cotton textiles. Further
duties imposed in 1818 and 1824 met with relatively little sectional
opposition. Farmers and would-be manufacturers saw eye to eye
because they were united in a common struggle against the depression: both wanted markets for their produce and both fell back
on the home-market idea and protectionism. In a speech to Congress
in March, 1824, defending the latest tariff, Henry Clay as spokes-
man of the West united the nationalists under his leadership for
the "American System": tariffs to protect native "infant industries"
and to stimulate urbanization and so to extend the market for farm
produce; federal internal improvements, financed mainly out of

tariff revenues, to ensure transportation for farmers and factory owners alike. Earlier Clay had succeeded in winning western farmers over to the idea of a new experiment with a national bank (1816). The alliance between Northeast and West was completed. Obviously the "domestic market" appeal for protection was more of a political success with western grain producers and eastern manufacturers than with the cotton planters of Dixie, dependent as they were on foreign outlets. In New England merchant and shipping interests kept the vote divided until about 1828, after which the section went over more solidly to the protectionist view. For instance, Daniel Webster of Massachusetts who spoke for shipping interests in opposing the tariffs of 1816 and 1824 made an about-face four years later and ardently supported the Tariff Act of 1828. Meanwhile, southern leaders became openly hostile to tariffs as the Cotton Kingdom became more entrenched in the Old Southwest. John C. Calhoun of South Carolina, formerly a Warhawk Nationalist, defender of internal improvements and tariffs, made a *volte-face* in the direction opposite to that taken by Webster in 1827. Calhoun originally supported protectionism because he had hopes that tariffs would encourage South Carolina to diversify and strengthen its economy through manufacturing. The tariff did not produce this miracle, and the South as a whole seemed to become increasingly dependent on the North. So in 1827–1828 when a bill was introduced to extend protection to wool manufactures, Calhoun came out strongly in opposition. The 1824 Act had brought tariffs up to an average level of 33⅓ percent; the "Tariff of Abominations" opposed by Calhoun in 1828 fixed an average rate of 41 percent with especially heavy duties on imported woolens and iron goods. The southern outcry was immediate, and Calhoun, who valued the United States almost as much as he valued his individual conception of liberty, had a tough job keeping in line southern extremists who proposed to break up the American Union. Many Southerners placed their faith in the newly elected President, Andrew Jackson of Tennessee. He was, after all, a plantation slaveholder. The Jackson party, which claimed to champion the "common man," was ostensibly democratic and opposed to all forms of monopoly; but it combined widely divergent groups, ranging from western farmers who demanded low interest rates to ex-Jeffersonian "hard-money" men opposed to the United States Bank, from southern states'-

righters demanding tariff reductions to urban workers and captains of industry alike. What unity "Jacksonian democracy" possessed seemed derived only from a common negative reaction against varied aspects of the Hamiltonian system (as extended by the Clay-Adams group of "National Republicans"). So it was not "King Andrew" but the wise compromiser Henry Clay who introduced downward amendments to the Tariff of Abominations.

Congress did finally cut the tariff to an average level of 33 percent in 1832, but the hated principle of protectionism was left intact and the southern secessionists once roused could not be mollified. In November, 1832, the State of South Carolina declared the federal tariff legislation of 1828 and 1832 to be null and void, and threatened to secede unilaterally from the Union if federal authorities used force to execute the national laws. On December 5th President Jackson was reelected, and his attitude toughened. He issued a "Proclamation to the People of South Carolina" that denounced the nullification ordinance as an "impractical absurdity" (December 10th). Calhoun resigned his Vice-Presidency, and South Carolina failed to win the support of her sister states. Jackson insisted that the Union was inviolable and was given congressional authority to use the army if need be, in the Force Act of 1833. Happily, the act remained a dead letter thanks to the acceptance of Henry Clay's compromise tariff after private negotiations between Clay and Calhoun. It has been suggested that Jackson's "firm stand" in this case was foolhardy and would have led to bloodshed except for the statesmanship of Clay and to a lesser degree of Calhoun; others would say that not everything is preferable to violence and that to uphold national laws was worth some risk of sacrifice. (Given the somewhat parallel situations that have arisen in recent years over the enforcement of national civil-rights legislation in the South, the nullification crisis of 1832–1833 is of more than academic relevance.)

The compromise Tariff of 1833 was a temporary victory for the South, and the tariff trend was generally downward until war broke out. Duties were cut to a maximum of 20 percent by 1842. A slight increase by the Whigs in that year was lopped off by the Walker Tariff three years later, and further reductions were made in 1857. These cuts did not have a noticeable overall impact on American economic growth.

Central banking: yes or no?

In the year that fiery South Carolina threatened to quit the United States and Andrew Jackson took a positive stand for the preservation of the Union, the national-Bank issue came to a head once more. Jackson's position on this was more negative. The charter of the Second United States Bank came up for renewal in 1832, and Jackson promptly used his veto to destroy the Bank forever.

The Second United States Bank had been founded in 1816, supported by Clay, Calhoun, and the same "agrarians" who only five years earlier had applauded the death of its predecessor, Hamilton's bank. In the years between had come the 1812–1814 War, financed by extravagant loans rather than by taxation. This cumulative over-borrowing by the federal government, coupled with ineffective taxation and a flood of bank notes issuing from state banks, produced the highest inflation of the century. In the summer of 1814 cash payments were suspended. Postwar currency was made up of a mass of bank notes and a smaller number of Treasury notes, all of fluctuating value. Out of this disturbing and unhealthy situation came an urgent demand from all sides for some national form of banking institution. An earlier bill was vetoed by President Madison, but Calhoun's scheme was finally enacted in March, 1816. The charter was broadly similar to that of 1791, with a twenty-year lease of life, a capital of $35 million (one-fifth subscribed by the federal government), and twenty-five directors of whom five were to be presidential nominees. As with the First Bank, public revenues were to be payable in United States Bank notes, redeemable in specie. State banks were thus forced to resume specie payments, and the banking system churned into full activity.

Why (apart from personal inclination) did Andrew Jackson destroy the Second United States Bank in 1832? The hostility of rival state-chartered banks once more came into play. For instance, various state legislatures followed Maryland's lead of 1817 and decided to tax the branches of the United States Bank within their borders. In 1819 a Maryland branch of the national Bank refused to pay a state annual tax of $15,000 on its note issue. The case went before the United States Supreme Court, which decided unanimously

(*McCulloch* v. *Maryland,* March 6, 1819) in favor of the United States Bank. Chief Justice Marshall in a superb nationalist analysis drew heavily on Hamilton's doctrine of implied powers and a broad construction of the Constitution. The Bank was now taken over by a more capable president, Langdon Cheves of South Carolina. Cheves restricted credit very severely and brought financial soundness once more before he resigned in 1823. His successor was Nicholas Biddle, Jackson's great protagonist a few years later. Biddle, forceful and aggressive, began with a complete reversal of Cheves's policy: he expanded the Bank's circulation, its loans, deposits, stock, and real-estate investments. What Biddle wanted was to create a real central Bank with control over the nation's money market. By 1828 he had the Bank earning a surplus of $1½ million and by 1831 its note circulation was up to $19 million (as opposed to $4½ million when he took over). Until its charter expired in 1836, the Bank managed to pay dividends at the rate of 7 percent a year.

In at least three ways the Second United States Bank contributed to stable economic growth. By upholding specie payments for its own notes and cajoling the state banks to do likewise, it encouraged the creation of a stable national currency. By using capital raised in the East as a basis for its business in other sections of the nation, the Bank made credit and currency available where it was most scarce. Finally, the Bank gave speedy and economical loans to the federal government in time of need.

Contemporary Americans had little understanding of these real and significant achievements. No action of the national Bank could satisfy some people. Debtor groups and rival state banks, for instance, were implacably hostile to the very idea of central banking. When Langdon Cheves reduced credit between 1819 and 1823 and had to foreclose securities on unpaid loans, the United States Bank became by default the chief owner of real estate in several western cities, and was bitterly lampooned as "the Monster." State banks had been making money out of the postwar inflation and currency chaos and had little real desire to return to a stable system of cash payments until they were forced to do so by pressure from the central Bank. Deflationary bank policies were blamed for the crash of 1819 when it came, which in all truth they could only have accelerated. Yet, in contrast, when Biddle took over and reversed this policy, going all out for credit expansion, he met concerted opposition from the "hard-money" men (especially after Jackson took over the White House in 1828). The restrictionists distrusted all banks and all paper currency in a wonderfully indiscriminate way, and blamed them for inflation, speculation, and cycles of boom-and-bust. Biddle's expansion of United States Bank business rapidly became as hated as Cheves's contraction of business had been. The state banks still felt able to cry out against central Bank pressure on their operations; the growing class of businessmen and manufacturers now demanded laissez faire and free banking, condemning "monopoly." At no time was the national Bank struggle a clear-cut fight between Northeast (in favor) and the other sections (against). The creditor, commercial and industrial sector did not always lend the Bank its support, and often doubted the benefits of control over local banks and over inflation by a centralized monetary system. Neither did the debtor western and southern farming sectors always defend a decentralized monetary system, credit expansion, and free local banking. If the United States Bank was supposed to represent in some measure public opinion on financial matters, how could it ever hope to determine that opinion at any given stage in the game?

Still, economic growth is a very complex matter, with many dynamic variables. There is little proof that strong central banking is invariably more conducive to growth than decentralized free banking. The fact is that the United States Bank charter was not renewed in 1832, and who can honestly demonstrate that the path of American economic history would have been smoother if Jackson had not used his veto?

"Tsar Nicholas" Biddle was no diplomatist, and he probably mistimed his application for charter renewal and totally misunderstood the change in the United States political climate since Jackson had come to power. The charter still had four years to go in the presidential election year of 1832 in which Biddle—pushed by Clay —decided to ask for a renewal. To veto the charter was a political maneuver that Jackson would scarcely fail to use: the "common man" was solidly against Biddle's Bank. Jackson's veto stood the risk of losing him some sectional votes in Pennsylvania, but in the general election that followed the Jacksonians captured 219 electoral college votes; the combined opposition forces did not muster 70. Henry Clay was thoroughly trounced (49 votes), and the second United States Bank was doomed, not to be revived.

Until its charter lapsed four years later, the Bank was torn by an internal struggle between its dictatorial leader and its administrative officers. Trying desperately to impress the nation with the need for a national Bank, Biddle opened a deflationary campaign in August, 1833, and restricted credit as stringently as he dared. The crisis he managed to produce in 1834 only worked against him and convinced the remaining waverers that the Bank was a power for evil in the land. Two years later Biddle's Bank expired as the "Bank of the United States." Henry Clay tried to create a third United States Bank in 1841, but President John Tyler vetoed it. Instead the federal government continued its practice of using state banks as government depositories. For good or for evil the United States faced the age of mass production with no formal centralized banking structure.

The people and the corporation

The two American experiments in central banking (1791–1811 and 1816–1836) made use of a mixed type of business enterprise that combined public with private investment and employed government directors on the board alongside private businessmen. The corporate form of organization made such cooperation possible.

Given the pressing need for government aid to finance social overhead investments like the railways, the corporation became a key institution in American life and an instrument of intercity and interstate rivalry. Mobile Americans with mobile interests found in the system of transferable, salable shares an ideal means of participating in business growth.[1] Understandably, the corporation spread much more rapidly in the United States (where it was most needed to scrape together scarce capital) than in Britain: the problems of American capital development were much greater and the United States was much poorer to begin with. By 1800, when Britain had an estimated twenty-odd corporations, the United States had three hundred.

Most of these early American corporations were organized in the fields of real-estate banking, insurance, public utilities (water supply), and transportation. Few corporations before the Civil War were in manufacturing, though during the industrial "take-off" of the 1850's their number was very likely doubled. In particular, primary industries (concerned with basic extraction and conversion of raw materials—iron ore, timber, coal) did not attract the corporate form of organization and finance for many years because they were slower to mechanize. Corporations were formed at first under special acts of state legislatures, which granted individual charters. It might seem a tedious matter to have to push a special act through a state assembly in order to set up a corporation, but in Britain, where an Act of Parliament was required, the process was much more time-consuming and costly. The decentralization of political authority in the American federal system greatly favored corporation growth. Anyway, by the 1830's many states had adopted general incorporation laws: under the terms of a single standardized charter any number of corporations could be created merely by payment of a legal fee. Limited liability, an essential attribute of company enterprise, came early in United States corporation history. This meant that if a firm should "go broke," each investor was legally responsible to help pay off the corporation's debt only up to the total extent and value of his shares. His other personal property could not legally be touched.

With all these privileges it would be wrong to think that corporations were popular in prewar days. They were not. Americans generally were highly suspicious of corporations, especially in the Jacksonian era. Writing in 1820, the welfare economist Daniel Raymond found himself for once on the Jackson side:

. . . All money corporations are detrimental to national wealth. They are always created for the benefit of the rich, and never for the poor. The poor have no money to vest in them and can therefore derive no advantage from such corporations.

Actually, the general incorporation laws were intended not to make incorporation easier so much as to impose well-defined statutory limits to corporation functions and give state authorities a better check on corporation activities. For long stretches of time and over large parts of the United States, the corporate image was hated and feared—as a tool of monopoly and privilege and as the worst enemy of individual opportunity and private enterprise.

Image of America

How can we explain this irony? United States public opinion denounced the corporation as a danger to free enterprise! And yet that same public opinion twice scuttled the central Bank and slashed the industrialist's protective tariff. What kind of business enterprise would most people have respected? What was the ideal business image of pre–Civil War Americans?

At last we have a question with an unambiguous, categorical answer. Rural Americans idealized the small entrepreneur: the family farm, the independent business, the modest partnership. Theirs was a homely image, fired in the small-town forge and hammered out on the frontier. It was the ideal of a farming and trading people. Adam Smith had provided its objective rationale, and Thomas Jefferson its spiritual sufficiency.

The free-enterprising, laissez-faire, self-equilibrating model society of the classical school of economics has never existed in history. But the nearest approximation to that kind of economy was reached in America's prewar years: the thirties, forties, and fifties. During this short space of time something like Adam Smith's upwardly mobile, petty bourgeois entrepreneur was to be seen at large in American society, creating wealth. He was accompanied, for good measure, by a near model of Jefferson's independent yeoman farmer.

But already in the antebellum decade the corporate form of business organization was beginning to invade the "privacy" of small enterprise. The early American critics of corporations witnessed the widening gap between investors and directors, the spread of speculative stockownership, the failure of ill-attended and ill-informed stockholders' meetings to control company policy, the emergence of a self-perpetuating elite group of wealthy corporation directors like the Lowells, Appletons, Jacksons, Cabots and their familiars. The new corporate order that spread throughout the economy after the civil conflict was brought to an end had little similarity to the prewar image, though for political and polemical purposes it would borrow the small-town philosophy that buttressed the image. "Free enterprise," "individualism," "laissez faire" (without its free-trade dimension, of course)—these would continue to act as political passwords. In the 1870's, 1880's and 1890's the unprecedented social problems created by industrialism were blithely ignored, and in his very concrete "realistic" fiction Howells depicted the transition from a Golden to a Gilded Age. In different terms the transition was from small business to large business, from entrepreneur to corporation, and (eventually) from "capitalist" to "bureaucrat." Antebellum society, a palpable, personal world of face-to-face business operations in which ownership and responsible control were fused in one person, gave way to a paper world of impersonal corporate finance in which business ownership was a mere accounting concept. Right or wrong, the popular critics had enough foresight to see that the corporation was more than a new way to organize production and marketing: it was a new way of life.

2. ECONOMIC PERFORMANCE

The precorporation economic system was not without its own faults. The "Golden Age," like its supposedly debased gilt successor, was subject to alternating cycles of boom and slump, prosperity and depression, the unhappy product of a poorly regulated and unplanned economic system. Lacking the "built-in stabilizers" of today's system, Victorian capitalism in both its early and its later phase performed very erratically and unevenly. This was true of capitalism in other parts of the world, in Britain, Belgium, France. But the United States was made especially sensitive to cyclical fluctuations by the sequential nature of the westward movement— speculative investment crazes in land associated with each stage of frontier development. Unstable financing, a weak banking structure, and credit problems also brought about frequent minor economic breakdowns with potentially cumulative effects. Rapid extension of the market area, the transportation revolution, city growth, interregional economic flows, while producing economic growth, made the various sectors of the nation so heavily interdependent that it became as impossible to localize economic disturbance within the nation as it later became to localize military disturbance in the world at large.

The machinery breaks down

Up to the First World War American capitalism suffered at least six major breakdowns, sufficient to cause widespread human suffering, unemployment, business failure, and social dislocation: the

crises of 1819, 1837, 1857, 1873, 1893, and 1907. Insofar as one can
isolate factors in any meaningful fashion, monetary overinvestment
had much to do with the three pre-Civil War panics and the years
of depression that followed. The 1819 panic climaxed several mal-
adjustments that followed the War of 1812–1814. A forward surge
of economic activity came in the three years 1815–1818, with rising
export prices for southern cotton and the opening up of new western lands. In 1818 about 3½ million acres of the public domain were
sold, and export volume and prices reached a new peak. In the following year Europe's demand suddenly slackened, and United
States terms of trade became much less favorable. Cotton prices fell
in international markets, and since the demand for western foodstuffs was regulated in those years chiefly by the state of economic
health in Dixie, the trade cutback had widespread depressive re-
percussions. Specific financial difficulties were first felt from the
middle of 1818, at the second United States Bank. When Langdon
Cheves took over, as we have seen, he imposed a stringent policy of
restricting all credit. His foreclosures and other deflationary measures were aimed at financial stability, and would not have been
necessary but for the previous speculative overexpansion. When
cotton and wheat prices (no longer artificially maintained by the
unusual war and postwar European demand) fell by a half and the
market collapsed, the United States Bank became a useful scapegoat.
The middle Atlantic states and Ohio Valley suffered terrible rural
unemployment and debt, and in the port city of New York one in
every ten persons went on poor relief. The ensuing depression took
about four years to lift, but by 1823 prosperity was returning and
Biddle took over the United States Bank to inaugurate a new policy
of economic expansion.

About ten years later another boom cycle got under way. The
early 1830's brought favorable international trade terms, rising cotton and grain prices, great investments in canals and railroads, a
proliferation of note-issuing banks, an abnormal influx of foreign
capital, and the wildest speculation in western lands yet to occur.
Over 20 million acres of the public domain changed hands in 1836
alone. The actual financial collapse of 1837 was precipitated by
Andrew Jackson. His *Specie Circular* (July, 1836) directed government land agencies to accept nothing but cash in payment for public
lands. This act pricked the speculative activities that had been

covered by the inflated bank-note issues. The market collapsed in May, 1837, when New York's banks suspended cash payments. There had already been trouble in Britain owing to overexpansion in transportation there (the railway mania of 1836), coupled with a capital drain to the United States, and American export prices had fallen heavily. Again, as in 1819, it was the middle Atlantic, western, and southern states that felt the blow most, not New England. The panic of 1837 was one of the three worst economic disasters of the nineteenth century, and the aftereffects were prolonged because the rally of 1839 was followed by a further collapse. This was marked by the final death throes of Biddle's Bank (as the "United States Bank of Pennsylvania") in 1841 after a vain attempt to keep up the price of cotton. In 1843 prices fell to a new low. Many state authorities simply repudiated their debts, and again thousands of workers were thrown onto a choked labor market and again banks and businesses by the score failed.[2]

The economy did not begin a sustained recovery until 1845—a full eight years after the panic. This recovery and the expansion of the 1850's that followed saw the "take-off" of New England's cotton textile industry, stimulated by rising domestic prices, the opening up of the Far West, and the largest inflood of European migrants to date. The tragic potato famine in Ireland in 1845-1846, Sir Robert Peel's relief measures, and rising export prices brought an increase in United States trade. Prices climbed especially steeply after 1852, banks flourished, and there was a fresh land boom in the West and Southwest. Bad European harvests in 1853 and the Crimean War (1853–1856) between the European great powers further enhanced United States prospects. In the South the price of cotton and of slaves mounted to higher levels. In the Far West gold and silver were discovered, bringing mining settlements, trade, and then permanent agriculture. California gold production in 1850 ($36 million) exceeded the annual average world output of the preceding ten years. In the mid-Northwest railway construction on a great scale brought rising land values and the emergence of Chicago and its sister cities.

The third collapse, acute and financial rather than persistent and industrial, came in August, 1857. The Ohio Life Insurance and Trust Company, which had $5 million involved in railway construction loans, failed to meet its eastern liabilities. New York banks immediately began to contract their loans, and by October most of them had agreed to suspend cash payments. Banks all over the nation followed their lead (except in New Orleans), and failures were numerous. Railroad companies found themselves unable to obtain credit to meet interest obligations, while at the same time their traffic in many new regions could not be expected to yield a fair return for long enough. As many as fourteen companies failed within one month, and the New York and Erie, the Illinois Central, and the Michigan Central filed petitions of bankruptcy. All railroad building ceased, land speculation was cut short abruptly, imports declined, and men were thrown temporarily out of work. Once more the lesson of wild banking, overhasty railroad building, and rash speculation was being taught very painfully (but little was being learned). The government under President Buchanan did little or nothing—on principle. Buchanan's economic policy consisted in the posting of troops to protect federal buildings in New York City. Though he understood that overextension of credit had helped to bring about the crisis, he did not believe it was the function of the federal authority to regulate state banks. Still less would he have regulated production. The cycle worked itself out pretty quickly, however, in this case. Expansion had led to speculation; a sudden tightening of credit after a brief scare on Wall Street in 1854 had injected doubt and loss of confidence;[3] one large failure then brought a chain reaction. Credit was curtailed, production halted, workers were sent home, and a period of liquidation and depression followed. Finally, the contraction of credit and a certain degree of financial reorganization led to a recovery, and the process was ready to begin all over again—except that America went to war in 1861. Most banks resumed specie payments in 1858, and about two years later (December 20, 1860) South Carolina seceded from the American Union.

Americans react to changing economic conditions

Periodic breakdowns of the economic machinery were common in several parts of the world in the Victorian Age. The American people had little alternative but to live with the existing system; and the United States economy, judged in other respects, seemed vastly superior to that of any other nation. Its day-by-day achievements in producing wealth in a relatively open society were tangible and obvious and could not be denied. The living standards of Americans were comparatively high and were constantly increasing. On the other hand, the public-supported privately managed economy left large sections of the populace in unprotected situations, especially the growing class of urban workers inside and outside the factory system, and of course the Negro. The white workers of the skilled and semiskilled type then dominant began to band together and organize to defend themselves against the solidifying economic and social power of the large employer group.

Skilled workers organize

Trade-union growth was hampered in early United States history by the employers' use of the legal concept of "conspiracy." This British common-law doctrine, developed in the Middle Ages and taken over by American jurisprudence, stated, first, that the government could legally fix the level of maximum wages and, second, that laborers could in effect be compelled to work. The idea was legalized at a time of acute labor shortage in Europe in the Statute of Laborers (1351). If workingmen associated or took action to force a rise in their wages above the average or standard level in their particular occupation, they could be found guilty of a criminal conspiracy at common law. For instance, in 1806 in the Philadelphia case *Commonwealth* v. *Pullis*, the court tried a group of shoemakers who had struck for higher piece rates. The indictment declared:

[They] were not content to work at the usual prices and rates for which they and other workmen and journeymen in the same art and occupation used to work. . . . But . . . did combine, conspire, confederate and unlawfully agree together that they would not work except at certain large prices and rates.

The luckless cobblers believed in what is called nowadays a "closed shop" policy (employment of union members only). On this count they would run into similar legal trouble today in some states of the Union. But the general count of conspiracy to raise wages could scarcely be used to crush workers' demands in the twentieth century economy. Embedded in the indictment is a purely European view of society in which each profession and trade has a certain clearly defined social status, and the "just wage" is that which maintains the social hierarchy in its fixed and unchanging form: a place for everyone and everyone in his place (which was, of course, his father's before him). This idea was somewhat at variance with the facts of American economic life—the mobility and opportunity, land policy and the frontier, labor scarcity. In fact, even in medieval England economic circumstances (again a pressing labor shortage) had made it well-nigh impossible to freeze wages at a given level.[4] However, in the legalistic atmosphere of the young American Republic the judge found the Philadelphia shoemakers of 1806 doubly guilty:

> A combination of workmen to raise their wages may be considered in a twofold point of view: one is to benefit themselves, the other is to injure those who do not join their society. The rule of law condemns both.

That great legal scholar and pragmatist of the Progressive Era, Roscoe Pound, pointed out that United States legal authorities had to experiment in the adaptation of English common law to American conditions and that other groups in American society also suffered during this period of testing. But it is also true that courts of law are frequently several decades behind public opinion and that nineteenth century judges, being men of property, thoroughly assimilated the laissez-faire, natural-law dogmas of the classical school and, to put it simply, were antilabor. *Commonwealth* v. *Pullis* contained as many references to the *Wealth of Nations* and the alleged laws of market competition as it did to the common law and conspiracy. Moreover, a few years later the same decision was followed by a New York court in *People* v. *Melvin* (1809–1810).

Legal anomalies and the anxieties of the propertied groups failed to prevent the growth of trade societies of craftsmen early in American history—though no genuine labor "movement" or feeling of social solidarity extending beyond any one single trade can be traced until 1827. A genuine strike had occurred as early as 1786 when Philadelphia printers demanded a minimum wage of $6 a week, but the strike actions that followed were piecemeal and local. They brought no permanent results. One of the first properly organized official strikes took place in 1799, led by the Federal Society of Journeymen Cordwainers—the Philadelphia shoemakers who were dissolved by the 1806 judgment. By the 1830's the leading skilled trades of the Atlantic coastal cities had their own societies: bookbinders, printers, hatters, plumbers, cobblers, ships' joiners, millwrights, glassmakers, and their colleagues.

The year 1827 is significant in the history of the American worker because the first central labor organization was founded, combining several crafts and trades: the Mechanics' Union of Trade Associations of Philadelphia. Carpenters had struck for a ten-hour day, and were joined almost immediately by sympathetic glaziers, bricklayers, and painters. The association they formed came to include as many as fifteen different unions. Other central bodies sprang into being in New York, Boston, and other leading cities, and the 1830's even saw the rudimentary beginnings of national unions among the shoemakers, combmakers, carpenters, printers, and handloom weavers.

This short-lived radical phase of labor history in the 1830's stimulated the first entry of organized workers into politics, aided by a wide extension of the franchise in new and revised state constitutions (for instance, Massachusetts, 1820; New York, 1822). The Philadelphia Mechanics' Union suggested to other unions that labor candidates should be nominated and supported in the 1828 election. With Jacksonian backing they did, in fact, have some success in the city. Labor political parties were founded in about fifteen states, together with several labor newspapers in the late 1820's. By 1833 the political movement had largely collapsed through divided and inexperienced leadership; but unionization increased continually in the years of prosperity and buoyancy that culminated in the collapse of 1837. The general air of well-being favored union demands for a larger share of the national cake and their concern for the extension of union protection to different branches of labor. However, the great panic and the long depression it created set back the whole union movement: first, it closed the doors of factories and workshops and caused mass unemployment; second, it wiped out union treasuries. Local, city, and even quasi-national unions (like the National Trades Union established in the city of New York in 1834) went under in 1837.

A modern labor leader would find little to recognize in these early societies because they were not organizations of factory workers. As noted, the earliest factory workers were young ladies of New England, organized by the Waltham Plan and housed in genteel dormitories under a somewhat false aura of philanthropy. The allegedly model boardinghouses of Massachusetts provided a useful means of despotic social control over the workers. The take-home pay of a factory girl, after stoppage for spartan board and lodging, was but two dollars. For this two dollars she had labored for seventy-five hours in a dangerous, noisy, and unhealthy factory. Employers combined to fix wages and hours and to blacklist the less docile "operatives." Some attempts were made by girls of this sort to protect themselves against exploitation, concealed or open; and one or two predominantly male crafts had counterpart female societies, like the Female Society of Lynn and Vicinity for the Protection and Promotion of Female Industry (1853–1854), of the shoe binders. A Female Union Association in New York and a United Seamstresses' Society in Baltimore were both established by 1835. For the most part factory women were not eager to unionize, and were made to labor hard throughout the century.

Schemes to rebuild society

The 1830's and even more the 1840's were years of intellectual and social ferment. All sorts of creed and eccentricity lived out ephemeral careers in a constantly changing society, though the one central theme was abolitionism, the elimination of human slavery. Some of these influences were of "foreign" origin, some were not. In any case, given the flood of immigration, what is alien and what native depends largely on your viewpoint. Many American writers have joyously accepted Adam Smith's Scottish economics and the English Industrial Revolution—in a word, capitalism—as "American," but have rejected socialism (fathered by the Welshman Robert Owen and also nurtured in England) with equal fervor as being "alien." Robert Owen, in fact, took time off from his welfare work in Britain to lecture in the United States, and with his son Robert Dale Owen founded the socialist community of New Harmony in Indiana. The "communitarians," whether recent immigrants or not, saw in the United States the world's hope for a "fresh start," and bravely established their backwoods utopias, often in the most difficult circumstances. One group, the Associationists, were disciples of the French socialist thinker Charles Fourier; throughout the

1840's and 1850's they advocated peaceful social reconstruction by
establishing "phalanxes"—small communities with partial common
ownership of property on a voluntary basis. Perhaps the most famous was Brook Farm, founded in 1841 by a Unitarian, the trans-
cendentalist minister George Ripley, and supported by Nathaniel
Hawthorne, Albert Brisbane, and Horace Greeley. Greeley, who is
said to have originated the phrase "Go West, young man!" and who,
as editor of the New York *Tribune* employed Karl Marx as a free
lance in the 1850's, also supported an ephemeral Pennsylvania
phalanx in 1842. The Associationists, whose zeal for productive
efficiency somewhat relegated the problems of just social distribution to second place, have perhaps been remembered more than
other utopians mainly because they associated with the transcen-
dentalist writers, including Emerson himself. Robert Owen was more
of a socialist than this; he believed not that social reorganization
was necessary to increase productive efficiency, but on the contrary
that industrialized Man's heightened powers of production demanded a new social and political framework. From his experience
as a successful manufacturing capitalist, Owen claimed that the
only hope for civilization was that cooperation should replace
wasteful competitive industry and that both large cities and solitary
farms should be abandoned in favor of independent associations—
planned cooperative communities that united farming and industrial
pursuits in an ideal balanced whole. Several Owenite and countless
other kinds of religious and social communities were established in
the 1840's, but few managed to survive the pressures of the wider
society for very long.

Apart from the craft unionists and the utopians, labor and radical
spokesmen presented a multitude of programs before the Civil War.
They demanded franchise reform—though rarely asked for the vote
for women and never for Negroes. They pressed for the ten-hour
day, full legalization of the strike and collective bargaining, the
abolition of "truck," and for safety regulations in factories. According to their sectional background they would advocate immigration
restriction, antimonopoly measures, a national cheap or free land
policy, and the abolition of imprisonment for debt. From Germany
come Joseph Weydemeyer in 1851, a disciple of Karl Marx, who
founded a newspaper to spread Marxist ideas. (Not being too successful with his Germanic philosophy among American workers,

Weydemeyer eventually fought in the Civil War as a lieutenant colonel in the Union Army.) Following the early success of the British example, an American cooperative movement got under way in 1845 with the New England Protective Union. Producers' and consumers' cooperatives numbered about eight hundred by 1861, but the war temporarily eradicated the movement. G. H. Evans's National Reform Association and his vociferous paper, the New York *Workingmen's Advocate*, demanded land reform; Neal Dow's temperance movement won great success in rock-ribbed Maine where the entire state went "dry" in 1846, to be copied before 1861 by a dozen or so like-minded states.

For the most part these varied and conflicting trends were a great distraction to the labor cause in the United States and impeded the rise of a unified movement. Not all radical energies were siphoned off into cranky or sterile campaigns, however. Trade unionism began to pick up strength in the later 1850's with the increase of railroad building, the gold discoveries, and the general revival of business. At least ten new national organizations included the Typographical Union (1850), the Hat Finishers' (1854), the National Union of Machinists and Blacksmiths (1859), and the National Molders' Union (1859). Only three of these new, more practical, and better-organized national unions managed to live through the crash of 1857, but the effects of this crisis were not prolonged. Meanwhile, the courts had shifted their line of attack on labor organizations from the question of whether unions were "criminal conspiracies" to the question of what were the reasonable means that labor could be permitted to use in order to achieve its legitimate aims. This slight softening of attitude was illustrated in the earlier decision of 1842 in *Commonwealth* v. *Hunt*. Chief Justice Shaw of the Massachusetts Supreme Court rejected the doctrine implicit in the 1806 decision against Pullis that unions were in themselves illegal combinations. Shaw's decision in effect legalized trade unions, but the courts clung to the employers' philosophy for years to come. They remained strangely silent on the question of the aims and means of the employers' associations that appeared in the 1860's, and left many questions about the aims and means of workers' organizations open to widely varied local interpretation. Was the "closed shop" legal, for instance? Some states recognized strike action to keep a workshop entirely unionized; others did not. And what about picketing in strikes and use of the boycott technique? For decades legal controversy of this sort involved trade unions in costly and crippling litigation. As they expanded with the natural growth of the economy and the spread of the factory system, the unions had to meet this threat through improved organization and the rise of a class of professional labor lawyers.

Gradually—much later than the corporations, and not fully until the New Deal—the unions would evolve their own bureaucracy.

Tangibles and intangibles: the living standard of Americans in 1860

Labor unions had to struggle hard and long for legal recognition and a place in American life. But in concrete terms, what the economy gave the worker without much struggle was good wages— relatively high and usually rising. The economy did *not* give him an easy or comfortable life, especially in prewar decades. Hours were long and working conditions were far from perfect. On the other hand, it did provide two highly valuable intangibles: a healthy atmosphere of social equality and a rising horizon of expectations (founded on real economic opportunity).

Economic historians seem to agree nowadays that American real wages (money wages balanced against the changing cost of living) probably increased by at least a quarter or a third between 1820 and 1860. Consequently, workers were able in 1860, if and when employed, to buy more goods from a much wider selection. The economist Alvin Hansen's index of real wage rates (based partly on the *Aldrich Report*, Senate Committee on Finance, 1893), showed in 1925 that the real wages of United States workers went up in the 1820's, 1830's, and 1840's, declined somewhat in the 1850's, and then continued to rise.[5] A later study of Harold G. Moulton at the Brookings Institution indicated that the Civil War demand pushed up prices at a quicker rate than wages, but that when the war ended prices fell to about their former levels, while wages fell much less steeply and were maintained for the rest of the nineteenth century at much higher than their pre-war levels. Such estimates make more sense under continuous full employment—an unrealistic assumption considering the degree of technological displacement of labor and cyclical unemployment in the history of the period.

A British visitor, Harriet Martineau, claimed in the mid-1830's that "all the strikes she heard of" were on the question of hours, not wages. In 1830 men commonly labored twelve or thirteen hours a day. Agitation to reduce this average had begun in Jackson's days and received wide support in the 1840's. In 1840 Van Buren decreed a general ten-hour working day for federal laborers and mechanics on public works, in the teeth of strong conservative opposition. A "New England Convention" at Boston in October, 1844, strongly urged the adoption of a ten-hour labor law for other workers too, and meetings continued throughout the 1840's. Political agitation, labor walkouts, and combined local pressures on state legislatures forced the enactment of ten-hour laws by several states—New Hampshire, Pennsylvania, Maine, New Jersey, Ohio, Rhode Island, California, and Connecticut having done so by 1855. The acts they passed were usually merely permissive rather than compulsory in character, and did not involve an efficient inspectorate system. In any case the measures were badly drafted and easily evaded. After relapsing for a while, the ten-hour-day agitation picked up again in the 1850's, led mainly by middle-class humanitarians. Public opinion forced even the large textile mills of Lowell to reduce hours of work to eleven a day, and by 1860 at least the *idea* of a general ten-hour laboring day was widely accepted.

Along with the tedium and strain of a ten- or twelve-hour day at work went bad working conditions, inadequate housing, and little or no provision for health and welfare. Leaving aside the ill-ventilated factories, unguarded machinery, and perilous mines, let us consider, for instance, public health. The first state board of health was not even established until 1869 (Massachusetts), although a private body—the American Medical Association—had been founded in 1847 partly to encourage good medical practice. Since hospitals were thought of as places for the poor, they were few in number and ill-equipped. To some extent the causes of the unhappy medical and health picture were non-economic: the great discoveries of men like Pasteur and Lister had not yet transformed the world's knowledge and control of bacteria and infection. It is not surprising that over 5,000 New Yorkers died of cholera in 1849 or that Memphis was practically wiped out as a city by yellow-fever plagues in the 1870's.[6] Perhaps these epidemics could have been better controlled however with greater public investment in medical social overhead

capital. The most chronic problem was a shortage of specialist doctors and of nurses; there was no provision for regular nursing training and education until 1873 (Bellevue Hospital, New York).

The incidence of disease was magnified by an enormous housing
problem, particularly in the eastern coastal cities swamped by immigrants from the 1840's onward. Most of the foreign-born factory
workers were crammed into filthy tenements in overcrowded communities like New York, Boston, and Baltimore, or in the mill towns
of New England. New York City housed over a million in the 1860's,
and half its total population managed to live in about 15,000 tenement houses. Another 18,000 or 20,000 were packed into 8,000 leaky,
unventilated, and unsanitary cellars. If there was vertical mobility
in American society, it was very tough on the way up; and for the
first generation, at least, the United States was often hard to distinguish from the Old Country. For those who could afford something better than the tenement existence, housing was considerably
improved by 1860, and several innovations had even made individual private houses more available in price. New methods of
timber-conversion, new types of saws, and nail-making machinery
cut the cost of lumber and of construction, while the lighter "bal-
loon-frame" house (a cheaper version of the solid old New England
frame house, using the new mass-produced nails instead of expensive
craftsman-made mortise-and-tenon joints) was introduced in the
1840's. In urban residential areas, however, much timber was being
replaced by brick, especially with the mechanization in the 1840's of
brick production, or with the brownstone of the Connecticut Valley
and elsewhere (according to the disenchanted Edith Wharton "the
most hideous stone ever quarried").

It seems that economic growth brought certain quantitative material improvements in the life of the average American; but we
must agree with Professor G. R. Taylor (and with the mass of evidence) that it also brought qualitative changes of a very disturbing
nature. The enormous social and psychological impact of unprecedented urban-industrial transformations on the very quality and tex-
ture of life itself—the roar of machinery and the daily discipline of
the factory, the destruction of privacy in huge city dwelling houses,
the divorce from the soil and the rhythm of the seasons—this complex of problems was scarcely discerned in dim outline, let alone
understood and faced by public policies in 1860. All over the face

of the United States today we still hear the reverberations of the technological, transportation, urban revolutions.

The American worker labored hard and long and was inadequately housed. But his wages were good, and there were the intangible benefits conferred by the economy: social equality and a degree of opportunity. Not that reactionary forces did not exist. American employers as much as their European counterparts had at hand convenient and widely accepted economic fictions and theories to support wage cuts and freezes, such as the "wages fund" theory which "proved" conclusively that the wages of any one group of workers could only be raised at the expense of other men's wages, because the total amount of capital funds available within the economic system for wage payments was fixed and final. This Malthusian "Iron Law" of wages went along with the legal doctrine of "conspiracy" already noted, to rationalize "tough" policies toward workers. But it is difficult to grasp what was really happening in the United States if we confine our attention to the domestic scene and to the public statements of native manufacturers, employers, or judges. One must take a comparative view, remembering the telling remarks of Charles Dickens on the Lowell factory girls, for instance,[7] or those of the stream of European commentators who all attested invariably to the upward mobility and relaxed social democracy of America. It was a society structured loosely by status, not rigidly by class or caste. Michel Chevalier (who did take note of a segregated Negro school in Cincinnati, by the way, during his two year visit of 1833–1835) unequivocally declared:

The United States are certainly the land of promise for the laboring class. . . . Nothing is impossible for the American worker; all his objectives can be achieved.

Perhaps the abundance of natural resources and the constant seller's market for labor can explain why, in Chevalier's words, the American worker's objectives could all be achieved. Yet have not other economic systems existed with abundance of land and scarcity of labor, systems of which it could not reasonably be said, as did Chevalier: "Here the condition of the richest merchant and that of the mechanic and farmer are not essentially different; the difference is merely one of degree and not of kind"?

The United States of the mid-century, then, was a relatively democratic, relatively open society. Its growing population com-

manded an unrestricted free-trade market area spanning a continent, rich natural endowments, and a high land-man ratio. Its
culture indulged in dreams of rags to riches, and favored rapid economic exploitation, if necessary through direct government intervention in the form of land grants to private corporations, through
tariffs, and even through state and public enterprise. In such a social
and economic framework there were perhaps few safeguards for
groups that were not politically organized. American skilled labor
began to learn this lesson very early. Large-scale industrialism in the
later nineteenth century would create new underprivileged groups
and throw into relief the problems of older sections. Masses of unskilled and overworked factory hands emerged in a new kind of
unionism; American womenfolk organized themselves to fight for
legal, social, and political equality in an essentially male world;
various waves of immigrants rose group by group up the social
ladder, not without violent adjustments on all sides; the American
Negro, his progress circumscribed by race and delayed by peculiar
regional economic conditions, began to come into his own only in
the twentieth century.

The struggles of these adjusting groups are as much problems of
fundamental human relations—of religion, race, and culture—as
they are of economic organization. They are problems of American
democracy as much as they are problems of American capitalism.
Purely as an economic system, the local version of capitalism that
had grown up in the United States before 1860 was fairly successful.
Perhaps the way the economy acted was erratic, subject to alternating boom and slump, highly uncertain. Perhaps the United States
was more highly favored than most nations by geographical and
human circumstances. Yet its success was not entirely circumstantial.
The system, after all, did make full use of its opportunities, did
create a high rate of economic growth. What is more, it seemed in
the very nature of American history that the fruits of that growth
should be fairly widely distributed among the people.[8]

3. WAR

The rhythm of economic development was broken in 1861 when
Americans took up arms against each other in the tragic and bitter
War Between the States. For those who want to understand the his-

tory of America's wealth the Civil War seems to beg two major questions. First: Was the war "caused" by economic forces? Second: Did the war delay or did it accelerate future economic growth?

We can ask the second of these questions more conveniently at the beginning of Part III of this book; the answer can provide a convenient vantage point from which to survey United States economic development before and after the war. To the first question there is no outright answer, and of course the question itself is too simple-minded; but at least we can try to indicate some of the complexities involved in formulating a more realistic question, or set of questions.

Civil war: the economic setting

Historians have said many different things about the origins of the Civil War. In the late nineteenth century partisanship kept alive the devil theory of war and the view that the struggle was a great "moral conflict" over human slavery. In our century the forces of Good and Evil are less easily distinguished; and grander, more sophisticated mechanisms of interpretation have been evolved, ranging from cultural anthropology ("culture conflict") to quasi-scientific economic determinism.[9] The field of social psychology, for instance, has been systematically raided for material to back up historical methods that often seem flimsy and sweeping. We shall never agree on an "ultimate" explanation of any sort—cultural, legal, psychological, political, or ethical. No modern economic historian would imagine that his own discipline had found the "answer" by applying an economic analysis to the sectional conflict. Perhaps the war is one thing and sectionalism another; the "causes" of sectionalism and the "causes" of military conflict are not necessarily the same. Anyway, sectionalism was on general economic grounds as much a force for national unity as for national disruption. Economic rivalry between sections was balanced by intersectional economic flows and increasing economic dependency between sections. The resort to military action in 1861 can only be explained empirically and politically, and on very specific premises.

This does not mean, of course, that economic analysis can be ignored. The Civil War took place in a special economic and sectional setting. The South, for countless years the leader of the nation, was, as we have seen, "fighting against the census returns" in the antebellum decade. Tied to an agrarian economy of staple crops heavily dependent on foreign demand and northern business organization, and failing through social inertia and rigidity to diversify its economic life, the South became a "conscious minority." The dynamic Northeast, undergoing a "take-off" into industrial growth accompanied by massive immigration and urbanization, became a conscious majority and could afford to moralize about southern institutions, especially about slavery (around which all antisouthern ideas revolved), because as a section it had found slavery to be uneconomic and unsuited to its style of production many years earlier. When the economic interests of the sections clashed, as they did over internal improvements, the national Bank, the protective tariff, and the development of public lands, crises occurred.

It is true that "cultural nationalism" underlay many of the economic and political arguments used by southern leaders. Comparing the growth of economic wealth in North and South before the war, we can see how different patterns of agricultural and industrial production helped to structure different styles of social life, different cultures. Technological changes (like the cotton gin in the Old Southwest and the metal plow in the Old Northwest) reacted on physical-resource endowments to give distinct "comparative advantage" to the two broad regions, the South for raw staple production and the North (and its new partner the West) for foodstuffs and manufactures. Patterns of monoculture in Dixie failed to bring about sustained regional economic growth. For example, overconcentration on cotton, rice, or tobacco production restricted the proliferation of division of labor and growth of specialized skills in other sectors of southern economic life; and this inhibition, taken with the legal enslavement of over one-third of the total population, kept large numbers of people virtually outside the market economy. We have seen in the previous chapter how plantation slavery supported a fairly narrow landed elite in a highly stratified society and produced a "skewed" income distribution: the majority of southern folk lived by almost self-sufficient farming and by purchase of basic necessities only, while the rich minority spent much of their income on luxuries imported from outside the region. The wealth earned by its major exports was not put to productive use for the South itself.

Therefore only slight encouragement was given to the growth of secondary and residentiary industries. There was little "induced" investment because the cotton growers did without any high degree of native social overhead capital—such as internal transportation lines, warehouses, ports, public education, business facilities, and steamship lines. Such matters were left in the hands of Yankee brokers, bankers, and shippers.

The normal growth of aggregate regional wealth that one can expect from an expanding foreign trade sector unhappily did not take place in the South. Southern profits (if they were not eaten up by slave investments) tended to flow north and west or abroad before 1860, and had minimal "multiplier" investment effects on regional income; in turn, the rate of growth of income and consumption was too slow to produce the "accelerator" feedback effect on investment spending. In the Northeast we see the direct antithesis of this picture. There, a business elite favored technological innovation, and in contrast with the rural squirearchy of the South, was ready to support public investment (where both the tax cost and the potential benefits would be spread widely), in such important long-term growth factors as education. Moreover, profits were plowed back creatively into existing manufacturing, while the export base was simultaneously widened. A greater variety of raw materials was processed and a growing regional domestic market was built up. More equitable income distribution in the North and West meant a broader range of demand for goods and services in those areas, more induced investment, a greater growth of trading centers, and accumulation of business skills. Secondary and residentiary industries developed on a wide front, and the growth of northern social capital was unprecedented.

Industrial expansion and the extension of the railroad into new western territories made the agrarian South feel that she was rapidly becoming an "economic colony" of the North. (According to one estimate, the burden of southern indebtedness to the North in 1861 totaled about $200 million.) Politically, southern prestige and power in national affairs seemed on the decline with the North's growing domination of the federal government. To avoid becoming a mere political colony too, southern politicians adapted a narrow constitutionalism—the states'-rights doctrine. If Southerners were to lose their traditional hold on the federal authority, then the best policy was to deny that authority itself.[10] However, many Northerners who were prepared to compromise over slavery as a southern institution were not prepared to countenance disunion. Ironically, the states'-rights dogma backfired on southern leaders: intended as an ultimate safeguard for slavery and the "southern way of life," when pushed to its logical extreme (secession and the denial of federal authority) the doctrine produced more unity in opposition to the South than slavery alone ever could. The waverers and doubters in the North and West went over, to "save the Union."

The antislavery movement

It is doubtful that Americans would have gone to war in 1861 over the one issue of slavery in the southern states. Even in the North abolitionists were usually regarded as extreme fanatics, as indeed many of them undoubtedly were. Before about 1830 the basis of abolitionism was clearly religious, and the Quaker preacher Benjamin Lundy was perhaps the most famous reformer of the period. By 1827 slavery was prohibited throughout the northern states, and the abolitionist movement seemed to be ebbing away. But the 1830's saw a rapid revival in the North (with cotton expansion in the Southwest), and the new generation of leaders replaced Lundy's moral and religious persuasion with outright and ferocious denunciation. Men like William Lloyd Garrison, Wendell Phillips, Theodore Parker, and Theodore Weld, for the most part blind to the injustices felt by factory laborers in the North and capable only of extremely polarized vision, broadened the attack to a general vilification of southern society and southern people. Garrison shouted in his paper the *Liberator*, on January 1, 1831:

> On this subject I do not wish to think, or speak, or write with moderation. . . . I am in earnest—I will not equivocate—I will not excuse—I will not retreat a single inch—AND I WILL BE HEARD.

Men like Garrison and women like Harriet Beecher Stowe (who wrote *Uncle Tom's Cabin* in 1852, based chiefly on Weld's pamphlet *Slavery as It Is, the Testimony of a Thousand Witnesses*, 1839) did most to perpetuate the stereotypes and popular myths that filled the literature and debates of antebellum years. To many Yankees their southern cousins were made up of planter-aristocrats, uneducated yet overbearing and conceited braggarts, violent of passion, self-indulgent, impatient, jealous, and avaricious, improvident, idle, and sadistically cruel. So they were portrayed by the abolitionist historian Richard Hildreth (*Despotism in America*, 1840). To many Southerners, on the other hand, their northern cousins were wildly extreme Puritans, hypocrites, and misanthropists with no feeling for life and culture, living in "moral deformity and hideous gloom" and unfitted for the exercise of true civil and religious liberty because of their "fierce, fantastic intolerance." So they were portrayed by the leading southern journal, *De Bow's Review*, in 1860. The *Review* went on to say that for all their "human" failings, the southern planters were in contrast a gallant, high-spirited, chivalrous, and generous race, direct descendants of Anglo-Saxon blood; in the South the source of all law was the Holy Bible, in the North, the Almighty Dollar; the southern social system (including slavery) was "founded on the revealed laws of God," . . . and so on.

Soon after the *Liberator* was founded, antislavery societies sprang into being all over the North and West, and a federation of such groups was organized in Boston in 1832. One year later, a larger federation, the American Antislavery Society, was established in Philadelphia by Garrison and his disciples. By 1840 about 175,000 active abolitionists were enrolled in 2,000 societies, and the wild and stormy period of abolitionism was over. No longer derided and feared, the movement was now well-organized, with a definite propaganda, and was able to attract the membership of leading men of liberal disposition—the poets Whittier and Lowell, the scholars W. E. Channing and F. Wayland. In Cincinnati a student faction from the Lane Theological Seminary broke away to form Oberlin College, which swiftly became a western center of abolitionist thought. As late as October, 1835, Garrison had been dragged forcibly through Boston streets wearing a halter; common opinion rejected his extreme demand for northern secession and his vilification of the federal Constitution as "A covenant with death and an agreement with Hell."

Land policy

This combination of slavery with other sectional disputes (like land policy, tariffs, the national Bank, and federal internal improvements) was easy for politicians to make, because in the national arena the slavery controversy took the form of northern opposition to the extension of slavery to the new territories continually being added in the West. Slavery became inextricably mixed up with the fierce sectional politics of federal land policy, for instance. As we have seen earlier, Congress had no authority to make laws about slavery inside any state of the Union, but it had the power to do so in the "Territorial" phase of a state's evolution. Therefore, each time a new Territorial government was formed, a congressional crisis broke out, because the position secured for slavery in the new Territory was very likely to decide its status when that Territory became a full-fledged state. As the population and wealth of Dixie suffered a relative decline toward 1860, so did its political strength in Congress. Any Territory that became a "free" state added still another two senators and several representatives to Congress who would represent northern interests. Southern politicians wished to prevent this and to expand the slaveholding area in a western and southern direction. The political crises and compromises of 1819–1820 and of 1850 were stages in the evolution of this problem.

What about the land itself? The cheap (and eventually free) public land policy already described was a burning sectional issue throughout prewar years. Up to about 1830 sectional alignment over land policy was that the Northeast (manufacturing and trading states) generally favored high-priced public lands and feared a labor shortage might be caused by the westward drain on manpower if the government made land too easy to buy. On the other hand, northeastern businessmen did not want Washington to make so much revenue out of high-priced public land sales that the government would no longer need or favor high tariffs. So they cleverly demanded that land should be more highly priced but that the profits from land sales should be allocated to individual states on the basis of population. Settlers in the West, of course, wanted a cheap or free land policy. In the South the coastal states maintained at this time a fairly neutral position before 1830. After that date a change came in the sectional lineup over land policy. As antislavery agitation grew, the South came to oppose a cheap land policy because such a policy was meant to encourage rapid settlement of the West by small pioneer (and therefore nonslaveholding) farmers; but the Northeast was willing now to support pro-western cheap land policies in order to win the cooperation of the West on other issues, particularly tariff protection.

Sectional voting for the Preemption bill of 1841 was thus: North-east (Connecticut, Delaware, Maine, Massachusetts, New Hampshire, New Jersey, New York, Pennsylvania, Rhode Island, Vermont, and Maryland)—72 for and 44 against; South (Alabama, Georgia, North and South Carolina, Virginia, Louisiana, Mississippi, Tennessee)—18 for and 62 against; West (Illinois, Indiana, Kentucky, Missouri, Ohio)—27 for and 12 against. Sectional interests were very clear. Twenty years later war broke out, and the newly elected Republican Congress passed the Homestead Act, which brought its pro-western policy to the logical conclusion: free land for all settlers.

Tariff policy

Protection as a sectional dispute was most controversial in the "middle" period, the 1820's and 1830's, when it led to the second threat of secession from the Union. The idea of secession had first been raised in New England, as we have seen during the War of 1812, and the "Tariff of Abominations" of 1828 resulted in an adoption of the same threat by South Carolina. Despite the Nullification Ordinance, however, a compromise tariff was hammered out in 1833. The South's feeling was that she paid tariffs to protect northern industries and to support the prices of northern goods that she had to buy herself. Though the tariff issue had largely passed by the time of the antebellum decade, it had given much publicity to the notions of "southern rights" and secession. Voting on the tariff of 1828 (April 22nd) showed a clear sectional trend, even though the anti-tariff group could expect some Northeastern support because of the wool tariff and the traditional concern of some coastal towns (for example, Boston) for freedom of trade. The Northeast[11] voted 73 for and 34 against the tariff (although Maine opposed it unanimously, and Massachusetts with a vote of 2 for and 11 against); the West voted for the tariff, 29 to 1; the South opposed the tariff, with a combined vote of 3 for and 59 against (the only 3 votes for the bill coming from Virginia).

Banking policy

The disputes about the United States Bank were not so clearly sectional, as a brief backward glance at an earlier chapter would show. It is very generally true that the Northeast as a creditor area favored a centralized monetary system, with control by a central bank over the note issue of local banks in order to check inflation, and that the South and West, as debtor areas lacking capital and currency, opposed the central-bank idea and did not like control over local credit issues. But state banks in New York and the Northeast, as well as those in other sections, were extremely jealous of both Hamilton's United States Bank (1791–1811) and the Second United States Bank (1816–1836). Northern workers opposed the Bank as the supporter of paper-money policies; but people who supported paper money also opposed the Bank because it restricted local issues. Western hatred of the Second Bank was particularly strong in 1819 when, as we have seen, it earned the name "the Monster" by calling in western loans. Nevertheless in 1832 it was only President Jackson's veto that prevented the Second Bank from having its charter renewed. The vote of July 3, 1832, in the House of Representatives was 107 for and 85 against: the Northeast favored the renewal of the charter 68 to 35 (Maine and New Hampshire opposing almost unanimously, New York opposing by a good majority); the West cooperated with the North; the southern states (with the exception of the three southwestern states, Mississippi, Louisiana, and Tennessee, which were evenly divided, 8 to 8) opposed the rechartering with a vote of 12 for and 35 against.

Internal improvements

Probably the most important of all the sectional issues except slavery and extension of slavery was internal improvements. Certainly it was the most dangerous to the South, for it was ultimately to split the old alliance between South and West, and thus ensure the victory of the North in any conflict that might occur. The scheme detailed in the report by Gallatin, the Secretary of the Treasury (1808), which suggested using the enormous surplus revenue at the rate of $2 million a year for ten years, to build turnpike roads and canals and to improve rivers, was a long-term plan for public enterprise unequaled in America until the twentieth century. But it was not accepted in 1808.

The construction of a national road, authorized by Congress in 1806, did not begin until 1811 and did not cease until 1838. This

was the Cumberland Road, from Maryland to Illinois, mentioned
previously. Other developments were slow, but Henry Clay hoped to
combine the question of internal improvements with those of tariffs
and the United States Bank, and to bring about the cooperation of
Northeast and West on this program: the "American System." His
plans, and the progress of federally aided improvements, suffered a
setback in 1816 when the Bonus bill was vetoed by President Madison. The bill had meant to use the surplus of $1½ million, paid by
the United States Bank to the federal government, for the building
of national roads and canals. Furthermore in 1831, a year before he
prevented the rechartering of the United States Bank, President
Jackson vetoed the Maysville Turnpike bill, which had been passed
by Congress to give financial aid to the building of a road from
Maysville to Lexington, both in Kentucky. The Jackson administration, however, was forced by changing economic circumstances to
spend more federal money on internal improvements than ever before: the West continued to grow at a huge rate and demanded such
improvements, and federal surpluses were increasingly heavy. Between 1829 and 1836 over $25 million were spent on roads, canals,
fortifications, rivers and harbors, lighthouses, and public buildings.
The policy of making federal land grants to railways as well as roads
and canals, begun openly by the Act of 1850, was forced through
Congress by a temporary alliance of southern and western states.

Sectionalism: an overview

Let us summarize the changes we have considered in earlier
chapters. Economic growth brought a shift in sectional alignment
by causing cleavage between West and South. The rapidly expanding population of the West, with no immediate seaboard, found
freight rates excessively high. What was already a large output
was thus being cramped. The river link with the South was becoming inadequate for western needs; some direct and cheap connection with the East and with Europe was obviously required. Under
Henry Clay the whole of the Ohio Valley was solidly united for
internal improvements. Clay managed to reconcile farmers and manufacturers to the idea of a national economy, though he had difficulty with planters and shipowners. Moreover, the actual success of

internal improvement schemes had the effect of linking Northeast and West by main lines of communication, such as the Erie Canal from New York, the double line of canal and railway from Philadelphia to the river Ohio, the Baltimore and Ohio railway from Maryland, and the Chesapeake and Ohio Canal from the same state (although this never finally reached Ohio). A new alignment between Northeast and West was thus clinched, and what was in effect the "removal of the Alleghenies" counteracted the political and economic consequences of the Mississippi, and set up new economic flows.

Up to about 1830 the most logical sectional alignment seemed to be an alliance of the West and South: the seaboard South felt much more strongly about low tariffs than she did about land policy and was willing to give way on the latter to obtain western support for the former; similarly, the West was more interested in cheap lands than in tariff policy, and the Southwest was in any case in favor of a low tariff. The Northeast, with its demands for high tariffs and dear land, its general support of a national bank, and its lack of deep interest in internal improvements until the late 1820's, seemed unlikely to come to political terms with the West. Between 1830 and 1860 came the distinct realignment of sections: the Northeast whipped up enthusiasm for internal improvements and began to support (with rather less enthusiasm) a cheap land policy, thus retaining western support for higher tariffs. So northern voting for the Maysville Turnpike bill of 1830 was 63 in favor, 35 against, although in 1817 its vote for the Bonus bill had been almost evenly divided, 52 to 51. Western approval of the Maysville bill was almost unanimous (27 to 1); but southern opposition to internal improvements had grown considerably, alienating the West with a vote in 1830 of 12 for, 51 against the bill. (In 1817 southern voting had been less marked in its rejection, 24 to 28.) Similarly, on the public land question, the southern view became after 1830 further and further removed from that of its former western ally. Three factors helped to cause this: the development of northern attacks on southern institutions, the fierce defense by the South that this produced, and the expansion of cotton production. Southerners refused to allow western lands to be disposed of in such a way that slavery and slaveholders were precluded, either by economic or by political pressures.

So it was that an alliance of West and Northeast defeated the

South in the election of 1860, and in the war that followed shortly after. In the years immediately preceding the outbreak of war, it seems clear that the processes of history had produced a unique situation; two events occurred in 1856 that illustrate this. First, the most important prairie railroad was completed: the Illinois Central, managed by Yankee capitalists and partly financed by them and by congressional grants, reached Cairo (where the Ohio joins the Mississippi) from Chicago. Second, a new political party emerged, the Republicans, with a platform uniting West and North.

Lincoln's election

The presidential election of November, 1860, brought in Abraham Lincoln of Illinois. During the antebellum decade the last bonds of Union had seemed to snap when the national political parties and national churches split and reformed on sectional lines. The Whigs disintegrated after 1852; the Democrats finally split in 1860; and the Republicans emerged as the party against the extension of slavery on an openly avowed sectional basis. Lincoln became a minority President, and it seemed to the South that her drifting decline would now be hastened and completed unless action was taken. After the failure of the compromise maneuvers of 1860–1861, war broke out on April 12, 1861, at Fort Sumter, in the harbor at Charleston, South Carolina.

Were the Southerners correct in their belief that Lincoln's election was an immediate menace to southern institutions? He was the very opposite of a fanatic. The abolitionist minority of the North had little influence in the Republican party, which they had scorned and disowned. Southern political power had a long tradition, and was still quite firmly entrenched, except in the executive branch of government. Finally, many northern vested interests were opposed to extreme action of any kind. Slavery itself was in any case limited geographically; the struggle over the extension of slavery was one over "an imaginary Negro in an impossible place" because western physical conditions would not have permitted the development of plantation slavery on an economic basis—the terrain was geographically unsuitable. It was precisely the secession of the southern states and the outbreak of war that empowered Lincoln to do all those things the South feared.

Nevertheless, although no immediate menace existed, there was good reason to believe that a more distant threat was implied by a Republican victory. There was little guarantee, for instance, that the northern Democrats would remain proslavery voters, or that the Republican party would not exclude the South from all share of the patronage. Politics had openly assumed a sectional character, and the South had come to the end of its long period of political control over the federal government. If such considerations were not tangible enough, there was always the South's complaint that she had become a mere "economic colony" of the North. Among the numerous exponents of this view was James L. Orr of South Carolina, who pointed out in the *Charleston Courier* of April, 1855, how the South depended on the North for all its manufactured goods and most of its bare necessities of life. He wrote:

Where came your axes, hoes, scythes? Yes, even your plows, harrows, rakes, axe and auger handles? Your furniture, carpets, calicos, muslins? The cradle that rocks your infant to sweet slumbers, the top your boy spins, the doll your little girl caresses . . . all are imported [from the North].

T. P. Kettell, however, author of *Southern Wealth and Northern Profits* (1860), marshaled an imposing array of dates and statistics to show that the South was the great wealth-producing region and the North an economic leech, dependent on southern raw materials yet drawing the lion's share of the profits. Kettell argued that this economic inequality resulted from the concentration of manufacturing, banking, shipping, and international trade in the North. New York was the center for the marketing of export crops, not New Orleans or Charleston. The southern planter was paid by English importers in bills of exchange, the market for which was in New York, where ready money could be obtained for them. When the demand for bills was low, this negotiable paper would be depressed; if the demand were high, on the other hand, some Yankee speculator rather than the southern producer would reap the profit. Southern planters were convinced of vicious speculation in this cotton paper, the factor of risk carried by northern brokers in giving money for a future claim (payable in sixty or ninety days) being ignored. In addition to monopolizing the foreign export business, the North almost completely controlled the banking system, allegedly to the detriment of the South. Heavy tribute was paid to Yankee shipping interests, which controlled the bulk of the American carrying trade.

The importance of King Cotton in world trade was, however, often exaggerated by Southerners: *De Bow's Review* once claimed that cotton furnished the basis of world trade and "ruled the commerce of the whole civilized globe." Southern "nationalists" failed to understand their own economic weaknesses, their lack of liquid capital, for instance, because wealth was tied up in slaves and land. It is true that an economic regime that made business depression nationwide rather than localized, and produced a host of middlemen, seemed unjust and inefficient. After such panics as that of 1857 the South had reason to view itself as an innocent victim of wild northern speculation. But there was no alliance between northern businessmen and laborers and western farmers against the planters of the South. Many northern businessmen, after all, were intimately tied by social and economic bonds to the South. They feared dissolution of the Union and disruption of normal trade relations much more than they disliked slavery or hoped for control of the federal government. During the secession crisis of 1860–1861, Congress was bombarded by compromise proposals from northern business groups. The claim of southern extremists, therefore, that Yankees were systematically robbing the South and provoking her to warlike action, must be accepted with the same reservations with which one accepts the northern claim of a vast "slave-power conspiracy." Above all, the agrarian conservatism and lack of resilience of southern institutions impeded any self-help such as moves to diversify the southern economy. Several southern commercial conventions were held, but little came of their proposals to establish direct trade with Europe, to encourage the growth of southern ports such as New Orleans, to improve commercial education, to enact better banking laws, and to improve methods of marketing cotton. Such reforms were never carried out intelligently by state or local governments. The remedy for southern economic grievances, other than self-reform, lay solely with time.

For this, the South refused to wait.

3 LABOR AND CAPITAL
1860 to 1920

Self-Sustaining Growth:
The Extension of the
Postwar Market

Whatever may have been the origins of the Civil War, its outcome was clearly a total political victory for the forces of industrial
capitalism. The political group that led the northern states to their
shattering victory—the Republican party—was born in 1854 in a
wave of popular feeling against slavery and fear that the institution
might be extended into Kansas and Nebraska territories. But the
Republicans, once they grasped control of power in 1861, swung
directly into action in defense of industrial and business interests.

1. THE SETTING

The Republicans vote for industry

Who can doubt the importance of economic factors in generating
the war when one of the first acts of Lincoln's party was a heavy
protective tariff? The Republicans dominated the new Congress,
which convened on the first Monday in December of 1860. Their

leader from Illinois was not to be installed as President of the United States until March 4, 1861. Two days before Abe Lincoln took the oath, his supporters pushed through Congress the Morrill Tariff Act —the first really thoroughgoing protective measure in United States history. An elaborate schedule imposed specific duties on all iron and steel products from abroad and on imported woolens, cottons, linens, and carpetings. Generally, Representative Morrill's act raised duty levels by 5 percent or 10 percent. The wall protecting northern manufacturers was buttressed by further tariff measures during the war, and in 1864 the average level of import duty had reached 47 percent. Southern prophecies on this score seem to have been justified.

The outbreak of open war between North and South did not deter the Republicans in their program of economic development; in fact, once the southern states seceded from the Union and their representatives abandoned Washington, the field was left wide open in Congress. Accordingly, several measures held up by southern opposition before the war now became the law of the land.

In 1862 the Homestead Act, pro-western and calculated to speed up economic exploitation, capped a land policy dating back to colonial days and bitterly opposed by southern spokesmen for the previous thirty years. The Pacific Railway Act of the same year gave the federal government the power to incorporate two companies (the Union Pacific and the Central Pacific) to build a transcontinental railroad financed by huge grants of public land and by federal loans. (In addition, in 1862 the Legal Tender Act allowed the federal government to issue "United States Notes"—the first "greenbacks," and the Department of Agriculture was established to take over and expand the work of the Patent Office's agricultural division, boosting the further commercialization and mechanization of farming.) The National Bank Act of 1863 (revised in 1864) was intended, as we shall see later, to provide the businessman with an adequate and dependable currency and to create a stable national banking system with adequate reserves to protect depositors. Having given business enormous encouragement by its land policy and transcontinental railroad policy, and having provided a national currency and banking facilities for capitalist expansion, the Republican Congress even tried to supply for industry that rare factor of production in nineteenth century America, labor. Lincoln's Contract Labor Law of

1864 (officially an "Act to Encourage Immigration") gave the binding force of federal law to contracts "whereby emigrants shall pledge the wages of their labor for a term not exceeding twelve months, to repay the expenses of their emigration." This was in effect to revive the indenture system that had died in 1817, and contract immigrant labor was not prohibited until 1885 (after trade-union pressure). The open intention of Congress to provide cheap labor for industry came to very little: the number of men involved under the Act of 1864 was not great and was mainly confined to British skilled immigrants. Competition in the labor market from cheap contract workers was acute, however, in some sectors, like the iron industry.

Economists have argued that a necessary political factor in economic revolution is the existence of an elite or leadership group favorable to capital investment and regulated by a positive scale of values conducive to economic growth. Judging by the legislative measures of the wartime Republican Congress, Lincoln's party was such a group.

The Civil War and economic growth

Apart from the effects of acts of Congress, did the Civil War contribute to the growth of America's wealth or did the war destroy more than it created? Two contradictory points of view can be taken. Either the Civil War was the "War of the Industrial Revolution," the great national effort that stimulated economic enterprise, increased production to a "breakthrough" point (through voracious military demand), and created enormous profits that could be "plowed back" into business—or the war was a bitter and destructive interruption of a process of more orderly and normal economic growth whose roots went back beyond the conflict itself. All the historical evidence examined in the earlier part of this book seems to support the second point of view. The United States economic breakthrough had already occurred in the 1840's and 1850's.

Werner Sombart (1863–1941), the famous German scholar of Berlin University, strongly believed that war stimulates economic growth through the accumulation of capital, military supplies, and large armies. War and the national spirit it engenders dissolves normal resistance to technical change and so affects long-run productive capacity as well as short-run industrial expansion. Accepting Sombart's view, one would try to show how large capital investment in United States wars—the Revolution, the War of 1812, and the Civil War—produced secular growth. More recently historians like the American J. U. Nef, for example, have been less impressed with this kind of evidence than they have with the economic dislocations caused by modern war, its reduction of the labor supply by death, disablement, and conscription, its utter waste and dissipation of physical resources and human talents, its depressing effects on living standards and human culture. Of course, the physical destruction caused by war is minimized when the nation is lucky enough not to suffer invasion or aerial bombardment, and in this respect the United States economy has been singularly fortunate up to the present time as far as the first two world wars are concerned—less so with the Civil War.

In 1869, four years after the war was over, David A. Wells, the special revenue commissioner, estimated its money cost as over $4,000 million, a sum fifty-two times greater than the national debt outstanding in the year 1861. To this initial $4 billion he added estimated Confederate costs and losses, war pensions, and the expenditures of individual state and local governments: about $9 billion was the total, said Wells—a sum in excess of the entire increase of national wealth in the boom decade from 1850 to 1860.

Furthermore, the financial management of the war was poor on both sides. The Union government paid for the conflict mainly by unhealthy loans (bond issues) and by currency inflation (the use of paper "greenbacks") rather than by the only more-or-less "efficient" way to finance a war: direct taxation. Even if accepted in principle by the people, a direct income tax might not prove a very effective revenue or anti-inflation measure in a largely agrarian economy with a national income of only about $140 a head; but the very principle of direct taxation was then in question, and the first United States experiment with a federal income tax (1862–1872) was beset by criticism on grounds of constitutionality.[1] Consequently, the Union government managed to raise only 22 percent of its income from taxes, and the Confederacy only 5 percent. At the outset the North believed the military struggle would be short and decisive, and therefore made no long-term financial plans. Salmon P. Chase, Lincoln's Secretary of the Treasury, unwisely depended on short-term loans, and the government was thus obliged to raise funds continuously throughout the long, tedious, and costly years of war, while at the same time meeting short-term obligations as they became due. Private individuals like the optimistic and patriotic speculator Jay Cooke made their fortunes. Cooke sold a large number of the United States war bonds marketed in 1861, and Chase appointed him as general agent for the sale of the 6 percent bond issue authorized by the Loan Act of February, 1862. With a team of 2,500 agents, Cooke swept the North with a publicity campaign that garnered $364 million by January, 1864. He reaped a personal profit, of course, very likely much more than the $220,000 he publicly claimed, and the success of his technique certainly earned him the title "the financier of the Civil War." (In his railroad scheme of a few years later, Cooke was not so lucky, and helped to precipitate the Crash of 1873). In the Confederate States the financial picture was very much worse. With much weaker credit and a less fruitful tax base, the South financed its campaigns largely by issuing floods of paper currency that very soon became inflated and almost worthless.[2]

Southerners held an exaggerated belief in the need of the outside world for cotton, a need they hoped would be so pressing that it would yield a triple return: aid to Dixie from European nations, the means to finance secession, and the ultimate acquiescence of the North. But when hostilities began, European cotton importers were rather overstocked and able to manage for some time. Europe needed wheat from the Northwest almost as badly as cotton from the South, and soon the Union blockade of southern ports would hinder exports of all sorts. Blockade and war did stimulate a temporary quickening of the Confederate economy, however: household industries revived, small munitions factories sprang up, and some of the plantations tried to switch from cotton to foodstuffs (an uneasy change with slave labor) to make up for the tragic drop in cotton output from 4½ million bales (1861) to 299,000 (1864). But blockade and war proved to be far more destructive than productive in the long run. Devastation of the southern countryside by such deliberate acts of "total war" as Sherman's march through Georgia and then northward through South Carolina, and the heavy losses felt by planters and farmers in the ebb and flow of war, reduced the South to a near morbid condition. Once the restraining and temperate hand of Lincoln was removed, the postwar military regime imposed by the victors perpetuated this condition until 1877. It has been said that certain "quietly constructive" social and political developments took place during these years of so-called "Reconstruction" in the South, but the achievement was minimal. For Dixie the Civil War brought three stunning economic and social problems: the abolition of slavery (which cost $3 billion and left the racial problem and the question of genuine economic independence for the American Negro wholly unsolved); the disruption and decay of the plantation system of agriculture; and the collapse of financing.

By contrast, while the South made painful, slow attempts to rise from the chaos, tragedy, and destruction caused by the war and exacerbated by Reconstruction, the North underwent remarkable industrial expansion. Northern military strategy during the campaign had been to encircle the South, blockade her ports, and defeat her armies inland. Against a Confederate population of 9 million (over one-third being slaves) the Union presented 22 million, and immigration from Europe continued throughout the war, so that 400,000 immigrants fought for the North. Against an undeveloped railroad and transportation network and a highly specialized, decentralized planting economy, the North presented an articulated railroad system, a navy, and a diversified, adaptable economy. Yet the North failed to make the fullest use of its productive capacity, and fell back essentially on superiority of manpower. The northern army could have been much better equipped and mechanized than it was, and as the comparative number of men in the field did not reveal impossible odds (at the peak about 1,000,000 Union troops facing 666,000 "Johnny Rebs"), the war itself was scarcely a "pushover" for Lincoln.

Finally, it was the common man—on the battlefield and at work —who paid for the Civil War. He paid as cannon fodder and he paid real economic costs in a falling standard of living, made worse by the fact that the government resorted to indirect taxes (which affected lower-income groups) more than it used the democratic graded income tax. Wages lagged behind living costs, and inflationary financing drove up all prices. From 1863 onward a considerable number of strikes broke out for more pay, and labor activities began to increase. Moreover, the war probably delayed population growth —a fact that might seem strange to those who have seen the opposite effect on population of the Second World War. Despite maintained immigration flows, the rate of population growth slackened during the Civil War with a decline in the birth rate. The economist Chester Wright has calculated that there would have been over 1¼ million more Americans in the decade 1860–1870 if they had not gone to war in 1861. (The casualty total was over 600,000.) Obviously, this delayed economic growth in the United States, although it would be difficult to measure by how much. Perhaps some wars have accelerated economic expansion in participant nations (those not invaded or bombed); perhaps World War II stimulated the United States economy, for instance. But the American Civil War—keeping in mind the boost to heavy industry and to existing labor-saving devices in the Northeast and the application of reapers, mowers, and farm machinery in the West, and the stimulus to specialized mass-production industries like canning and food processing, clothing and munitions (encouraged by military contracts)— this war consumed natural resources, devastated the plantation export sector, disrupted finances, produced currency inflation, delayed population growth, and therefore future economic expansion, and reduced the living standards of Americans.

A physical framework for growth

With the Civil War out of the way, the northern and western economy boomed. Its gigantic growth was based on vast supplies of raw materials and means of power—almost half the world's iron resources, two-thirds of its copper, one-third of its lead; plentiful coal supplies, both anthracitic and bituminous; wide prairies yielding agricultural abundance, and deep forests rich in timber. Large accumulations of capital, at the command of captains of industry for investment, and a versatile, growing labor force acted creatively on all this natural wealth.

By 1900 a westward and southward internal move was taking place, toward raw-material sources: iron ore, timber and cotton for instance. Iron and steel replaced timber and cotton, however, as the basic American industries, although in 1914 meatpacking was still at the head in product value. United States leadership as a whole had by the twentieth century shifted from fine work to mass production, and the American people had made their homeland (inherited or deliberately adopted) the world's outstanding industrial nation. Naturally, behind this expansion was an ever-growing domestic market created and maintained by the spreading railroad and communications network, the increase of population, and complex economic organization.

2. THE MARKET SPREADS

The Iron Horse from coast to coast

The Gilded Age was to a large degree the Railroad Age, for the railroads characterized American economic life in the late nineteenth century: as corporations they played an important part in the business image; as sources of profit they produced the family fortunes of men like E. H. Harriman, James J. Hill, and Leland Stanford, millionaires who symbolized American expansion and opportunity; as a highly efficient form of transportation railroads put on display the geographical and regional variety of the continent to its people and to the world, and bound together with bands of steel the sprawling diversity of America.

The 30,000 miles of operated track laid down during the years 1830 to 1860 had become over 400,000 miles by 1920. Mileage constructed each year fluctuated continually, but in years of peak building like the late 1860's and early 1870's or the late 1890's and the 1900's, an average of 4,000 or 5,000 miles a year were completed —7,439 miles in 1872, for instance, and 6,026 miles in 1902.[3] United States mileage in 1920 exceeded that of the whole of Europe and was a third of the global total; American railroad corporations in that year provided employment for over 2,000,000 workers.

The outbreak of the First World War put an end forever to the long, enthusiastic years of railroad construction. The main cause was not wartime retrenchment, however, but the ebullient expansion of the Gilded Age that brought, for the railroads as for agriculture, too much, too quickly. Archenemies, the farmer and the railroad manager ironically faced the same problem: they were both too successful. Food production outstripped demand, and railroad extension outstripped population growth. The wild scramble for franchises, land grants, and government aid, and the exaggerations of speculators, led to unwise construction, the laying down of competing or even of totally unnecessary track in barren, unpopulated areas. Building surpassed saturation point, and the railroad corporations found themselves in slippery financial circumstances at the precise moment when the competition of newer forms of transportation was being felt. The internal combustion engine enjoyed revolutionary success and brought the competition of motor-vehicle traffic into the passenger and the short-haul freight business. Between the two world wars more miles of track were abandoned than constructed—over three times as many.[4] The 1930's brought chronic near insolvency to America's railroads.

Today's tragic plight of the great railroad corporations should not blind us to their brilliant technical achievements in the Gilded Age. Apart from multiplication of mileage, the outstanding feature was the completion of a transcontinental line in 1869. Further innovations were Pullman's sleeping car (first designed in 1864); George Westinghouse's compressed-air brake (patented 1869) and his later electric signaling devices, both of which made high-speed rail travel possible and safe; the refrigerated freight car (1875); the adoption of uniform gauge (4 feet 8½ inches between rails) in the 1880's; and the introduction of four standard time zones for the United States in 1883.

Under the terms of the Pacific Railway Act passed by the Republican Congress in 1862, charters were issued to the Union Pacific Railroad Company to build a line westward from Nebraska, and to the Central Pacific Railroad Company (managed by two famous figures, Leland Stanford and C. P. Huntington) to build a line eastward from Sacramento, California. The two roads were to meet in the middle, and were subsidized by the gift of ten alternate sections of public land on each side of the track for every mile of line actually constructed, together with official loans of from $16,000 to $48,000 per route mile. American iron only was to be used in all construction jobs. Two years later Congress doubled the land grant and extended its credit to the corporations, because the investing public was slow to subscribe for stock. After bitter competition and almost open warfare, the two corporations finally met at Promontory Point, Utah, on May 10, 1869, and their lines were joined by a gold spike driven in with a silver sledgehammer, amid great pomp and circumstance. The Union Pacific's 1,086 miles and the Central Pacific's 689 miles linked up a system that brought the Atlantic within a week of the Pacific by land. The "iron horse" now rode from coast to coast.

In the meantime, Congress had given charters to other corporations. The Northern Pacific (1864) from Lake Superior to Puget Sound (Washington) was first managed by Jay Cooke of Civil War fame, who managed to lay about 500 miles of track before he failed financially in 1873 and was succeeded by Henry Villard, who used German capital to help out the line and completed the link in 1883. The Atlantic and Pacific (1866) was intended to build westward from Springfield, Missouri, but after its financial collapse it was merged with the more successful "35th parallel" route, the Atchison, Topeka and Santa Fe (1863), directed by Cyrus Holliday. This line stretched across the deserts of New Mexico and Arizona and made contact with the Southern Pacific of California in 1881. Another southern route that linked with the Southern Pacific was the Texas and Pacific (1871), which built westward from Marshall, Texas, and linked at El Paso, establishing a through route to the Pacific coast at San Diego.

The sweat and brawn of hundreds of immigrant laborers— Irishmen on the Union Pacific and Chinamen on the Central Pacific —went into the immense engineering accomplishment of the first transcontinental. Work was organized by construction companies controlled by the men who also happened to be the leading stockholders of the lines concerned—a convenient dual role that gave them great strategic advantage for personal profiteering. For example, the UP was built by a Pennsylvania corporation, the Crédit Mobilier Company (1867), which had finagled the contract through its liaison man, Oakes Ames, a promoter-congressman with financial interests in both sides of the deal. In effect Ames and his partners were making contracts with themselves, at profits of up to $23 million. Because Ames thought it judicious to place stock "where it would do most good," and forestall criticism by implicating other members of Congress, he offered some of his Washington colleagues shares in the Crédit Mobilier Company at par, though their market value shot up 400 percent by February, 1868. Occasionally Ames even went so far as to lend money to enable politicians to buy stock. Bribery charges were brought against congressmen in the presidential campaign year of 1872. The New York *Sun* attacked leading figures (Vice-President Schuyler Colfax and Representative James A. Garfield a future President of the United States) for accepting Crédit Mobilier stock, and an investigating committee revealed among other tidbits that the corporation had been paid $73 million for work that cost under $50 million. Ames was censured but not expelled from the House. As for the Central Pacific, its construction corporation, the Crocker Company, charged an average of $100,000 per mile, said to be at least twice the actual cost.

Historians have not come to agreed conclusions yet about railroad financial scandals, and the statistics are not easy to investigate. Perhaps the railroads have had a poorer press than they deserved. In their role as corporations we shall have cause to discuss them again in a later section. Essentially the point here is that the companies got the transcontinentals built and in a very short time. Later individual "empire builders" consolidated and rationalized regional systems, extending and deepening the national market still further. A prime example, James J. Hill rescued the Northern Pacific in 1893 and, aided by two Canadian aristocrats, proceeded to build up the Great Northern system without benefit of government land grants. The economic prosperity of the northwestern states of Minnesota, North Dakota, and Montana was entirely bound up in Hill's railroad system. He founded communities complete with churches and schools; he encouraged farming, bred cattle, opened banks and, after reaching the Pacific coast, built a fleet of ships to deal directly (as an extension of his railroad lines) with the distant markets of the Far East.

America's waterways in decay

Railroads extended the market and built up American wealth even more after the Civil War than before it, but the waterways did not recover from the initial shock of rail competition. Inferior in speed, in long-distance freight haulage, and in the passenger-carrying field, and subject to climatic hazards, the canals and river steamboats fell behind in the economic race. Moreover, American railroad corporations, like those in Britain, were only too happy to gain financial control of canal and steamer lines, either to operate them as legitimate subsidiaries or simply to close them down deliberately. After 1880 Mississippi River traffic declined steeply. More than half the canals built before 1909 have been totally abandoned since.

Traffic on the Great Lakes, in contrast, did not fall off, and from the 1880's began a long increase (mainly iron-ore traffic). On the whole it has been on the increase ever since, and the recent (1959) opening of the St. Lawrence Seaway is likely to transform future traffic (as we shall see in Part IV of this book). In 1908 the report of Theodore Roosevelt's Inland Waterways Commission, and in the years 1904-1914 the intermittent building of the Panama Canal, kept interest in waterways alive and even caused a slight canal revival with moves to deepen the Erie, Oswego, and Champlain lanes. Yet one could expect little in the way of economic growth from America's decaying inland waterways in the age of finance capitalism. Revolutionary change came from quite another direction.

Rebirth of the highways: the automobile revolution

Railroads exerted their hegemony over all other forms of transportation in the late nineteenth century, but after 1900 or so the real competitor of the iron horse appeared on the scene—that most individualistic, equalizing, "American" phenomenon, the mass-produced automobile. Experiments with land vehicles other than the railway engine had been going on for some time. Andrew Hallidie invented the cable streetcar in 1871, and San Francisco adopted it a couple of years later; in 1874 S. D. Field's electric streetcar made its debut in the streets of New York. Many attempts had been made to build a successful steam-driven automobile since Henry A. House's model of 1866, but the popularity of both steam and electric power for automobiles fell away once the first patent for a practicable gasoline-engined motorcar was taken out by George Selden in 1895.[5] In the 1890's and later, men like R. E. Olds, the Duryeas, and Henry Ford designed internal-combustion automobiles, and in 1903, when Selden's licensees tried to restrict manufacture under the patent laws, independent producers (especially Ford) fought hard; the Selden patent was virtually set aside in 1911. By that time American production was already almost 200,000 cars a year. Nine years later (1920) the output nearly reached 2 million, and in another nine years (1929) it stood at about 4½ million (not counting 880,000 trucks and buses). Manufacture of automobiles under continuous-flow mass-production schedules will be considered later; at this stage we are interested chiefly in the impact of the motorcar on transportation, mobility, and market growth.

Perhaps the three most outstanding features of the automobile in this respect were: the United States policy of producing cheap cars en masse for the general population (the "Ford Revolution" which greatly increased the social depth of the market); the greater freedom of movement given to labor within the economy—the increased lateral mobility of the population—through the automobile; and also, the improved highway building that was demanded by the new form of individual transportation. Highway surfaces had been improved before the coming of the internal-combustion engine: asphalt was introduced (New York City) in the 1870's, Portland cement in the 1890's; in fact, the federal government was moved to enter the highway field, and created an Office of Road Inquiry in 1894 (later renamed the Bureau of Public Roads) to experiment with the latest road-building techniques. In 1916 Congress began its policy of federal aid to major highway constructions.[6] In urban areas local electric tramways gave way to more efficient bus companies with better adaptability and coverage. By 1930 the United States had over 26 million registered vehicles on her highways and byways. (Compare 1957: 67 million registrations). The greatest stimulus to road building and increased travel must surely have come from the perfected automobile; without the internal-combustion engine the "road renaissance" of the twentieth century would scarcely have surpassed in economic impact that of the turnpike revolution over a hundred years earlier. What is more, the automobile very soon became, in itself and apart from its impact elsewhere, a major sector of the American consumer market.

3. THE MARKET THICKENS

The population and the labor force

No less effective an element in the expansion of America's wealth between 1860 and 1920 than the favorable political atmosphere of the Gilded Age and the lateral extension of the market by improved transportation was the overall growth of United States population and its increasing concentration in urban centers. Three times as many Americans made up the total economy of 1920 (106 million) as made up the economy of 1860 (31 million). In addition, more than half the population of 1920 was defined by the United States Census as "urban" compared with under one-quarter of the 1860 population. That is to say, the size of the urban market had grown from 6 million to 54 million since the Civil War.[7]

A larger population meant more producers as well as more consumers, a larger labor force as well as a denser market. Social and economic change brought the addition of women to the labor force in considerable numbers, though not so noticeably as in the years since 1920. The characteristic role of female labor in modern economic life has been in the proliferating field of "office work" where breakthroughs occurred in organization and method as well as in mechanical aids like the typewriter and calculating machine. According to Census data, women made up about one-sixth of the labor force in 1890, about one-quarter in 1920, and about one-third in 1940. While this addition was taking place, the school population was growing and children were being drawn out of the labor force by increased educational opportunities, child-labor laws, and rising standards of living; in addition, retirement practices were becoming standardized, and therefore a balance was maintained. In any case female labor added an element of flexibility to the overall labor force, since women could be utilized when needed and reabsorbed into the nonworking sector of the population without insuperable difficulty later. (This happened, of course, in various nations during the two world wars.)

The labor force of 1920 was therefore larger and more adaptable in size than that of 1860. What is equally important, it was much more efficient and more efficiently placed. First, capitalization per worker was greater—that is, jobs were more mechanized; there was more horsepower behind the elbow of each worker. Second, labor migration and mobility produced a long-term shift from low-output jobs to those that produced the most output for the least strain and hours. A prime example was the move from the country to the city, out of farming and into manufacturing, transportation and commerce. The efficiency of the labor force was maximized, as economists would say. Ironically, as hours of labor were gradually diminished, output per manhour (and the absolute output of labor) greatly increased. America's wealth was the fruit of high labor productivity.

The American as immigrant

The growth of United States wealth would have been slower and less certain without the boost it received from immigration in the late nineteenth and early twentieth centuries. About 30 million immigrants were added to the American population between 1850 and 1920—surely the largest migration in world history. The vast majority of these new Americans were of working age: they added directly to the labor force and not to the dependent section of the population, and they brought help at a critical time when declining native birth rates and death rates were making the population older and increasing the ratio of dependents to workers.

Not only did the immigrants add directly to the productive powers of the American nation; they also added indirectly. From the economic point of view there are two socially unproductive periods of dependency in the life of each individual—childhood and old age—divided by a productive period of labor. Any economic system has to support the individual in all three phases of his life. But the 30 million immigrants who came to America had been raised abroad; foreign nations—Britain, Germany, Russia, Italy, and the rest—had borne the social costs of their childhood, and the United States received them "free."

Traditionally, the United States welcomed immigration under the Naturalization Act of 1795. Short-lived outbursts of nativism and anti-alien fears broke out from time to time, as in the restrictive legislation of 1798 and the "Know-Nothing" hysteria of the 1840's and 1850's; but down to 1921 an open policy was maintained (except for Orientals). However, the government's attitude was usually permissive rather than positive. Little was done officially to protect the immigrant masses from economic, political, and social exploitation. In fact, the only well-defined commitment the federal government ever developed toward immigration was to cut it off. We shall see later how the immigrant lived and how the "golden door" was slammed shut in the 1920's. For the most part there was little comprehension of the immigrant's contribution to United States economic growth.[8]

We need not be surprised at this, for even today economists are in some ways divided about "migration theory": Why do people migrate? What is the impact on the releasing and receiving nations? For instance, a British economist, Professor Brinley Thomas, in 1954 produced a brilliant study of Atlantic migration that emphasized the "push" rather than the "pull" in causing migration—that is, he correlated a mass of statistical data to show how depressive factors in Europe rather than attractive conditions in America lay behind each of the four principal waves of migration which he isolated between the 1840's and the First World War. Each Malthusian dilemma and the migrant flow it engendered from the Old World stimulated investment in the New World—capital was poured into transportation improvements, basic construction work, and mass-production machinery that could be used by polygot, heterogeneous, unskilled labor. It seems from Thomas's figures that booms in the United States were associated with years of declining investment and contraction in Europe, the two conditions being compensatory to some extent, and recurring in twenty-year cycles. The main factor in Europe conditioning migration was periodic pressure of population: there is, he argued, a distinct relationship between the birth rate and emigration statistics. If we accepted Brinley Thomas's findings, they would not necessarily contradict existing knowledge about the internal westward movement. Apparently settlers moved west in good times, and not (as previously believed) in times of economic depression in the East. The moves west could therefore coincide with immigrant flows from Europe.

Apart from the general impact of immigration on United States growth, each national and ethnic group made its own distinct social and economic contribution.

Four million Germans, for example, who came to escape from oppressive taxation and military service and to seek political freedom and economic opportunity in the American Midwest were excellent farmers; they added enormously to United States agricultural wealth (to say nothing of the great brewing industry they established in midwestern cities).[9] German immigration, stimulated by the fiasco of the 1848 revolutions, reached its numerical peak in 1882 and declined after about 1890 as Germany itself began to emerge as an industrial power.

The Scandinavians were also first-class farmers, driven off their small and increasingly uneconomic farms in the homeland by a disastrous series of poor harvests and encouraged by the publicity of transatlantic steamship lines and United States railroad corporations to settle in Minnesota and the surrounding regions.

Earlier, the Irish usually moved into urban areas and worked in industry, mining, and commerce. They furnished much of the tough manual labor needed to build railroads and canals—an initial contribution to America's Industrial Revolution that they had also made in England. Irish immigration was heaviest in the 1840's and 1850's, and declined after the mid-nineties.

The British migrated to America in increased numbers from the late 1860's onward, three or four million of them. These were chiefly skilled workers from Britain's factories and mines, who rapidly moved into commanding positions as foremen, managers, and trade-union leaders. Men from Sheffield trained machine-tool workers in Connecticut; Mancunians directed textile mills in Massachusetts;[10] Welshmen and Cornishmen mined and quarried coal, slate, and ores in Pennsylvania and on Lake Superior's southern and western shores; Scotsmen dominated the shipping yards. They came for cheap land, independence, and high wages, but after about 1890, with the official "closing" of the frontier, the British migrant tended to seek land in Canada or elsewhere in the Commonwealth instead of in the United States. In any event, Britain experienced her socialist revival of the 1880's and 1890's, and in 1900 the Labour party emerged. For the British common man, the United States of those years no longer seemed, as in the past, a beacon of democratic freedom, but a fortress of monopoly capitalism. American employers began to lose patience with British workers who, one manager claimed, were "great sticklers for high wages, small production and strikes." The British for their part were often already unionized before they emigrated, and refused to be used as strikebreakers. About 108,000 of them came in the peak year of 1888, but after that date their numbers fell away and more use was made of the tractable, conservative, peasant labor from eastern and southern Europe.

On the other hand, an unfavorable image of the United States did not impede the two million Canadians who emigrated to lumbering and textile regions of the United States in the first quarter of the twentieth century (over 200,000 moving southward in the peak year 1924); moreover, the bulk of them were Protestant Canadians rather than French *Canadiens*.

After 1900 also came the flood of migrants from southern and eastern Europe, the Russians, Poles, Italians, Hungarians, Greeks, and others who settled mainly in large industrial cities and ports and who provided the bulk of the cheap manufacturing and mining labor of the early century. Over 70 percent of the immigrants of the 1900's came from southern and eastern Europe as compared with about 20 percent in the 1880's, and large-scale industry could not have continued expanding without them. They composed at least 80 percent of the labor force in Pennsylvania's bituminous coal mines, for instance, and 50 percent or more of the population of industrial centers like Lawrence, Massachusetts, in 1910.

The disdain of the native-born and the well-established, housing discriminations, group emigration, and religious or linguistic difficulties produced ghetto-like cities within cities—continuing a trend already in evidence before the Civil War—and American society became more and more diverse and varied. Meanwhile, in the Far West Chinese immigration increased in the 1850's and reached a peak in 1882 when almost 40,000 came in one year. A restrictive policy was then established against them (described in a later chapter). In addition, from America's neighbor to the south came three-quarters of a million official Mexican immigrants between 1900 and 1930, seeking to make a decent living by using their skills on the cotton, rice, citrus, beet, and vegetable farms and in the construction and railroad industries of Texas, California, and especially Arizona.

Massive immigration satisfied the hungry cries of the American West and of the "American system of manufacture" for labor; it gave more—a fascinating, bewildering, and rich cultural diversity to American civilization. The many millions of migrants formed the basic construction materials for building American society according to the blueprint that Walt Whitman, among others, had read out so often.

The city in American life

While several million immigrants imposed a special character on American culture, the cities in which they concentrated came to dominate American society. In 1860 there were 93 cities of over 10,000 souls; in 1920, 752 (and 12 of these housed over 500,000 each). Naturally, urbanization was unevenly distributed: nine out of ten people in Massachusetts were city folk, eight out of ten in New York State, but only one out of ten in the deep South or the Dakotas. We have already taken note in an earlier chapter of the emergent urban civilization of the Ohio Valley (Cincinnati, Louisville, Pittsburgh), of the Lakes (Chicago, Detroit, Toledo, Cleveland), and of the Mississippi River (St. Louis, Memphis, and the great southern port of New Orleans). All these cities were nodal centers, mechanisms of trade, valves in the network of interregional flows that was the respiratory-circulatory system of the economy.

Among the greatest cities, Chicago was by 1890 or so second only to New York, and its position exemplified the westward migration of the population and of political and economic power. Far away on the Pacific coast, San Francisco commanded the world's largest land-locked harbor; the shanty town that sprang up overnight during the gold-rush frenzy of 1848 was now a fine city, linked by land to the East (by pony express since 1860 and by the Union Pacific Railroad since 1869) and by sea and the Panama Canal (opened 1914) to the commerce of the globe. Asian and European immigrants had flooded in—the city today contains the largest Chinese community outside the Orient—and San Francisco heroically survived the tragic earthquake of 1906, rebuilt 20,000 new buildings within three years of the disaster, and emerged as one of the three or four most colorful and distinguished cities of the nation. Many miles farther south, Los Angeles came into prominence somewhat later with the railroad expansion of the 1870's and 1880's, the oil discoveries of the 1890's, and the motion-picture and aviation developments of the early twentieth century.

During the course of American history these urban areas and others like them underwent a continuing process of evolution: small market towns in rural settings became bustling commercial centers; commercial centers became larger industrial cities with outlying dormitory suburbs; and eventually in our day industrial cities transformed themselves into gigantic "conurbations" ringed by suburbs and a wider commuters' hinterland of "ex-urbs." Articulate American opinion was usually highly critical and skeptical about the whole process—so deep did the waters of Jeffersonianism run, and so strong, that conservatives and progressives alike found themselves defending the agrarian tradition against the evils of the city.

Yet, ironically, whatever Americans said and wrote about city life, they abandoned their farms and flocked from the countryside in multitudes. In practice the agrarian ideal failed to match up to the urban reality. Farm life was tough and brutally lonely; the countryside offered few opportunities and little education for the ambitious and talented young; and agriculture, subject as it was to fluctuating (and usually falling) world prices for farm staples, was even more chancy and uncertain than city employment. In the city the country boy or girl would find opportunity, education, community. Where population density could support a higher degree of division of labor and specialization, there would be the hospitals and doctors, the theaters, the libraries, the wider marriage opportunities, the salaries and the consumer benefits of an expansive economy. Here men came to make the "rags-to-riches" ideology a reality. To put it mildly, at the hands of American public opinion the city has had a raw deal.

The city and the frontier

Frederick Jackson Turner's famous "Frontier Thesis" of American history (1893) already mentioned was partly a reaction against the "European" interpretation of the origins of American civilization; but Turner also gave expression to deep American disregard for the city and frontier suspicion of "the East." His thesis was that American democracy was born on the western frontier, in the backwoods and out on the plains, in the cooperative struggle with Nature. A "westward marching army of individualistic liberty-loving backwoodsmen" was the real driving force of American history. It has been said that Turner took no heed of frontier movements in other nations—Canada, Argentina, Australia, for example—and thought the American experience was unique. Furthermore, he probably exaggerated the role of the "West" as a "region of revolt"; after all, few innovations or radical political ideas came from the frontier, which never gave the vote to Indians, Negroes, or women until its very end and which derived most of its institutions from eastern models. From the East came the antislavery movement, prison reform, missionary enterprise, and the concern for the "common man"—a concern born in eastern cities.[11] Turner emphasized the frontier farmer but chose to ignore the frontier landgrabber, the miner, the artisan, and the millowner. The rise of cities he rarely mentioned at all, except insofar as he believed the frontier provided a "safety valve," an outlet for the discontented common people who could move west when things were too bad in the eastern cities. In truth, the exact reverse was more likely the case: the West was settled, not by unemployed city folk moving in times of depression, but by independent farmers (who could afford the $1,000 worth of equipment, food, and supplies to migrate) moving in times of prosperity; the city acted as a safety valve for the farm population that began to migrate from the countryside in times of agricultural depression, and has not ceased to do so ever since. Turner's thesis was nevertheless very attractive to Americans, and he gained many disciples.[12]

The American as frontiersman

In 1860 there were already two "frontiers." First, the traditional westward-moving line, halted since the 1850's on the edge of the Great Plains—from central Minnesota to the southeastern corner of South Dakota, through eastern Nebraska and Kansas, excluding Oklahoma, but dividing Texas; this line of 1860 is a boon to "geographic determinists" because it follows the "edge" of the Plains with remarkable closeness, especially in Texas. Second, the Far West "mining frontier," hardly a line at all but comprising a few thousand settlers between the Rockies and the Pacific coast, lured by gold to make a perilous overland journey across the Great Plains, a long sea trip around the Horn, or a sea and land voyage across the Isthmus of Panama. Between these two settled areas lay the High Plains—the "Great American Desert"—treeless and often waterless "prairie," inhabited by herds of wild buffalo and nomadic Indian tribes. The story of the last frontier is chiefly that of how ranchers and then farmers filled in the great intervening space.

In the spring and summer of 1849 thousands of war veterans and adventurers had made their way to California, in search of gold. By 1850 the population of the area numbered about 100,000, and it was admitted as a state into the Union. The western slopes of the Sierras were scattered with more or less ephemeral mining camps, and during the next fifteen years various gold "rushes" followed upon discoveries in Colorado, Nevada, Arizona, and Idaho. Few miners were lucky, the majority remaining to exploit the wealth of less precious minerals or to supply goods and services to the mining communities and farms. Enough migrants remained behind to form the Territory of Jefferson (1859), which had a population of some 35,000, according to the Census of 1860, and was admitted as the State of Colorado in 1876. Meanwhile, silver was discovered—the richest deposits in the West—in the extreme western part of Utah Territory[13] in 1859. This "Comstock" Lode attracted sufficient settlers to establish Nevada as a State of the Union within five years (1864), and for long remained the basis of Nevada's economy.

The advance of the eastern frontier line was delayed, as we have seen, by lack of transportation, water, economical fencing, and a plow sturdy enough to cut the hard prairie sod. The Plains had long been regarded as desert (although suitable in fact for maize and wheat cultivation and for dairying) and until the 1850's pioneers had encountered mainly well-watered and wooded land and had conditioned themselves to meet the requirements of such an environment; but the Plains offered quite a different terrain, lacking timber for houses, fences, implements, and fuel, and lacking water for crops, cattle, and humans. In addition there were the Indians. So it was that until the 1870's and 1880's the Great Plains were merely "the highway to the Far West," and were left, undisturbed except by passing migrants, to the Indian and the buffalo.

With the eastward advance of the mining frontier and the extension of the network of transportation came a revival of the Indian Question, first in the mountain lands and eventually in the Plains themselves. In a series of bloody wars the Indian tribes were tragically depleted in numbers and herded into small "reservations." Two principal factors explain the defeat of the red men by the white men: first, the latter's superior strategy and improved weapons; second—and a much deeper explanation—the rapid extermination of the buffalo. The nomadic life of the Indians was closely intertwined with that of the buffalo, without which that life would not have been possible. The beast provided the native with hide for clothing, meat (eaten fresh or preserved in the form of "pemmican"), bowstrings, lariats, and fuel.

There were two vast herds, one north and one south of the central overland route, and their destruction began in earnest after the Union Pacific Railroad was connected with the Central Pacific at Promontory Point, Utah, in 1869. For two years after this, the white man continued to hunt buffalo for sport, but in 1871 a powerful economic incentive was added: a Pennsylvania tannery found a method of using buffalo hides for commercial leather. Hired teams of hunters were sent out, and by the mid-1880's the animal was practically extinct. Its numbers had been reduced from a roughly estimated total of about 13 million to a mere specimen handful of thirty-four by 1903.

The Indian wars themselves were sporadic, drawn-out, and bloody affairs that took place in two chief areas—mountains and plains—each having northern and southern sectors.

The subjugation of the natives of the northern mountain zone (Snake and Bannock tribes in Oregon and southern Idaho, and Ute Indians in Utah and Nevada) followed the pattern adopted in earlier years by the Forty-niners, who murdered most of the 130,000 peaceful Digger tribe of California. The miners intermittently fought, bribed, and cheated the tribesmen between 1850 and 1855, and in 1861 the Ute eventually ceded most of their territories to the federal government, in return for a small "reservation." The Indians of the southern mountain area were not so easily subdued; the ferocity and tenacity of the Apache and Navajo warriors kept prospectors out until the 1850's, when military invasion took place. Haphazard fighting in those years gave way to serious war between 1860 and 1864. Both tribes were defeated, the Navajo being dispatched to a reserve at Fort Sumner (1865) and the Apache to a number of small reserves in New Mexico and Arizona (1871–1873). During this war the famous Colonel Kit Carson trapped as many as 7,000 Indians at one time. Nearly 9,000 were captured and over 600 killed in one year alone, 1863–1864.

The Indians of the Plains were even more intractable: they were excellent horsemen and warriors, and their bows were more effective than the muzzle-loading rifle. (In the 1850's the Colt six-shooter helped to weight the scales in the white man's favor, however.) The idea of retaining the whole of the Great American Desert as "one big reservation" fell through with the gold discoveries and transportation improvements of the 1850's and 1860's; the demand grew to "clear" Kansas and Nebraska, which were organized as

Territories in 1854. By 1860 this demand was fulfilled, but the movement did not end at that point. A gold discovery in Colorado brought the invasion of 100,000 miners from the East, urged on by the slogan "Pike's Peak or Bust!" who proceeded to oust the Cheyenne and Arapaho from their territory—despite the entente of Fort Laramie (1851) in which the federal government had promised to preserve definite tribal boundaries. Refusing to accept a further imposed treaty (Fort Lyon, 1861), many Cheyenne and Arapaho took to the warpath in Colorado, Wyoming, and elsewhere. There was much savagery on both sides, especially in the winter of 1864-1865,[14] but peace was secured in October, 1865. The two tribes accepted new reservations, and the Kiowa and Commanche surrendered all claims to central Texas, Kansas, and eastern New Mexico. Uneasy peace reigned in the Southwest until the Red River War of 1874–1875, which signified complete defeat for the Indians.

The chief battles in the northern area of the Plains were fought in the Sioux wars of 1865–1868 and 1876. A federal attempt to connect Montana to the East by the "Powder River Road" was the immediate cause of the first; the advance of the Northern Pacific Railroad, the Black Hills gold rush (1875), and corrupt administration of the Indian reservations were the causes of the second. It was in the war of 1876 that Custer foolishly disobeyed orders and was forced to make his "last stand" at the Battle of the Little Big Horn (June 25th). Despite this victory the tribes surrendered in October, and Chief Sitting Bull fled to Canada, to add to the worries of the overworked "Mounties." This marked the end of major Indian wars, although an epilogue, as it were, was the religious revival of the Teton Sioux of South Dakota and the "battle" of Wounded Knee (1890), in which the white Americans used the Hotchkiss rapid-fire gun with murderous effect.

In the East there was a considerable body of pro-Indian, humanitarian thought, led by reformers like Carl Schurz and Helen H. Jackson, whose *A Century of Dishonor* (1881) played a role in the Indian question similar to that of *Uncle Tom's Cabin* in the Negro question. The Congressional Committee on the Condition of the Indian Tribes (1865) decided it was cheaper to keep Indians in reservations at federal expense than to fight them, and from 1871 a policy was developed of breaking down tribal barriers and dealing with Indians as individuals rather than as separate nations. This culminated in the Dawes Severalty Act (February 8, 1887), the first genuine attempt to "civilize" the Indian and educate him in the essentials of agriculture and social life. Land was to be divided among tribal members, those receiving grants to be admitted to full citizenship. In 1901 the "Five Civilized Nations" of Oklahoma were given citizenship, and in 1924 all remaining Indians received it.

Before the eastern line of settlement could continue from where it had halted in the 1850's, it had not only Indians and technical difficulties of the terrain to face. Federal land policy encouraged the land speculator rather than the "homesteader," and between the late 1860's and the late 1880's ranchers used the great intervening Plains, and refused to give way to farmers.

Eight hundred million acres of the public domain were "alienated" between 1860 and 1920. A rapid rate of alienation after 1860 was governed by a series of acts, including the Preemption Act of 1841 (repealed in 1891), Homestead Act (1862), Morrill Act (1862), Timber Culture Act (1873), Desert Land Act (1877), Timber and Stone Act (1878), Carey Act (1894), and National Reclamation Act (1902). Huge federal grants were given to states and railroad corporations, and smaller areas were given over to Indian reservations and forest reserves or national parks.

The central measure was of course the Homestead Act of 1862, which had legalized the donation of free land by the government to bona fide settlers and was the culmination of the traditional "cheap land" policy. The act gave to any United States citizen (or intended citizen) 160 acres of free land if he had been settled on it for as long as five years and if it showed definite "improvement." Although it prohibited the raising of loans against "homestead" land until possession was legally confirmed, the act put no restrictions on transfer of ownership or maximum size of holdings. Its commuting clause was seriously abused, speculators obtaining vast tracts at only $1.25 an acre; the General Land Office was inefficient and the State Land offices often corrupt. Much of this failure was inherent in the act itself. Written by Easterners, it ignored the real geographical and economic conditions of the West. For instance, conditions of low precipitation west of 97° demanded either small-scale irrigation farming or large-scale "dry" farming—more often the latter. A tract of only 160 acres was thus quite useless except east of the 97th meridian. West of this, 3,000 acres might have been a more economic

size for a farming unit, but the federal government failed to take
this into account until after World War I. The land given to individual states under the Morrill (agricultural colleges) Act of 1862
was eventually sold on the open market to the highest bidders, and
the homesteader could not possibly compete in such sales. Landholding in fact became concentrated at an early date, and before
1890 only 3½ percent of the land west of the Mississippi went to
actual homesteaders. The Homestead Act was thus only a theoretical
triumph for the notion of small-scale landholding. The holdings of
speculators tended to cause a widespread dispersion of population,
which necessitated the construction of railways across sparsely
populated areas and raised the costs of local government. A constant
feud raged between settlers and speculators, resident and absentee
owners. On the other hand it must be admitted that "speculation"
was not necessarily inimical to resourceful colonization and economic growth.

Cowboy economics

Finally, another enemy of the settler was the cattleman. The
extermination of the bison and federal victories over the Indians in
the late 1860's and early 1870's made the Great Plains available for
the range cattle industry. It was discovered quite fortuitously that
cattle could survive the bad winters of the Kansas, Nebraska, and
Wyoming region and fatten up on the pasturage afforded by the
Plains. Almost simultaneously an opportunity of marketing the
cattle from the same region was supplied by the transcontinental
railroad. Texas ranchers thus began to send their yearling "steers"
each spring "on the hoof" to the central and northern Plains,[15]
guided by cowboys along the long and arduous trails. Fattened on
northern pastures, the cattle were then shipped to the packers of
the midwestern cities. This was transhumance on a scale unprecedented in history.
    At first costs were negligible owing to lack of competition; ranch-
ing spread rapidly, the strain of stock was improved, and eastern
or foreign capital was introduced. By 1880 the industry was firmly
established throughout the Plains, and cattle were being bred in the
northern region. A "longhorn" costing $7 or $8 in Texas would

breed (if satisfactorily crossed) steers fetching up to $50 or $60 in the North. The cattle population of Kansas increased between 1860 and 1880 more than sixteenfold (to over 1,500,000). That of Nebraska multiplied thirtyfold (to over 1,000,000), and in Colorado, Wyoming, and Montana numbers increased from negligible amounts to 790,000, 520,000, and 430,000 respectively.

The "Cattle Kingdom" lasted no more than a couple of hectic decades. In the twentieth century it was to provide—posthumously —a boon for the film industry; but its real as opposed to its romanticized existence was conditioned by several hard economic factors. In its beginning was its end: the railroad that shipped its cattle to market eventually brought back in return settlers and farmers. Furthermore, good transportation and communications played no small part in the immense speculative "mania" of 1882-1885. As the cattle boom developed uncontrollably, prices soared and capital poured into the industry from the East and from Europe. In 1881 the Prairie Cattle Company of Edinburgh, Scotland, declared a dividend of 28 percent. Bidding in the East for cattle with which to stock western ranges was bitterly competitive. The demand was so overwhelming that between 1882 and 1884 the numbers of eastern cattle transported westward as range stock balanced the numbers sent east to market. During the mania thousands of would-be "ranchers" and millions of cattle swarmed over the Great Plains, and neither men nor beasts could be supported. Veteran ranchers began enclosing their ranges to protect them from the new invaders, and countless "stockbreeders' protective associations" were organized.

The basic conditions for a slump existed by 1885: the Plains were heavily overstocked. There were 9,000,000 head of cattle in Wyoming alone in 1886—a figure beyond comparison with those given above for 1860 to 1880. A series of historical accidents provided the "immediate" cause of the collapse that came between 1885 and 1887: the bad winter of 1885–1886, the withering hot summer of 1886 and the almost legendary winter of 1886–1887 that killed off cattle in their thousands. The great "livestock corporations" that had emerged could not stand the strain, and went under in 1887.

Meanwhile, from the Southwest, over the Rockies by way of New Mexico, came sheep farmers, and sheep in their hundreds of

thousands. More important still, from the opposite edge of the
Plains the homesteader moved inexorably on, enclosing and farming, adapting himself at last to his new environment—with the help
of barbed-wire fencing (first patented by J. F. Glidden of Illinois in
1874 and by the 1880's made cheap owing to heavy competition in
the wire industry), steel plows to cut the resisting prairie (in general use by the late 1870's), and windmills to pump water (not in
general use, however, until the 1890's because of the high cost of
drilling operations). By 1890 the Great Plains were in the possession
of the farmer, and the "rancher's frontier" was at an end.

In the same year the Superintendent of the Census stated that
the "unsettled area" had been "so broken into by isolated bodies of
settlement that there can hardly be said to be a frontier line."
Officially, the frontier was "closed." That is not to say that the westward movement came to an abrupt end. It did not. There was perhaps little first-class free land left in 1890, but there was still much
inferior land from which modern methods could extract a yield,
and there was an abundance of cheap land. The closing of the frontier, therefore, brought no sudden or emphatic economic changes.
The fact remains, however, that large-scale territorial expansion on
the North American continent was now over. Many writers have
pointed to this when analyzing the "great aberration" of the 1890's
that turned the American Republic into an "imperialist" nation.
More than any other single factor except immigration, the existence
of a boundless area of unoccupied land to the West helped to
differentiate the economy of America from that of Europe. It helped
to shape the monetary, banking, and transportation systems, and
dictated the direction and content of America's foreign trade. It
allowed a free expansion of population and the absorption of masses
of immigrants, and, ironically, it stimulated the growth of those very
cities that the "Frontier Thesis" ignored.

Meeting the needs of an urban market

Urban growth in the late nineteenth century provided a highly
concentrated and accessible mass-consumer market with a variety
of needs. Those needs were met in part by a development and
sophistication of the techniques in evidence before and during the

Civil War in the field of wholesale and retail distribution—the one-price methods already described, adopted in New York City by Stewart, Macy, Constable, and Lord & Taylor. In the 1870's Philadelphia witnessed the rise of Wanamaker's and Chicago the rise of Marshall Field's. Integrated department stores of this sort, usually completely situated in one building, with unified management and accounting, with a team of their own buyers linking the manufacturer directly with changing consumer needs and tastes, and able to handle masses of goods at quantity discounts, led the field in market organization, advertising, and diversification. Food could be served to 2,500 customers in Macy's restaurant in 1908; the store had 91 departments by 1914.

Vigorous competition and an expanding consumer market produced two other developments in addition to the large department store: the mail-order business and chain stores. Curiously enough, the first mail-order house in United States history grew out of the farmers' social-protest movement of the 1870's: this was Montgomery Ward, established in Chicago (1872) to sell supplies to the Grangers. Its great rival, Sears, Roebuck, began as a small firm selling cheap watches in the rural market (1886); in 1897 the company moved to Chicago, taking its five- or six-hundred-page catalog with it. America's first chain store was the A&P (the Great Atlantic & Pacific Tea Company), which opened the doors of its first branch in New York City in 1859 and had opened 400 stores by 1911. Trade resistance and jealousy were very strong: as early as 1870 the first edition of the *American Grocer* launched an attack on large tea stores, alleging that they sold inferior (and even once-used!) tea. Bitter complaints of price-cutting were probably justified, since the chain stores enjoyed distinct economies of scale in buying—F. W. Woolworth, for instance, tried to establish monopsony (monopoly buying power) in some cases by guaranteeing to purchase the entire output of a given producer, thus reducing costs all round. Woolworth's was a special kind of chain store, a "five-and-ten-cent store" aimed at the cheapest possible mass market, a low profit margin, and a rapid turnover. After a false start in Utica, New York (1879), Woolworth moved to Lancaster, Pennsylvania, where a good site and the technique of laying all his goods out on display for customers to examine at will brought wealth untold. Woolworth's (and its rival, Kresge's) was a kind of "self-service" store, since sales effort was reduced to a minimum and all the emphasis was placed on open display. Before the First World War he had built up a corporate empire of 600 stores and erected the tallest and most spectacular skyscraper in the United States (1913).

The forty-two floors of the Woolworth Tower seemed all the more remarkable since they represented the fortune of a $60,000,000 or $70,000,000 corporation that had never sold a single item for more than one dime. Such was the power of the new urban market.

4. THE UNITED STATES IN WORLD TRADE

The strategic market factor in the growth of American industrial capitalism in the years 1860–1920, as in the years that followed, was a vast domestic demand: when that demand faltered the economy faltered; when that demand flourished (as it normally did), the economy flourished. The role of foreign trade in United States growth was therefore very much reduced after the Civil War. Colonial economic life had revolved around international trade, and economic change had been initiated in the export sector. This state of affairs was no longer true in the late nineteenth century, when the pattern and composition of America's foreign commerce was more a reflection of domestic economic changes within the nation. A declining merchant marine was one illustration of this shift of significance.

The merchant navy fails to compete

Crushed by the Civil War, American merchant shipping did not revive until it felt the direct stimulus of World War I and federal encouragement. The inner cause, however, was not the Civil War itself, but, as we have seen in the case of the ephemeral Yankee-clipper boom, an essential failure of the American industry to compete.

Shipping was revolutionized in the later nineteenth century by steam and steel; in this revolution the United States lost ground to European competitors. World steam tonnage (increasingly in steel rather than iron hulls) surpassed world sail tonnage in the 1890's. Refrigerated ships had already been introduced for long-distance food transportation about 1880, and twin-screw engines came in 1883. The twentieth century brought the internal-combustion and turbine engine, and increased use of fuel oil rather than coal in merchant shipping, a move that released space for cargo and lowered fuel costs. Meanwhile, several nations had pioneered the building of specialized freighters, such as oil tankers and ore vessels. Britain led the way: in 1870 her *City of Brussels* steamed the breadth of the Atlantic in under eight days. The opening of the Suez Canal in 1869 altered the geographic balance of world trade. United States sailing ships could not negotiate the canal and were simply cut out of the trade, while British vessels of advanced design took over. Britain's original cost advantage in her developed steam-power and iron-plate industries was maintained in the Age of Steel by the cheap Bessemer process perfected in Sheffield in 1856 and by direct government aid. In most European nations the shipping industries received government subsidies and contracts, but in the United States heavy wartime shipping taxes were not removed until 1868, subsidies were not given, and when the last contract to carry United States mail lapsed in 1875 no steps were taken to renew it until the Ocean Mail Act (1891) almost twenty years later. Unlike many of America's manufacturing industries (which received the "hidden subsidy" of tariff protection), shipbuilding was left to the vagaries of the market economy, and private capitalists were not interested in investing in that area. They put their money into more attractive foreign shipping lines or into the coastal trade, or into even richer manufacturing fields at home.

The outcome of all this was that by 1913 American ships carried only 9 percent of the value of United States foreign trade, as compared with about 75 percent in 1860. Well-organized British companies carried about half and Germans about 14 percent. In the absence of an efficient merchant navy of her own, America's overseas trade was heavily dependent for ocean transport on the services and prices of foreign shipping rings.

With the outbreak of war in Europe in 1914, Congress abolished an Act of 1789 that had prohibited the right of American registration to foreign-built ships, and after declaring war on the German Empire in April, 1917, commandeered all German and privately owned shipping, created an Emergency Fleet Corporation, and launched a record-breaking shipbuilding program under the terms of the Shipping Act of 1916, at considerable financial cost to the nation. In 1920 the Jones Merchant Marine Act sold much of the accumulated tonnage left in federal hands after the war to private corporations on very liberal terms, and the proportion of American foreign trade carried by native ships was now higher in the 1920's (30 percent or 40 percent).[16]

America takes on colonies

There is no more dramatic "extension of the market" than the capture of colonies. Lack of a merchant marine did not delay the United States decision—which one historian has called a "Great Aberration"—to join in the great scramble for colonies inaugurated by the world powers in their "grab for Africa" of the 1880's. Officialdom was cajoled into the great aberration by a new school of imperialist thinking led by writers like Captain A. T. Mahan, and commanded during the process by leaders like Teddy Roosevelt.

This "New Imperialism," under whatever euphemism it masqueraded ("the white man's burden" or "Manifest Destiny"), was basically a question of economic exploitation of undeveloped areas of the globe by advanced nations who had come to some solution of the production problem and were in search of new raw materials, new outlets for surplus capital, new markets. Toward this goal Britain rapidly added an extra 5 million square miles to her jurisdiction, France 3½ million, Germany 1 million. By a roundabout and rather indirect route, the United States followed suit in the Far East and Latin America.

The War of 1812 released certain nationalist ambitions within the United States, as we have seen, some of which were already directed toward Latin America, and the Monroe Doctrine (1823) confirmed a strong United States economic and political interest in the fate of her southern neighbors. In some ways the New Imperialism of the 1890's was but a revival of the earlier expansionism, but this time it had a stronger economic orientation. Cuba was the key.

Jefferson and John Quincy Adams, among others, had first grasped the island's strategic importance—close to United States shores, in command of the entrance to the Mexican Gulf—and President Polk had even tried to buy it (1848). Cuba's relationship with Spain was bitter and bloody: a ten-year war broke out in 1868 that ravaged the country, but somehow the Spaniards hung on. McKinley's Tariff Act of 1890 freed raw sugar—Cuba's staple crop —from United States import duties; but four years later the Wilson-Gorman Act reversed this policy without warning, cut off the United States market for Cuban sugar (which fell to one-quarter of its former price), and brought mass unemployment and tragedy to the island. A fresh anticolonial revolution flared up in 1895 when frustrated Cubans took to burning sugar plantations. By 1898 the United States was ready to intervene: first, there were important mining and sugar investments to protect, and, second, the burgeoning "yellow press" had whipped up public opinion to a frenzy over Spanish "atrocities" in Cuba and the mysterious sinking of the United States battleship *Maine* in Havana harbor (February 15, 1898). In April, 1898, Congress resolved that Cuba was an independent nation, and instructed the President to go to war with Spain to give credence to its resolution. The Teller Resolution added that control of the island would be guaranteed to the Cuban people. But things did not work out that way. From 1898 to 1902 the United States Army ruled Cuba, and before the island was finally handed over the Platt Amendment (1901) was inserted into the Cuban constitution, to stipulate that Cuba should never sign away its independence to any foreign power, would never contract any public debt it could not pay, would allow the United States to establish coaling and naval stations, and would grant to the United States the right of intervention at any time to preserve Cuban independence and protect "life, property and individual liberty."[17] In 1934 the amendment was abrogated, but United States economic interests in Cuba remained active—direct investment there totaled over $660 million in 1936.

A United States protectorate over Cuba was but one heritage of the 113-day Spanish-American War of 1898. Another was Puerto Rico as a colony. After about eighteen months of military government the Foraker Act (1900) gave Puerto Rico a quasi-territorial status, and two years later free trade with the United States was permitted; finally, the Jones Act of 1917 extended full United States citizenship to Puerto Ricans, together with an elected bicameral system of government with a Bill of Rights and an appointed governor. Transportation, sanitary, and educational facilities were developed, and the sugar, tobacco, and fruit industries expanded. The Puerto Rican economy, however, was very unstable, its two chief crops being entirely dependent on the mainland market and cultivated by absentee corporations that controlled 60 percent of total wealth and did not plow back sufficient profits into Puerto Rico itself. In the 1930's a class of landless proletarians emerged as farms were consolidated into larger tobacco and sugar plantations, and two-thirds of the population were left without jobs when the market collapsed. Puerto Ricans began emigrating to the United States, and many settled in New York City.

A third legacy of the Spanish-American War was renewed agitation for an Isthmian canal to link California and the Pacific with the East directly by sea instead of by the long passage round the Horn. An Anglo-American agreement of 1901 (the Hay-Pauncefote Treaty) gave the United States a free hand to build such a canal in Central America provided it were kept open to all nations on equal terms. Two years later, when Colombia refused to accept the terms of the Hay-Herran Treaty with the United States regarding payment for land to be ceded on which a canal could be built, a revolt broke out in that country (November 3, 1903), encouraged no doubt by the timely arrival of the United States gunboat *Nashville*. On November 6th the United States recognized the sudden independence of the Republic of Panama with rather unseemly haste and signed an immediate treaty with the new republic that gave her a Canal Zone ten miles wide in perpetuity, in return for $10 million cash and an annuity of a quarter-million. The Panama Canal was built by the United States Army Corps of Engineers and opened in 1914. Later the United States paid Colombia $25 million damages for the loss of Panama (1921).

Desire to protect American investments and political unrest in the areas concerned similarly produced an extension of United States protectorates over Nicaragua, Haiti, and Santo Domingo. United States marines landed in Nicaragua in 1912 and stayed until 1933 (except for the three years 1925–1928); Haiti was occupied in 1915 at a time of acute financial distress and political turbulence, and the marines did not leave until 1934; Dominican finances were influenced by the United States from 1904 and openly controlled from 1907, and the marines who landed to supervise elections in 1914 were in virtual control of Santo Domingo until 1924. Elsewhere in Latin America the new spirit of intervention was less official, except for the outright purchase of the Virgin Islands from Denmark in 1917 (for $25 million). Mexico was the scene of private enterprise rather than government maneuvers.

United States investments in Mexican mines, oil, transportation, and ranching were encouraged by the dictator Porfirio Díaz, and took place at an average rate of $40 million a year between 1897 and 1914, total investments multiplying by four to well over $850 million —a sum three times larger than British capital in Mexico at that period. International rivalries complicated the Mexican situation: fierce commercial competition against a background of tremendous profits, economic instability, and (from 1911 when Francisco Madero led a revolution against the autocratic Díaz regime) almost continuous civil conflict. Madero's rising was believed to be partly financed by United States oilmen angered at Díaz's policy of playing off the British and American oil interests against each other. Madero was soon assassinated by the conservatives, who achieved a counterrevolution (with British help, it was said). This conservative government was eventually driven out under pressure from President Wilson, and a new administration led by Venustiano Carranza found American support in 1914. After further bloodshed a remarkable constitution for Mexico was drawn up in 1917; it provided for an advanced secular educational system, and declared the inalienable right of the Mexican people to own their land, water, and subsoil resources. All alien ownership of land and water rights within specified coastal and frontier zones was prohibited, but not retroactively. In 1938 the Mexican government nationalized foreign oil concessions, and United States acceptance of this expropriation owed much to the better diplomatic climate then existing between the two nations.

In other parts of the Americas, United States economic expansionism limited itself to investment. United States capital was heavily sunk in the precious metals, copper, and oil of Peru, Chile, Venezuela, and Colombia, for example. But Canada was the leading field by 1914. United States investment in Canada increased steadily after 1900 or so. Corporations established direct subsidiaries in Canada in order to produce for that market with Canadian raw materials while avoiding Canadian tariff barriers. Thus United States capital has developed the Dominion's automobile, machinery, metallurgical, electrical, rubber, chemical, pulp and paper industries by taking over from the inside, as it were. The $860 million of United States capital in Canada in 1914 had become $3.6 billion by 1935 (compared with $3 billion in Europe and $2.6 billion in South America).

The Pacific and Far East were the second major areas of interest for American expansion at the turn of the century, and of course the Orient had figured very much earlier in the extension of markets abroad. Perry's voyage to Japan (1854) and American trips to Samoa (from which the United States got Tutuila with Pago Pago Harbor in 1899) kept alive the interest.

Hawaii (the Sandwich Islands) was first discovered in 1778 by Captain Cook. In the 1820's several Boston missionaries emigrated to the islands and with gradual intermarriage gained political power. Two groups of Yankees established close commercial contact with Hawaii—first the traders who sold its sandalwood to China, and later the whalers who used it as a supply base. From the 1840's sugar was grown in increasing quantities in the islands. Amity between Hawaii and the United States was assured by America's determined exclusion of England and France. In 1875 a reciprocity treaty placed Hawaiian sugar on the United States free list, exports to America thus increasing fifteenfold by 1890. However, Hawaiian prosperity chiefly favored the American beneficiaries who had invested heavily in the islands. A constitution advantageous to property owners was forced upon the king in 1887, thus giving even greater power to the American planters, who held the best land and worked it with imported cheap labor from China and Japan.

Then in 1890 the McKinley Tariff (placing all raw sugar on the free list and giving a bounty to native American producers) caused great anxiety in the Hawaiian sugar industry: sugar was almost halved in price, and property values slumped. When in the following year the new ruler, Queen Liliuokalani, demanded a democratic constitution embodying native rights, foreign capitalists panicked, demanded United States aid, and successfully brought about the abolition of the monarchy (January 16, 1893). A treaty of annexation was drawn up, but President Cleveland's liberal qualms prevented further action in that direction. Hawaii became an independent republic until 1898, when she was annexed under the administration of President McKinley—the same McKinley whose tariff had been the chief cause of Hawaiian distress eight years earlier. After 1900, canning was introduced, and Hawaii came to produce 80 percent of the world's output of canned pineapples. The islands were admitted to the Union as the fiftieth state in 1959.

The Philippine Islands and Guam[18] were ceded to the United States by Spain at the Peace of Paris, after an American payment of $20 million cash. Even before the treaty was ratified a Filipino revolution broke out (February, 1899). Despite the commercial potentialities of the islands for sugar, hemp, coconut oil, tobacco, minerals, timber, and rubber, their disadvantages were very great. Not only were there over forty different tribes speaking about ninety different dialects, but a large proportion of the population was illiterate, and transportation and sanitary conditions were extremely bad. A purely civil administration was established, with some native participation, and considerable material progress was made, even before the costly rebellion was put down in 1902. Once peace was regained a 25 percent tariff reduction was allowed to Philippine products. Seven years later free trade was conceded between the two countries except in sugar and tobacco, and in 1913 complete free trade was finally secured. The Jones Act (1916) gave a measure of home rule and promised American withdrawal on the institution of "stable government." There seemed little doubt that the Philippine adventure had cost and was costing the federal government much more than it gained in return, and in 1934 the Tydings-McDuffie Act—supported by American isolationists, agricultural interests in fear of competition, and the AFL—arranged for Philippine independence after a ten-year probationary period. This would have meant, of course, regular American tariffs, the imposition of an immigration quota, and the withdrawal of automatic United States military defense of the islands. But the Japanese put a stop to this by their invasion in World War II, which completely altered the situation: Philippine autonomy was finally confirmed on July 4, 1946, and the Philippine Trade Act of the same year promised United States–Filipino free trade for at least eight years.

American policy with regard to China was to check her territorial disintegration and maintain her economic integrity against the encroachments of Japan and Russia and the Western powers—Great Britain, France, and Germany. The conclusion of the Sino-Japanese

War in 1895 left Japan with Formosa and vague rights over Korea. In addition the other powers demanded long-term leases of certain ports from China. Encouraged by Great Britain, the American Secretary of State, John Hay, made an effort to keep the doors of China open to commerce. He sent notes to all the nations concerned on September 6, 1899, asking that no power interfere with any port within its "sphere of influence," that no tariffs be imposed other than those of the Chinese government, collected by Chinese officials, and that there be no differentiation between nations in harbor and railway rates. The Boxer Rebellion of 1900, in which the United States helped the other powers to suppress anti-alien riots, gave Hay another opportunity to affirm the "Open Door" policy of equal trading facilities for all nations. On July 3, 1900, he issued another circular message opposing further annexation of Chinese territory as a result of the rebellion, and declaring that the United States intended "to safeguard for the world the principle of equal and impartial trade with all parts of the Chinese Empire." This policy was generally upheld despite such intrusions as the Russo-Japanese War (1904–1905) and World War I, until the Japanese invasion of Manchuria in 1931. Taft's efforts at "dollar diplomacy"—the substitution of dollars for bullets by encouraging railway magnates like E. H. Harriman to invest in Chinese railways—came to naught. Similarly his proposal that all Manchurian railways be neutralized (November, 1909) was hastily rejected by Japan and Russia. In 1910 a British, French, German, and American four-power banking consortium was set up to share equally in all Chinese loans, but American membership was withdrawn by Woodrow Wilson. (Ultimately it proved impossible to substitute dollars for bullets in Far Eastern diplomacy; the door would have to be propped open with bayonets, it seemed, despite the strong reluctance of the United States and other powers to take military steps to halt Japanese aggression.)

For all its efforts in China the United States received little or no return. American investment hopes had centered on railroad construction and on the travelers' tales of "fabulous trade" in the Pacific and an "illimitable market" in China itself that was supposed to ensue from United States control of the Philippines. But the China adventure proved disappointing; Japan, with its greater stability and economic growth after the overthrow of the feudalistic Tokugawa Shogunate in 1868, offered a better opportunity for United States enterprise and investment. In China more American money was tied up in missionary work than in railroad development, and total investments came to a mere $59 million in 1914.

America's part in world trade

The colonial spree of the 1890's was fairly short-lived, and outside the mainstream of United States economic development. Most eyes remained on internal growth, despite the theoretical "closing" of the frontier, and the merchant navy failed to compete, mainly because neither Washington nor Wall Street was interested enough in it. On the one side, the United States played but a modest role in the world economy down to 1914, and a fairly passive role in world affairs generally. On the other side, the United States was more self-sufficient than the nations of Western Europe and had less need of foreign trade. The per capita value of her trade in 1914 was $43—that of Britain was $108, of Germany, $73.

Despite a rise (for obvious reasons) in the First World War, United States exports normally came to only 4 percent or 5 percent of her gross national product (4.8 percent in 1910, for example). Even farm exports themselves accounted for no more than 15.9 percent of farm income in 1910, a proportion that rose with food exports in wartime but fell in the late 1920's and 1930's to a low of 8.5 percent of the farmer's income in 1936. At all times total foreign trade remained but a fraction of domestic trade.

Still, United States exports and imports did multiply many times over between 1860 and 1920, and the nation was the world's third leading trader in 1910. Foreign-trade expansion more or less kept up with overall national economic growth, and of course it was an essential element in national health from the balance-of-payments point of view. Beginning in 1874, the United States exported more goods than she imported, and this favorable balance helped to make up in the international ledger for her deficits caused by the increased foreign travel and spending abroad of Americans, shipping payments, and immigrants' remittances (the money immigrants sent back home).

What were these goods exported by the United States? Raw cotton was still important, but manufactured and semimanufactured goods were now increasing in volume, and foodstuffs took a particularly great part in exports, reaching a peak outward flow in the last two decades of the nineteenth century. Industrial corporations, protected in their manufacturing by high tariffs, began to reorganize to capture foreign markets by creating direct subsidiary corporations to sell abroad with separate distributive structures and headquarters in the countries concerned. The United States Steel Corporation built its own fleet for this end, and in 1918 the smaller companies who had no existing foreign sales organizations were openly encouraged, by the Webb-Pomerene Export Combination Act, to combine together to reduce costs and crack foreign markets. Over 2,000 corporations took advantage of this relaxation of antitrust sentiment between the two world wars. Using new sales institutions of these kinds, American companies distributed sewing machines, steel, cash registers, soap, petroleum, meat products, and a host of other merchandise in many parts of the world.

The United States no longer in debt

But it was the First World War that set the seal on America's emergence into world leadership. That war set in motion waves of distress and change from which the British nation never fully recovered, and produced a massive westward shift in world economic power. New York replaced London as the world's financial center, and the United States became a net creditor on international capital account. For example, in the year the war broke out (1914) total investments by foreigners (mainly Britishers) in the United States amounted to $7.2 billion; American investments abroad, though growing, were half that figure ($3.5 billion). When the World War came to an end at last in 1919, the position was almost reversed: foreign investments in the United States totaled only $3.3 billion, and United States investments abroad were $7 billion.

Concluding on the theme of America's foreign markets in the years 1860–1920, we can see that the merchant marine declined, that most traffic was carried by foreigners, and that although international trade had less significance than it possessed earlier, it did manage to expand with the rest of the economy, and played an important part in the national emergence on the world scene. The

United States was no longer a mere supplier of raw materials to an industrial Europe; she was no longer a borrowing nation. Moreover, parts of the globe other than Europe began to take a large share of United States trade—especially the rest of the Americas and Asia.

The market area and the marketing techniques of 1920 were as different from those of 1860 as an urban-industrial-consumer economy of an established world power is from a rural, commercial, small-town economy of an obscure and struggling republic. They were as far apart as the Woolworth Building and Independence Hall.

The Wealth of Industrial Capitalism

The wealth of the pre–Civil War market had been overwhelmingly agricultural, though the nation did witness a manufacturing breakthrough in the textile industry and a spreading of large-scale productive techniques to other areas, such as meat-packing. Continued extension of the market after the war through the westward movement, transcontinental railroads, population increase and immigration, improvement of mass sales organization, and maintenance of foreign-trade levels brought an irreversible alteration in the productive balance of the economy. Agriculture became the handmaiden of manufacturing industry.

1. THE WEALTH OF THE WEST

While men built up the industrial strength of the United States, wrested precious minerals from the earth, drew upon untapped sources of energy, and fashioned a new technology, the unending struggle with Nature and the subjugation of virgin lands continued without respite "out West." On the American farm the "agricultural revolution," its foundations laid in the years before 1860, was consolidated and elaborated.

The agriculture of industrialism

Three great forces were at work on United States farming in the period 1860 to 1920: the westward movement and the bitter struggle already described between cattle ranchers, farmers, and Indians; the impact of technology and science; and the emergence of regional specialization. In their wake came widening currents of social and political change—outbursts of rural discontent and frustration, a demand for improved agricultural education, and deeper government intervention in the farming sector.

New technical know-how transformed American farms in two ways: through mechanization and through land reclamation. The combine-harvester, as it evolved through a series of increasingly efficient separate inventions for mechanical reaping and threshing, spearheaded farm modernization. Although countless patents were issued in the 1870's and 1880's for harvesting devices, McCormick's corporation (established in 1847 in Chicago) came to dominate the field. McCormick himself died in 1884 and never saw the perfected combine reaper-thresher-binder all in one; but his own mechanical reaper helped to sustain the Union government both financially and physically during the Civil War by increasing grain exports and home food production. Exhibited at the Crystal Palace in London (1851), the McCormick reaper stimulated the mechanization of Europe's farms. In 1902 six harvester manufacturing firms amalgamated in the giant International Harvester Company and came to control over 80 percent of all United States needs. Meanwhile, highly specialized plows and improved windmills were developed, and power was applied to existing machinery.

As a result of all this, the total value of tools and machinery on Unites States farms multiplied by 14 to $3,500 million (1860–1920). Total farm labor costs were soon cut to one-quarter or less, and the time spent preparing the soil and in sowing was reduced to one-fifteenth. It took 233 manhours to grow 100 bushels of wheat in 1840 and only 87 manhours in 1920 (says the United States Census); for corn the manhour reduction was from 276 to 113. Between 1860 and 1920 total farm output tripled in value. Wheat production multiplied by four or five, cotton and corn by three or four.

Great use of scientific fertilization improved yields per acre for some crops (though American agriculture remained extensive and its average yields low compared with the intensive farming of Europe). Much soil was regenerated by the increased use of commercial fertilizers, the national consumption of which leaped from almost nothing (164,000 short tons) to over 7 million short tons (1920). Within one decade (1910–1920) farm use of lime tripled. Interest in soil science encouraged the first real United States conservation movement (1877–1908) and brought increasing public attention to irrigation and reclamation schemes.

Irrigation was successfully practiced by Mormon settlers in the arid parts of Utah (copying ancient Indian stream-diversion methods), and farther south in the "Gadsden Purchase" area, which was by 1890 reclaimed through use of artificial reservoirs. The Desert Land Act (1877) revealed some degree of federal concern, but the act itself was distorted by fraudulent irrigation corporations and benefited only herdsmen. Some of the more obvious abuses were checked by the Carey Act (1894), which made water rights an inalienable part of land title. The desert states were offered a million acres each on condition that reclamation be carried out. Some states took advantage of the Carey Act, but its scope was limited mainly to the most fertile and easily irrigated public lands. As a reclamation measure the act was inadequate, and its framers did not envisage conservation as a general public policy. In 1902 federal irrigation schemes were begun in Arizona, Colorado, Utah, and California, over 2 million acres of desert wasteland being made to bloom. Within ten years these states were growing large quantities of fruit and grain—adding directly to America's agricultural wealth. But many problems remained in the conservation areas: flooding, dam reconstruction, and lack of real interstate cooperative action.

Meanwhile, well-defined and recognizable farming "zones" had appeared, though the extremes of monoculture were to be seen only in the cotton belt. For instance a truck-farming area lay along the Atlantic coast from South Carolina to Massachusetts. A hay and dairying belt extended westward from New England to Michigan, northern Illinois, and Iowa. South and west of this stretched the vast, monotonous corn, winter wheat, and meat-product lands, reaching from Kansas-Nebraska in the West to Pennsylvania and Virginia in the East. North of this belt but to the west of the Great Lakes lay the spring wheat belt, covering the Dakotas, Minnesota, and Wisconsin, which sustained the domestic United States market together with an export surplus of 20 percent for abroad.

Farther south the cotton belt extended west-east from Texas and Oklahoma to Georgia and the Carolinas. Despite cotton's rigid climatic requirements, the growing area has tended to move northward and westward in this century, mainly to escape the breeding grounds of the destructive boll weevil. The weevil migrated from Mexico to Texas about 1892, and spread rapidly over the entire cotton belt. Insofar as it has forced southern farmers to diversify, the beetle has not been a total disaster.

The mountain states and semiarid parts of the Plains formed another belt of specialized farming (Montana, Idaho, Wyoming, Nevada, Utah, Colorado, Arizona, and New Mexico), the chief investment being in wool and livestock. Washington, Oregon, and California—the Pacific coastal zone—provided grain, fruit and lumber.

Clearly these specialized belts could rarely devote themselves exclusively to the crops that characterized them. Even the cotton belt produced much fine timber and corn, as well as wheat and livestock. An important citrus fruit industry grew up in suitable parts of California, Arizona, the Rio Grande Valley of New Mexico and Texas, and in Florida; and there was, too, the dynamic range cattle industry previously described.

The "agricultural industries"

Farm machinery, soil reclamation, and regional specialization drew agriculture closely into the market economy, released farm labor for expanding industries, and speeded up western settlement. Agriculture also had its own industries: meat-packing; the manufacture of farm tools and machinery; "processed" food, fruit and vegetable canning, and flour milling. The combine harvester not only increased grain production; it also dictated a revolution in the techniques of handling, shipping, and storing vast loads of grain. With great economy the gap was filled by steam power, the grain elevator (capable of storing a million bushels and of loading ships at the rate of 10,000 bushels an hour), and cooperative bulk handling. Using such methods export totals leaped upward until the United States supplied half the needs of the world's wheat-importing nations.

The meat-packing industry still contains corporations whose origins go back to 1865 and beyond, such as Swift, Armour, and Morris; but it was Civil War contracts that gave the industry its principal boost. In 1850 Chicago was not an important meat-packing center; by 1865 it led the nation and had left Cincinnati far behind. Canal and rail connections, war demands, the growth of the range cattle industry, and a changeover in the Chicago area from wheat to corn cultivation all account for Chicago's rise. Corn implies (in the United States) hogs, since they are chiefly fed on it; so the shift from wheat brought a huge expansion in hog numbers in the belt after the Civil War.

Packers in both Chicago and Cincinnati handled mostly pork, since its demand was more stable than that of beef, until refrigeration was introduced. By 1870, however, many of the large abattoirs had rooms chilled with natural ice; ten years later refrigerated freight wagons were common, and sale of fresh western beef was now possible in eastern markets. Between 1875 and 1890 the number of cattle slaughtered in Chicago doubled twice, and the city became the world's largest abattoir—pictured grimly in Upton Sinclair's unrelenting novel of 1906, *The Jungle.*

The packing industry followed the national pattern of vertical integration by taking over farms and transportation facilities; it achieved great economies of scale and put to good commercial use many fatty and "waste" materials formerly discarded—manufacturing by-products like lard, soap, glue, tallow, and fertilizer. After about 1890 new packing centers appeared farther west, including Omaha and St. Joseph, and in Texas itself the cities of Fort Worth and Dallas.

Pioneered in Europe, the canning industry saw its greatest development in the United States, especially in Maryland and California before 1900. When Gail Borden opened his first condensed-milk canning plant in New York (1861), its entire output was immediately snapped up by the Union government. Military contracts also stimulated commercial experiments in fruit and vegetable canning. Later elements in the industry's growth were the use of calcium chloride (to give higher temperatures and extend the range of cannable foods), the mechanization of can making (1885),[1] increased bacteriological knowledge and control methods, the growth of cities, two global wars, and regional farm specialization (for example, Maine for sweet corn, Wisconsin for peas, Alaska for salmon, Hawaii for pineapples). Even before World War II Americans were ripping open 45 million cans every day of the year. With the automobile and the domestic refrigerator, which came a little later, the can was an established and prominent feature of modern American life.

Flour milling in immediate post–Civil War days was concentrated in three states, New York, Pennsylvania, and Illinois, but during the next twenty years Minnesota captured the home market and invaded foreign markets by use of newly developed milling processes. By 1890 Minneapolis was turning out 7 million barrels of flour a year—90 percent of it controlled by four mighty corporations. Milling interests encouraged and exploited railroad growth and made Minneapolis the wheat market of the entire Northwest. But in turn Minnesota felt competition from still newer milling cities in Kansas (America's chief wheat state by 1892), Texas, Oklahoma, and New York State. Since 1930, in fact, Buffalo has taken the lead, having the advantage of cheap power and first-class transportation facilities by lake, canal, and rail between Canada or the Northwest and the Atlantic. The relative decline of Minneapolis after 1900 was symptomatic of the decline of the Northwest itself as a wheat area, the falling competitive quality of its grain, and the switch to dairying on a large scale.

Changes like these, which affected the balance and productivity of the entire economy and the ultimate living standards of the American people, were matters of deep concern to federal and state authorities. Government sought to ally itself with economic forces by encouraging the trend toward specialization and a more scientific and rational farming.

An education for modern farming

The heart of this particular problem was agricultural education. As early as 1802 (the Ohio Enabling Act) the federal government had taken steps to finance public education: one "section" of land out of each "township" was given to the state government for this purpose. But the first state college intended specifically for agricultural science was not opened until 1857 (Michigan). The Morrill Act (1862) made the land-grant college system more general: each state was given a land grant of 30,000 acres for each representative and senator it had in Congress, provided that state authorities opened a college within five years. Most states managed to procure around $1.25 an acre for the public land, but on the whole the new colleges were short of funds and could not find well-trained agricultural science instructors for many years. They had to fight the rooted opposition of older, traditional colleges. The second Morrill Act of 1890 relieved some of these pressures by giving federal cash grants to the new colleges and by liberating funds to create separate Negro colleges in several southern states. Morrill's legislation was supplemented later by the Smith-Lever (1914) and Smith-Hughes (1917) acts, and alongside the colleges grew up agricultural research stations. Connecticut (1875) had the first publicly owned station; the Hatch Act (1887) gave a small federal grant to each of the land-grant college states that chose to provide a research station.

Further work in applied science for agriculture was encouraged by the federal Department of Agriculture (1862) and the later Bureau of Animal Husbandry (1884) for research in animal diseases. Of the individual states, Georgia was the leader in establishing its own Department of Agriculture (1874), and others followed her example.

The great farm dilemma

Government scientific aid and the improvement of technical education helped to make agriculture more efficient and productive; but it could not guarantee a good life for the American farmer. In fact, the more efficient and commercialized he became, the more unstable his living standard seemed to be. How can we explain this? Why did the subjugation of a rich continent and the creation of a vast agricultural domain not create a wealthy class of farmers? What happened to the Jeffersonian ideal—the "agrarian democracy" of self-sufficient, independent, and sturdy family farmers, owning the land they tilled?

The crux of the "farm problem" was price. Commercial farming is coupled to the national economic machine (and to the world economy) by the mechanism of price. Fluctuations in the world or nation became exaggerated in farm prices; the farmer was fighting against blind "economic forces" beyond his individual control.

Unstable (and usually low) prices for farm products were the root cause of farm distress and poverty in both of the great agrarian depressions of United States history—that from the Civil War's end to the late 1890's, and that of the 1920's and 1930's. In the former depression, prices were relatively low because industrial productivity, for all its dynamism, did not grow fast enough to outstrip farm productivity. Spread of the cultivated land area and growth of farm output—if you like, the very success of the American farmer —was too great for the market to bear, despite the steady rise of output and income in the nonfarm sector. So, national farm prices were low. As for the international market, Americans had to face growing competition from Canada, Argentina, Australia, and New Zealand with their "comparative advantage" of rich virgin soils; and although farmers exported two or three times as much (dollar value) at the turn of the century as in 1870, the overall demand "gap" was hardly affected. Foreign sales did help to keep the farmer going, but they absorbed only a small fraction of total United States output. The real trouble lay at home, in the domestic market, where (terrible irony!) thousands of city dwellers and immigrants were forced to eke out a precarious existence on a substandard diet.

Small wonder that many Americans began to question the "American Dream"; they saw that "equality of opportunity" is not always quite the same thing as "equality." The capitalist system that helped to provide the opportunities was seen to work arbitrarily and unevenly. Some radical revision seemed to be necessary, in favor of true equality and social justice. Farm leaders began to demand the same sort of privileges and special government protection that businessmen had been receiving from Republican administrations. Apart from farm prices, which they hoped the government would stimulate by a "managed currency" policy of an inflationist character (use of paper and silver money), farm protest movements wanted action to curb high interest and mortgage rates, real or imagined railroad corporation abuses, and the large rakeoff of middlemen. Like other underprivileged people in history, they were sometimes wrongheaded, and instead of seeking out true economic causes they "personalized" their attacks.[2]

This weakness is criticized in a rather complacent way by some modern writers judging after the events and with the aid of today's more sophisticated economic analysis. It is now fashionable to drain the humanity out of nineteenth century farm problems and discuss them in the cold light of "agricultural economics"—demand inelasticities, capitalization per farming unit, fixed-variable cost ratios—in terms that make only too evident the "structural," built-in nature of the problems. But life is uncertain, and it might be wise not to fall into a fatalistic worship of the economic "forces" we uncover. Can we fairly dismiss the farm protest movements as being ill-directed, misplaced, or "doomed" from the start? Perhaps economic forces are not so "blind" or totally incapable of being directed by men; and however naïve the economic notions of farm leaders may appear, some of them were adopted in later years.

Farmers help themselves

After the Civil War American farmers learned the essential lesson of any underprivileged group in a democracy: self-help. It was a lesson learned earlier by would-be capitalist entrepreneurs when denied rightful political and social privileges under monarchy and oligarchy; one learned by factory hands pressed under a system of long hours, shutouts, and wage cuts;[3] one learned later by women in their struggle for justice between the sexes; and today a lesson learned by American Negroes so long denied first-class citizenship. The farmer's self-help was expressed in the Granger and Greenback movements, the Farmers' Alliances and Populism. Each of these was motivated by particular empiric grievances rather than an overall plan; they worked through ephemeral "third parties" and by pressure on the two major parties.

The Patrons of Husbandry, the first significant protest group to emerge, was a secret "fraternal" order or club begun in 1867 by Oliver H. Kelley, an agent of the new Department of Agriculture. The Patrons' ritual, titles, and constitution were based on rural life, and their aims were mainly social and educative. In 1868 local lodges were established, called "granges," from which the members received their more frequent name, Grangers. Kelley's hope was to improve social and cultural conditions in rural communities and induce farming men and women to adopt scientific ideas.

At first the order grew but slowly. Then, in the early seventies, the creeping paralysis of economic depression made itself felt: 8,500 local lodges were established in the crisis year alone (1873), and by 1875 the National Grange could claim as many as 20,000 branches. Accelerated growth was accompanied by a distinct change in outlook. Farmers of the Northwest had seized upon the Grange as a means of attacking a particular problem of great concern to them at that time: railroad abuses. The Patrons of Husbandry had become a vehicle in the war against transportation monopoly.

But this was not their only concern. Grangers tried to encourage the use of cooperative enterprises (dairies, warehouses, grain elevators), for instance, and spread a deep hostility to "middlemen," retailers, and the artificially maintained monopoly prices of manufactured goods. State granges operated insurance companies, banks (as in California), agricultural implement factories, packing plants, and cooperative retail shops. These ambitious cooperative schemes failed disastrously in the spheres of both distribution and production. The "Rochdale Pioneers" plan did not take root so well in the Midwest as in England: the Granger industrial concerns came up against the powerful hostility of railroad corporations and private manufacturers.[4]

Despite this misfortune, the Grange did give the farmers valuable experience in cooperative effort, and stimulated the spread of farmers' political parties, especially in the years 1873–1876. These gained control of several state legislatures and managed to force through "Granger laws" (restricting the activities of transport and elevator corporations) in Illinois, Wisconsin, Iowa, and Minnesota. The new state constitution adopted by Illinois in 1870 proclaimed:

> The General Assembly shall pass laws to correct abuses and to prevent unjust discrimination and extortion in the rates of freight and passenger traffics on the different railroads in this state, and enforce such laws by adequate penalties.

Accordingly, in 1871 the state fixed maximum passenger rates, required freight charges based solely on distance, and set up a regulatory board of railway and warehouse commissioners. When the Illinois Supreme Court invalidated the law, the Grangers simply voted a recalcitrant judge out of office, passing a more efficient law in 1873. The next year an elaborate code was passed by the Iowa Legislature, dispensing with the commission idea and fixing instead by direct statute the rates for all railroads within the state. California, Missouri, Nebraska, and several southern states put condemnations of railroad abuses into their revised constitutions in the seventies.

The United States Supreme Court upheld the Granger laws against the railroads in four cases in October, 1876, the most famous of which were *Munn* v. *Illinois* and *Peik* v. *The Chicago and Northwestern Railroad*. On the whole, though, the laws were difficult to enforce, and the powerful railroad companies employed very skillful lawyers. In any event the depression of the seventies temporarily slowed down railroad building and caused some anxiety lest construction stop in the West altogether. Rate wars, moreover, resulted in a permanent lowering of freight rates, and this weakened the position of the Grangers. Ten years after it had sanctioned the laws, the Supreme Court reversed its view in the case of the *Wabash, St. Louis and Pacific Railroad Co.* v. *Illinois* (1886). Its decision destroyed 90 percent of the state railroad rate laws by explicitly limiting the authority of individual states to intrastate commerce. Only Congress could regulate interstate commerce, by legislation that was national in scope. The federal Interstate Commerce Act (1887) that was the logical outcome proved a disappointment.

The decay of the Granger movement was to some extent the measure of the resurgence of the currency issue. Western farmers were anxious about the currency. They found interest rates high and loans difficult to obtain; they felt controlled by eastern financiers; they had to accept eastern prices for their crops, and submit to arbitrary railroad rates. What happened in the sphere of monetary policy was therefore of central importance to them, and in the 1880's they became involved in the Greenback, Free Silver, and Populist movements.

At first farmers were slow to accept the inflationist notions adopted by the Greenback and Free Silver men. The pro-Greenback party called the National Labor Union, for instance, appearing in 1866, had been chiefly an industrial wage earners' movement. Its failure in the presidential election of 1872 (when its candidate O'Connor polled under 30,000 votes) caused the initiative to pass to agrarian interests, and by 1876 a new group had formed, mostly with farm support. This was the Independent National party established at Indianapolis with Peter Cooper (the famous ironmaster-philanthropist, then eighty-five years old) as its leader, and representative members from Illinois, Indiana, Michigan, Iowa, Kansas, and Missouri. In the election of 1876 Cooper gained a negligible 82,000 votes (but an increase over his predecessor). Finally, the Greenback Labor party was founded at Toledo in 1878, with strong agrarian support from all the Midwest; it gained 1,000,000 votes and 14 Congressmen in the congressional elections of that year. An avowed agrarian, J. B. Weaver, was the party's presidential candidate in 1880, and he polled 307,306 votes, almost all of which came from the upper Mississippi Valley—the former stronghold of the Grangers.

The Greenback party, lacking support from the urban proletariat, could not withstand the return of prosperity, the rise in prices, and the effects of the Specie Resumption Act (1875), which provided for the resumption of cash payments on January 1, 1879, and made paper money circulate like gold. The party declined rapidly in the early 1880's, and its most prominent leaders later joined the Populists.

The currency question was now changing to one of free silver, and former Greenbackers adopted the idea of the free and unlimited coinage of silver (at a ratio to gold of 16 to 1) to replace their discredited "greenbacks." Silver-mining interests[5] and debtor western farmers combined to urge the remonetization of silver, the former because they believed this would increase the value of silver (which had fallen owing to vast silver discoveries like the Comstock Lode in Nevada) and the latter because they believed that free coinage of silver would mean a cheaper dollar.

At the same time the vacuum in social action caused by the collapse of the Granges was being filled by the Farmers' Alliances which were modeled upon them—the National Farmers' Alliance in the Northwest and the Farmers' Alliance and Industrial Union in the South. The southern group, which fused various spontaneous unplanned growths (for example, the Agricultural Wheel of Arkansas, the Texas State Alliance, and the Farmers' Union of Louisiana), was established in 1888 to prevent the "encroachment of concentrated capital and the tyranny of monopoly." The northern group, less closely knit, was first formed in 1880 by Milton George, a Chicago editor of a farmers' paper, the *Western Rural*. Within a decade it was fully organized in ten northwestern states, the bulk of its power coming from the wheat areas of Minnesota, the Dakotas, Kansas, and Nebraska.

A convention at St. Louis in 1889 failed to unite the two wings

of the movement, the rift being the result mainly of conflicting economic needs, such as the competition between northwestern lard
and butter and its southern substitute, cottonseed oil. Furthermore,
the southern alliance created hostility by refusing to cooperate with
the 1¼ million membership of the Colored Farmers' National Alliance established at Houston in 1886. But resolutions were drafted
that included demands for "free silver," nationalization of the railways and telegraph companies, land reforms, government subsidies
to agriculture, and a hint of tariff reform. In the election struggle
of 1890 the Farmers' Alliances merged into the now more prominent
third party—the People's party, or Populists.

In the decade after 1887, agricultural depression returned to the
Midwest in an intensified form. Drought on the Great Plains cut
Kansas corn production from 158 million bushels (1885) to 55 million (1890). The Farmers' Alliances were reluctant to enter the political arena, and it seemed that nothing was to be gained from either
of the two major parties. The result was the appearance of the
People's party, more or less informally, in 1890 in Kansas, Nebraska,
and South Dakota. The Populists of the Northwest allied themselves
at first with the Democrats, and despite the Knights of Labor element in the party, it was on the whole an agrarian movement demanding currency inflation and attacking silver demonetization as
the "crime of 1873." Several federal senators and representatives
and one or two state governors were elected in 1890 on platforms
that favored the Populists, and in Kansas the party secured a working majority in the state legislature. This victory urged on the zeal-
ots, and a national political party was formally announced at the
Cincinnati Convention of May, 1891.

Although Populism ended in a whimper, it certainly began with
a bang. The St. Louis Convention (February, 1892) declared:

> We meet in the midst of a nation brought to the verge of moral, politi-
> cal and material ruin. Corruption dominates. . . . The people are demoral-
> ized. . . . The newspapers are subsidized or muzzled; public opinion
> silenced; business prostrated, our homes covered with mortgages, labor
> impoverished and the land concentrating in the hands of capitalists. . . .
> From the same prolific womb of governmental injustice we breed two
> great classes—paupers and millionaires.

About 1,400 delegates in Cincinnati had already pledged themselves
to a program in which many of the aims of industrial labor (such

as the eight-hour day, universal manhood suffrage, and the direct election of the senate) stood side by side with agrarian demands. The *National Economist* was begun as the official organ of the party, and during the summer of 1892 western and southern sections, temporarily united by the enthusiastic spirit of the day, wholeheartedly cheered the "Omaha Platform." This conceived three great reforms: in finance (free silver), in transportation (nationalization), and in public land policy (opposing excessive grants to private corporations). Additional demands were: a graduated income tax, postal savings banks, the Australian ballot, the Initiative and Referendum, and the "Sub-Treasury" Scheme produced earlier by the Southern Alliance (government loans to farmers, based on crops deposited in federal warehouses and elevators).

General James B. Weaver, the former Greenback nominee and Civil War veteran, headed the Populist ticket in 1892, and he could expect support throughout the West and parts of the South, whether the local party title was "Industrial," "Independent," or "People's party." The soil was well prepared by rural rabblerousers like Tom Watson of Georgia or Mary Ellen Lease, the "Kansas pythoness," who roused lethargic farmers to "raise less corn and more Hell!" Defections occurred, especially in the South where "white supremacy" came before all other political issues. Ben Tillman ordered his South Carolina supporters to vote for Cleveland (gold standard and all!) to keep the state "white," even though he was radical in other matters and promised to stick his pitchfork in President Cleveland's ribs two years later.

Nevertheless, 1892 was the high tide of the Populist faith despite "Pitchfork Ben's" capricious ways. The People's party swept Nevada, Idaho, Colorado, Kansas, much of Nebraska and parts of Wyoming; carried off ten seats in the House of Representatives and five in the Senate; put about 1,500 county officials and state legislators in office, won over a million popular votes and 22 electoral college votes for Weaver, and triumphantly predicted an irrevocable victory of the "people" over the "plutocrats" for 1896.

That year did not bring revolution. The tide of Populism was receding, and the scurrilous presidential campaign of 1896 had very little to do with farm protest; Populist supporters were led astray by the monetary issue, voting for western and southern Democrats and fiery William Jennings Bryan. McKinley captured the Presidency for the Republicans on a platform that stood for the gold standard, protective tariffs for industry, and a "firm hand" in foreign affairs. Sixteen solid years of Republicanism followed (McKinley, Theodore Roosevelt, Taft). Farm prices began to rise because of poor harvests in Europe and India; general foreign trade expanded with United States output; and the strain on gold was adventitiously relieved by a threefold increase in world gold production. Money in circulation increased in volume in the United States itself, and the Currency Act of 1900 established the gold standard.

Like the Greenbackers, the Populists were wiped away by the return of prosperity and the natural growth of the economy. Recent interpretations of their faith have played up its negative side (the disturbing racist streak, for instance, which produced the South's segregation laws). But many of the constructive aims of Populism have since been realized—post office banks, railroad regulation, federal intervention for farm prosperity, direct election of senators. On the other hand, the agrarian radicals conceived of no plan to regulate society as a whole; their vision lacked nobility. Except for railroad nationalization the Populists expended energy wastefully on local and fleeting issues. Their empiricism was not the empiricism within a general plan of, say, the British Fabians; they had little to offer that could hold a party together over any considerable length of time—little that could outlast a mere upward swing of the economic cycle.

The horrors of pure competition

If competition in the sense of "classical" capitalist economics exists anywhere, it is in the farming sector of the economy. Here one finds the necessary conditions: comparatively free entry into the business, and production of relatively undifferentiated[6] goods by many small units. Chicken farming, for instance, is a wide-open industry in which five or six million producers compete with each other, like the five million farmers who grow corn and the two million who plant cotton. Ironically, large sectors of industrial America thrived by openly abandoning free competition, while the farmer suffered through an excess of it.

First, farmers were so numerous and geographically scattered that it was very difficult for them to combine effectively in their own interests: neither farm labor unions nor farm employer organizations were very successful. Yet the capital and consumer goods the farmer had to buy were manufactured increasingly by unionized labor and trustified industries, protected in Washington by the lobbies of manufacturers' associations, and very often fixing their own sales prices.[7]

Second, the great number of small producers in agriculture meant that action by any one farmer had no visible effect on the price system: so, being unable to control prices, the individual farmer had little choice if prices fell but to increase his output and make enough to survive. Similarly, if prices rose he would naturally increase his output to make the most of this advantage. The result was continuous pressure to "overproduce" at existing demand levels.

There were technical problems too: first, heavy overhead costs. American agriculture has experienced a relatively high capital-output ratio,[8] and apart from mechanization costs most farmers were burdened by heavy mortgages (entered into in good times of rising prices and due for repayment quite often in appreciating dollars when times were bad). The margin between success and failure in farming was dangerously narrow—one or two poor harvests or a severe illness in the family could hold up debt payments and bring the whole enterprise into the hands of its creditors, the country merchant or eastern banker. Second, the farming temperament, together with dependence on Nature and uncertain markets for staples, made rational economic planning very rare in agriculture. Efficient cost accounting and planned output were scarcely to be found on western homesteads and southern cotton plantations. Moreover, animals and crops take time to grow, and farm production usually lags behind changes in consumer demand. Third, the stimulation of home demand was the key to American farm prosperity; but with rising living standards, farm food products experience relatively low price and income elasticity of demand.[9]

The pity is that such technical problems are obscured in the "good times," when insurance measures of some kind should really be taken. After 1896 the good times returned, and, with the help of a world war, remained until about 1920. As time advanced, the "farm problem" became less and less ideological and more and more technical. In the depressed 1920's and 1930's farmers' organizations

appeared in Washington, D.C., quite conservative and staid in outlook and pursuing prosaic, businesslike aims. Like that other response to modern industrialism, the labor movement, the farm
protest movement became bureaucratized and respectable.

2. MINES, POWER PLANTS, AND FACTORIES

The Victorian capitalism of the 1870's and 1880's in which farming folk struggled to adapt and survive was built solidly on coal,
iron, and steel, and heavy steam-powered machinery. Toward the
close of the old century and in the first two decades of the new, the
emergence of strange new industries (chemical, automotive, electrical) and the growing technical complexity of the productive
process made the former industrial capitalism seem clumsy and
obsolescent by 1920.

Native mineral wealth

Outstanding in the industrial history of the United States after
1860 was the gigantic rise of a $7 billion (1920) group of mineral
industries, on which the whole economy became crucially dependent. Mines were deepened and extended; "new" ores came into
industrial use (like bauxite for aluminum); traditional minerals
received wider application; and coal finally replaced timber as the
principal industrial fuel.

Massive demand for machinery, rails, domestic utensils, and
constructional material had a drastic effect on the United States
iron and steel industry. Iron-ore output increased more or less steadily from about 3 million long tons (1860) to about 27 million (1900),
and then to over 70 million during World War I; pig-iron production jumped from under 1 million short tons to 15 million (1900)
and then to over 40 million during the war. Apart from new demand,
this enormous[10] gain was due to the invention of new processes for
converting iron into steel, and to the discovery of new resources of
ores. (Also, federal tariffs on foreign iron and steel were almost
prohibitive—a sizable indirect subsidy to the industry.) In the 1860's
and 1870's the use of timber (charcoal) rather than coal in the

smelting process became no longer profitable, and in the steelmaking process the Bessemer converter was applied extensively (using the nonphosphoric and nonsulphurous iron ores of New Jersey and of Lake Superior's shores). In Trenton, New Jersey, Peter Cooper (Greenback president and candidate of 1876, as we have seen, inventor of the "Tom Thumb" railway engine for the Baltimore and Ohio in 1830, and an early ironmaster to use the Bessemer converter) began to roll wrought-iron "I"-beams for building uses (about 1860). Cheap steel rails were rolled in Chicago in the 1860's, and Cleveland, Toledo, and Milwaukee became important steel centers on the Lakes.

But the city that came to dominate the world of steel was Pittsburgh, the former Indian village and French fort (Duquesne), wonderfully located where that east-west artery the Ohio River is created out of the Monongahela and the Allegheny, well placed for transportation by water and by rail, rich in oil and gas and at the very heart of the Appalachian coalfield. Out of the Pittsburgh region today tons of coking coal from the mines of the Alleghenies are shipped to the other great centers of America's heavy industry: to Chicago, to Detroit, Toledo, and Cleveland at one end of Lake Erie and to Buffalo and Erie at the other. Into Pittsburgh and into Wheeling, West Virginia, comes the soft red iron ore from the opencast pits of Lake Superior. Duluth, Milwaukee, Toledo, Pittsburgh —all are made one by the Great Lakes waterways and railroad connections. A dozen widely scattered major cities in what was once the "Old Northwest" now form part of a vast industrial complex responsible for a large share of United States heavy-goods output.

The Pittsburgh complex has no monopoly, however, for in the 1880's and 1890's the Industrial Revolution eventually hit the southern states, and in Alabama the city of Birmingham (which was not even founded until 1871) emerged as a great steel center, exploiting the coal, iron, and limestone seams of the southern Appalachians. Birmingham would have sprouted sooner still, except that the nearby iron ore was too phosphoric to be changed readily into steel. Fortunately, in the 1890's the use of a process other than Bessemer's spread very rapidly: this was a combination of European innovations by Siemens and Martin (1866) and by Thomas and Gilchrist (1878) —the "open hearth" process which produced steel at a slower rate, but in much larger quantities and in addition allowed the re-use of scrap metal. The furnace was lined with limestone to absorb phosphoric impurities. It was this open-hearth method that caught on in Birmingham and helped to make that city great.

The southern steel industry suffered from one other disadvantage, however, and this was more intractable, being human: namely, a deliberately colonial attitude on the part of northern steel corporations. Once the South proved the profitability of steelmaking in Alabama and Tennessee, northern bankers stepped in to finance consolidations, and very rapidly the control of the industry passed into the hands of steel men in the North—mainly by way of the Tennessee Coal and Iron Company, which was captured by United States Steel in the panic of 1907. Not only was the South limited to the manufacture of bar iron and steel rather than finished metal products, but a purely fictitious additional charge was added to the price of southern steel—the so-called "Pittsburgh Plus" or "basing point pricing" technique. The Federal Trade Commission later found that Birmingham's product was 26 percent cheaper than the North's, yet the industry quoted all steel at the Pittsburgh production price *plus* the cost of transportation from Pittsburgh to the user (even if the steel came from Birmingham and the consumer worked in Alabama). As a result, manufacturers using steel would locate as near to Pittsburgh as possible and keep out of the South. The regional cost advantage of Birmingham's industry was simply eliminated.[11]

Such a policy was bad for the South, and ultimately it was bad for the firms themselves that were using resources foolishly and uneconomically, mainly out of anxiety—a feverish drive to establish stable output and prices that motivated many large corporations in an era of monopoly. Nevertheless, America's productive achievement in steel was remarkable, and by 1937 she overtopped the combined output of Britain, France, Germany, Italy, and Japan. Despite its peculiar internal price structure, the United States industry surpassed Britain in quantity, technique, and cost; it achieved economies of scale that kept its products at competitive prices in world markets; it was eager to apply chemical science to iron and steel production and to use electric furnaces.

This all came about with extensive vertical and horizontal integration of the industry, until in 1901 Carnegie retired and sold out to the giant United States Steel Corporation, a billion-dollar monopoly. United States Steel owned and mined 65 percent of Lake Superior ores, owned five large docks and an extensive fleet, ran its own trains on its own railroad system, and produced 50 percent of America's steel. The corporation was capitalized at $1,400 million, and by 1924 had made an aggregate net profit of well over $2 billion dollars. Vertical integration (control by a single firm of all the elements going into the making of a single product at all levels— raw materials, transport, manufacture, distribution, finance, and advertising) gave an enormous degree of freewheeling independence. Horizontal integration (the combination of all the manufacturers of one product) made it easy to control price and levels of output. United States Steel combined all these advantages.

Open-hearth steel rapidly outstripped Bessemer steel production in the 1900's and soon became the acceptable method in the United States (in 1950, for instance, 4 million long tons were Bessemer steel but 77 million were open hearth). As for iron-ore supplies, the Lake Superior deposits (first surveyed at Marquette, Michigan, as early as 1844) formed the real basis of the industry; but the fields in Michigan and Wisconsin declined in significance after 1900 as the amazing 100-mile-long Mesabi Range of northeast Minnesota was opened up.

The rich Lake Superior lands also yielded tons of copper, a metal that became highly valuable as an essential raw-material source for the flourishing electrical industries of the 1880's and continuing decades. With the invention of the telegraph, too (1844), had come a demand for miles of copper wire, augmented by the success of the transatlantic cable service publicized in 1858 when Queen Victoria exchanged suitable greetings with President Buchanan. From the early 1880's came electric-light bulbs, electric motors, and all types of apparatus for industry and the home, not to mention Alexander Graham Bell's telephone, perfected in 1884. The future prosperity of the copper industry was assured. A copper "fever" reached its climax in northern Michigan in 1846. In southeastern Tennessee and adjoining parts of Georgia a similar speculative boom broke out in the 1850's, but Michigan dominated, producing 75 percent of all United States copper around 1860. After the Civil War the center of copper mining migrated west to the Rockies. Montana surpassed Michigan in copper output by 1890 and was in turn surpassed by Arizona. The Anaconda Corporation at Butte, Montana, operated the most fruitful mine in the United States by 1887 and forced the Calumet and Hecla Corporation of Michigan into a bitter "war" that slashed copper prices to one-half. Meanwhile, national output continued to multiply (150,000 short tons—1890; 300,000—1900; 1 million tons—1916), and the United States led the world in copper production.

Large monopolistic businesses have dominated the copper industry, and before the First World War the profits to be reaped in copper were enormous—Calumet and Hecla's *average* annual dividends to its lucky shareholders amounted to 143 percent. Four large firms dominated the mining of the ore, and four large firms (two of them from the first two) controlled the smelting. Anaconda not only mined and smelted but (through a subsidiary) also manufactured finished copper products; its assets in 1929 totaled $750 million.[12]

Minerals rarely occur singly. For example, Butte began (1864) as a gold-miners' camp, but the fortune hunters found silver, zinc, and lead, as well as copper in abundance. Zinc is widespread, and usually a geological associate of other minerals, mined from the same source. Lead appears with zinc and also with silver; it was one of the first metals adopted for man's use centuries ago, and, like iron, has been worked in America since colonial days. In southern Missouri vast seams of low-grade lead ore were discovered by prospectors in 1869; in the Rockies the metal has been successfully mined in Nevada, Utah, Colorado, and Idaho, and the states of California and Illinois now produce important lead supplies too. Nevada and Utah became lead-mining states after completion of the railroad link in 1871, and they tripled national output in five years, 1871–1875; and in the 1880's Leadville, Colorado, rose to fame for its fabulous lead seams with high silver content, but was damaged by Cleveland's repeal of the Sherman Silver Purchase Act in 1893; in the 1890's, Coeur d'Alene, Idaho, already famous for its gold rush of the previous decade, emerged as a lead center.

Bitter competition led to the formation by American producers of a master trust in 1889 which became regularized as the National Lead Company in 1891 and reportedly managed 95 percent of all United States output. As with copper, the United States meanwhile became and remained the world's top producer, with Mexico a close second and Africa rising in recent times. Lead is a poor conductor and absorbs radiation—an essential metal for the electrical and atomic-energy industries—and America's native output is far below national needs.

Another strategic metal of which the United States is the world's chief producer but has to import large quantities for its consumption needs is zinc. From almost nothing before the Civil War, zinc output reached 25,000 short tons in 1880, 124,000 in 1900, and about 600,-000 short tons in 1920. Nineteenth century zinc output was stimulated by the "galvanizing" process: coating iron and steel with zinc to prevent rusting. (In the preelectric kitchen the washtub was usually of galvanized metal.) But the critical role of zinc is in the makeup of metal alloys.[13]

Aluminum, an essential light, general-purpose, and structural metal of the modern world without which the aircraft industry could not have achieved greatness, was scarcely manufactured at all in the United States before 1886 when C. M. Hall (1863–1914), an original founder of ALCOA, invented the electrolytic process for reducing aluminum from bauxite ore on a commercial scale. Within a decade the industry was established, and costs fell consistently. Aluminum replaced cast iron in the dome of Philadelphia's City Hall in 1891 and reduced the weight of the tower by 400 tons. Though the United States produces over half the world's aluminum, and although native bauxite output has increased fourfold or more since 1940, the nation still has to import three times as much ore as it can find at home. (British Guiana, Surinam, and Jamaica are important world bauxite sources.) The aluminum industry is controlled by three large corporations established near sources of hydroelectric power (great heat is needed in the reduction process) in the Tennessee Valley, in Washington State, and around Niagara. Meanwhile magnesium, another light structural metal, is gaining popularity. Both are first-rate investments today.

Salt, sulfur, coal, and oil were the four chief nonmetallic minerals of economic consequence developed by American industrialists and miners in the decades between 1860 and 1920. Salt came into great demand with the rise of the chemical industries. Up to 1886 under 1 million short tons of salt were sold or used in any one year; by 1900 the annual figure had tripled; by 1920 it stood at almost 7 million tons (and since that year it has more than tripled again). Used in meat preservation and in the household before the Civil War, native salt had been found chiefly around Syracuse (upper New York State) and in the upper reaches of the Ohio Valley. But more than half the American consumption was imported from

Britain and elsewhere. Salt mining experienced as an industry no major technical innovations—the main processes normally being to drill, force water down the bores, and pump up the brine. What happened was that after 1860 fresh strata of rock salt were discovered in New York, Louisiana, and Michigan, and these fields were exploited as the rising demand for chemicals found greatly enlarged industrial uses for common salt as a chief source of sodium compounds and chlorine. Also, the tariff on imported foreign salt (repealed in 1807) was renewed at a high rate to protect the native industry. Salt played an incidental role in the rise of Chicago as a meat-packing center: it was useful ballast for the return journey of ships carrying western grain down the Erie Canal from the upper Lakes.

Sulfur is a mainstay of the chemical industries as a source of sulfur dioxide, sulfuric acid (for the dye, drug, fertilizer, petroleum, explosives, electrical and metal industries) and sulfate salts; the match industry and the paper and rubber industries also depend on sulfur. Its production increased rapidly in the later nineteenth century but was based almost entirely on the importation of pyrites from Spain and elsewhere until the 1900's when vast strata of native American sulfur were discovered in Louisiana and Texas. The first shipment abroad of United States crude sulfur left Louisiana (for France) in 1904, and the nation has been an exporter ever since. A happy combination of circumstances brought great prosperity to the sulfur industry—a German immigrant chemist (Herman Frasch) devised a superior sulfur-mining technique; the "Frasch process," adopted exclusively in modern mines, demands gallons of hot water under pressure: cheap fuel for heating was provided by the nearby oil industry of Texas (which had arisen simultaneously) and the oil producers in turn received the benefits of abundant sulfur supplies for their own processing needs. War demands gave the sulfur industry a massive push (it doubled production in one year 1916–1917), and except for slight contraction in the early 1930's its output has been on the increase ever since, tripling since 1940.

The fuel resources of a continent

Two of America's richest minerals in the later nineteenth century were also major fuels—coal and oil. Most of the machinery that produced modern industrialism and the railroads that articulated the system were powered after 1870 or so by coal, usually of the bituminous ("soft") variety.

We have noticed (pp. 82-83) that an abundance of timber kept down the demand for bituminous coal until the 1860's and 1870's, especially since the industry's chief clients, the ironmasters, had learned the trick of smelting with anthracite ("hard") coal. Anthracite from Virginia and eastern Pennsylvania was the foremost industrial fuel of the antebellum decade. Vertical and horizontal integration characterized the mining industry; by 1870 a small group of coal buyers (railroad corporations) owned most of the anthracite districts ("captive" mines, these were called).

Bituminous mining in western Pennsylvania, eastern Ohio, West Virginia and Kentucky, Tennessee and Alabama was structured differently. The geography of soft-coal mining did not favor such a degree of integration: bituminous deposits are much more extensive and scattered;[14] conditions fluctuated, and organization was varied if not confused. Large captive mines belonging to steel and railroad corporations and supplying only company needs contrasted with "snow-birds" (irregular little mines working only in season); complex coal-mining companies contrasted with simple "wagon mines." In 1920 the anthracite business was composed of under 200 units; the bituminous industry had well over 12,000. Cheaply mined opencast bituminous coal cost under a dollar a ton; its heat and power lay behind the industrial growth of Pittsburgh in the mid-nineteenth century. Shipped from the bituminous mines of western Pennsylvania via navigable tributaries of the Ohio River system, it performed a similar function for Cincinnati and Louisville.

Bituminous production surpassed anthracite in the 1870's: total coal output in 1860 was about 20 million short tons, of which over half was still anthracitic; by 1920 the total was 658 million short tons, of which a bare 90 million were anthracitic. Soft coal was the principal industrial fuel at the opening of this century; it provided 70 percent of America's energy needs. But coal production was declining by World War I, beginning in anthracite and becoming severe in soft coal too in the 1920's. Coal could not meet the fierce competition of newer fuels—natural gas, petroleum, and electric power.

The coal industry in the United States under free enterprise and private control had developed its capacity far in excess of reasonably estimated demand, and chronic idle capacity with un- (or under-) employment of men and plant was the result. The general effect of large idle capacity was to depress prices, profits, and wages in the industry, which as a result has historically been an "under-privileged" sector of the economy. In justice one must say that the miners increased their plant capacity in both world wars in response to national needs, and found themselves in trouble when those wars ended. (Farmers suffered from the same fate.) In addition, bituminous producers have been too numerous to cooperate effectively against the bargaining power of a few large buyers or against the ill-effects of idle capacity. During the years 1946–1949 bituminous coal provided a heavily reduced proportion of United States energy needs (39 percent), while natural gas provided 14 percent and the great competitor petroleum provided 32 percent.

Coal's losses have been the gains of petroleum ever since the mid-1880's when oil-drilling rigs began to sprout up in widely scattered parts of the continent. For all practical purposes the oil industry was born in a field at Titusville, Pennsylvania on August 27, 1859.[15] Ironically, Colonel Edwin Drake, its pioneer, had already given the order to quit when the gusher blew.

An immediate oil boom followed, and within a decade similar wells were sunk in several foreign nations—Canada, Russia, Romania, and Italy. By 1900 central Europe, Latin America, and the East Indies were added to this group. (Today's chief producers are the United States, Venezuela, Soviet Russia, and the Middle East.) Within the United States the leading position of western Pennsylvania was challenged and taken over in 1895 by Ohio, which in turn was supplanted by California in 1903. Later came equally dramatic strikes in Texas, Louisiana, Oklahoma, Kansas, and an erratic boom (1905–1908) in Illinois.

Spectacular industrial growth of this order implies great elasticity of demand for oil even before the automobile. Gasoline did not become the chief product of the oil industry until after World War I. In the 1860's such demand came from the machinery world, crying out for a modern lubricant, and from concentrated urban populations desperate for a cheap form of lighting. Mineral oil supplanted whale oil in both these markets. Down to the 1920's crude oil was refined by fractional distillation, but since then the adoption of the "cracking process" has enormously widened the range of by-products of the oil industry, creating a new industrial sector, "petrochemi-cals"[16]—a twentieth century investment certainty matched only by the new structural metals.

As an energy source petroleum dominates this automobile, cen-tral-heated age, and even the railroads have abandoned coal for diesel power. America's insatiable energy needs since the last cen-tury, however, have created a market vast enough for natural gas and electric power too. Electricity was first used only for lighting, and was derived mainly with the use of coal. Thomas Edison in-vented the first incandescent electric light bulb that really worked in 1879, and two years later, encouraged by the experiments of pre-vious pioneers like W. A. Antony of Cornell University (1875), Edi-son's company built America's first commercially practicable dynamo to generate electricity. In the 1890's steam turbines were introduced to drive the dynamos, and increased production now made it pos-sible to adopt electricity for power as well as for illumination—hence the flourishing of electric street railways, and the electrifying of textile mills (especially the mills recently constructed in the "New" South).

Electric machinery had enormous advantages: it dispensed with the complex mass of overhead belts, pulleys, and linkages needed in steam-powered factories and made machinery less heavy; it dis-pensed with boilers and "warming-up" time—power was now at hand immediately at the touch of a switch, and individual machines in a series could now be left standing while others worked. On the human side, electric power and lighting greatly reduced fire hazards and made the factory a cleaner, quieter, and more pleasant place to work in.[17] What is more, the American home was revolutionized be-tween the two world wars by electrical gadgets, as we shall see. And yet, during its first twenty or thirty years electricity spread only slowly: generating plants were expensive and required assured, well-organized markets. The coming of hydroelectric power schemes (like the one at Niagara—surely an obvious site—around 1894) did much to reduce costs.

Factory production: the "Ford Revolution"

Though each is fascinating in its own way and rich in human interest, we do not have space here to deal in turn with all the major modern industries that came upon the American scene before 1920, fed by the prodigious mineral wealth and energy supplies just described. By 1914 meat-packing was the leading United States industry in value of total product. Of the manufacturing industries it is useful to consider automobile production because the automobile itself has had such an extraordinary impact on social history and because the fundamental principles involved in the industry were a logical extension of ideas already well established by 1860 in the so-called "American system of manufacture." (See pp. 83-85.) We reviewed the revolution wrought in transportation by the automobile in the last chapter; the revolution it encouraged in manufacturing methods was equally sweeping.

The automobile industry arose after 1900, when the largely experimental and inventive period of automobile history (the European period) was over and when imaginative and farsighted United States producers took the accumulated wisdom of German, British, and French inventors and allied with it the American system of mass production pioneered by Oliver Evans, Eli Whitney, and others.[18] It was not Henry Ford but R. E. Olds who was the earliest American entrepreneur to mass-produce cars by detailed division of labor tasks and use of an assembly line. Olds was the first to "assemble" cars from quantity-bought parts rather than to hand-build them. Four thousand Oldsmobiles were manufactured in 1904 when the Ford Motor Company of Michigan (incorporated 1903) was still struggling and its manufacturing policy was still divided between large, expensive cars and lighter, popular models. Ford's special genius was to push all preceding ideas to their logical conclusions, and to insist eventually on the production of the world's cheapest automobile. Meanwhile, he was trying to make the name Ford widely known by building and driving huge racing cars, like the "999" which roared to success in a race in 1902 with the daredevil cyclist Barney Oldfield at the tiller. (Ford had to teach him to drive.)

The Ford Motor Company turned out over 8,000 cars in 1907, the year of the so-called "rich man's panic." Slump and a cutback in 1908 caused them little lasting pain because plans were already laid for a new automobile that would sweep the nation, the "Model T." During these early years of uncertainty when countless companies went bankrupt trying to manufacture cars, Henry Ford was convinced that the secret of success was to crack open "the other 95 percent" of the market—the mass of potential customers not yet reached at all by existing models. The Model T was a car for the common man, not a European plaything for the rich. Ford persuaded his firm to devote its entire resources to the manufacture of a single automobile, made up of totally standardized and interchangeable parts—like those pioneered by H. M. Leland in the Cadillac, but Ford parts were to be priced so low it would be cheaper to replace than to repair them. Like the retail stores for the urban mass market, Ford aimed at low profit margins but quantity sales. The stripped-down Model T, sturdy, simple, reliable, would provide personal transportation at the world's cheapest price. At the onset, however, the Model T was no cheaper than some of its competitors: in fact, the first 800 models produced in 1909 cost $950 while cars made by the veteran R. E. Olds were selling at $650. What sold the early Model T was not price but reliability and endurance: it was a tough little car, with its three-point suspension and vanadium steel. Ford captured the market in 1910, and from that date the price of the "Tin Lizzie" began to fall, to a low of $360 in 1917 and down to the lowest ever, $290 in 1924—a year that produced 1½ million Model T's and 200,000 Ford trucks. Cost reductions, new internal operating efficiencies, and hence reduced sales prices were virtually forced upon the company by the mounting pressure of demand.

For almost twenty years the basic form of the Model T remained unchanged, and Ford violently and personally resisted all attempts from within his company to experiment with more expensive or advanced models. In all, 15 million Tin Lizzies flooded America's highways between 1908 and 1927.[19] Two years after the Model T was introduced, Ford began to lay out a special plant near Detroit to make his own steel and glass from basic raw materials shipped on the Great Lakes system to Ford docks. This River Rouge plant, to which the assembly process was later moved, became the world's model continuous-flow "scientific" mass-production factory. The company had at first used the static assembly process, in which the car remains stationary and labor gangs specializing in certain tasks take turns to work on it; at River Rouge, Ford's manager and workmen perfected the line-assembly technique by adopting continuous-belt-conveyors to bring the job to the worker. Mechanical tasks were routinized and broken down into a series of elementary motions; each worker was strictly limited to the performance of one or two of the movements; and productivity could be increased at the employer's will by speeding up the endless belt.

Continuous-flow mass production, with its intensification and "speed-up" of unthinking, repetitive tasks, was a heavy price for American labor to pay.[20] Automobile workers had a tough time and the industry an unhappy labor history; the turnover at Ford was unusual—to maintain a labor force of 14,000 involved the hiring on average of 53,000 men. Inducements had to be high, especially since Ford bitterly resisted unions. In 1914 he announced a spectacular eight-hour, five-dollar day. After all, the workers of 1914 could assemble a Model T in under one hour; the once-revolutionary static assembly line had taken them 12 or 14 hours.

Scientific management: Frederick W. Taylor and Elton Mayo

In the fully developed Ford system raw materials (such as coal, limestone, iron ore) entered one end of a plant and finished automobiles were driven out of the other.[21] The lesson was not lost on other United States industrial leaders, and the continuous-flow mass-production technique spread to iron and steel, paper, chemical products, petroleum, electrical goods, domestic utensils and processed foods. Methodical plant layout, combined with worker time-and-motion study was the essence of mass production. Its great exponent was Frederick Winslow Taylor, the father of "scientific management."

Taylor was a Bethlehem Steel engineer who had already made a significant contribution to the development of high-speed tool steels before bringing his cool, rational mind to bear on the problems of work organization. A paper of 1895 on piece rates led him toward a comprehensive philosophy of plant management summarized in his presidency-acceptance speech to the American Society of Mechanical Engineers in 1902 and more fully expounded in a book of 1911, *The Principles of Scientific Management:*

In the past [he wrote] the prevailing idea has been well expressed in the saying that "Captains of industry are born, not made." . . . In the future it will be appreciated that our leaders must be trained right as well as born right.

Taylor proclaimed, in other words, the death of the Heroic Age of American business. The Great Man was defunct; his greatness was broken down into rational principles, just as intensified division of labor and mass production had broken down complex work tasks in manufacturing industry. Those principles could now be taught in specialized schools like the Tucker School at Dartmouth (1910) or Harvard's earlier graduate school of business administration (1908). In Taylor's own words: "In the past the man has been first; in the future the system must be first."

Perhaps few "organization men" would state the case so baldly today. Taylor advocated minutely detailed analysis of job movements, experimentation to determine the optimum size and weight of tools,[22] complete standardization, correct layout of the physical plant with regard to ventilation, lighting, and production flows, correct routing of work, accurate scheduling of production orders, a differentiated incentive structure, and use of bonuses. All this (and much more) now exists in many sectors of United States industry, but Taylor's blunt book got a mixed reception in 1911. Factory workers were justifiably suspicious of time-and-motion study, which was motivated to maximize labor output with low regard for welfare. In this respect there seemed little to choose between "Taylorism" and Russia's "Stakhanovitism" of later years: both were speeded up, closely timed, and supervised work systems.

But in the 1920's a new gloss was being added to "scientific management" when Elton Mayo of Harvard made his study of organizational behavior at the Western Electric Company (outlined in the Lowell Lectures and published in 1933 as *The Human Problems of an Industrial Civilization*). Taylor had brought engineering to bear on management problems; Mayo brought elementary social psychology—"human relations." His work on the selection of a management class, and on fatigue, monotony, and factory morale qualified and sophisticated some of the earlier crudities of Taylorism. For instance, Mayo complained:

In the US we have travelled rapidly and carelessly from simple social and economic organization to a form of industrial organization which assumes that every participant will be a devotee of systematic economies and rigid logic. This unthinkable assumption does not "work" with us, it does not "work" in Russia; it has never "worked" in the whole course of human history.

Elton Mayo and the lesser men in the fashionable field of personnel and labor management, which has flourished between the wars and since, were able to temper the brash expectations of previous "social engineers." They managed to convince many American business leaders that increased "welfare" meant increased efficiency, that bigger "fringe benefits" (from washrooms to employee stockownership) brought bigger profits.

Frederick Taylor's desire to seek efficiency in systematic management "rather than in searching for some unusual or extraordinary man" would strike a European as very American. In 1911 the great liberal jurist Louis Brandeis (1856–1944), for years an adversary of big business and a defender of labor, came out in favor of "the Taylor system" in his case before the Interstate Commerce Commission against an increase of railroad freight rates. Brandeis strongly argued that scientific management was the answer, not higher rates; he got a leading Taylor disciple (Harrington Emerson) to testify that greater efficiency would save a million dollars a day for the nation's railroads. Emerson may well have been right.

Before the days of Henry Ford and Frederick Taylor, big business had rarely been methodically planned—it had "just growed." The textile-factory manager of the 1850's and 1860's was essentially a salesman, a seeker after markets, not a technically trained engineer. What the late Victorians saw, however, was the rise of the engineer, the man exemplified by Taylor and idealized by Veblen. The manager of 1920, unlike his counterpart of 1860, needed technical training, a solid background in pure or applied science, or at least in the occult lore of "business administration." The intuitive rule-of-thumb of the old-style individualist entrepreneur in a personalized business world could not survive the advent of continuous-flow mass production, could not resist the pressures of an enormously expanded continental market.

The Nature of Industrial Capitalism

To determine the nature of the pre–Civil War market economy, we reviewed (in the last chapter of Part II) national economic policy and performance, and the public's reactions. The same method can be applied to understand the greatly altered postwar economy that is often called "industrial" or "Victorian" capitalism. And since this period also comes to an end in military conflict, we can usefully adopt precisely the same tripartite division of our material: economic thought and policy, economic performance, and war.

1. ECONOMIC THOUGHT AND POLICY

The central theme of United States economic policy after as before the Civil War was the ambiguous question of the role of government in the nation's economic life, and the divergence between thought and practice on this score was scarcely less acute. Rather, the functions of government were reduced to the barest minimum during the twenty years of fastest and most chaotic economic growth immediately after the war (when the average rate of growth was around 9 percent a year). Gilded Age corrupt politics, widening economic inequality, a cult of distorted "individualism" and complacency, and conservative Social Darwinism in popular thought characterized these decades. The next major burst of economic growth, in the late 1890's and 1900's (at a reduced annual rate of about 5 percent and then of about 3 percent),[1] as well as the depressed years between the two cycles, brought a very gradual reversion to older American ideals, the reinstatement of social conscience and reemergence of some degree of positive government—all of which flowered into "Progressivism."

The "Gospel of Wealth"

Formal political economy had precious little influence on national policy. The general climate of opinion highly favored industrial capitalism and a lax business code; the ideas selected for use in defense of laissez faire were taken not from economics so much as from popular religion and popular science. Among the chief victims of this pillage were St. Paul and Charles Darwin: Paul for his doctrine of "stewardship" and Darwin for his "survival of the fittest." A true Baptist, John D. Rockefeller, declared quite simply, "The good Lord gave me my money and how could I withhold it from the University of Chicago?" Elsewhere, defending the tough business tactics of the Standard Oil monopoly, he explained:

> The growth of a large business is merely a survival of the fittest. . . . The American Beauty rose can be produced in the splendor and fragrance which brings cheer to its beholder only by sacrificing the early buds which grow up around it. This is not an evil tendency in business. It is merely the working-out of a law of nature and a law of God.

The most famous and perhaps the most sincere and telling combination of Pauline stewardship with Social Darwinism was achieved by Andrew Carnegie—a thoroughgoing and articulate apologist for laissez faire who by enormous philanthropy lived up to his beliefs. An agnostic himself, Carnegie secularized the doctrine of wealth. Previously, Protestant clergymen struggling to maintain congregations in an age of growing materialism and doubt concentrated their resources on the ruling economic groups in American society and preached political and economic orthodoxy in the language of the upper and middle classes. Henry Ward Beecher (1813–1887), the popular Congregational preacher whose sister wrote *Uncle*

Tom's Cabin and who was himself a genuine abolitionist, feminist, and civil-service reformer, found it possible to announce categorically in 1877, that lean and tragic year of depression:

> God has intended the great to be great and the little to be little. . . . The trade union, originated under the European system, destroys liberty. . . . I do not say that a dollar a day is enough to support . . . a man and five children if a man insists on smoking and drinking beer. . . . But the man who cannot live on bread and water is not fit to live.[2]

Asceticism of this sort could never have become the principal religious argument in favor of economic inequality in a nation that had written the "pursuit of happiness" into its very Declaration of Independence. More useful was the stewardship line that equated poverty and failure with sin, wealth and business success with virtue. "In the long run," said the Episcopal Bishop of Massachusetts William Lawrence, "It is only to the man of morality that wealth comes. . . . Godliness is in league with riches." And a famous public lecture, "Acres of Diamonds" (given six thousand times) by the Reverend Russell H. Conwell, published in 1890, contained the comforting thought that "the number of poor who are to be sympathized with is very small. To sympathize with a man whom God has punished for his sins . . . is to do wrong, no doubt about it."

However, Carnegie was more attracted to the works of Herbert Spencer, the evolutionist philosopher whose ideas found poor response in his native Britain but an amazing and widespread success in the United States. Spencer's extreme and crude application of Darwin to human society bordered on philosophic anarchism, and would deny the government any role except the maintenance of order; even the post office was considered too "socialistic" a notion. Upon reading Spencer, said Carnegie later:

> Light came as in a flood and all was clear. . . . Not only had I got rid of theology and the supernatural but I had found the truth of evolution. "All is well since all grows better" became my motto, my true source of comfort.

The writings of Andrew Carnegie cannot be dismissed lightly as "guilt pangs" or as a rationalization of enormous wealth—for Carnegie after all was an immigrant boy and (with a good deal of help to be sure) he did find and take opportunity in America, and even more important he had a real vision of his adopted country.

"The old nations of the earth creep on at a snail's pace; the Republic thunders past with the rush of the express," he proclaimed at the opening of *Triumphant Democracy* (1886). He exemplified and expressed a thoroughly American faith in social mobility, and though a stout defender of private property he characteristically rejected inheritance.

Yet there remained an element in Carnegie's thought and in the Gospel of Wealth as a whole that was at odds with the mainstream of American democratic life. This was the elitist suspicion that ultimately government by the majority (and by implication, the mediocre) was inferior to government by a "natural aristocracy" of ability—ability to *survive*, that is, in the Victorian marketplace. (A somewhat similar kind of suspicion of the masses and of the democratic process was expressed later in Herbert Hoover's writings.) Historically the age of late nineteenth century industrial capitalism, when government reached its lowest ebb and the economy was left in the hands of private empire builders, must be regarded not as the true model of pristine American capitalism but as a purely temporary aberration.

Business and politics

The American Beauty rose notwithstanding, the power, influence, and prestige of business in late nineteenth century American culture cannot be explained merely by Social Darwinism. After all, Darwinian arguments did little to restrain the discontents of the Grangers, Alliancemen, and Populists on the farm; in colleges the conservative evolutionism of William Graham Sumner was soon matched by the reform Darwinism of Edward A. Ross; and even to the churches came a new working-class orientation and the Social Gospel. The prestige of business was partly based on its actual performance in raising real overall living standards despite growing social inequalities. Partly, too, it was based on a prestige vacuum in American society. Which groups could compete with the businessmen for social status? The United States lacked an aristocracy of title or blood; no "Establishment" maintained a closed shop or class control of the upper echelons of government, the foreign service, the military, or education; there was no established church with a single clerical hierarchy. Law and politics alone (and they were often the same thing) offered any true competition for social place to the successful merchant, manufacturer, or financier, and as a group political leaders remained loyal to business. They always accepted, even if they sometimes modified, the basic assumptions of economic progress, private property, and the dream of rags to riches that buttressed American capitalism.

During the Civil War the triumphant Republican party with its body of radically probusiness legislation did almost as much institutionally for American capitalism as Alexander Hamilton. This we have examined, but no noticeable change in the close relationship of business and politics occurred after the conflict. In fact from the Civil War to the First World War Republicans dominated the Senate, had great influence in the House, and controlled the Presidency itself for all but eight years (Cleveland, 1885–1889 and 1893–1897). With its tariffs, gold standard, and land grants the party served the business community very well—making sure, naturally, to entrench itself in office by a careful use of patronage. Not that there was a great deal to choose between the two major parties. Democrats and Republicans agreed on the conservative fundamentals of political life, such as the gold standard, aid to business, opposition to labor, and extravagant exploitation of natural resources. Though a rather unfortunate difference of opinion did seem to arise on the tariff issue in the 1880's, no mere concern for principle was allowed to divide old friends for long. Reform—except for the bland Pendleton civil-service measure of 1883—was left to ephemeral third parties, without which the political history of the late nineteenth century would indeed be dreary.[3]

Economic policy: tariffs

Senator Penrose, Republican state boss of Pennsylvania, once addressed himself to business in the following pithy manner:

I believe in a division of labor. You send us to Congress; we pass laws under . . . which you make money; . . . and out of your profits you further contribute to our campaign fund to send us back again to pass more laws to enable you to make more money.

Penrose loved to quip; but his remarks present a not too inaccurate description of the relationship between business and politics under old-style capitalism. This relationship was nowhere more clear than in tariff policy.

Under Republican auspices, by 1864 the average level of import duties had risen to 47 percent, as noted earlier. From that date strenuous lobbying by manufacturing interests and the useful argument that workers must be saved from the unfair competition of foreign "pauper labor" ensured the continued success of a high tariff policy.

In 1867 after pressure from the Woolen Manufacturers' Association, Congress increased duties on woolens; in 1869 the copper interests gained an increase of duties, although their profits were already huge. Momentarily an increasing Treasury surplus and the growing agitation of western farmers operated in the opposite direction, and in 1872 a reduction of 10 percent was made on the protected industries—iron, wool, and steel among them. This liberalizing movement was vitiated, however, by the crisis of 1873, and in 1875 high tariffs were again restored.

The embarrassing federal surplus of 1882 reached over $145 million, and President Arthur's suggestion of a tariff commission was accepted by Congress. Curiously enough, the commission, though composed chiefly of businessmen and presided over by the secretary of the Woolen Manufacturers' Association, recommended a substantial tariff reduction of from 20 percent to 25 percent in the interests of consumers and of "general industrial prosperity." The 1883 Act that ensued, however, has been justifiably called one of the silliest in the history of the American tariff. It was pushed through within hours of the end of a session by a Congress desperate to do something to stave off the possibility of more radical measures being taken in the new session—measures more in line with the commission's views. Nominal reductions were made in some duties; others were substantially raised.

Grover Cleveland was elected to the Presidency in 1884. His party, the Democrats, had supported lower duties since the time of President James K. Polk (1845–1849), but even so, by the 1880's had a protectionist wing. Cleveland managed to startle both his party and the country by devoting the whole of his annual message of December, 1887, to the question of tariff revision. The Democrats rallied, and passed by a strict party vote the Mills bill, which hoped to reduce duties on pig iron, cotton goods, and other articles and place raw materials on the free list. The Republican-dominated Senate refused to concur however, and Cleveland fought the electoral campaign of 1888 on the issue, gaining a popular majority but losing the Presidency to the inoffensive Benjamin Harrison, who captured the electoral college.

The victorious Republicans immediately decided to stifle adverse criticism from one quarter by extending "the protective system" to agriculture. The McKinley Tariff (1890) raised the average level to 49.5 percent. Duties on wheat, corn, dairy products, meat, barley, hemp, and flax were increased, and on woolen and cotton goods and linens. Powers were given to the President to impose duties on sugar, molasses, coffee, tea, and hides (all of which were on the free list) if he should decide that duties imposed by foreign exporters of these goods were unreasonable. At the instigation of Secretary of State Blaine, who feared for America's foreign-trade relations, a reciprocity clause was inserted in the Act.

The McKinley Tariff stimulated prices almost immediately, and as congressional elections were held in the following month (November), consumer reactions helped to return the Democrats to power with an overwhelming majority. This tied President Harrison's hands, and prepared the way for a Democratic victory in the presidential election of 1892. McKinley had asserted in his hour of triumph that his act was "protective in every paragraph and American in every line and word." In answer the Democrats claimed to denounce it as "the culminating atrocity of class legislation." Cleveland was returned to the White House with an outstanding popular vote and a considerable majority in the electoral college, giving the Democrats full control of both executive and legislature for the first time since the Civil War. The hour of free trade seemed to be at hand.

The Wilson-Gorman Act (1894) that resulted was a complete fiasco. In retrospect the long struggle of the Democrats and their final return to power in 1892 seems little more than an involved preface to a great unwritten work.

What happened was that the reformist Wilson bill passed the House but came up against strong opposition in the Senate from the protectionist wing of the Democratic party, led by Senator Gorman. The bill was radically altered in favor of protection, and despite Cleveland's public strictures it became law without his signature. Two years later the Republicans regained power and rapidly introduced the Dingley Tariff (1897), which imposed an average level of 57 percent—the highest of the century—and remained the unaltered law of the land for twelve years.

Economic change in the opening years of the new century, rising prices, and America's industrial expansion and emergence as a great power placed the high-tariff protagonists increasingly on the defensive. Also, the Dingley Tariff was severely criticized as "the mother of all trusts," while the growing expenses of federal government made it inadequate from the revenue viewpoint. Some attempt at revision was made in the Payne-Aldrich Tariff (1909), but the Senate hacked about the original bill, adding 847 changes in rates, chiefly upward. The result was a slight extension of the free list to include hides, wood pulp, and petroleum, the institution of a Tariff Board, and a tax of 1 percent on net corporate incomes of over $5,000.[4] The Payne-Aldrich bill precipitated a split in the Republicans that led ultimately to the emergence of the Progressive party and the victory of the Democrats under Woodrow Wilson in 1912. As part of his "New Freedom" policy, Wilson aimed at tariff revision. The Underwood-Simmons Act (1913) left the system still highly protectionist but at least made the first serious breach since the Civil War. Over a hundred articles were added to the free list, and rates were lowered on nearly a thousand, including necessities —food, clothing, and raw materials. The average rate was reduced to 29 percent.

The First World War, like previous wars, brought an aftermath of protectionism. The Republicans replaced their opponents in 1921 and under Harding immediately enacted the Fordney Emergency Tariff, reimposing high duties on wheat, corn, wool, meat, and sugar. This they regarded as a temporary stimulant, a stopgap to give them time to set about the complete rebuilding of their old protective system. In this reconstruction farmers and the new industries that had sprung up during the war ("war babies") would be the chief beneficiaries. The Fordney-McCumber Tariff (1922) established the highest rates yet in American history, its only compromising feature being a special provision for flexibility, allowing the President to raise or lower duties by 50 percent to equalize production cost differences in the United States of America and competing nations. The plan was ludicrous because neither Harding nor Coolidge had the slightest intention of lowering tariffs. Between them they made 37 changes: 32 upward (butter, cheese, pig iron, chemicals) and 5 downward (live bobwhite quail, paintbrush handles, mill feed, cresylic acid, and phenol!).

Many other changes were still "under consideration" as late as 1930 when the act was superseded by the Hawley-Smoot Tariff. This brought even greater increases: the average rate on agricultural products was raised to 33.6 percent, that on metals to 35 percent, and that on woolens to 59.8 percent. The economic effects of the acts of 1922 and 1930 were disastrous. At home they stimulated monopoly, and abroad they made it well-nigh impossible for European nations to repay their indebtedness to America in the form of goods, and brought reprisals such as the increased duties imposed on American products in France in 1927 and in Great Britain, Canada, and elsewhere later. The Hawley-Smoot Tariff was clearly one of the decisive factors in the breakdown of the European economy in the 1930's.

Economic policy: currency and banking

Lincoln's party, it will be recalled, also took decisive steps to strengthen the currency (Legal Tender Act, 1862) and banking (National Bank Acts, 1863-1864) systems; but here the question of economic interest was less obvious and much more complex; for the most part the policy makers were working in the dark and knew not what they did—especially in the case of currency reform.

The "Greenbacks" of 1862 were legal-tender paper money issued on government credit and without metallic backing. Wartime issue of $450 million in Greenbacks brought their value down very rapidly to about 43 cents each (1864), an inflationary tendency that was countered in the immediate postwar years when banking and business creditor groups were successful in having some paper withdrawn. Farm interest in currency affairs was partly explained, as we have seen already, in the unfortunate fact that those who had borrowed on a 40- or 50-cent paper dollar found themselves obliged to repay interest demands and principal on an appreciating 80- or 90-cent dollar—and this while commodity prices continued to fall steadily. The Specie Resumption Act of 1875 aimed at a further contraction of paper money (to reduce Greenbacks specifically from $382 million to $300 million) and at resumption of cash payments by January 1, 1879. Provoked by this policy and by the lean years after the 1873 crisis, the inflationist reformers—"Greenbackers"—fought their hard electoral struggle of 1876, and won many local triumphs despite Peter Cooper's miserable popular vote as presidential candidate and the victory of that dull mediocrity, Rutherford B. Hayes. Two years later the inflationists emerged anew at Toledo in the Greenback Labor party with strong farm support and captured their 1,000,000 votes and 14 congressmen.

Nonetheless, the opposition plan to resume cash payments at the opening of 1879 went forward. The United States returned to a metallic standard after seventeen years of irredeemable paper currency, and in the teeth of inflationist antagonism. Weaver's disastrous presidential campaign of 1880 heralded the decline of the Greenbackers, their loss of working-class support to the Knights of Labor, and the vitiation of their specific monetary arguments by rising prices, improved harvest profits, and the upward movement of the business cycle. Paper money circulated like gold (under the 1875 Act), and the old inflationist technique disappeared to be replaced by a new obsession: Free Silver.

The aim of the Free Silver men was to inflate the currency by reestablishing the free and unlimited coinage of silver at a ratio to gold of sixteen to one. Free, unlimited silver coinage was first approved by the Act of 1792. From 1834 until 1873 its ratio had been sixteen to one, which overvalued gold. As a result silver was driven from circulation, and in 1873 the federal government, recognizing a *de facto* situation, discontinued the free coinage of silver. There was no protest at this time. But in 1871 Germany had adopted the gold standard, to be followed later by Holland and the Scandinavian countries. Furthermore, in 1874 the Latin Monetary Union (France, Italy, Belgium, Switzerland, and Greece) limited silver coinage. Much silver bullion came on to the market as a result, precisely when American silver mines were increasing output, especially in Nevada. As the price of silver rapidly dropped, agitators in the silver-mining states and in the debtor West and South began denouncing demonetization as the "Crime of '73." In 1878 the inflationists were powerful enough in Congress to pass the Bland-Allison

Act over the veto of President Hayes. This empowered the Secretary of the Treasury to buy between $2 and $4 million worth of silver bullion per month and to coin it into dollars at a ratio of sixteen to one. But although nearly 380 million silver dollars were coined in this way between 1878 and 1890, the price of silver continued to fall.

In 1888 the Republican candidate, Benjamin Harrison, became President. The inflationist faction from the silver states had supported the McKinley Tariff and were accordingly rewarded with the Sherman Silver Purchase Act (1890). This authorized purchase by the Treasury of still more silver (about 4.5 million ounces a month, or most of the United States output), to be paid for in a new issue of paper money, the "Treasury Notes of 1890," redeemable either in gold or in silver and to be fully accepted as legal tender. But the Free Silver men remained unsatisfied; nothing short of "free and unlimited coinage" would quiet them. The "Omaha Platform" of the Populists in 1892 was headed by this measure, and in the election of that year the former Greenbacker J. B. Weaver polled over one million popular votes for them.

The monetary struggle was brought to a climax by the crisis of 1893 and the ensuing depression in which, by 1896, prices reached their lowest point for half a century. Furthermore, President Cleveland (who had been elected in 1892) was a "gold Democrat" and, convinced that currency uncertainty was a principal factor in the economic collapse, he called a special session of Congress which repealed the Sherman Silver Purchase Act on October 30, 1893. Finally, the famous presidential campaign of 1896, that roused more excitement and attention than any since Lincoln, put an end to the long bimetallist controversy. The western and southern Democrats managed to displace Cleveland, and supported instead a man much more in their favor, William Jennings Bryan. The Bryan Free Silver Democrats were joined by the Populists. On the opposite side the Republicans, led by McKinley, defended gold, protective tariffs, and a "firm" foreign policy (meaning intervention in Cuba, control of Hawaii, and purchase of the Danish West Indies). Bryan, the orator —"five feet deep and a mile wide at the mouth," like the river Platte from which he came—made the underlying forces very clear, perhaps too clear, in his famous "Cross of Gold" speech:

> You come to us and tell us that the great cities are in favor of the gold standard; we reply that the great cities rest upon our broad and fertile

prairies. Burn down your cities and leave our farms, and your cities will spring up again as if by magic; but destroy our farms and the grass will grow in the streets of every city in the country. . . . You shall not press down upon the brow of labor this crown of thorns, you shall not crucify mankind upon a cross of gold.

The vote was cast on clear economic and sectional lines. Bryan won ten western states, the eleven states of the South, and a "border" state, Missouri; but he lost the election to McKinley.

After 1896 the farmers' demands for inflation disappeared in a period of relative prosperity when the price level at last began to tilt upward. Many outside factors were at work here: poor harvests in India and Europe (1896–1897) which improved demand and boosted prices for United States staples; growing United States industrial output; trebling of the world's gold supply by 1900, through technological innovation in gold mining and the development of new mines in the Klondike and South Africa; and an overall increase in the amount of money in circulation.

The Currency Act of 1900 legally established a monometallic gold standard. In future all forms of currency must be maintained at parity with the gold dollar (25.8 grains, nine-tenths fine). To redeem Greenbacks and the "Treasury Notes of 1890" a reserve fund of $150 million in gold coin and bullion was set aside. Silver dollars replaced the Treasury Notes in circulation. The Free Silver controversy was over.

Banking policy between the Civil and First World wars was even more experimental and *ad hoc* than currency policy. Bray Hammond, one of the most readable banking experts, has said that lack of homogeneity, independence of foreign examples, great experimental originality, and fundamental discontinuity characterize United States banking history, as the system has seemed to evolve from one of privileged, atomistic individual businesses issuing bank notes and largely unregulated, to one of competitive, organically related units using demand deposits and the check system, regulated by legislation.

Concretely, the main issue in the banking history of these years were the National Bank System, the role of the Independent Treasury in monetary policy, the organization of the Federal Reserve System in 1913, and the growing power of investment bankers. The last is treated more conveniently as an aspect of business organization history in a later section.

The National Bank Acts of 1863 and 1864 were, as noted, an attempt to provide for business an adequate and stable credit system and to provide for the Union government revenue by the sale of Civil War bonds. In the United States Treasury a new department was created—that of the Comptroller of the Currency—which could issue federal (rather than state) charters to empower any groups of not less than five stockholders with a certain amount of capital to establish "National" banks. These banks, with federal bonds as security, would be the source of a uniform paper currency —National Bank notes. The stockholders could issue National Bank notes up to 90 percent of the current market value of the bonds they had been made to deposit with the Comptroller (bonds equal in amount to one-third of their capital). Total issue of all National Bank notes was restricted to $300 million, and to safeguard depositors all National Banks were to maintain certain reserves: those in central-"reserve cities" had to keep a reserve of 25 percent of their deposits, made up of "lawful money" and held in their own vaults. Banks in other cities also had to maintain a 25 percent reserve, but half of it in their case could be kept on deposit in the banks of central-reserve cities. Country banks must keep a 15 percent reserve of which three-fifths could be kept on deposit in city National Banks of either category. Hoping to make the National Bank notes fully convertible and stable, the government sought to drive the notes issued by state-chartered commercial banks out of the market. Accordingly, a federal tax was imposed on the note issue of non-National Banks in March, 1865. By October, 1866, there were 1,644 National Banks, with a note circulation of over $280 million.

The most significant outcome of Civil War financing was this National Banking System. But its history was by no means smooth. Unlike the earlier United States Banks, it established a large number of relatively small banks scattered throughout the nation rather than a single central controlling bank. The act faithfully reflected the centrifugal, individualistic tendency of the time, and the strong suspicion of consolidated authority in banking. Perhaps this was its chief weakness. Local control implied less experienced control; decentralization implied less unity of policy, and hampered the formulation and execution of decisive action in times of financial crisis. In addition, the state-authorized commercial banks continued to exist, complicating the situation.[5] Moreover, although the currency secured by the act was sound, it was inelastic. This was the second major flaw in the system. The amount of federal bonds held by banks—without which they could not obtain charters and National Bank notes—bore little or no relation to the demand for money. Looked at another way, this meant that instead of fluctuating with business demand, the number of National Bank notes in circulation tended to vary with the price of the federal bonds that were needed to obtain them—because this considerably affected the profit gained by issuing them at all. So when bonds were cheap in the 1870's note issue was easy and profitable; but when bonds rose in price as many were redeemed in the 1880's, note issue was difficult and unprofitable. The anomalous situation therefore came about that during the prosperity of the 1880's, when more currency was needed, less National Bank notes were available.

The notes were as unresponsive to short-term requirements (harvests, Christmas expenses, and other seasonal demands) as they were to long-term requirements—a weakness disastrously well illustrated in times of financial panics. Other circulating media were also inelastic, and but for the growth of deposit banking and the expansion of the check system[6] the need would have been very stringent indeed.

The failure of the National Banks to provide an adequate money supply, especially during the crises of 1873, 1884, 1893, 1903, and 1907, led almost directly to the passing of the Federal Reserve Act of 1913. Several ineffective attempts were made in the interim to strengthen National banking. The Resumption Act (1875), for instance, removed altogether the "ceiling" figure of total notes to be issued ($300 million), and in 1882 steps were taken to improve the competitive position of the National Banks by allowing those with a capital of under $150,000 to deposit only one-quarter (instead of one-third) of it in bonds with the Comptroller. In addition, the Currency Act of 1900, insofar as it affected the banking system alone, permitted National Bank notes to be issued up to the full par value of the bonds (instead of 90 percent), reduced the minimum capital needs for banks in towns of under 3,000 population, reduced the tax on all bonds yielding under 2 percent, and refunded the existing national debt in thirty-year 2 percent bonds.

National Bank-note circulation, which had reached over $340 million in 1874 and then fluctuated around that figure for a decade, began to decline after 1884, while other forms of money increased.

Later on, increased loans to cover such expenses as the Spanish-American War brought it up again, and by 1913 it was not far below $716 million.

Neither increased circulation nor reforms managed to avert a large-scale overhaul of the banking system in 1913. The federal government had already made a foray into the banking field (after a long armistice of almost half a century) when it created postal savings banks by an act of 1910. But although it met some opposition from government critics as a "socialistic" measure, this act was not their chief object of abuse. Those who distrusted and feared the growth of federal authority were greatly displeased even with conditions during the truce. Under the National Bank system the central government possessed no fiscal agent, and with the lack of central bank control over credit, the Independent Treasury (the government's chief depository established in 1846) was forced to assume responsibility for various central banking functions. When in 1871–1872 it took steps to meet a public demand for currency by issuing over $6 million in paper, opposition to the move was severe on the grounds that Congress alone should decide monetary policy and its authority should not be delegated to an uncontrolled Treasury official. From 1890 to 1912 the Treasury acted as a genuine central bank, being considered as a lender of last resort. Serious doubts soon arose as to its true place in the monetary system.

The Federal Reserve System set up by the act of December, 1913, did not adopt a central bank—despite the recommendations of a National Monetary Commission in favor of such a move. Instead, the nation was divided into twelve Federal Reserve districts, each with one Federal Reserve Bank to act as a clearinghouse and bankers' bank for the member banks of the system. All National Banks were compelled and all other commercial banks encouraged to participate by subscribing to the capital fund of their Federal Reserve District Bank. They were to buy district bank stock amounting to 6 percent of their capital and surplus (a cumulative dividend of 6 percent to be paid on each share). District banks were empowered to issue Federal Reserve notes secured by 100 percent commercial paper and a reserve of 40 percent in gold or gold certificates. Their earnings in excess of 6 percent were to be shared equally between their own surplus funds and the federal government. A Federal Reserve Board with headquarters in the Capital was to supervise the whole structure, its seven members to include five presidential nominees, the Secretary of the Treasury, and the Comptroller of the Currency.

The Federal Reserve System: "open market operations"

How did this American compromise, this quasi-centralized, privately owned banking system responsible to the federal government function? Over time its functioning has in fact evolved. At all times the system deals exclusively with member banks and not with individuals. It influences monetary policy in three major ways: through the legal reserve requirements of its members, through "discount rate" policy, and by "open market operations."

Changing the legal reserve requirement of member banks (a power given to the Federal Reserve System in the 1930's) is not a means of daily control over monetary policy: it is a powerful tool with emphatic results, kept for special occasions. Raising legal reserve requirements in boom times tightens credit and curbs expansion; lowering the ratio in slack periods makes credit easier and encourages economic activity. Changes in the "discount rate" (the interest the Federal Reserve District banks charge on the loans they give to member banks) affect economic activity in much the same way. If the discount rate is lowered, money is cheaper; if it is raised, credit is scarce. The discount rate is watched continually by the money market, and changes are very effective, but the rate follows rather than leads the market trend. The rate is usually raised by the Federal Reserve authorities only after general interest rates have risen, and is usually lowered only after a general fall in rates. As a source of discretionary authority the Federal Reserve discount rate is much less powerful than the British (central) "bank rate."

More important for continuous stabilization management is the fact that as a clearinghouse for member banks the Federal Reserve could adopt "open-market operations" (as it did after 1922) to stimulate a sluggish economy or temper a boom. "Open-market operations" consist essentially in the judicious purchase or sale of federal bonds by the Federal Reserve's "Open Market Committee." To curb the economy and to "squeeze" credit the committee sells federal bonds to dealers and brokers in the open money market, thereby diminishing its own liabilities and assets and reducing the reserves of member banks.[7] To expand credit the committee takes the reverse action: it buys federal bonds, thereby increasing its own liabilities and assets and adding to the reserves of member banks. The broker who sells the bonds receives a Federal Reserve check which he deposits in his bank, adding to that bank's credit with the Federal Reserve System and ultimately increasing the nation's total money supply.

The technique of open-market operations was used in conjunction with discount rate changes with some success in 1924, but in 1929 restrictions were applied too late to be of any use—a stunning failure. (J. K. Galbraith's study of the Great Crash condemns the top personnel of the Reserve Board of "wilful helplessness" in such matters as failing to press for stricter margin requirements for stock speculators.) However, the Federal Reserve System was an undoubted improvement over the previous National Bank–Independent Treasury patchwork. The system failed to justify the hopes of the Comptroller of the Currency at its inception (that future financial panics would be "mathematically impossible") or the hideous fears of the American Bankers' Association (who damned the act immediately as "socialism"). Yet it did provide a more rational central control of elements essential to national economic health—the discount rate and gold stock—and was a credit source for banks in emergencies as well as a fiscal agent linking the banking system with the Treasury. Moreover, its Federal Reserve rates gave the United States a more elastic currency.[8]

During the 1930's the Federal Reserve did not adopt a tough anti-depression line, and in World War II it became largely the handmaiden of the Treasury, losing its independent role in monetary policy in order to sustain government bond sales. This subservience seemed to continue for too long after the war, and with the outbreak of a new conflict in Korea (June, 1950) the board looked on in impotent anxiety (presumably) while panic consumer sales and credit extensions leaped. A more healthy independence was gradually allowed to the Federal Reserve, however, and it took a tight credit stand in 1952–1953, followed by an easy, expansive policy to combat the recession of 1953-1954.

Today the Federal Reserve System—if it chooses to be—is an essential discretionary weapon in the armory of so-called "stabilizers" for economic growth and the mollification (if not the elimination) of the capitalist business cycle.

The changing nature of American business

The Federal Reserve Act of 1913 was a major structural change in the United States economy, as was the income-tax amendment of the same year. But they both came at the end of the period. The laissez faire mythology of the Gilded Age had begun to crumble twenty or more years earlier. Whispers of change were to be heard in popular thought even in the 1880's, and they grew louder in the 1890's. And with the emergence of holding companies, investment banks, and large insurance houses (Lenin's stage of "finance capitalism"), American capitalism itself shed a chrysalis.

The physical and industrial basis of the changing nature of American business in these years has already been described. By 1900 the United States produced half as much as all Europe and about double the total industrial output of Great Britain. In all the key industries giant productive combinations arose, as we have seen, like United States Steel, International Harvester, Standard Oil, and Anaconda. Capitalization per firm rose eightfold between 1850 and 1880, for example. Cumulative technical innovations made the adoption of large-scale operations imperative from all viewpoints: mechanical, labor, and capital. We have seen how the continuing transportation revolution—railroad, postal services, telegraph and telephone, automobile and radio—vastly expanded the marketing area, while old-fashioned steam engines gave way before the high-speed compound turbine and electric power, and the growth of urban complexes brought new mass-sales techniques.

Business consolidates

From one point of view, then, the growing size of American business units seems totally justifiable—even unavoidable and essential. The evolution of new forms of industrial organization capable of handling large operations, and of raising the capital to begin them, seems in the logic of economic history. Two qualities—limited liability and flexibility of management—were essential to the life of these new corporate structures. Their complex business operations were facilitated by such mechanical office aids as the typewriter, cash register, and adding machine[9] and by the study of scientific management that was given such a boost by F. W. Taylor.

But these general background circumstances do not tell the whole story. More specifically, consolidation was a conscious attempt by United States businessmen to increase their share of the national income, which seemed to be a falling percentage. Entrepreneurial earnings did not undergo an increase comparable with rising productivity and living standards, mainly because of erratic growth with "overproduction" gluts and sudden price falls, and the long-drawn-out deflation. According to the studies of Warren and Pearson (published in 1933), the general wholesale price index was more than halved from 1865 to 1890—falling almost without respite from 185 to 82 (1910–1914 = 100). The wholesale textile index fell from 266 to 103; the metals and metal-products index from 306 to 123.

An unrelenting and steady price fall presents severe financial problems to corporations with topheavy cost structures and large overheads, like the railroads, mining and heavy metals industries. A fall in sales brings heavier costs per unit of output, especially when the firm has to bear the financial weight of interest on capital, rent of large plants, depreciation on fixed capital assets (in years of ever-changing technology), and growing upward pressure on wages and salary bills because of the emergence of strong unions and the need for larger clerical and technical staffs. These economic problems were genuine, and to meet them corporations would go in for price "wars" to undercut their competitors. Standard Oil devised a merciless and masterful strategy of price cutting. Eventually business leaders grasped the danger of this and realized that it could prove fatal to continue "overproducing" during a time of surplus in the hope of somehow meeting their costs. Rockefeller's hatred of competition was based on this realization. Why not combine—cooperate instead of compete—and stabilize the market? Combination could bring benefits threefold: an increase of profits by cutting competitive losses, a monopoly power to raise prices and counteract deflation, and still greater "economies of scale" that would lower production costs. Usually the uppermost aim was price and market control rather than cost reduction, though in justice it must be said that major technical improvements did occur in steel, mining, textiles, and some other industries when a larger scale of operation was achieved.

Business leaders were encouraged and abetted in their desire to trustify industry by federal patent laws, tariffs, land policy, and legal structure. Patent laws gave inventors the exclusive right for seventeen years to make, sell, lease, or simply shelve any original invention, which encouraged the "collecting" of patents by firms with monopolistic intent. Thus the United Shoe Machinery Company became overlord to the shoe industry simply by buying up 6,000 patents covering all aspects of shoe manufacturing, and dictating the terms on which it was prepared to lease them. Corporations that owned leading technical patents could, of course, fix high prices for the industry as a whole. Protective tariffs helped to encourage several monopolies, especially the American Sugar Refining Company whose president in giving evidence before the Industrial Commission at the end of the century admitted that the Dingley Tariff of 1897 was "the mother of all trusts." Federal land-grant policy also favored the growth of private monopolies in natural resources, for obvious reasons. And the legal system, with its division of powers and differences between individual states, made it almost impossible to prohibit combination generally. New Jersey, West Virginia, and Delaware welcomed monopolies, and the seven greatest combines in the United States were incorporated in New Jersey between 1891 and 1902—American Sugar (1891), Amalgamated Copper (1899), American Smelting and Refining (1899), Standard Oil (1899), Consolidated Tobacco (1901), United States Steel (1901), and International Mercantile Marine (1902). Many of these "mergers" began as more or less informal arrangements for limiting production or fixing prices but gave way gradually to more permanent institutional forms—industrial pools, trusts, and holding companies.

Pools, trusts, holding companies

How did these various forms differ? Each one is difficult to define in exact terms. (Most writers on the subject begin with careful distinctions but end up in general confusion). Any given "merger"

—Standard Oil, for instance—may be difficult to catalog at any given moment in its complex legal history. Roughly, very roughly, pools were the main kind of merger from the crash of 1873 to about 1887, and though they continued thereafter, trusts dominated the 1880's and early 1890's and holding companies were most favored from 1897 to 1904. Yet all three forms were revived in the 1920's.

Pools have been a perennial form of merger because they offer certain advantages but do not impair the independence of individual corporations. Essentially loose agreements among autonomous firms, pools are most commonly established to fix prices and control supply. Usually a central administrative committee assesses penalties for "overproduction" or underselling. Sometimes sales areas are allotted to specific firms, in relation to their estimated capacity to produce—as in the meat-packers and wire-nail pools. (In 1902 this device reached international dimensions by an agreement between the American Tobacco Company and the Imperial Tobacco Company of Great Britain.) Sometimes a pool will go so far as to establish a central selling agency. Early pools were agreed upon in the cordage, salt, and anthracite industries, and later in gunpowder and in whiskey production. The Michigan Salt Association was founded in 1868, the steel-rail pool in 1887, and the Associated Pipe Works in 1894.

Pools were essentially "gentlemen's agreements," and when the gentlemen chose to agree no longer, their informal contract was not enforceable in courts of law. In their looseness lay their ultimate weakness, and pools frequently dissolved only to form once more and then dissolve again. As "conspiracies in restraint of trade" they were contrary to the common law, and after 1890 they were also forbidden by statute—the Sherman Antitrust Act.

Seeking a firmer and more durable type of combination, business leaders of the 1880's turned increasingly toward the trust. Standard Oil (1879) was the first example, followed by the Cotton Oil trust (1884), the Distillers' and Cattle Feed—"whiskey"—trust (1887), and similar mergers in sugar, cordage, and lead. The word "trust" has the vaguest connotation of all these terms, but its specific meaning is a form of combination that goes beyond the pool but remains true to the letter, at least, of the various state laws that prohibited any one corporation from owning the stock of another corporation. In a trust, voting stock in competing concerns is surrendered to a "board of trustees" in return for "trust certificates." The firms combined are then managed as a whole by the "trustees," and the certificate holders receive a part of the general proceeds. So the individual investor is no longer concerned at all with the financial condition of any one particular company in the group, and the board of trustees has its hands free to dismantle plant, discontinue lines, buy new companies, and expand or contract business in any direction. These advantages were gained by Standard Oil in 1879.

In time several legal decisions against trusts mounted up, and they also came under heavy fire from social reformers and "muckraker" journalists, like Ida M. Tarbell, Henry Demarest Lloyd, and Henry George. "Trust-busting" became a major political plank in Teddy Roosevelt's "Square Deal" program and was the central theme of Progressivism, as we shall see. The Sherman Act of 1890 declared that joint action of any sort in restraint of trade was illegal; all attempts to monopolize interstate or international commerce were criminal offenses; the Attorney General, public authorities, and private individuals could proceed in the courts against "injurious combinations," and violation of the act was to carry a fine of $5,000 or a year in jail, or both. These clauses sounded tougher than they really were, because they were seriously weakened by the impossibility of defining, in a dynamic economy, such phrases as "restraint of trade" and "monopoly." Lacking precise legal meaning, their interpretation was in practice left to the courts, and true to its Victorian character, the Supreme Court kept the interpretation within very narrow limits, violating the spirit of the Sherman Act in order to uphold its letter. The first case under the act to come before the Supreme Court was a federal suit against the American Sugar Refining Company for having acquired the stock of E. C. Knight & Co. and three other independent corporations, with the aim of controlling over 95 percent of all refined sugar production in the United States (*US* v. *E. C. Knight & Co.*, 1895). The Court rejected the government's suit on the grounds that the Sherman Act applied only to monopoly of interstate "commerce," not to monopoly of "manufacturing." The Justices went on to add gratuitously that the act contained no federal prohibition on the rights of corporations to hold stock and control property—thereby seeming to validate holding companies. As a result this form of merger became very popular during the years of greatest monopoly growth, 1897–1904 when the act was at its weakest. The Court decision of 1895 remained in force until the Northern Securities Co. case of 1904 clearly extended the act's jurisdiction over monopolies created by property transfer.

The holding companies that developed after the E. C. Knight decision, McKinley's election (1896), and the Dingley Tariff (1897) spread very rapidly once corporation lawyers realized the new form enabled existing trusts to transform themselves into legal bodies. A holding company was a firm that acquired control over manufacturing concerns by outright purchase or majority stock control. State legislation in New Jersey (1889, 1893), New York (1892), Delaware (1899), Maine (1901), and elsewhere legalized this procedure. In such a company ultimate control is centralized, but actual administration is decentralized. The member firms remain ostensibly independent, and thus beyond the reach of antitrust laws; but the directors of the holding company (which is purely a financial rather than a manufacturing affair) have voting control over the members. There is also the "interlocking directorate" in which one man is on the board of directors of many companies (a practice still common today). This was not illegal before 1914, although the House of Representatives' Pujo Committee of 1913 disclosed extensive interlocking among the largest corporations, banks, and insurance houses. The directors of 18 banks (180 individuals) held 746 directorates in 134 companies with a combined capitalization of $25 billion. In 1914 the Clayton Act limited interlocking but did not prove too effective; the Transportation Act of 1920 prohibited interlocking in its own sphere except by permission of the Interstate Commerce Commission—which promptly granted over 2,500 permissions between 1920 and 1928.

United States Steel was the largest holding company of the period. Standard Oil, which was attacked as a trust by the State of Ohio and invalidated in 1892 on common-law grounds, was held together by the astute Rockefeller on the basis of "community of interest" until 1899, and then became a holding company.

Financial go-betweens: the power of investment bankers

When industrialists chose to combine, they did so in order to make more profits, or simply to survive in a harshly competitive world. But the financiers who promoted mergers had very little interest in production matters and no concern for their survival. As a group they gained more pure profit than any party to the merger transactions.

Growing need for capital as industry became more complex gave enormous power to the specialists who had the financial resources and contacts to sell large security issues. Capital was still relatively scarce in the United States, and stocks were not easy to sell. Only large dealers with good foreign sales outlets could handle stock issues of up to $10 million at a time. Such sales successfully conducted made millionaires out of the financial go-betweens, the investment bankers. Their eager pursuit of financial gain was often an important reason for the very formation of individual mergers. For instance, in his classic study of the trust problem Eliot Jones estimated the stock-market profits of the "underwriting syndicate" that promoted the merger of United States Steel in 1901 at the incredible figure of $62,500,000.

Behind this syndicate loomed the enormous financial power of J. Pierpont Morgan, the man who created General Electric, International Harvester, and International Mercantile Marine—the sworn enemy of competition, and the almost unchallenged leader of the United States financial world. Morgan, apart from his own brilliance, had all the necessary background advantages, including foreign sales branches in Paris and London and close contacts with distributors (banks, brokers, insurance companies) at home in the New York City money market where so much was concentrated. His power over the market and over his great rivals, such as Kuhn, Loeb (experts in German investments), or Lee, Higginson, or Kidder, Peabody, was always informal and unsystematized. Odd luncheon meetings with James Stillman (head of the National City Bank whose $200 million resources financed raw-material industries—metals, oil, meat) and George F. Baker (head of the First National Bank of New York which controlled manufacturing and railroad deposits) were deemed to be adequate to hold things together.

Morgan's influence was floodlit by the stock-market panic of 1907 when several leading banks got into difficulties. He demanded a purge of some of their staff before agreeing to help; then, choosing what he regarded as the best turning point in the market, Morgan marshaled the financial community to pool emergency resources, managing to dominate even his biggest contemporaries (including

Rockefeller). The affairs of 1907 brought public fears of a vast "money trust" that were later reinforced by the discoveries of the Pujo Committee. Morgan controlled 72 directorships in various large corporations in 1910 and had appointees working for him on the boards of the manufacturing companies for whom the stock was sold, and the insurance and banking houses to whom the stock went —to say nothing of his large personal holdings of stock in these houses. Often, it seems, Morgan was virtually trading with himself.

Arguments against such a situation are obvious enough on social, economic, political, and moral grounds. But looking back to the years before his death in 1913 one cannot help noticing that the truly remarkable thing about Morgan and his investment banker colleagues is not the casual enormity of their economic power so much as how little they really used it.[10]

Standard Oil

On the industrial side of the merger movement, the best example, and one that rapidly came to symbolize all the successes and evils inherent in monopoly organization, was Standard Oil.

John D. Rockefeller, its founder, was born in 1839 and began work at the age of sixteen as a bookkeeper in a commission merchant's office in Cleveland, Ohio. In 1859 with his savings and parental aid he supplied half the capital for a business in grain, hay, and meats: Clark & Rockefeller. The firm made some $17,000 a year during the Civil War, and in 1863 John D. took up oil refining, buying out his partner two years later. The new business, Rockefeller & Andrews, had a capital stock of $200,000. The Englishman Andrews dealt chiefly with the manufacturing, and Rockefeller with the buying and selling. A critical moment was experienced in 1867, but disaster was averted by a timely injection of capital from a rich Ohio brewer, Harkness. In 1870 the title Standard Oil Company of Ohio was adopted, and the capital stock of a million dollars had multiplied fivefold by 1877.

Oil refining was bitterly competitive. From the start Rockefeller grasped the need for stringent internal economies. He undertook to maintain all incidental and related services rather than to pay other producers. Standard Oil sought to possess its own tank cars, storage depots, plumbing and drayage service, and its own cooperage plants for the making of oil barrels (the timber for which came from forest land owned by the company, the iron hoops being also of its own make). Small articles, such as barrel bungs, were subject to strict economy and supervision. But economy alone was insufficient to make a great company: Rockefeller also speculated. For instance, he purchased new fields in Ohio where the oil had an unsuitable sulphur base—but in a short time Standard Oil chemists had overcome the difficulty, and a large profit ensued.

In his relations with the railroads Rockefeller typified the mental attitude of the monopolist of his day. In 1873 there were three major railroads competing in the oil regions for the lucrative traffic afforded by the industry. These railways served three cities, each of which was determined to dominate the refining stage of the industry: Cleveland, Pittsburgh, and Philadelphia. In addition refineries existed in New York and Baltimore. The eventual success of Cleveland in establishing its hegemony was the result not only of natural advantages but also of Rockefeller's relentless ingenuity.

While Cleveland had the advantage of summer transport by water and good rail-canal connections to New York by the Erie and New York Central railroads and the Erie Canal, Pittsburgh was well placed near the source of the raw material and had the Allegheny River for transport, and Philadelphia was best located for the eastern market and export trade. In the 1860's and 1870's open bargaining and discrimination in freight carriage rates by shippers and railroads were widespread, although a "common carrier" had theoretically no right to show partiality. Rockefeller was neither the originator of "rebates" nor the sole refiner who demanded them from carriers; but he was certainly the most successful and unscrupulous in negotiating for preferential treatment. After failing to secure sweeping rebates in the notorious South Improvement Company scheme in 1872 (judicially quashed by the Pennsylvania Legislature after complaints from small companies), Rockefeller managed in the summer of the same year to cajole refiners to form a pool—the National Refiners' Association—with himself as president. This pool controlled during its existence some four-fifths of America's refining capacity. As it threatened to reduce still further the price of crude oil, the oil producers opposed the refiners' pool by halting pumping. Eventually an agreement was made on both sides to check output of both crude and refined oil—the "treaty of Titusville" (December 23, 1872)—but this broke down, and Rockefeller's refiners' pool was dissolved six months later (June 24, 1873). Standard Oil merely continued to strengthen its position in the industry by entering the pipeline field, continuing rebate contracts with railways and building or acquiring large eastern plants and terminals. Rockefeller bought out nearly all the Cleveland concerns, and between 1874 and 1877 took over extensive refineries in Philadelphia, Pittsburgh, and New York. By 1879 Standard Oil refined 90 percent of American oil, and Rockefeller's real aim was to set up an interstate combination without getting into the public eye; so the trust was formed. Ever since 1872 the new acquisitions of the company outside Ohio had been placed in the hands of a "trustee," usually H. M. Flagler, the company secretary. The acquisitions remained nominally independent, but the profits went to the Ohio company, despite the laws prohibiting ownership of corporation stock by another corporation. But this device was too vague and very doubtful in law. What was Flagler a trustee for? The situation was regularized when the Standard Oil Trust was established in 1879. Nine trustees received the stock of the forty component concerns, giving trust certificates to shareholders in return. The combination was now capitalized at about $70 million. In 1892 the trust agreement was invalidated, as we have seen, and seven years later Standard Oil became a holding company.

Having gone through most of the chief forms of combination, it dominated the oil industry for several decades. In 1911 the government charged that Standard Oil of New Jersey practised price discrimination throughout the United States, operated at least seventy companies under the guise that they were independent, and paid $326 million in eight years on an original investment of $70 million. It would undercut prices of competitors in some districts and recoup losses by imposing higher charges in others, where its monopoly was more complete; it employed espionage on competitors and bribed first-class men working for rivals; it bought up companies surreptitiously and thus obtained trade secrets; it tried to cut off supplies of crude oil to its rivals and force transport companies to deny the competing refiners access to markets. On the other hand, Standard Oil management was more efficient and its leaders were undoubtedly men of vision and high administrative ability, even though these qualities alone are not sufficient to explain the rise of the giant oil monopoly. The Supreme Court ordered the trust to be dissolved on May 15, 1911.

2. ECONOMIC PERFORMANCE AND SOCIAL REFORM

The condemnation of Standard Oil in 1911 was symptomatic of hostility that had developed against the newly evolving industrial and financial structures of late-Victorian capitalism. Public opinion reacted most violently against industrialism after breakdowns in the economic system, like those of 1873, 1893, and 1907.

The fatal flaw: boom and slump

Like earlier panics of the nineteenth century, that of 1873 was preceded by heavy overinvestment, this time in railroad companies, and unstable financing. "Railway mania" between 1865 and 1873 doubled the total national mileage and stimulated a wild boom in heavy metals, land, and agriculture. A total increase in national income associated with a high "marginal propensity to import" and consumer extravagance brought an 82 percent rise in imports (to $642 million) with an export rise of only 57 percent (to $522 million). In addition to the resulting capital outflow, specie was drained by the need to pay annual interest rates on foreign capital ($130 million).

From 1871 money was very scarce and interest rates unsteady and high. The crash came in September with the failure of a major firm, Jay Cooke & Co., following that of several smaller concerns engaged in railroad financing. Cooke, despite his earlier successes in financing the Civil War, had managed to overinvolve himself heavily in Northern Pacific railroad securities. His bankruptcy precipitated a swift panic that closed the doors of the New York Stock Exchange for ten days, suspended cash payments at most banks, and ruined the livelihood of many stockbrokers and bankers. In Washington the Grant administration scraped together all its collective imagination and decided to liberate $13 million in currency by the repurchase of federal bonds! By October, financial injections from the rest of the nation and from Europe restored New York to some kind of health, cash payments were resumed, and the crisis deepened into a depression.

For about five years the country suffered severe unemployment, wage cuts, strikes, bread lines, the closing down of many manufacturing concerns (especially in the iron and steel and coal industries) and steeply falling agricultural and industrial prices. Distress was so universal and severe that two congressional committees were appointed to investigate the "causes" of the depression; they found, and failed to resolve, nearly two hundred. Nevertheless a favorable balance of trade was achieved by a reduction of imports and expansion of exports encouraged by falling home prices and income, demand elasticity for (luxury) imports being high. From late 1878 to 1883 there was a recovery, in which perhaps the central factors were foreign crop failures in 1879 and 1880, increasingly heavy American exports, and an influx of gold. Railroad building and manufacturing revived and prices began rising. An acute setback was the financial crisis of 1884, again the result of wild railroad financing. The ensuing depression lasted a year, but there was no suspension of cash payments. About a million workers were thrown out of employment. Besides the railroads the main industry affected was iron and steel. However, the same two industries featured in the boom that soon developed out of the rapid recovery. There was also in the late 1880's a speculative boom in western lands and a renewed inflow of foreign capital.

In 1890 the economy paused slightly in its stride; in 1893 it staggered. Monetary factors were of particular significance in this second major crisis. Anxiety about American policy over the gold standard (owing to the bimetallist controversy and the Sherman Silver Purchase Act) led to withdrawal of considerable amounts of foreign capital, which together with the bankruptcy of several railroad companies (such as the Philadelphia and Reading) overtaxed the banking system. Western and southern banks withdrew funds from New York, where cash payments were halted in July. A general contraction of the money market ensued. Almost 600 banks failed in 1893, the interior bearing the brunt of the strain. Commercial failures were three times the 1873 number, 15,242 houses going down. Railroad construction ceased, 74 companies collapsed, and by 1895 no dividends were being paid on 60 percent of railroad stocks. Factories and mines closed their gates and an estimated 3 million workers were unemployed (1894). European demand for wheat fell off, and poor American harvests caused distress among the farming community.

The depression that followed the panic lasted nearly four years, prices reaching their bottom level in 1896—the year of the great Bryan-McKinley presidential campaign. The "hard times" explain much of the bitterness in that election and the severity of the Pullman strike of 1894.[11] Inflationists and westerners claimed that the depression could be ended by increasing the currency through the free coinage of silver; conservatives blamed the crisis itself on silver. The former thought silver policy had not yet gone far enough; the latter thought it had gone too far. The conservatives forgot that most failures occurred in the West, where they could hardly be ascribed to a lack of confidence in the currency arising out of silver policy; the inflationists did not realize that much of the nation's business was transacted not in currency but through checks and demand deposits. President Cleveland, however, had the Sherman Silver Purchase Act repealed in October, 1893, to protect gold and stop the drain on the Treasury. Although the drain in fact continued and the federal government had to buy gold (by selling bonds) on at least four occasions, conditions did improve during 1896 when the Treasury's financial position became more favorable and the gold drain ceased. A business revival began in the following year.

The Panic of 1907 is attributed nowadays chiefly—sometimes exclusively—to a banking failure. Contemporary opinion, however, was conflicting: the currency was once more blamed (the Aldrich-Vreeland Act of 1908 being the outcome); Roosevelt's "trust-busting" policy was claimed by businessmen to be the central factor; rumors and blind fear in the financial world came in for severe castigation from newspaper cartoonists. The so-called "rich man's Panic" of 1907 had been preceded by a smaller scare in 1903, felt most by the iron and steel industry and brought about mainly by the rapid overexpansion of holding companies and other mergers. In 1907 not only were heavy foreign and domestic capital funds concentrated in New York, but under the National Banking System many provincial houses had redeposited their reserves with New York banks, which practice had two dangerous results: first, both depositing and depository banks counted the same funds as reserves;

second, the concentration at New York made reserves immobile and caused a tightening of the New York money market and a rise in interest rates twice a year, as farmers' deposits were withdrawn to meet the seasonal needs of sowing and harvesting. So in August and September, 1907, when bank loans had reached a peak and reserves were cut down to the legal minimum (stimulated by speculation in holding company securities, as in 1903), interest rates began to creep up and the Treasury had to make widespread deposits of federal funds (amounting to $28 million) in various banks to ensure that harvesting would take place. In October the Mercantile National Bank ran into difficulties which when investigated revealed a case of wilfully irresponsible speculation. This led to a general panic disclosure of weakness among other institutions and a run on the Mercantile spread elsewhere. On October 22nd the giant Knickerbocker Trust Company, the largest in New York and one that held in alleged safekeeping the deposits of 17,000 Americans, valued at about $50 million, closed its doors.

A full-scale banking crisis followed with a sharp fall in business activity and tragic unemployment. The New York Clearing House members suspended cash payments and the government took steps to relieve the stringency by depositing $36 million of federal funds in the National Banks of New York. The credit pool that J. P. Morgan came to dominate was established with federal help, to extend loans to solvent companies in need. (Incidentally, President Roosevelt allowed United States Steel to assimilate the Tennessee Coal and Iron Company—a maneuver that did not escape public notice.) The depression was brief, and by 1909 business had revived, along with prices. A recession in 1911 was followed by renewed growth until the outbreak of war in Europe.

Labor seeks a solution

Erratic and uncertain progress in the economy had its parallel in the field of labor organization. Labor leaders alternately embraced and rejected political action, accepted and discarded various theories of social regeneration from the Single Tax on land values to philosophic anarchism, and inconsistently demanded labor unity but left out the masses of unskilled, casual, and Negro workers.

While the Civil War and postwar economic transformations broke down localism and encouraged nationwide labor organization, and while 32 national trade unions were established by 1872, union membership never exceeded one-fifth of the labor force. Despite the violent strikes of 1877 (railroads), 1886 (mines and railroads), 1892 (steel), and 1894 (Pullman), American workers found the "class warfare" ideology indigestible and, in the American culture, unrewarding. More was to be gained by piecemeal reform and fighting to keep open the channels of economic opportunity.

For instance, there was the continuing struggle for a civilized working day. The National Labor Union led by W. H. Sylvis in 1866 aimed at a federation of labor and reform organizations for the eight-hour day (an advance of two hours on the prewar ideal). According to the philosophy of Ira Steward, the Boston machinist:

> Whether you work by the piece or work by the day
> Decreasing the hours increases the pay.

Steward aimed to absorb all profits into wages by a series of gradual enactments, and in 1866 he established the Grand Eight-Hour League of Massachusetts, copied in other states. Two years later President Andrew Johnson signed a bill proclaiming the eight-hour day for federal employees on public works, thus setting a similar example to that of Van Buren in 1840. Eight-hour legislation was enacted by several states in the 1860's, but was nearly always weakened by the lack of provision for inspection.

The other aims of the National Labor Union included producers' cooperatives and the admittance of Negroes, newly emancipated, to trade unions. The majority of its members favored arbitration and conciliation rather than strike action, and were mildly "reformist" in outlook. They involved themselves not only with the "co-ops" that became discredited in the late 1860's and early 1870's, but with such "third party" movements as the currency agitation. The prestige of the N.L.U. with industrial labor declined rapidly, no trade union sending a delegate to the congress of 1871. As we have seen, it suffered disastrous political defeat (as the National Labor and Reform party with a Greenback platform) in the presidential election of 1872.

In Professor Perlman's phrase, two "nuclei" survived the crisis of 1873 and depression of the 1870's that dislocated most of the organized labor movement. These were the Noble Order of the Knights of Labor and several unions grouped around the International Cigarmakers' Union which eventually became the American Federation of Labor.[12] The Knights of Labor were founded in Philadelphia in 1869 by Uriah S. Stephens, a tailor and former candidate for the ministry. It began as a secret, ritualistic group with a threefold aim: to educate public opinion on the need to give labor a just share of the wealth it created, to advance legislation "to lighten the exhaustiveness of toil," and finally to give each other mutual aid in times of distress. The order grew quickly, and by 1873 had eighty local assemblies. A centralizing move was made in that year, the seat of control being called "Assembly No. 1." During the 1870's the Knights gained many new members owing to the defection of trade-union organizations. (The number of national unions was reduced from over thirty to six by 1878, and total membership reduced to one-tenth, from about 500,000 to 50,000.) In addition, the miserable failure of the railway strike of 1877, followed by wage cuts and retaliatory "blacklisting" of prominent unionists by employers in Baltimore, Pittsburgh, Chicago, Toledo, and St. Louis, produced a kind of general strike accompanied by wild disorders.

In the anthracite region of eastern Pennsylvania the defeat of a miners' union in 1869 led to the growth of a secret organization— the Molly Maguires—which used terrorism and assassination. Its leaders were caught and executed in 1876. It is now known that part of the violence was instigated by the employers themselves, as an excuse to dissolve the organization. In Pittsburgh a pitched battle developed; the militia killed seventeen demonstrators, and $5 million worth of damage was done to railway property.

Employers everywhere took heavy reprisals—and the secrecy of the Knights attracted new followers. During the 1880's the order grew to five and a half times its former size, and returning economic prosperity in 1879, together with the election of a new "Grand Master Workman" (T. V. Powderly), brought about the abolition of secrecy. The "hard times" after 1884 led to further increases in membership and forced the leaders to accept, albeit reluctantly, the notion of "industrial warfare"—the use of strike and boycott. Under the leadership of Powderly the Knights of Labor became a national force and took an important part in many national strikes. A strike against wage reductions was called in February, 1885, on three railways of the Gould system—the Wabash, the Missouri Pacific, and the Missouri, Kansas and Pacific. It was successful in preventing the reductions, and forced from the unscrupulous Jay Gould a promise that he would not use the blacklist, and would in future submit disputes to arbitration. These sensational results swelled membership to 700,000, and the Knights even managed to squeeze from Congress a law prohibiting the importation of cheap contract labor.

In the following year, though, they overplayed their hand. A strike was called in March, 1886, on the Gould railroad in the Southwest that brought business to a halt and alienated public opinion. In May the Knights were forced to the point of unconditional surrender. The year 1886 was one of great upheaval generally: the nation was swept by "sympathetic" strikes and lockouts, and waves of destruction. The rank and file of the Knights of Labor gave their support to the May Day strikes organized by the Federation of Organized Trades and Labor Unions of the United States and Canada,[13] in favor of the general adoption of the eight-hour day, and three days later the Haymarket Riot (Chicago) came as the calamitous climax.

A mass meeting was called to protest against the killing of strikers of the McCormick Corporation by the police. Anarchist speakers (members of the so-called "Black International") addressed the crowd, and tempers became frayed as the police advanced to disperse the meeting. A bomb was thrown. One policeman was killed, seven civilians were fatally injured and fifty or more wounded. After a trial that caused an outcry in labor and socialist circles in Europe as well as America (for example, in William Morris's paper *Commonweal*, in England), eight men were convicted of murder and four actually executed.[14]

The Knights of Labor, along with other labor groups, were wrongly blamed for the Haymarket affair, and 1886 proved to be the turning point in their history. The order had included too many conflicting demands and pressure groups. It had supported, during its existence, the eight-hour day, "free soil," feminism, officially recognized arbitration machinery, cooperation, abolition of child and convict labor, a graduated income tax, post-office savings banks, nationalization of railroads and telegraph services, full legal protection for trade unions, factory and mines acts, public health codes, abolition of the contract system for public works, and the setting up of a Bureau of Labor Statistics. These diverse social reforms were too attractive to its leaders, who gave little time to trade-union affiliation and organization. No reserve fund was maintained, and strikes were called with little or no preparation. Moreover, the failure of the great southwestern strike of 1886 and of all the two hundred cooperative enterprises begun by the Knights (none were left by 1888) had a bad effect on internal morale and external prestige. Nothing succeeds like success. At the opening of 1886 the Knights of Labor had seemed strong, unified, and well directed; at the end of the year the same organization seemed overcentralized, torn by internal dissensions and jealousies, and lacking in sound leadership.

In 1893 when the last blow was struck—the replacing of Powderly by a farmer-editor—membership had dropped to 10 percent (70,000). But a new organization had already established its hegemony over the American labor movement. This, the American Federation of Labor, was firmly fixed on a craft basis. An idealistic hope of uniting labor of all skills, creeds, and colors was certainly not the "unspoken major premiss" of AFL philosophy. Far from it. Leaders trained in European (and especially British) methods, like Gompers, Strasser, and McGuire, were motivated by a hard-bitten, "job-conscious" attitude quite unlike the Owenite enthusiasm of the "Knights" of Labor. Their principal goals were to secure decent wages and fair hours, build up closely knit unions of skilled artisans, and legalize collective bargaining. Very similar in aims to the conservative "Junta" that ruled the TUC in Britain until the socialist revival of the 1880's, the AFL made no attempt to become a comprehensive labor movement and eschewed politics or the notion of independent labor representation.

The AFL was first organized in Pittsburgh in 1881 and then reorganized five years later. Gompers, who became its president from 1882 until his death in 1924 (except for one year), had already experimented successfully with the International Cigarmakers' Union, concentrating on building a national union of artisans with a well-organized central authority and paid secretariat, a union fund, regular union dues, and a mutual "benefit" system covering illness and death. Gompers's basic philosophy was simply: "More! —Now!" By 1879 the Cigarmakers' had become a "model" union on these lines. Membership of the AFL was restricted to trades and labor unions, representation in the federation being based on membership numbers. A three-cent subscription per head was to provide a permanent revenue. Membership increased from 50,000 (1884) to 190,000 (1890) and gained heavily from the decline of the Knights of Labor. At the outbreak of World War I, the AFL had fully 2 million members, and most of the national trade unions were affiliated to it. It had fought stiff opposition in the 1890's and suffered defeat in two steel strikes.[15] It was weakened by the crisis of 1893 and ensuing depression. But it had led a successful revival of the eight-hour movement and in at least one member union, the Stove Molders', permanent arbitration machinery was set up, officially recognized by the employers (1891). The greatest period of growth up to World War I was after 1895, and especially in the five years 1900–1905, when membership trebled.

Homestead and Pullman: two strikes

Meanwhile about 24,000 strikes had occurred between 1880 and 1900, half of them ending in the defeat of the workers and a third of them being successful. A spectacular outbreak was the famous Homestead strike (June 30 to November 20, 1892), organized by a powerful union, the Amalgamated Association of Iron and Steel Workers, at a branch of the Carnegie Steel Company. The trouble was over a wage disagreement. The employers fought bitterly, hiring 300 Pinkerton "detectives" who staged a pitched battle with strikers. About ten people were killed, and the Governor of Pennsylvania ordered the National Guard to stand by. An attempt on the life of an unpopular member of the steel company's staff (H. C. Frick) by an anarchist turned public opinion against the Homestead men, and the strike ultimately failed. Only a fifth of the 5,000 strikers were reemployed by the firm, and those taken back had to renounce their union membership. Other steel firms in the Pittsburgh region also refused to have dealings with the Amalgamated Association of Iron and Steel Workers; this once-proud union was shattered, and its leaders blacklisted.

Even more important was the Pullman strike in Chicago in 1894, organized by the American Railway Union (an early example of a "vertical" or industrial union) under the radical socialist Eugene V. Debs. This strike was a microcosm of industrial labor relations under old-style capitalism. First, it illustrates the three chief forms of intervention in disputes at that time: use of state militia and federal troops (increasingly common after 1877); use of the judiciary (although the courts made no lasting contribution to industrial peace, favoring capital as they did); and use of public mediating and conciliating agencies. Second, the strike presents typical examples of the conduct and opinion of both capital and labor. Third, and like many of its kind, it involved the participation of groups not parties to the original quarrel, and focused intense local and national feeling on several sensational "incidents." Finally, the Pullman strike marked the beginning of a legal and legislative struggle extending over many years.

The prelude to the trouble at Pullman's Palace Car Company was the crisis of 1893. Prices fell, failures were numerous, unemployment was widespread, and strikes almost continuous. In May, 1894, a year after the depression began, a serious strike occurred at Pullman—the town that housed Pullman workers in dwellings built and owned by the company. Wages had been cut, although salaries remained untouched and profits totaled $4 million. Even so, the strike might have worn itself out if both employers and workers had not had affiliations with larger and stronger groups, the actions of which turned a local dispute into a national crisis.

Several weeks before trouble broke out, about 4,000 Pullman men had joined the new American Railway Union. The union held a convention in June, and because they could make no headway in negotiations with their employers, the Pullman workers appealed to the convention for help. Response was readily made: a complete boycott of all Pullman coaches. As these coaches were included in almost all United States trains, a nationwide railroad strike was threatened unless they were detached. When the threat of boycott proved to be inadequate, the ARU called a full-scale strike, and at one point in the proceedings (in July) it seemed possible that all organized labor in America would join in the strike sympathetically. Gompers, in his capacity as president of the AFL, put a stop to this at a conference in Chicago, and limited AFL action to a strongly worded statement supporting the strikers. It is probable that he thought the battle was already lost.

But the scope of the strike continued to widen as the federal and state governments became active participants. The central government was implicated because Olney, the Attorney General, had to safeguard the passage of regular trains carrying United States mails, and take legal action against any person obstructing them. On the advice of several district attorneys and local federal judges, President Cleveland ordered troops to the troubled zones. Almost immediately a constitutional dispute arose between the state governor and Cleveland regarding the rôle of federal and state action in industrial disputes.

A further complication was added by the intervention of the judicial arm. The aim was to prosecute Debs and his associates in one of two ways. first, by claiming they had violated federal criminal laws (for example, obstruction of the mails and "conspiracy in restraint of trade"), and, second, by inculpating them through civil law, by use of the "injunction." The main criminal charge of "conspiracy" fell through, but the civil charge was more successful. An "injunction" is an order issued by a court of equity commanding someone to do, or restraining him from doing, an act that would violate the personal or property rights of someone else.[16] The violation of an injunction constitutes contempt of court and is thus punishable by fine or imprisonment. On July 2nd the government secured a "blanket" injunction from a federal court forbidding "all persons whomsoever" from interfering in any way, even indirectly, with the operation of the railroads. Debs and three colleagues were then arrested (for the second time) on the charge of contempt of court, and the case was eventually carried to the Supreme Court, which, by its decision, promptly placed the use of the injunction in labor disputes upon a strong legal basis (May 27, 1895). Debs served a six-month prison sentence.

The meaning of all this was not lost on industrialists, and during the following two decades the injunction was used as one of the most formidable weapons in their armory in the struggle with labor. Woodrow Wilson promised to restrict its sphere of action in his "New Freedom" program, and the Clayton Antitrust Act (1914) exempted non-profit-making labor and agricultural organizations from the "restraint of trade" clauses. The act had little practical effect, however, and no genuine relief came for labor until the Norris–La Guardia Act (1932) put a halt to the misuse of federal judicial power by prohibiting the issue of injunctions in cases of official, publicized strikes financed by orderly trade unions, and in cases of "peaceable assembly." All cases of contempt springing from violation of injunctions were to be assured of trial by jury.

The significance of the Pullman strike of 1894 lies also in the fact that it heralds the beginning of the emergence of the federal government in its function of mediator in industrial disputes. President Cleveland established an investigating commission, and some of its recommendations were embodied in the Erdman Act (1898), a measure that set up machinery for arbitration between certain classes of railwaymen and their companies and strengthened the mediating powers of the central government. In 1913 the Newlands Act extended these provisions, and there has been ever since a growth of government responsibility in conciliation and arbitration.

Three further groups in the world of organized labor up to 1917 were: the United Mineworkers of America, a powerful "industrial" union entirely outside the AFL; the four great Railway Brotherhoods, also outside the AFL, and consisting of the Locomotive Engineers (organized at Detroit in 1863 and first called the Brotherhood of the Footboard), the Order of Railway Conductors (founded 1868), the Locomotive Firemen and Enginemen (founded 1873), and the Railroad Trainmen (founded 1883); and third, the Industrial Workers of the World, otherwise known as the IWW, or "Wobblies."

The IWW was formed in 1905 from various dissident radical and socialist splinter groups such as the Western Federation of Miners and the Socialist Trade and Labor Alliance. It was headed by William D. Haywood, who in 1907 was acquitted on a sensational murder charge arising out of a violent labor dispute, and who had assimilated the principles of French syndicalism. He was supported, though splits were soon to appear, by the Marxian socialist Daniel De Leon (leader of the Socialist Labor party) and by Eugene V. Debs, already famous for his generalship in the Pullman strike. The aim of the Wobblies was, according to their manifesto:

> One great industrial union embracing all industries, providing for craft autonomy locally, industrial autonomy internationally, and wage-class unity generally.

In fierce reaction to the craft conservatism of the AFL, they appealed to the unskilled (as did the "New Unionists" in England after the triumphant Dock Strike of 1889). Textile workers, migratory harvest hands, western lumberjacks and exploited immigrants—everybody found a place among the Wobblies. Ignoring the vigorous attacks launched upon them by Gompers (who feared for his respectability) and the AFL, they advocated a revolutionary program aimed at the complete abolition of the "wage system." Nothing short of a general strike could solve the social problem, for their motto was "an injury to one is an injury to all"—in direct contradiction to the *sauve-qui-peut* policy that had emerged among the craft unions. Perhaps the chief activities of the IWW were the Lawrence strike of 1912 and the unsuccessful Paterson textile strikes of 1912–1913. It achieved little else, mainly because of its heterogeneous membership and complicated internal dissensions. The Western Federation of Miners seceded in 1907, only two years after the founding of the movement, and in 1911 joined the AFL. The "rump" split into two sections in 1908 with headquarters in Chicago and Detroit, one favoring revolutionary political action and its rival "direct" industrial action. Government persecution, further dissensions, lack of financial support and the "anti-Red" hysteria of 1917–1920 drove the group out of existence. At no time had its membership exceeded sixty or seventy thousand.

During World War I, which America entered in 1917, employment figures were high, and the government and industry eagerly sought the cooperation of the trade unions. In the space of five years (1915–1920) the AFL increased its numbers from two million to over four million, and there was a flowering of "labor relations" councils and the like, in an effort to step up productivity. From about 1920 to the New Deal, however, a very different state of affairs existed. Only the strongest unions survived the depression and the all-out attacks from employers; AFL membership fell to well under three million by 1925, and many unionists turned once more to the radicalism they had rejected earlier. Such bodies as the League for Progressive Political Action (dominated by the railway unions) sprang up, and the AFL executive made Robert La Follette, the Progressive leader, its presidential nominee for the election of 1924. This failed, but in the 1930's economic distress infused the AFL with further radicalism, and the most impatient unions broke away to form the CIO.

Character of the American labor movement

Looking back from about 1920 over United States labor history, an insistent question recurs: What happened to socialism in America? Why did the United States not develop an independent socialist-labor party, like some other democratic nations? The answer is not simple. Many factors uniquely American come into play—immigration, the westward movement and sectionalism, federal political structure and a written Constitution.

Unrestricted immigration provided cheap and manipulative labor, that was sometimes a useful tool for "tough" employers to use against unions, and it has also been said that immigration delayed unionization because the later immigrants (pictured by Oscar Handlin as conservative, apolitical peasant folk) refused to join. But as unskilled laborers there were no unions for these people to join anyway until very late in labor history; and it is doubtful if immigrants created fewer jobs as consumers than they filled as producers —the number of jobs multiplied threefold (1870–1930), while the total population only doubled. Immigration did add to the religious and ethnic complexity of the nation and created "group" rather than "class" loyalties. While the inflow continued (to about 1920), such loyalties were strongly maintained in the teeth of conformist pressures and the spread (through modern mass media) of common standards of taste and value in education, domestic life, dress, and leisure. Since the 1920's ethnic conflicts within the trade unions have been greatly reduced. In contrast, the Negro's problems (in the railroad brotherhoods, for instance) seemed to increase rather than diminish as Negro unionization became a real possibility at last.

Whether the westward movement retarded labor organizations or not has been greatly debated. The old "safety-valve" theory of the frontier has been more or less exploded; but the existence of free land out West—however expensive it was to farm—is but one aspect and symbol of American opportunity. Economic opportunity and social democracy must certainly have dissuaded workers from joining radical reform parties. As far as the "capitalist class" was concerned many Americans aimed not to fight it, but to join it.

From the British point of view, therefore, the United States labor movement lagged behind by half a century. Not only were American unions too weak to enter the political field, but the federal political structure and the enormous complexity and expense it entailed for any major welfare reform discouraged all moves in that particular direction. In Britain, with a unitary form of government, the problem was comparatively simple. Throughout these years "the Constitution" hung around the neck of United States labor leaders.

More important still, American labor history was much more discontinuous and *ad hoc* than the British experience. The long struggle for universal suffrage in Britain, permitted in gracious stages down the social order from 1832 (upper middle class) to 1867 (urban workers) to 1884–1885 (rural workers), gave the British radical movement a unity and a character American workers (receiving their voting rights on a platter) did not have to forge.

The "American Dream"

What is more, was not "Americanism" in some ways at least a kind of substitute socialism? Did not the American Dream promise much that socialism promised, and offer in the hand much that socialism in "class"-bound Europe could only hope for? The good life: the world's highest (and rising) living standards; social equality (of a kind that could fulfill the dream of Britain's noble pioneer Keir Hardie that someday "workingmen" would be treated as "men"); a society which rewarded hard work, talent, and character more than it honored background, blood, or rank.

Later historians and sociologists have questioned the "myth" of rags to riches on which Victorian popular thought thrived, the faith that goes back at least to Ben Franklin and received such a boost from the cult of "success" books in the later nineteenth century— like the hundred or so written by Horatio Alger. A careful study of the social origins of America's leading businessmen before 1920 would reveal the not so startling fact that the average example was neither poor nor foreign nor a farm boy. On the contrary, he was born of "Anglo-Saxon" American parents usually in a city environment in the Northeast; he attended a decent school and an "acceptable" Protestant church (Episcopal, Congregational, or Presbyterian); he enjoyed a stable childhood in a fairly well-to-do family that valued reading and public affairs and believed in giving their child a good start in the business!

But what does this latest research mean? It is good that we should know the truth about old-style capitalism; there is little statistical evidence to support the rags-to-riches folklore in its extreme form. Few immigrant and/or farm boys of poor background and education could climb in one generation from the poverty line to great wealth. Furthermore, industrialism and big business had increased inequality and widened the range of incomes. But the *prima facie* evidence is overwhelming from all sides that movement up the social scale, of a less drastic kind perhaps than from the bottom to the top, was the norm. No boy was tied to his father's "class" or job. Within the extremes of wealth American society was, to claim the very least, more "open" and less stratified than any society then existing.

Some elements were lacking in the United States economy which the as yet untried socialist commonwealth promised—such as full employment with economic growth, or the elimination of the tragic capitalist cycle of boom and slump. But even in these directions native forces were tentatively at work within the country to bring more social justice and economic efficiency to old-style capitalism.

The urge to reform: Progressivism

The Progressive Era, roughly from about 1890 to the First World War, forms the second of the three reform periods of United States history, the first being the 1830's and 1840's and the third the 1930's. Each period had its prophets of social doom and regeneration— which on the whole it ignored. Each period was characterized by one central, empirical issue: abolitionism, or federal intervention to halt the Great Depression, or (as in the case of the 1890's) "trustbusting," which gave it a curiously *ad hoc* character.

While "the trusts" had come to symbolize all America's social ills by the period of Progressivism proper, a whole gamut of reform ideas was in the air between 1860 and 1920. William H. ("Coin") Harvey and William Jennings Bryan advocated currency reform; E. L. Godkin, D. A. Wells, and others demanded civil-service reform; Tom Johnson, "Golden Rule" Jones (Mayor of Toledo, Ohio), and a host

of writers, including Lincoln Steffens and the Anglo-American W. T.
Stead (*If Christ Came to Chicago*, 1894), urged a "cleansing" of
urban government; Jane Addams led the social-settlement movement
and founded Hull House in Chicago (1889); Edward Bellamy's fu-
turistic novel of utopian socialism (*Looking Backward*, 1887) was
so successful he based an influential movement on it; Marxism was
interpreted by several writers for American consumption, most effectively by Laurence Gronlund (*Cooperative Commonwealth*, 1884);
various shades of anarchism brought joy to Johann Möst, Emma
Goldman, and the philosophical Benjamin Tucker (*Instead of a
Book*, 1893); Christian socialism and the English-type Fabian socialism were expounded by H. Demarest Lloyd, various clergymen
and academics and the Reverend W. D. P. Bliss—the encyclopedist
of American social reform. Widening circles of intellectual disturbance spread to all spheres of human activity.

The economists stir

First, and quite apart from the impact of Karl Marx (whose economics technically was rather old hat), a quiet revolution was taking
place in the staid academic halls of economic science. It was a revolution in thought that reflected some of the institutional changes
already described.

A new generation of economists, some of them trained in Europe
like Richard T. Ely of Johns Hopkins, came deeply under the influence of the German "historical" school of Wilhelm Roscher and Gus-
tav Schmoller. This school rejected the concept of "natural laws" and
the deductive, abstract quality of mind that characterized classical
economics. Seeking to understand economic man in society as he
really was, the "historicists" emphasized a detailed study of institutions and economic policies.

Turning away from theoretical principles to a positive analysis
of the existing social framework, American economists established
the American Economic Association in 1885 which promptly declared:

We regard the State as an agency whose positive assistance is one of the
indispensable conditions of human progress.

Popular economic thought had become so out of touch with the
realities of pre–Civil War history that this declaration was regarded

as something new in the United States experience. What is more, Ely, who like several economists and economic historians in Britain and the United States at that time was a Christian Socialist, went on to dismiss laissez faire as a doctrine "unsafe in politics and unsound in morals." The first president of the AEA was Francis A. Walker (1840–1897), a typical member of the historical or "institutional" school: a practical-minded statistician and Superintendent of the 1870 Census who rejected the "wages fund" theory.

More important in the history of technical economics was John Bates Clark (1847–1938) who made great contributions to value and distribution theory from the new viewpoint of "marginal utility analysis." Clark's demands for antitrust regulations was fully within the new institutionalist position in American economics, but his later distinction between economic science and reform policy, and all his theoretical work, led him much beyond historicism. (In fact, the German historical school regarded the new marginal utility theories with some rivalry, especially since the Austrians—Karl Menger, Eugen Böhm-Bawerk, and others—had helped to develop them.)[17] This second cat among the pigeons, marginalism, helped to bring economic change in the United States because it upset classical orthodoxy even more profoundly than institutionalism did—not by rejecting economic theory but by questioning the essential core of classical doctrine itself. Finding an overinsistence on costs and supply, the marginalists developed a subjective theory of economic value around the demand factor. This quite naturally led to a new intellectual interest in the theoretical problem of distribution, which also (not by accident) was one of the two major real problems of late-nineteenth century economic life.

The second major real problem, boom and slump, received more and more scientific study from the statisticians and theorists alike, and gradually "business cycle theory" became an accepted part of economics in the twentieth century, as did the theory of "imperfect" or monopolistic competition (also after the event).

The writers revolt

While the economists fashioned new theoretical tools and built up a body of detailed knowledge about the economy, a new group of publicists, novelists, and journalists attacked America's social problems more directly. These "writers" included two mavericks: Henry George, whose radical *Progress and Poverty* (1879), advocating a single tax on all land values (since these are socially created), became the world's best seller in popular economics and the handbook of self-educated workingmen all over the world—Denmark, Britain, New Zealand, China; and the unclassifiable offbeat Thorstein Veblen (1857–1929), the alienated midwesterner trained in the social scientism of the new graduate schools, who dissected the pecuniary values of America's business culture with sardonic, semiserious detachment.[18]

The novelists who filed their "minority report" against the social evils of unregulated industrialism at the turn of the century, approached social criticism through the new literary "realism" and naturalism. They owed much to that more gentle and sedate utopian, William Dean Howells, but spoke in stronger, stranger language. Outstanding examples were Stephen Crane's *Maggie: A Girl of the Streets* (1893), Theodore Dreiser's *Sister Carrie* (1900), Frank Norris's *The Octopus* (1901), Upton Sinclair's *The Jungle* (1906), and Jack London's *The Iron Heel* (1907), portraying slum degradation in the cities, railroad chicanery in California, grim Chicago packing plants, and a prophecy of revolution. As novels they are terribly uneven, and some of them contain streaks of prejudice and even racism distasteful to modern readers. London and Norris in particular were superficially attracted by changing currents of popular psychology, pseudoscience, and boiled-down "irrationalism." What is significant about the novels of the social realists, however, from the viewpoint of economic history, is their bitter denunciation of those prejudices of the day which they did *not* share.

"Muckrakers"

Writers other than novelists attacked social problems head on in the Progressive Era, for these were years of great and courageous American journalism. Certain outspoken magazines, such as *Collier's*, *McClure's*, the *American, La Follette's Weekly,* and *Everybody's* (working on the principle "Publish and be damned!"), printed regular exposés of corrupt politics, business practices, and monopoly in all fields from finance and insurance to transportation and copper

mining. Their leading writers, dubbed "muckrakers" by Teddy Roosevelt, included the indefatigable Ida M. Tarbell and Henry Demarest
Lloyd whose article on Standard Oil in the *Atlantic Monthly* in 1880
led him on to a complete book on the subject, *Wealth against Commonwealth* (1894), which gave plenty of ammunition to the "trust-
busting" movement. For Sam McClure, Lincoln Steffens wrote *The
Shame of the Cities* (1904), a telling collection of articles on six
leading United States city governments, now a classic in the history
of journalism.

More specifically "humanitarian" were the colorful, personal and
touching writings of Jacob Riis on slum life in New York City. Land-
ing from Denmark in 1870, Riis spent seven years in poverty and
twenty-two years as a police reporter for city newspapers. His powerful book *How the Other Half Lives* (1890) won Riis the friendship
and aid of Theodore Roosevelt in the long battle for what we now
call "urban renewal." Riis was an unsophisticated, harsh writer not
far removed from the prejudices he was fighting against, but he
painted an untarnished picture of city life as it really was for thousands of Americans.

Efforts repaid: improvements in old-style capitalism before 1920

In politics the "Progressive party" was a faction of the Republicans led by Roosevelt; but Progressivism appealed more widely than
this—its exponents were the Democrat William Jennings Bryan, the
Republican Robert M. La Follette, the Republican Theodore Roosevelt, and the Democrat Woodrow Wilson. Many of the positive
achievements of Progressivism were made under T.R.'s "Square
Deal" and Wilson's "New Freedom" programs.

Roosevelt's "Square Deal" was not quite all it should have been,
considering the fuss he made about it. T.R.'s noisy "trust-busting"
campaign for instance was little more than a smokescreen. Looking
at the cold facts rather than at the speeches, we see that the Sherman
Antitrust Act had already been passed in 1890, eleven years before
Roosevelt took over after McKinley's assassination. The second most
important trust-busting measure, the Clayton Act of 1914, did not
come until six years after Teddy had abandoned the White House
for the wilds of Africa. More federal actions were brought against

monopolies by the administration of the avowed conservative Taft than under his rambunctious predecessor Roosevelt. (T.R.'s administration introduced 37 cases under the Sherman Act, Taft's 43, and Woodrow Wilson's 53.) Yet such was the success of T.R.'s publicity campaign that his name is forever linked with "trust-busting."[19]

Wilson's "New Freedom"

It was Woodrow Wilson who eventually tried to plug the holes in the leaky Sherman Act. Winning the United States Presidency for the Democrats in 1912 after a successful presidency of Princeton and two years as reform governor of New Jersey (a state that needed reforming), Wilson presented in his inaugural speech a far-reaching plan for economic reconstruction: the "New Freedom." Currency and banking, tariffs and business regulation ranked high, and Wilson did not seem to waste time. The Underwood Tariff (1913), pushed through Congress with the help of patronage, gave the United States the lowest tariff rates since 1857, a reduction in the average level from 40 to 29 percent.

Along with the tariff cuts came the federal income-tax amendment, ratification of which was at last completed. Wilson's income tax was low and evasions were widespread, but its introduction signified a major structural change in American capitalism: the right of the federal government to tax incomes directly without reapportionment to the states. Taxes according to income are not only the most) democratic and just variety, but they are ultimately redistributive.

Meanwhile, when American Tobacco and Standard Oil were dissolved by the Court in 1911, the judges introduced a new interpretative gloss—a distinction between "reasonable" and "unreasonable" trusts. Wider powers were left to the justices to decide on "reasonability," and the Sherman Act was explicitly limited to "unreasonable" contracts in restraint of trade. So in 1914 Wilson pushed for two measures to strengthen antitrust laws: the Clayton Act and the Federal Trade Commission Act. These were the core of the New Freedom. The former supplemented the Act of 1890 by prohibiting certain listed monopolistic practices not previously specified, such as certain kinds of price discrimination and exclusive-dealing agreements, and the acquisition by a company of its competitor's stock.

The latter measure set up the Federal Trade Commission to enforce and administer the trust laws and to investigate cases in order to make recommendations to the President, the Attorney General and Congress.

Samuel Gompers of the AFL saluted the Clayton Act as the Magna Carta of labor because it sought to limit the use of antilabor injunctions and exempted nonprofit labor and farm organization from the "restraint of trade" clauses of the Sherman Act. His rejoicing was rather premature. As for mergers they were as powerful as ever in the 1920's, mainly because after World War I the courts adopted a very restricted interpretation of the law and were hesitant to dissolve established combinations. In cases concerning the United Shoe Machinery Co. (1918) and United States Steel (1920), the judges decided that mere size was no condemnation, and that however large it might be, no merger could be considered illegal unless it engaged in secret agreements or patently unfair competitive practices.[20] But the responsibility for this attitude, right or wrong, cannot be laid at the door of the New Freedom.

A more lasting structural achievement was the Federal Reserve System already described. Other domestic reform legislation included the Federal Farm Loan Act and the Federal Warehouse Act, both of 1916, to provide official credit channels for farmers and reduce their excessive load of debt; La Follette's Seaman's Act (1915) regulating safety precautions and working conditions for sailors—an act that crowned years of struggle by the Seamen's Union; the Adamson Act (1916) which began the eight-hour day on interstate railroads; the Keating-Owen Child Labor Act (1916) which tried to limit the use of children under sixteen years of age in mines and quarries, and those under fourteen in factories (declared "unconstitutional" by the Supreme Court in 1918);[21] the Smith-Lever (1914) and Smith-Hughes (1917) Acts providing federal aid for farm education and demonstration work; the Rural Post Roads Act (1916) and the Alaska Railroad Act (1914), the first giving federal aid to the states to build local roads and the second envisaging railroads in Alaska built, owned, and managed by the federal government.

This was an enormous mass of legislation, and American capitalism—pushed by the Progressive spirit—may well have transformed itself still more if it had not been for World War I. This did not happen, however, and the ultimate judgment of the pre-1920 economy must rest on its actual performance in raising living standards and per capita real income.

The living standards of 1920

The American living standard of 1920 is no easier to gauge than that of 1860. Once more we face the problem of judging intangibles —qualitative as well as quantitative elements. And the quantitative elements are not easily ascertained anyway, given the weakness of most historical statistics.

Per capita real income probably doubled between 1860 and 1920. But most of the growth came in the thirty years before 1890, when (according once more to Hansen's index) real wages rose 70 percent. The evidence conflicts in some ways, but it seems clear that during the years of Progressivism (1890 to the First World War) the rate of increase of the whole economy slowed down and real wages were more or less constant. Robert Hunter's classic study made in 1904, *Poverty*, estimated that 13 percent of the population, or 10 million Americans, were living on or below the bare minimum poverty-line income of $300 a year (South) or $460 (cities). In addition, the risk of not being allowed to earn a living at all—through unemployment, displacement, shutouts, and strikes—was very much increased under industrial capitalism, both because of its inherent economic instability and unplanned nature, and because fewer means of supplementing food supply or low income were available to the uprooted city worker. The unity and privacy of family life came under pressure from the need of women and children to go out to work and the growing practice of accepting "boarders."

Old-style capitalism was not a great success at providing stability or security, and perhaps even traditional American equality of opportunity was impaired in the late nineteenth century by the rise of great industrial dynasties and the advantages of inherited wealth. By 1890 at least six private fortunes exceeded $100 million each and over sixty exceeded $20 million. (After 1900 two fortunes certainly overtopped $500 million.) By 1892 more than 4,000 individuals were worth a million dollars apiece. At the end of the period grossly uneven income distribution still remained. In 1921, for instance, according to National Industrial Conference Board figures, the bottom 10 percent of the United States population received only 2 percent of total income, while the top 10 percent received 38 percent.

How were Americans reconciled to this situation? Perhaps the major part of the answer lies in the *dynamism* of the economy and its overall upward sweep. In three major areas there was undoubted and obvious improvement by 1920: leisure time, health, and education.

Down to 1890 working hours were not reduced very noticeably. Despite the idealistic hopes of Ira Steward immediately after the Civil War, unionized workers as late as 1890 were fortunate to be on a 9-hour (not an 8-hour) day. Ten hours was more typical, and for nonunionized labor the working day could be even more drawn out. A long and relentless struggle by organized groups eventually reduced the 60-hour working week by five hours to 55. That is to say that by 1920 many workers labored only 8 or so hours a day. This increase in leisure was an enormous gain in human terms, in Professor C. W. Wright's view one of the outstanding factors in America's high living standards.

Medicine made more advances after 1860 than ever before, and in the United States considerable wealth was poured into research. The great discoveries, like those of Pasteur (disease control) in France and Lister (antisepsis) in England, were quickly made available to American patients. Needless pain and incorrect treatment were reduced by improvements in anesthesiology and diagnostics, while the number of doctors, nurses, medical schools, and hospitals multiplied. In public health the most notable step was the creation in 1912 of the United States Public Health Service.

As a direct result of medical advances, better diet, and increased leisure, expectation of life at birth was prolonged from about 40 years (1860) to about 55 years (1920)—a 15-year gift of life, of which about ten years were added after 1900.[22] More of these precious years were spent at school than in 1860. The number and quality of elementary and secondary schools improved, and teaching methods altered greatly. Secondary-school enrollment doubled every ten years from 1890 to 1940; public high schools proliferated after 1880 and state universities after about 1890. In effect, rising material standards created a strong demand by Americans for a chance to share in the cultural and intellectual heritage so long monopolized by a fortunate elite.

Leisure, longevity, health, education—continuing achievements like these helped old-style capitalism to overcome its failures during business cycles, the harshness of its industrial discipline, the rigors of its city and farm life. Though a new Tocqueville might have discovered greater inequalities of wealth in this later America and looked askance perhaps at the huge concentrations of private financial and industrial power within the democratic state, capitalism had begun to reform itself from within. Above all, despite setbacks, America's wealth refused to stop growing.

3. WAR AGAIN

On April 2, 1917, President Wilson read his war message to Congress, and four days later the legislature passed its joint resolution declaring war on the German Empire. The fate of Progressivism was sealed, and the reform movement that was transforming the United States economy was terminated, not to be revived until 1933. For after the war came a decade of unprecedented prosperity, a deep conservative reaction, and ossification in domestic policy. Yet the 1920's were the first true years of "consumer capitalism," and were sufficiently different to justify using the war's end as a stopping place in this history.

Even though the United States was involved in World War I for a mere nineteen months, her economy was seriously affected by the conflict from the moment of its outbreak in Europe in 1914. Heavy demands by belligerent nations for American supplies and equipment sent up United States export figures for munitions, iron and steel, copper and brass goods, raw materials, foodstuffs, motor vehicles, and animals for transport. Once these orders began to come through, the depression of 1914 was quickly dispelled. In 1916 United States total exports were almost $5,500 million and exceeded imports by well over $3,000 million. In 1917 total exports reached well over $6,200 million, exceeding total imports by over $3,280 million. The result of war demand was to expand the volume of American foreign commerce and create an extremely favorable trade balance.

All was not well, however, for the Allies were running short of cash. Gold poured into the United States from Europe during 1915 and 1916; the British government and its American fiscal agent, J. P. Morgan and Co., could not maintain sterling exchange, and the rate fell. The result, after much congressional debate and disagreement, was the extension of United States loans to the Allied governments, which by 1917 amounted to almost $2,000 million. This financial help made a huge breach in the policy of strict neutrality laid down by Wilson in 1914. It became increasingly clear that it was impossible to uphold neutral trading rights in such a war, and American opinion moved gradually in favor of the Western Allies. An alteration of feeling was undoubtedly stimulated to some degree by economic interest: the war boom of 1916 was based on trade with the Allies financed by credit extended to them, the British blockade having prevented Germany from effective participation in such trade. A German victory would simply wipe out Allied debts to United States creditors.

American industrial and commercial organization had not been in any way readapted to meet the needs of this new European demand, and one of the first aims of the Wilson government after declaring war was to impose some plan on the chaotic struggle of private enterprise to fulfill its obligations. But even before America entered the war, certain changes had been made. First, the European demand for war materials had caused a partial industrial turnover to wartime production; second, the federal government had taken steps to improve national defense, which included a Council of National Defense, consisting of the Secretaries of War, Navy, Agriculture, Commerce, Interior and Labor, its main function being to coordinate economic resources for national security and welfare and to create the conditions necessary for rapid economic mobilization at any moment. An additional advisory body of seven unpaid experts was chosen by the President to provide the Council with information. The "experts" included the president of the Baltimore and Ohio Railroad; a successful Wall Street man, Bernard Baruch; a prominent surgeon; the president of Sears, Roebuck and Company; and Samuel Gompers. The Council proved to be the parent body of·most of the innumerable control agencies established after official American hostilities opened.

National crisis always emphasizes the necessity of collective action. Twentieth century war, being the supreme crisis, produces a universal need for government regulation of private economic and political activities. But no single or decisive line of action was taken by the American government during World War I; the question remained undecided whether key industries should be taken over wholesale or whether private producers should be persuaded or cajoled to adopt their activities to the needs of the nation.

A series of empirical compromises followed, and a mass of controlling and advising agencies were set up, transforming the mighty economy into a more or less regulated war machine—just as in the 1930's a similar mass of agencies managed somehow to fabricate a more or less national effort to beat the depression.

The alphabetical agencies

Of all the agencies the most important—and the nearest approach to a central coordinating body—was the War Industries Board. Set up by the Council of National Defense after the dismal failure of the short-lived "General Munitions Board," it was to coordinate military estimates. Because it lacked any executive authority, the WIB made little headway at first, and plans were even advanced to replace it with a "Munitions Department" similar to Lloyd George's Ministry of Munitions in the United Kingdom. However, Wilson did not accept the idea. Instead he reorganized the WIB, made it independent of the Council of National Defense, gave it executive commission to coordinate the national industrial, agricultural, and financial effort, and placed the energetic Bernard Baruch in charge (March 4, 1918). In a short time Baruch became a kind of economic supreme commander, and the board itself an economic general staff. "War Service Committees" were set up for each industry, somewhat similar to the "Code Authorities" under the New Deal, to act as liaison bodies between the WIB and producers. The board's four principal means of control were: issuing "priority" orders (following the British example) to ensure the production and distribution of essential commodities; enforcing conservation and standardization in industry; price fixing; and commandeering. Baruch never in fact used the last method, although it was always useful as a threat to recalcitrant producers who refused to keep prices down to reasonable limits. As it was, the WIB proved to be successful in its industrial expansion policy, but failed in its price-fixing policy to prevent inflation or the amassing of large, easy profits by many industrialists.

The Fuel Administration (set up under the Food and Fuel Control Act of August, 1917) had as its foremost problem the unusual and severe shortage of bituminous coal, caused partly by its universal wartime demand, by traffic congestion, by an increase in normal domestic consumption during the harsh winter of 1917–1918, and by labor shortage in the mines arising out of poor working conditions and the call of military service. By rationing luxury users, breweries, less important industries, and the like, and by mediating in labor disputes and exempting miners from the draft, the Fuel Administration succeeded in increasing overall coal production and productivity per manhour underground. Average production per miner underground in 1914 was 833 tons a year; by 1918 it had reached 1,151 tons. There was always a coal shortage, however, until the war came to an end.

The Shipping Board was established in September, 1916, and its subsidiary, the Emergency Fleet Corporation, in April, 1917. These two bodies came in for heavy criticism for procrastination and delay, but they did enable the government to take over all private shipping, and to seize enemy and commandeer or purchase neutral vessels. Internal transportation was controlled by the federal government through the Railroad Adminstration, which took over all rail and inland water transport facilities from January 1, 1918. Several schemes, including the "Railroads' War Board" voluntarily established by the companies themselves, had already failed. The Railroad Administration was on the whole, and for the purpose it served, a success. W. G. McAdoo (the Secretary of the Treasury) was put in charge, and an act of March, 1918, guaranteed to each company a fixed return based on the average earnings of the three years 1914–1917—years of high profits. Although a heavy deficit arose during the two years of government operation (mainly owing to a much slower rise in freight rates than in costs and wages), large additions were made to plant and a degree of "rationalization" took place that would not have been otherwise possible. Facilities were interchanged, wasteful crosshauls were excluded, needlessly competitive lines withdrawn from service, equipment standardized, and accounting coordinated.

The Food Administration was created in August, 1917, only after

bitter debate in Congress in which representatives of the farmers and
the immense food-processing and distribution industries took a major
part. These groups were thriving as a result of the huge expanded
demand and the doubling of American food exports and agricultural
prices. The Food Administration (under Herbert Hoover) did not
establish retail rationing or price control; it tried instead to eliminate
speculation in the wholesale markets, regulate wholesale prices, and
hasten the flow of distribution. The Food and Fuel Control Act of
1917 made it illegal to hoard, waste, or charge excessive prices for
essential foodstuffs, but the administration relied mainly on propaganda and persuasion rather than on compulsion. "Hooverizing"—
being economical in the use of food in the home—became a patriotic
byword. For wheat and sugar, however, it was thought necessary to
create two special bodies: the Grain Corporation, organized with a
capital of $150 million, abolished competitive purchase by buying
grain from the producers (at a minimum guaranteed price) and allo-
cating it to all mills according to the average "grind" of each for the
three prewar years; the Sugar Equalization Board similarly bought
raw sugar from the producers—in the United States, Cuba, and
Hawaii—paying varying prices according to local conditions, but
selling it all at one price to American refiners, whose profit margin
was regulated.

Labor in wartime

So much for industry, fuel, transportation, and food; but what
of manpower in wartime, on both the military and domestic fronts?
On the military front the main federal measure was the Selective
Service Act (May 18, 1917) which demanded that all men between
twenty-one and thirty should register. About 10 million men were
rapidly registered, of which nearly 3 million were taken immediately.
Deferments were allowed generously in such employments as essential war industries and agriculture; unemployed able-bodied men
were given a choice, under the "work or fight" order of May, 1918,
between national service or essential labor. Altogether about 16 percent of the American male labor force was diverted into the armed
services. On the domestic front this, together with the cutting short
of immigration, exacerbated an already difficult labor problem. After
a year of confusion and labor wastage characterized by a high turn-

over, the government at last recognized the need for national standardization of wages and working conditions as far as possible. The
National War Labor Board was established on April 8, 1918, consisting of five labor and five employer representatives, and two joint
chairmen—former President W. H. Taft and a prominent liberal,
Frank P. Walsh. The board worked. Its arbitration decisions on disputes were widely accepted. In addition a War Labor Policies Board
dealt in more detail with questions of labor mobilization, and a
Housing Corporation had begun building workers' homes when the
war ended.

Labor was eagerly sought during the war; there was an out-
growth of labor-relations councils and productivity boards, and trade
unions flourished, the AFL increasing its membership from 2 million
to over 4 million between 1915 and 1920. This state of affairs soon
altered in the 1920's, but not all the advances made by labor in the
war were lost in the peace. The eight-hour day, for instance, became
more or less general once the pressure of wartime production was
eased, and the notion of a half-day on Saturday began to spread very
gradually. As far as real income is concerned, advances were very
uneven, and the skilled and salaried groups or those workers in
nonwar occupations found that their spasmodic wage increases were
inadequate to meet the rising living costs, especially during the inflation of the immediate postwar years. Professional people and those
on fixed incomes found it increasingly difficult to make ends meet
during the war.

Financing war

Meanwhile, the federal government had its own financial problems. After 1917 it took over the financial task of waging the war, at
a total cost to the nation (April, 1917, to July, 1919), excluding normal estimated peacetime expenditures, of about $32,700 million—
according to Professor E. R. A. Seligman.[23] This figure should be
compared with that for other wars: the Civil War (though it lasted,
from the American viewpoint, twice as long) cost the government but
an eighth or a ninth of the World War I total; the Second World War,
on the other hand, cost eleven or twelve times as much (well over
$360,000 million).

About 31 percent of the total cost of the First World War was raised by taxation, the rest by loans. The Secretary of the Treasury, McAdoo, believed that taxation was the best means of war financing from the economic viewpoint because it cut down consumer purchasing power, and would help to keep prices down. At first he hoped to derive at least 50 percent of wartime needs from taxes, but deep antipathy to the idea existed in the country and prevented it. Taxation was a slow and lengthy process that did not provide immediate revenue. From the start the Treasury had to fall back on borrowing. Currency inflation (the issue of paper money), as adopted in the Civil War, was not envisaged at all in World War I.

In an attempt to aid businessmen and farmers, Congress established the War Finance Corporation on April 5, 1918. It was given a capital stock of $500 million, all subscribed by the government, and was empowered to make advances of credit to banks, trust companies, building and loan associations, and indeed to any concern or individual engaged in essential war work. Farmers were assisted through the Federal Farm Land Banks set up by the Act of 1916. The War Finance Corporation was assisted by a Capital Issues Committee, the function of which was to prevent diversion of credit into unwanted channels.

Government borrowing took two principal forms: first, the sale of short-term notes or certificates to banks at frequent intervals; second, the sale of long-term "Liberty Bonds" in biannual, organized popular "drives," not unlike the Jay Cooke campaigns of the Civil War. The four Liberty Loans yielded $17,000 million, and an additional "Victory Loan" (March, 1919) a further $4,500 million—a startling revelation of the wealth reserves at America's disposal.

This type of borrowing resulted in credit inflation, which revealed itself in rising prices. The Bureau of Labor Statistics index number of wholesale prices (July 1914 = 100) showed a marked rise from 106 in December, 1915, to 187 in July, 1917. Government price controls then began to operate and cut down the rate of increase, so that by November, 1918 (the war's end), the index stood at 206. Even with the control policy, wholesale prices were more than twice as high at the end of hostilities as in 1914. (This inflation must be taken into account when any comparison of prewar and postwar conditions or any evaluation of gains and losses is being attempted.)

Business and war

Business corporations—and especially their leaders—gained most from World War I. Business acquisitions revealed themselves partly in the payment of increased dividends to investors but also (perhaps chiefly) in the building up of huge "undistributed" surpluses. Many devices were adopted to evade taxation, and the "official" figures given by firms themselves are not always a sound guide. These surpluses did enable companies to continue paying out dividends to investors during the later depression, when other sections of the community were not so fortunate.

The most significant industrial gain was the large expansion of physical plant and equipment brought about by the war. Together with the stimulus given to the movement for standardization and interchangeability of parts, this physical expansion led to a total increase in America's productive capacity. On the other hand, growth was uneven, and while the automobile industry quadrupled, the rubber industry trebled, the canned milk industry more than doubled, and the iron and steel, meat-packing, and petroleum industries heavily increased their respective outputs, there was a severe contraction of house construction and (once the war was over) an equally drastic reduction on the artificially boosted war industries —especially shipbuilding and aircraft production.

Agriculture also had considerable gains during the war. Total farm output did not increase in any startling way, but it was maintained while prices for farm goods rose rapidly. For instance, the prices of raw agricultural products were 106 percent higher in 1918 than in 1913. Even marginal farms prospered in a period when the real income of farmers increased 29 percent (1915–1918). Farm laborers were not so lucky, their real income rising by only 2 percent in the same years. In agriculture as in industry expansion was very uneven. The cutting off of the British market dealt a solid blow to southern cotton, for instance. Moreover, the farmers' gain in real income was often invested in further land acquisition rather than used to raise current farm living standards, and these investments were tragically swallowed up in the depression years.

World war and United States economic growth

Did the First World War help or hinder the growth of America's wealth? Looking back to the economic theories we considered in the case of the Civil War, and making comparisons, two "advantages" of World War I stand out. First, it did not involve physical destruction of economic potential at home. Second, it enhanced America's international competitive position by depressing that of other nations, noticeably Britain.

Nevertheless it can be argued that the First World War did create imbalances by overencouraging agriculture, shipbuilding, and uneconomical war industries at a high cost to the American people; that it brought inflation and disrupted the normal rate of population growth; that it wasted physical and human resources in pure destruction. And the main cost of the war was not directly economic or financial.

War psychosis left the nation with a hangover—isolationism, bigotry, and lack of faith—that persisted for ten or more years. This was the ultimate "social cost," and though intangible it could sometimes be measured in very concrete terms—for instance, the continuing loss to the population caused by deliberate exclusion of immigrants after the war (the quota system).[24] Postwar economic policies also served to make matters worse rather than better abroad, and certainly helped to bring about the insane economic conditions in central Europe that bred fascism. But this is part of the story of the twenties.

4 CONSUMER CAPITALISM
since 1920

NINE

The American Market Since 1920

The First World War was a true "turning point" in the history of American economic life. Abroad, it marked United States emergence as a dominant force in the world economy. Postwar America now performed radically different international economic functions. At home the economy boomed into a "New Era," a consumer-oriented, expansionist decade of ballyhoo and advertising, which shared some characteristics of pre-1917 booms but was different in essence. The age of "industrial capitalism" had faced a central economic challenge, production: how to make enough of life's essentials to go around. The new age, one that is called here "consumer capitalism," had to face a new challenge: how to maintain aggregate demand.

The economy of 1920 was "mature." It had solved the production problems of mere survival. Small wonder that Herbert Hoover sincerely felt in the summer of 1928, "We in America today are nearer to the final triumph over poverty than ever before in the history of any land." These brave words were substantially correct; but few Americans grasped the extent of the change which had overtaken the United States economy, and Hoover was not one of them. The trouble was that 1928 was followed, in due course of time, by 1929. In that year the official "Committee on Recent Economic Changes" groped toward reality: ". . . . it is not sufficient to be able to produce abundantly; we must also be able to distribute intelligently."

1. THE TWENTIES

Climate of the "Jazz Age"

The decade 1919–1929 has a unity and a character all its own in American history. It was an age of prosperity and disillusionment, of jingoism and isolationism, of fundamentalism in popular religion and open corruption in democratic politics, of gangsterism and apathy, of good writing and bigoted thinking, of prohibition and heavy drinking, of "rugged individualism" and mass entertainment. Suffering a severe hangover from World War I, the nation delivered itself up to a wave of intolerance, hatred, and guilt. A witch-hunting hysteria broke out, textbooks were censored, aliens deported, pacifists denied citizenship, and radical movements (even socialism) outlawed by state governments. The virulent phase of this strange disease did not last much beyond 1920, but bigotry continued. In Georgia the Ku Klux Klan had been established in 1915; in Tennessee the fundamentalist William Jennings Bryan defended that state's right to prohibit the teaching of evolution within its sacred borders (Scopes "Monkey" Trial, 1925); in the Commonwealth of Massachusetts two Italian "philosophical anarchists"—Sacco and Vanzetti— were put on trial allegedly for murder but really for their opinions, for seven long years (1920–1927), and finally executed. After the war two measures were taken that set a deadening tone for the whole decade: prohibition and immigration restriction.

Yet there is another side to the 1920's, a more positive social aspect, for the consumer economy of the New Era with its previously unheard-of purchasing power was something new in history. And so much that is regarded as typical of American society today either was born or came to flower in the 1920's: consumer durables; radio and the movies; the spread of psychology (the "Freudian revolution"); jazz music and modern dance; the welcome decline of "Victorian" stuffiness and the relaxation of school and family discipline; "suburbia"; greater freedom for women.[1] An economic historian might be forgiven the temptation to see some vital connection between increased material well-being and the emergence of a social order marked by greater generosity of spirit and magnanimity in personal relationships.

Prohibition: gangster economics

Prohibition was enforced, insofar as this was possible, under the Eighteenth Amendment (ratified January, 1919), which forbade the "manufacture, sale or transportation of intoxicating liquors." The Volstead Act of the same year created a Prohibition Commission within the Bureau of Internal Revenue, and defined as "intoxicating" any beverage containing over half of 1 percent of alcohol—a great triumph for pressure groups like the Anti-Saloon League, which had been agitating since 1895. The results of this futile attempt to legislate other people's morals are well known: the inadequacies of enforcement agencies and their almost inevitable corruption; the rise of the "speakeasy," home-brewing and the "cocktail";[2] the probable increase in drinking because it became fashionable; above all, the support the illicit liquor traffic gave to mobsters. To this last result we might apply an "economic analysis" using Adam Smith's familiar thesis that specialization depends upon the extent of the market.

First, being a federal matter, prohibition created overnight a vast continental marketing area for "hooch"—with an absolutely assured demand. Second, the "primary" producers engaged in the manufacture and distribution of liquor achieved a good measure of both vertical and horizontal integration, and of necessity had to take over the "service industries" (extortion, blackmail, and murder) without which they could not for long continue. In the supporting industries two important technical innovations were put to use: the automobile ("get-away car," sometimes armored) and the machine gun (war surplus?). Competition was tough, but various forms of merger were possible to control price and output.

All this division of labor and training in special skills was made possible only by the power of the market, power that was illustrated when prohibition came to an end in 1933 (Twenty-first Amendment).

Federally organized crime was badly in need of some new market large enough to justify and sustain the "syndicate" structures already in existence; this has been one explanation of why they turned to certain sectors of the trucking industry and to certain labor unions. Prohibition made it possible for crime to become "institutionalized"; by the 1930's it was a going industry with heavy overheads and a momentum of its own.

Closing the "golden door": the quota system

Many large brewers, naturally, were families of German origin, and the ratification of the prohibition amendment was helped by a boost from anti-German feelings in the populace at large. This is not so shocking; one cannot be taught to hate "the enemy" one day and love him the next. (In Britain it was thought unpatriotic to play Beethoven!) But the transient anti-German sentiment was only a small part of the problem of ethnic and group relations in the United States. Never before had such a wide variety of peoples tried to live, work, and play in close proximity and to build one culture. Religious and ethnic hostilities built up over centuries of European (and Oriental) history had, somehow or other, to be resolved and working relationships discovered. This "great experiment," unlike the United States political and economic experiments, was unconscious and unplanned: the nation more or less drifted into it (though ironically it may prove to be the greatest experiment of all).

A clear sense of the purpose of America's history was to be found in the words of the New York City poet Emma Lazarus, inscribed in 1886 on the pedestal of the Statue of Liberty, that famous French gift to the United States people which stands on Bedloe's Island in the city harbor:

> Give me your tired, your poor,
> Your huddled masses yearning to breathe free,
> The wretched refuse of your teeming shore,
> Send these, the homeless, tempest-tost to me:
> I lift my lamp beside the golden door!

However, in the 1920's the words "wretched refuse" were given by some Americans an interpretation never intended by their author, and Congress voted to slam the golden door.

Much of the animosity against immigrants came from native workers who had seen how employers were prepared to use the newcomers to undercut wages and break strikes. Magyars were imported by the railroad corporations for this purpose in 1877; Poles and Slovaks helped to break a large coopers' strike at a New Jersey oil plant; Slav labor was deliberately introduced to Pennsylvania coal fields during a stoppage. Economic fears combined sometimes with racial antipathy, bursting the surface of society on tragic occasions like the Los Angeles race riots of 1871. Feeling was especially strong against Chinese labor (brought in to build the Central Pacific) on the Pacific coast and in 1877 an Irish drayman, Dennis Kearney, organized an anti-Chinese political party, the Workingmen's Trade and Labor Union. His movement gained the support of some employers too, after several enterprising Chinese had themselves become successful employers. Congress was brought to the point of enacting a Chinese Exclusion Act in 1879, but President Hayes vetoed it as contrary to the United States-Chinese Burlingame Treaty (1868) which guaranteed unrestricted Chinese immigration. The government of China appeared somewhat indifferent to the fate of its citizens in the United States, and agreed to draw up a new treaty in 1880. As a result the Chinese Exclusion Act of 1882 prohibited the entry of Chinese workers for ten years. Renewed several times, the act became permanent in 1902. Not until the year 1943 were people of Chinese origin allowed to migrate to the United States; they were then permitted an annual quota of 105.

With the new century a similar fate befell would-be immigrants from Japan, though by means of so-called "Gentleman's Agreements" (1900, 1907) between the two powers rather than by act of Congress. Finally, after attempts in California to use segregated schools (1906) and deny legal rights of landownership to Japanese (1913, 1920), the Act of 1924 officially excluded them as "ineligible aliens" who could never become United States citizens. In Tokyo the Japanese staged a national "Humiliation Day," and anti-American mass meetings. This remained the unhappy situation until 1952 when the otherwise restrictive McCarran-Walter Act abolished the veto on Asian and Pacific immigration.

For many years the exclusionists experimented with techniques for controlling not only Oriental but all immigration. One such means was thought to be the literacy test, which it was hoped would act in favor of the more "advanced" and racially "acceptable" people of northern and western Europe. The act did not seem to work in this way, and in any case the coming of peace in Europe the following year brought great fear of a fresh wave of migrants. A new and more effective device was found in the quota system, first used in the emergency act of 1921.

The quota act of 1921 fixed the maximum number of immigrants to be admitted through the "golden door" in any one year (357,000) and this total number was broken down into "quotas" for each permissible nationality. A nation's quota was to be no more than 3 percent of the number of its people living in the United States according to the Census of 1910. A second quota act of 1924 *halved* the total figure and cut the national quotas to 2 percent of the Census of 1890—when there were far fewer people from southern and eastern Europe living in the United States. (Canada and Latin America were excepted from this system.) By 1924 "selective immigration" had received its full sanction, and one of America's oldest and most significant historical traditions had been abruptly overturned.[3]

Business as usual

The double victory of the prohibitionists and the immigration restrictionists struck a negative note that echoed throughout the twenties, and in the field of business the laissez-faire doctrine revived, phoenix-like, complete with the old Social Darwinism. Herbert Hoover's essay of 1922, *American Individualism,* despite its polite bow to social conscience, is the best illustration of this resurgence. The decade shares some other characteristics of the Gilded Age too. Its politics were often corrupt (the "Teapot Dome" fraud in the naval oil reserves of Wyoming in 1924, for example); its Presidents—especially Harding and Coolidge—were weak, mediocre, or lazy; its business conduct was not good; and its Congress truckled to the corporations at the expense of other sections of the community. Taxes were low and tariffs high. After all, in the words of that Vermont Yankee "Silent Cal" Coolidge: "The man who builds a factory builds a temple. . . . The man who works there worships there."

No time was lost in sweeping away wartime controls and institutions. In 1920 railroads were given back, and accumulated merchant shipping tonnage sold back on easy terms to private ownership (the Transportation Act and the Jones Merchant Marine Act). War contracts were canceled and the "alphabetical" agencies of control were immediately abandoned. Meanwhile the changed international position of the United States economy—its new creditor status and large export surplus—created bitter problems in the world at large.

Balance of payments: the tangled web

The question of war debts is an oft-told tale, easier to grasp if understood as a threefold problem involving Allied debts to the United States, inter-Allied debts, and German reparations. The federal government consistently refused to recognize the simple connection between the debts the Allies owed it and German reparations (which Washington did not itself demand of the Germans). It is true there was no legal relationship, but the *de facto* economic relationship was conspicuous.

At the war's end European private and governmental debts to the United States amounted to $12,600 million. The war had entirely disrupted existing fiscal and trade patterns and turned former creditor nations into debtors almost overnight. European nations wholly unused to debtor status lost income formerly derived from United States assets and all hope of increasing their net United States holdings. On the other hand they now had heavy liabilities, and the American government pressed them not only for current interest due but also for "amortization"—repayment of the original principal in regular installments. As United States industrial exports increased and Europe continued to demand cotton, grain, and tobacco, America's trade balance was always favorable. In fact the balance improved from $375 million (1923) to over $1 billion (1928).

Europe had a large gap in its balance of payments, and insufficient dollars even for its current needs from the United States. How was the gap to be filled? Three possible ways were: a drastic, perhaps tragic, cut in Europe's import of American products; a heavy United States import of European goods; international gold movements. The first might have produced starvation in Europe and severe dislocation in American industry and agriculture as a result; the second method was highly improbable given the United States climate of opinion in the 1920's and the crippling protective tariff imposed (the Fordney-McCumber Act of 1922); the third would surely drain Europe's already falling gold supply, disable her economy, and perhaps force her completely off any gold standard. And of course the United States immigration quotas of 1921 and 1924 made matters worse by closing off the last avenues of escape from a stricken Europe. Great Britain, in a vain effort to save the situation, agitated for the complete cancellation of all war debts—although she had herself lent out twice as much to the Allies as she had borrowed from the United States. But Washington refused to accept the idea. "They hired the money, didn't they?" Coolidge rasped.

Soon the impact of dollar shortage in Europe was felt on American farming. Europe's purchasing power was abruptly reduced, bringing to an end the fortunate years for United States agriculture of high prices and high demand. As farm produce flooded Europe in the early 1920's prices came down 50 percent within two years. True to type, and unlike businessmen, the farmers would not curtail production. Organized in their relatively small, scattered units, each tried to increase output still further and eke out a living. This simply made the situation worse, and they suffered badly throughout America's prosperous 1920's when others were doing well. To a degree the standard of living of the American farmer was sacrificed and Europe was saved from starvation, for European consumption of United States foodstuffs was maintained.

How could this be, if all three possible methods of closing the trade gap were not effective? How could Europe buy anything at all from the United States? The answer was heavy American foreign investment. United States capital was exported, in various forms: by purchase of foreign government bonds, for instance, or through the establishment abroad of foreign branches of United States manufacturers—like Ford and Standard Oil. In consequence $3 or $4 billion flowed outward in the 1920's, dollars that made it possible for Europe to buy essential imports—and incidentally, dollars that kept up the large exports of the United States and stimulated American economic growth in the New Era.

This peculiar circular method of payments, however, was purely a stopgap, and a highly unstable and dangerous one. It meant that

Europe's very life and America's exports were dependent on the willingness of United States businessmen to make foreign loans. From the summer of 1928 this flow of loans did peter out, and international economic life was virtually becalmed.

Americans had begun to make heavy investments in Europe partly as a result of the acceptance of the Dawes Plan in 1924. This scheme, on the whole a success, was invented to meet the immense difficulties in the German reparations problem. Briefly, Germany could not pay heavy reparations to the European victors and at the same time cope with her vast domestic problem of inflation. The Dawes Plan gave a gold loan to Germany as a basis for a new currency, and was sensible enough to recognize her total inability to pay reparations except insofar as she had an economic surplus to pay with. There is no doubt that this notable attempt to tackle reparations helped to encourage the flow of United States investments.

Grossly simplified, the payments flow after 1924 was something like this: Germany paid reparations to France and the United Kingdom out of the inflow of (chiefly) American capital; France was thus enabled to meet her obligations in Britain; in turn Britain, out of its French and German receipts, could pay its debt charges to the United States. This circular system broke down, with serious results for Europe, once United States foreign investments terminated.

New Era: the buildup

At home, once the severe but brief recession of 1920–1921 was out of the way, an upsurge of economic expansion began to build up from which few Americans could be distracted by the depressing complexities of international finance. In the frothy, ebullient Jazz Age nothing was more jazzy than this unprecedented boom. What was its economic basis?

First, it was founded on an "extension of the market"—an impressive rise in consumer purchasing power. To some extent this rise was an extension of wartime prosperity. Total personal consumption expenditures almost doubled between 1914 and 1919, fell somewhat in the postwar recession to under $56 billion (1921), and then climbed steadily to a peak of nearly $81 billion (1929). Looked at from the other side, between 1921 and 1929 disposable income (in current prices) increased from $60 billion to $83 billion—a height not reached again until 1941 ($93 billion). GNP in the same period (at 1929 prices) rose from about $72 billion to about $104 billion, or a per capita improvement from $660 to $857.[4]

Second, the Jazz Age was built on the expansion of certain industries: a newer manufacturing group and an older construction group. The construction-industries indices (thought to be a good guide to the general health of a modern economy) reveal expansive conditions for the 1920's. Total private and public construction nearly doubled in value in 1921–1927, from a low of under $9 billion to a peak of almost $16 billion—again a height not regained until 1941. Though she had not suffered wartime destruction, the United States shared with Europe an acute housing shortage; house building was cut back heavily during the war. Pent-up demand and favorable, rising rents (to 1925) stimulated an enormous real-estate and housing boom that reached its climax in the years 1926–1928. Growth was financed by an expanding market for real-estate mortgage bonds and a flowering of building-and-loan associations. Cities were greatly extended, and within them apartment blocks and giant skyscraper offices multiplied. Outstanding urban mortgage debt trebled, while urban America took on its now characteristic skyline.

One effect of the real-estate boom was to accelerate the emergence of southern California, Florida, and other resort areas. In Florida where the boom attained epic proportions, countless square miles of mud and swamp were sold with ease. Dealers made huge fortunes persuading people they could afford to "invest in the future"—until the bubble finally burst (with the aid of two hurricanes) in 1926. Florida's real-estate collapse seems to have had little dampening influence elsewhere, and the construction boom continued for a couple of years or more. Highway building may have had something to do with this. Under the Rural Post Roads Act of Woodrow Wilson (1916), federal aid was given to individual state governments for road construction, and by 1929 federal and state expenditures together had approached almost $2 billion. Behind this highway program can be seen the diffusion of the automobile.

We have seen in an earlier chapter that the manufacture of

what came to be called "automobiles" was already a major industry by 1917. But the war and postwar years saw the greatest expansion in the industry. In 1917, 1¾ million passenger cars were sold; nearly 4½ million in 1929—when total vehicle registration exceeded 26½ million. The automobile industry of 1929 consumed 15 percent of the nation's steel output and had an insatiable appetite for gasoline, rubber, glass, lead, and nickel; it employed over 7 percent of the total American labor force, paid nearly 9 percent of total factory wages, and created nearly 13 percent of the total value of manufactured output. And this is all in addition to the industry's impact on highway construction and the growth of suburbia. In the year of the Great Crash there was already more than one automobile for every six Americans.

Almost as important a feature in the consumer market as the automobile industry were the electrical and radio groups. Industry generally was adopting electric power, and the public demand for electrical consumers' goods was large, increasing, and still mainly untapped. Household gadgets, electric irons, vacuum cleaners, washing machines, and refrigerators came onto the market. Total output of electrical household goods and supplies tripled in value, 1921–1929, reaching about $177 million. Five million radios were marketed in 1929 (in contrast with a mere 190,000 six years earlier). Station KDKA in East Pittsburgh began America's first daily commercial radio program in November, 1920, and by 1924 (when NBC initiated the first nationwide broadcasts) 500 or 600 stations were in commercial operation. Meanwhile, total electric power output more than doubled, rising from 53 billion kilowatt-hours to nearly 117 billion (1921–1929).

By the end of the period eleven holding companies had emerged, in control of 85 percent of the electrical industry's installed capacity. In a bitter struggle reminiscent of the days of Progressivism, the power companies fought the state-established "public utility commissions" and tried to reject all attempts at public regulation. Under the Water-Power Act (1920) a Federal Power Commission was established with fairly limited jurisdiction over hydroelectric plants in federal areas. Eight years later an act authorized the construction by the federal government of the Boulder Dam project on the Colorado River. The idea was to produce cheap electricity for regional development and also to establish a standard rate for consumer prices all over the nation. Hostility from the private power companies in this case was nothing compared to the flare-up over a similar project at Muscle Shoals, on the Tennessee River in Alabama. Senator George Norris twice sponsored bills to enable the federal government to use the Muscle Shoals power plant (which had been built during the war), but these were vetoed by Coolidge and Hoover, respectively, and its capacity lay unused until Franklin Roosevelt became President in 1933.

The booming construction, automobile, radio, and electrical industries were the most noticeable areas of industrial growth, but the Federal Reserve Board's index of general manufacturing production also shows an improvement from a 1921 low of 30 to a 1929 high of 58 (1947–1949 = 100). Increased productive efficiency was the keynote of the New Era, with a keen application of F. W. Taylor's scientific-management techniques. Efforts to "put science into industry" brought forth concrete results in better productivity per manhour. The index of manufacturing output per manhour rose from 44.6 to 74.3 in the decade 1920–1930 (1947 = 100). High labor productivity, mass production, and mass distribution were the outstanding traits of the Jazz Age economy.

Spots on the sun

Ramsay Muir, the astute British Liberal, described the United States of 1926 as "a rapturous whirl of making and spending." Yet he was forced by the weight of evidence to declare, "Even the prosperity of America is not without shadows." Even the sun has spots.[5] The spots for Muir were agriculture, the coal industry, and "the decline of New England." Later analysis accepts these three but adds to the list.

To begin with, the New Era was weakest at the point of its most conspicuous achievement—mass consumption. Millions of automobiles and radios could not have been marketed, despite the growth of consumer income, without a large-scale recourse to consumer credit sales. Installment buying (what is called in Britain "hire-purchase," or more colorfully, the "never-never") became so popular that by 1929 outstanding installment debt totaled more than 3 billion dollars. This was the highest point until 1936, and about two-fifths of the total was automobile paper. The demand for consumer durables is fairly elastic: in times of austerity one can forget about a new automobile or refrigerator very easily. Such an elastic demand, sustained by heavy credit financing and stimulated by large advertising expenditures (which in 1929 totaled 3,426 million), was hardly a stable pivot on which to balance a nation's welfare. Even if the credit pyramid did not collapse or consumer demand did not unaccountably falter, the durable-goods industries were much more risky than those that produced perishable staple commodities essential to everyday life with constantly renewing demand. Advertisers tried to get around this obstacle by encouraging the speedy casting off and replacement of consumer "durables" and by forever introducing real or feigned "latest improvements." Rapid obsolescence, whether deliberately "built in" or not, was unable to stave off the demand failure and so-called "overproduction" of later years.

A second flaw in the economic structure of the twenties was the persistence of certain industrial trouble spots among which were the old-line Victorian industries: the railroads, shipbuilding, coal, textiles, flour milling, leather, and lumber. The trouble in part was one of adjustment to changed competitive conditions and new consumer demand. Coal mining and railroads for example both suffered from a heavy and complex cost structure, a pressing need to modernize plant and equipment, and tough competition from newcomers—oil, gas, and electricity or the automobile, truck, and airplane. Textile manufacturers faced the competition of man-made cellulose fibers. A. D. Little patented an American rayon in 1902 (the first rayon patent of 1884 having been taken out in France); the earliest commercial production of artificial fabric in the United States came eight or nine years later, and after 1920 rayons threatened to cut into popular demand for traditional woolens and cottons. Meanwhile, the migration of the textile industry to the southern states (for their cheap labor, long hours, and lax industrial regulations) was both a cause and symptom of New England's decline.[6]

Chronic or "secular" unemployment was one outcome of the rapid but highly uneven economic growth of the 1920's that advanced some industries while it left others standing. Overall employment percentages compared favorably with previous and later

history—the 11.9 percent out of work as a result of the 1921 recession falling as low as 1.9 percent at the height of prosperity (1926).
Average unemployment was under 5 percent of the civilian labor
force, 1920–1929, compared with over 18 percent for the years 1930–
1939. Other industrial economies like Britain (average unemployment throughout both decades, 1921–1938, at over 14 percent) and
Germany (almost 18 percent, 1923–1932) let their workers down
very badly and for a longer time. As in the years before 1860 or
1920, however, such comparisons were little comfort to those Americans perennially out of work in the stagnant sectors of the economy,
and their poverty was all the more acute in a society that was
booming.

A farmer's life

Farmers were in the same predicament, and agriculture was
probably the major "black spot" on the whole economy. Responding
to the needs of war and the stimulus of rising prices, American
farmers had increased output, taken out loans and mortgages for
improvements, and generally allowed themselves to expand. When
the war ended they were left high and dry. Without World War I,
however, the situation in the 1920's would still have been tricky.
In any event farm output was increasing in excess of effective demand, and even with a declining farm population[7] a food surplus
was still produced.

How was this achievement possible? Mainly through four factors:
the increased productivity made available by the reclamation and
irrigation reforms of the earlier years of the century; the spread of
"dry farming" techniques on semiarid lands, especially in the central
High Plains; sensible modifications of the Homestead Act of 1862 to
rid it of those defects that arose from its eastern authorship and its
ignorance of the need for much larger farm units in the West;[8] and
a continuing stream of technical innovations, of which the most
striking feature was the gasoline tractor. (By 1929, 827,000 tractors
were in use—four times as many as in 1920; their average price had
dropped to $1,000 each, and their general effect was to cut grain
prices and improve output.)

Productive mastery did not assure social reward to the farmer.

"Engel's Law" of the relative income inelasticity of demand for
foodstuffs (mentioned earlier) came into operation very force-
fully between the wars. Farmers still reacted to economic
fluctuations in the traditional manner, by striving to increase output
whether prices went up or down. In the 1920–1921 recession farm
prices fell to prewar levels but other prices did not; consequently,
the farmers' purchasing power remained reduced throughout the
decade. This gave rise to the demand for parity prices—for federal
action to guarantee the maintenance of farm prices on a par with a
standard based (usually) on the years 1909–1914. But prices did not
manage to reach prewar "parity" before 1929; their highest point
(June, 1928) was 93 percent of parity. Numerous farmer-owners
were forced into tenancy or driven off the land altogether, and great
numbers of farm bankruptcies were concluded, rising from 997 a
year in 1920 to a peak of almost 8,000 in 1925 (and not falling
below 1,000 a year until 1944). In many cases the banks that fore-
closed the mortgages had to go into farming themselves since they
could not find buyers for the land they had acquired. Though some
farmers turned to the production of luxury goods, not everyone (as
Professor Shannon dryly explains) could operate blueberry or skunk
farms. Demands for reform of all kinds soon arose, from tariff reductions to the greater use of agricultural cooperatives[9] and the
wider utilization of farm waste materials in industry. Corporation
and chain farming developed in an attempt to achieve economies of
large scale. A California orchard corporation worked over 60,000
acres; a British group bought 45,000 acres of Mississippi cotton
land; a Texas corporation established the largest rice plantation in
the world. By 1925 there were over 8,000 of these combines, owning
areas of up to 75,000 acres (at least in the wheat belt). Chain
farms (such as the 600 farms under supervised tenants operated by
the Aetna Life Insurance Company) were mainly the result of
mortgage foreclosure.

Since Populism had been wiped away by the rising tide of agricultural prosperity in the late 1890's, farmers had not been entirely
without organization. Of the various farmers' unions that had been
absorbed into the Alliances of the 1880's and thence into Populism,
the only one of any consequence that emerged intact was the
Grange. It grew steadily but unspectacularly after 1900, and by
1915 had about 540,000 members. On the other hand, groups very

similar to the early unions were revived on a fresh basis, including the Farmers' Union (established in Texas in 1902), the Farmers' Relief Association (organized in 1900 and merged with the Farmers' Union in 1906), and the American Society of Equity (founded in Illinois in 1902). There were several more or less unsuccessful attempts at national federation. During World War I a loosely federated Farmers' National War Council had existed in the capital. After the armistice the National Council continued to meet. Its postwar platform included nationalization of railroads, mercantile marine, grain elevators, and natural resources; reform of the meat-packing industry; a single tax on land values that would have brought joy to the heart of Henry George; an improved marketing system, and cheap farm credit. A more effectively organized rival body with very similar aims was the National Board of Farm Organizations, begun in 1917 principally under the auspices of the Farmers' Union. Like the National Council, it spent most of its time in lobbying, but it exceeded the council in influence. Four other groups representing farm interests in Washington were the Farm Bureau Federation, the Farm Bloc, the Nonpartisan League, and the Farmer-Labor party.

The Farm Bureau Federation was a wholly unintended off-shoot of the county organizations for local educational and demonstration programs under the Smith-Lever Agricultural Extension Act (1914). By 1918 these local bodies had formed themselves into several state federations to consider mutual problems on policy matters far transcending education. The movement was finally and officially launched in March, 1920, and by July of the following year its network covered forty-two states of the Union. Though it had a first-class national organization, its aims were middle-class and "reformist" and it had no particular appeal for the under-privileged or poorer class of farmers and farm laborers. After the war, for instance, it strongly supported the return of the railroads to private ownership, and in the 1920's the more radical agrarian organizations, such as the Farmers' Union, attacked the bureau for its friendliness to big business.

The Farm Bloc was an alliance between members of Congress representing farm states, organized in 1921 by Gray Silver, the Washington agent of the bureau. In many ways it became more radical than the bureau would have intended. Prominent members were Senators La Follette (Wisconsin), William Kenyon (Iowa), Arthur Capper (Kansas), and Ellison Smith (South Carolina). The bloc came to hold the balance of power in Congress and had considerable legislative success. For instance it forced through a group of measures in July and August, 1921, including two amendments to the Farm Loan Act, one to increase the capital of federal Land Banks and extend their credit facilities, the other to raise the interest on farm loan bonds to the investor without raising them to the borrower; an act subjecting packers and stockyards to regulations against monopoly and "unfair practices" (the Packers and Stockyards Act); an act revised later in 1922 and renamed the Grain Futures Act, to control speculation in grain markets; and, finally, an Emergency Credits Act to finance the export of agricultural surpluses through the revived War Finance Corporation. These minor congressional triumphs were of course totally inadequate to slow down the rate of agricultural decline.

A more direct attack was the McNary-Haugen scheme, presented to Congress as a bill five times (once each year, 1924–1928, inclusive), defeated twice in the House, shelved once, and passed twice in both House and Senate, only to be vetoed by President Coolidge. It went beyond the aims of the original members of the farm bloc by demanding a government export corporation for farm surpluses (not unlike the wartime Grain Corporation and Sugar Equalization Board in some respects) that would control marketing and virtually control prices. A year after the veto of the fifth McNary-Haugen bill, the new administration under President Hoover passed the Agricultural Marketing Act (June 15, 1929). This set up a Federal Farm Board financed by a revolving fund of $500 million, to extend credit to agricultural cooperatives and encourage "effective merchandising." The board was permitted to form "stabilization corporations" to control surpluses and uphold prices. It was too late for this plan to come to anything, however, and the structure it established was engulfed by the New Deal.

The Farmers' Nonpartisan Political League was founded in North Dakota in 1915 and spread into fifteen western states. In 1916 it gained control of the state government of North Dakota and began to execute a radical agricultural relief program: state-owned elevators and warehouses, a state bank, exemption from taxation of farm improvements, a hail-insurance fund, an industrial commission to organize state-owned and state-financed industries, and a Home Building Association to encourage home ownership by state loans to builders.[10] By 1922, however, the league had passed its zenith in North Dakota, and in that year it lost the gubernatorial campaign. Its decline was caused by administrative inexperience, scandals connected with the state bank, rumors of the league's pacifism during the war, and the opposition of eastern financial interests.

The Farmer-Labor party grew up partly out of the disfavored Nonpartisan League, but its main purpose was to unite farmers with industrial workers in a concerted agitation and program of reform— a very difficult task. The problem that taxed the imagination of Lenin and brought the moral collapse of his successor Stalin proved too onerous also for Parley P. Christensen, the Farmer-Labor party's luckless nominee for the Presidency in 1920. Christensen gained no electoral and a mere 265,000 popular votes. Nor did he prevent the separate nomination and campaigning of the able Eugene V. Debs (Socialist), or of W. W. Cox (Socialist-Labor) and R. C. Macauley (Single Tax). Two years later the party did elect one Minnesota candidate to the United States Senate. In the 1924 presidential campaign a loose alliance of Farmer-Labor men, AFL members, and Socialists supported La Follette on a Progressive ticket, and he won almost 5 million popular votes; but even in that election there was a separate Socialist-Labor candidate and a Workers' candidate.

For all their contribution to the growth of America's wealth, the farmer-reformers could win little political support from the wider community for radical measures in the age of consumer capitalism.

New Era: the falling-off

Hidden fissures in the economic structure were disclosed by a recession in 1927. American consumers checked their buying spree. Growth indices faltered, and the wholesale price index (Bureau of Labor Statistics) fell 4.6 percent. Along with lower rates of consumption came actual salary and wage reductions in the construction industries, mining and commerce, and a leveling-off in factory output and wages. Automobile production fell 23 percent below the 1926 figure and the housing boom slackened, throwing building workers onto the labor market. Unemployment rose from 1.9 percent to 4.4 percent, 1926-1928.

The 1927 cutback did not become a major affair; it signified reduced rates of expansion rather than absolute declines. Long-term restraining influences were at work, however. Slowdown in automobile sales implied that the market was saturated at existing demand levels—levels that were restricted by growing income inequalities and lagging wage improvements. While tax reductions and a 62 percent increase in corporate profits (1923–1929) favored the wealthy, and while the worker's productivity per manhour increased by about 36 percent (1920–1929), wages were fairly stationary. The average annual wage stood at $1,424 in 1920, and after fluctuations of $100 or so had only reached $1,489 by 1929. In agriculture, mining, construction, and transportation the average wage of 1929 was *less* than that of 1920.[11] George Soule has summarized the situation very aptly by rephrasing Karl Marx: the poor were not getting poorer but the rich were getting richer.

Two further long-term restraints were a shrinking rate of net capital formation and of population growth. Although dividends, interest, and rent continued to grow at the same or better rates, net capital formation did not. According to the studies of Simon Kuznets, 12.6 percent of national income went into net capital formation in the years 1899–1908 but only 10.2 percent in the years 1919–1928. This 20 percent decline in the rate of growth was associated perhaps with the slowing down of the population increase. Like many Western nations, the United States suffered anxieties between the world wars because her population did not grow as quickly as before 1917. (We have noticed already that demographers in these days prophesied future stagnation, as those of today in a reverse position prophesy future mass starvation.) The immigration quota system cut in half the average inflow of persons per year, from something under 900,000 a year (1900–1914) to about 450,000 a year or less (1920–1929). But economists seem generally agreed that immigration restriction should not be exaggerated; it is likely that the European inflow would have declined in any case, and immigrant numbers were less significant than natural increase. The birth rate fell from 32.3 (live births per 1,000 population) in 1900 to 27.7 in 1920 and to a low of 18.4 (1933, 1936) before recovering in the 1940's (to a high of 26.6 in 1947).

When the final crash came in 1929 and was followed by years of depression and mass unemployment, these factors—demand in-

stability, income inequality, declining net capital formation, and
falling population growth—helped to stimulate new approaches to
economic policy. In Britain the scholarly John Maynard Keynes was
developing a theory that he was well aware (as a letter to Bernard
Shaw reveals) would "revolutionize" economics. After twenty years
of unemployment in leading European nations, Keynes had come to
believe that secular stagnation had set in for the mature industrial
economies. Declining marginal efficiency of capital and falling population growth induce people to save instead of to invest. Aggregate
spending is thereby reduced, contracting the effective demand on
which economic prosperity is based. Hence unemployment and
decay. In the 1930's Keynes recommended vigorous government
steps to stimulate new investment, if need be through deliberate
public expenditures and deficit financing. Keynes became fairly
well known on both sides of the Atlantic during the 1920's (though
his two-volume *Treatise on Money* was not published until 1930).
The New Era generation paid little attention to his statements or to
those by alerted native economists; the growth indicators of 1928
picked up and America surged forward full tilt toward the Great
Crash.

2. THE THIRTIES

The decade of the 1930's opened in economic chaos and closed in
total war. Its character, at least in United States history, is handed
down in marked contrast to that which preceded it: earnest where
the twenties were giddy; reformist and didactic where they were
passive and shiftless; becalmed in economic depression where they
were driven headlong before the trade winds of prosperity; but
purposefully governed where the twenties lacked a moral and
political focus. The challenge to which Franklin D. Roosevelt's
leadership was the response must concern us first.

Crash!

On December 4, 1928, in his annual message to Congress, President Coolidge announced:

No Congress of the United States ever assembled, on surveying the state of the Union, has met with a more pleasing prospect than that which appears at the present time. . . .

Ten months later the worst financial crash in history hit the New York Stock Exchange and brought untold ruin and tragedy to thousands of Americans. Ten long years of depression ensued, which were brought to an end only by renewed global war. The panic of October, 1929, started a deflationary price spiral, and downward pressure was intensified by the heavy weight of farm and consumer debt, by a deflationary national wages policy (after 1930), by falling prices for primary products, and by many bank failures (owing to farm bankruptcies and to the sharp drop in inflated real-estate values). Bank failures—apart from the local tragedies they caused in those days before the existence of Federal Deposit Insurance— discouraged investment, consumed money and stimulated currency hoarding. These were the very factors, it will be noticed, that occupied the thoughts of the brilliant Bursar of King's (the future Lord Keynes) in his college rooms at Cambridge.

Through the boom years stock-exchange speculation grew heavier and more complicated. Familiarized to some extent with the techniques of investment and the vocabulary of exchange operations by the federal government's Liberty Bond campaigns, more Americans after the war thought in terms of stocks and bonds—though fewer members of the general public bought securities than was sometimes claimed. Securities sold with little difficulty, and the Federal Reserve Board followed a relaxed credit policy. J. K. Galbraith in *The Great Crash* has denied the long-held belief that credit was exceptionally easy (or that even if it were, this alone could induce runaway speculation). Savings were more important: since the marginal value of savings decline as they build up, speculation happens when savings are in excess of other outlets. This apparently happened in the late twenties. Business could make enough profit to finance itself by "plow-back" and did not need to go to the banks for loans to extend plant or expand facilities. Meanwhile, banking services were extended and modernized; "chain" and branch banking consolidations appeared. Even the large outflow of capital funds that had found investment opportunities abroad still left idle bank resources at home. A major charge against bankers has been that they used these excess funds not only for real-estate loans but to make large collateral loans for the speculative purchase of securities. For instance, in the three years 1925–1927 security loans of Federal Reserve member Banks increased 40 percent, investments 20 percent, and commercial loans only 12 percent. Bank resources were used to help finance speculation for its own sake. In normal times business corporations make new issues of stock (or refund old issues) because they need to acquire fresh capital for physical expansion. In the pre–New Deal bull market of the 1920's new securities were issued not because business needed extra capital for real investment but simply because such securities could be sold at a good profit rake-off. New securities were "manufactured" to be sold through nationwide advertising schemes. The system was upside-down. A speculative mania took shape—a bull market that was "artificial" and highly unstable because it was based on hasty selling and reselling of stocks irrespective of their yield potentialities and with no reference to the real business activities they were supposed to represent.

"Investment trusts" took quick advantage of the fantastic market conditions. One house, Dillon, Read & Company, established a special trust in 1924—the United States and Foreign Securities Corporation—which eventually made $30 to $40 million on an original investment of $5 million. On the basis of these rich pickings the bank then created a new trust, the International Securities Corporation. Some such trusts had ramifications so intricate and delicate both legally and financially that their very promoters knew little of how they operated or how much they were worth. All of them helped eventually to saturate the market with an excess supply of securities above the effective demand of public investors, even given the attenuated margin requirements of those unregulated days. Before this happened, stock prices zoomed. The price index for all common stock (1941–1943 = 10) shot up from 7.98 (1920) to 26.02 (1929)—a three- or four-fold increase. Railroads doubled (20.86 to 46.15), industrials and utilities quadrupled (6.50 to 21.35; 13.36 to 59.33). Corporate security issues magnified more than three-fold in value (1920: $2,788 million—1929: $9,376 million). Five times as many shares were traded through the New York Stock Exchange, which handled 58 percent of the national total in 1929. A few streets away, the Curb Exchange managed a further 25 percent, thus concentrating 83 percent of all United States stock sales within the same district of New York City.[12]

Who owned all these shares? The belief was long held that much of the speculation was by a flood of small investors—the "common man." J. K. Galbraith's study reveals, however, that no more than 1½ million people had active business with the exchanges, and of those less than 600,000 were trading on margin. Stock ownership was not widespread under old-style capitalism. Allowing for a 1929 population total of just under 122 millions, one could say that it was a pronounced minority of Americans that engaged in frenzied speculation during the months preceding the October crash.

On September 3, 1929, stock prices reached their utmost height. Two days later came the first check: the so-called "Babson break," a panic price fall on the exchange in response to some dismal public crystal-gazing by a familiar market analyst, Roger Babson. A fair amount of selling continued into late September and October and the market was ragged, but generally depressed. Professor Irving Fisher, the accepted oracle of prosperity, announced on October 15th—a day that sustained a 5- or 6-point loss—that stock prices stood on "a permanently high plateau." The decline could not last, he believed, and was the result of ignorant panic by the "lunatic fringe" of small investors. (In justice one should mention that in Britain J. M. Keynes himself thought for a time that the slump might usefully liquidate unsound speculation.) "Black Thursday," October 24, 1929, was the rude awakening: almost 13 million shares were traded, prices dropped precipitously, and the New York Stock Exchange was flooded by selling orders with the ticker tape running hours behind. Leading bankers, themselves deeply involved, met together at the J. P. Morgan offices and revealed to an anxious world their agreement to support the market: a "buying pool" was established. This should put a stop to the wild rumors of suicides, failures, and economic collapse. At one-thirty the vice-president of the Exchange, Richard Whitney, walked across the floor to the United States Steel specialist's post and made a show of buying 10,000 shares at the previous selling price. Whitney then did the same for several other stocks (buying at the last price instead of at the going bids, which were lower). As a result of this new injection of confidence prices rallied for a while, and late into the night skyscraper offices hummed with activity as hundreds of clerks labored steadily to catch up with the paper work.

In these early stages there were few business failures. Business did not depend on bank credit, and indeed some firms saw their cash balances expand as they called in loans. But on Monday the downward trend renewed, bringing severe losses to leading corporations. The bankers met once more but took no further action, and Tuesday, October 29th, was the worst day in the history of Wall Street. Over 16 million shares were traded, and giants like American Telephone & Telegraph, General Electric, American Can, Westinghouse and United States Steel felt the pinch. Topheavy investment trusts like Goldman Sachs Trading Corporation saw their stock deteriorate to half or one-third its former value, and some stock could find no buyers whatsoever—a most unusual market condition. During the grim winter stock prices continued to sink. By 1930 the price index of all common stock had fallen from its apogee (previously noted) of 1929 down to 21.03; by 1932 the nadir was plumbed—6.93. Industrials were cut to one-quarter of the 1929 value, railroads to under one-fifth. Utilities reached the lowest ebb in 1935 at a fraction over one-quarter of their price before the holocaust.

Between 1929 and 1933 about 90,000 businesses failed. Gross national product (total United States production) was cut by one-third, from $104 billion to $74 billion (at 1929 prices). In per capita terms this meant that America's wealth amounted to $857 a head in 1929, but only $590 a head four years later. The income of farmers was more than halved; the income of labor generally fell by 30 percent or 40 percent. At least one-quarter of the labor force was destitute and without work in 1933, estimates varying from 13 to 15 million workers. From 1931 right down to 1940 mass unemployment fluctuated above 8 million a year (except for 1937—7,700,000), and in five of those years it exceeded 10 million. Small wonder that rising economists like Alvin Hansen shared Keynes's anxiety about "secular stagnation." The depression persisted for about ten years.

Does a financial crash cause a depression? The answer usually is No. Most stock-market panics seem to follow rather than to initiate downward trends in the wider economy; there have to be fundamental weaknesses in the economic structure for the panic to exploit. The New Era had such weaknesses—these we have examined. Yet would there have been such a severe and drawn-out depression if the stock market had not crashed or if the bankers' "buying pool" had been effective? It does seem likely that a less disastrous turn of events on Wall Street might have been followed by a shorter period of paralysis. After all, the recession of 1927 did not lead to an enormous depression, and "structural flaws" were as much present then as two years later. On common-sense grounds one could argue that the essential difference must be in the *severity* of the two recessions, 1927 and 1929. The "Great Crash" is so called because it was the most severe, precipitous, and total collapse the financial world had ever known.

Lease of life: the New Deal

Thirty years or so after the New Deal the attitude of Americans to FDR and to his achievements appears somewhat ambiguous. Outside certain narrow business circles (which have learned to accept TVA, the SEC, social security, and the rest but still insist that Roosevelt the man "set class against class"), and perhaps outside certain equally narrow academic circles (the tiny clique of self-styled "New Conservatives" who prefer Professor Friedrich von Hayek), the great majority of the American people seem no longer stirred by thoughts of the thirties. The latest generation of college students, nurtured in an environment of growth and prosperity, never knew those years. Meanwhile, their parents' memories have been dulled by time, confused by the upheaval of world war and rockets to the moon, appeased by the emollient of "high mass consumption" since 1945. Among their professors feelings of deep and immediate involvement are gone and differences of opinion about the New Deal are usually marginal; their acceptance remains firm but detached, critical, and cool—a mild, unemphatic consensus.[13]

So different is the post–New Deal, post–Hitler's War economy that students have to exercise real imaginative effort in order to believe in the existence of the Great Depression. Was this country truly the United States, in which a Cabinet member advocated as public policy that those thrown out of work by the economic system be kept alive on garbage collected from restaurants? Was it here that Chicago's citizens grubbed for scraps of rotten meat and vegetables on the city's waste dumps? Was it so recent in this land of self-reliance and opportunity that men queued hopelessly and abjectly for hours and days at employment offices or stalked the railroad tracks in desperation? . . . where the young women of Connecticut labored a 55-hour week for under one dollar? Was it in these same prosperous exurbs, suburbs, and flourishing cities from which come the healthy and lively students of today, that young people were too poverty-stricken to marry, and married couples too scared and uncertain to raise families? . . . The statistics do reveal a 30 percent fall in the marriage rate (1929-1932) and the lowest birth rates in United States history during the 1930's.[14] Roosevelt had to cope with this desperate situation. The New Deal which was his means gave American capitalism a new lease of life. This was clearly his intention.

The economic history of the 1930's has three predominant trends: a long decline (from September, 1929, to the spring of 1933—Roosevelt's inauguration), during which business activity was more or less halved; an equally long, irregular uphill climb until the fall of 1937 (in which the economic peak of 1929 was almost reconquered); and finally a sudden, steep fall in 1937–1938 followed by a general resurgence of economic activity in response to European war demands and increased deficit spending. The long climb, 1933-1937, was of course directly associated with New Deal economic policies.

For those who wish to study it, the New Deal presents great problems, not the least of which is the overwhelming mass of historical evidence it left behind. Perhaps the best way to approach such a vast subject for our present purposes is simply to categorize the main problems the nation faced in 1933 and the principal solutions the New Deal offered. We might also keep in mind a very useful distinction made by a pioneer historian of the period (Basil Rauch, 1944) between the "First New Deal" to 1934, mainly concerned with relief measures, and the more radical "Second New Deal" from 1935, which centered on reform.

The pragmatic approach

In 1933 the depression was at its very depths. The ratio of employed resources to available resources was disastrously low. Thomas Carlyle's comment on Victorian industrialism—"In the midst of plethoric plenty the people perish"—or, nearer home, Henry George's classic title of 1879—*Progress and Poverty*—took on a new meaning. For the privation of the 1930's was not the product of nineteenth century scarcity but of twentieth century abundance. The world's most advanced economic machine had come to a grinding halt. The challenge to FDR was how to get it started again.

Six complexes of interdependent problems had to be met: overexpansion of capital plant and production, especially acute in farming; cyclical and technological unemployment and the need to improve labor's share of national income and stimulate mass purchasing power; unstable credit and banking structure; monopolistic practices, particularly price manipulations and corporate control of public utilities; economic trouble zones (like building and mining); and the crippling of international trade owing to tariff barriers and foreign-exchange difficulties. The New Deal consisted in a series of empirical, undogmatic, and experimental answers to these problems, administered by innumerable *ad hoc* agencies. This approach was thoroughly American in tone and traditional in practice. The "alphabetical agencies" were modeled closely on historical experience with the agencies of World War I; the nonideological, pragmatic spirit that infused them FDR inherited from the Progressives—his former leader, Woodrow Wilson, and the inspiring memory of Teddy Roosevelt (Eleanor's uncle). The very title that FDR chose for his program conjures up recollections of a *New* Freedom and a Square *Deal*.

In truth Franklin D. Roosevelt did not think at all like a professional economist. His program was deliberately eclectic. Even during the Second New Deal it could not be said for example that he was a "Keynesian." (In fact, a personal meeting of Roosevelt and Keynes proved to be rather a flop: there was little genuine communication between the two great men.) To the economic purist the New Deal might appear to be a curious political hotchpotch of logically unrelated and even mutually inconsistent ideas. The President did not even exclude the experience, such as it was, of the previous administration. Hoover's Agricultural Marketing Act of 1929, which concerned itself, through a Federal Farm Board, with agricultural surpluses and farm credit, although it was starved of adequate appropriations to do any good, was not very different in style from later New Deal farm measures. The more significant Reconstruction Finance Corporation that Hoover created in January, 1932, to extend credit to various economic sectors managed to lend out $3 billion in 18 months. Though the RFC was rightly satirized by La Guardia as "the millionaire's dole" because it gave aid to those who had helped to cause the collapse rather than to the masses, the economic principle on which the RFC operated was not essentially different from that behind some New Deal steps to revive capitalism.

The real weakness of Hoover's RFC was that it constituted his only major action. Conferences were held with business leaders begging them to maintain wages and employment; the rest of the nation was urged to nail the flag to the mast. Meanwhile, the mechanisms of private and local charity broke down under the strain, and internationally the Republican administration made a blunder of the first magnitude with its steep Hawley-Smoot Tariff Act of 1930. Sick and tired of Hoover's homilies on the virtues of thrift and tightened belts, the American electorate swept the man out of power in 1932. After an ambiguous and frustrating "lame duck" interregnum of four months FDR took over the nation's helm. The First New Deal began instantly.

A plan for industry

For industry the National Industrial Recovery Act (1933) set up a National Recovery Administration (NRA) to supervise the formation of "code authorities" by individual branches of business. The idea was totally alien to nationalization. Instead the act aimed to give industrialists the power and encouragement to police themselves through the code authorities that would work to ensure what was called "fair competition"—the acceptance of a code of business practice. Under the Act of 1914 the Federal Trade Commission had already come to terms with individual industries around the conference table concerning the working definition of "fair" and "unfair" practices. The NRA simply regularized these meetings and agreements and drafted a code for each branch (about 600 codes all told, some of them fairly picayune) which had precedence at law over the provisions of the Sherman Antitrust Act of 1890, should a conflict arise. Many code authorities legalized practices previously thought to be monopolistic (for example, "open price filing") and were theoretically in contradiction with the Democratic party's avowed antitrust policy; some of the NRA personnel were survivors of the old War Industries Board, and on the whole the organization was business-oriented.

In principle labor representatives were to share in formulating the codes and ensure that the regulations guaranteed freedom of collective bargaining and established acceptable maxima and minima respectively for hours and wages. In practice labor participation was rare, perhaps because the Act did not specifically command it. Section 7(a), the famous labor clause that gave solid legal status to trade unions and collective bargaining, had to be a part of all the codes: a great many codes did contain provisions for a 40-cent-an-hour wage minimum and a 40-hour basic working week. But workers who could not achieve even a 25-cent-an-hour wage without resorting to strike activity looked with despair to Washington, and soon began to call NRA the "National Run-Around."

Part II of the 1933 Act empowered the President to spend up to $3,300 million on public works, and was perhaps the most useful part of the measure, which was not a thoroughgoing success. It helped in part to bring about an ephemeral recovery of sorts in the summer of 1933, but (as Professor W. A. Lewis points out) its two aims were contradictory: to create a prosperous atmosphere and stimulate investment by raising prices, and to expand purchasing power (and therefore consumption) by improving wages. As it was effective to about the same degree in both these goals, they effectively canceled each other out. To the complaints of small businessmen and consumers (who were totally ignored by the act) and the disappointments of labor (expressed in the textile strikes of September, 1934) was soon added the overt hostility even of the larger industrial firms themselves, which by the fall were grumbling about too much "government intervention." But in its decision on the Schechter case, in May, 1935, the Supreme Court rapidly made this controversy a matter of interest chiefly for historians: it invalidated the National Industrial Recovery Act. This it did on two principal counts: that the act authorized the use of delegated legislation, which was unconstitutional, and that it exceeded the limits of federal authority over interstate commerce.

Perhaps New Dealers were not wholly sorry to see the NRA safely out of the way, for soon after they began chasing the trust-busting hare with renewed enthusiasm. In his second term Roosevelt enlarged the antitrust investigating staff and gave it bigger funds; trust-busting hit the headlines once more, after a considerable armistice. But despite the flurry of activity little was done to reverse the trend toward oligopoly that the New Deal had itself encouraged earlier.[15] No "return" was to be made to the semimythical pristine democracy of "free competition." World War II and the postwar prosperity were to reinforce the foundations of oligopoly in the United States.

Priming the American pump

As a general condition for recovery, prices had somehow to be stimulated. Roosevelt tried several devices besides the National Industrial Recovery Act. For instance, he took the United States off the gold standard by executive order in April, 1933, forbidding the hoarding or export of gold, and by a joint resolution (June, 1933) making all public and private debts payable only in legal tender, abrogating the gold clauses of contracts. The dollar depreciated on the foreign exchanges and the domestic price level rose. Gold was bought from abroad under the Gold Reserve Act (1934), which established what was virtually a "managed" currency, but left gold available for payment of foreign balances.[16] The day after the act was passed, the President devalued the dollar to between 50 and 60 cents of its former worth in gold. This inflationary policy was not so successful as was expected, and the government shifted its attention from the currency itself to credit.

The outstanding problem in this sphere was the complete collapse of the banking system in 1933, the year in which over 4,000 banks failed. On Roosevelt's inauguration day bank "holidays" had to be declared in the two chief financial centers, Chicago and New York. The first action he took on coming to power was to complete this tendency, by proclaiming a national banking moratorium (March 5th). In addition, other normal sources of credit, such as savings banks, insurance and trust companies, title and mortgage companies, had proved inadequate. It therefore proved necessary to expand the work of Hoover's RFC, to reopen commercial banks and enable them to achieve liquidity rapidly. A special session of Congress was called to sanction the President's action, and was immediately presented with an Emergency Banking Act (March 9th). This also gave him special powers to control monetary and foreign-exchange transactions, and strengthened the hands of the RFC by allowing it to buy up (or accept as collateral for loans) the preferred stock of banks in distress. Moreover, the act permitted solvent and near solvent Federal Reserve member banks to reopen under license, and enlarged their note-issuing powers. A further act augmenting the scope of the RFC was the Loans-to-Industry Act (June, 1934) sanctioning direct industrial loans of up to $580 million.

Two Banking Acts were aimed more directly at reform of the banking structure. The first (1933) introduced safeguards for depositors using Federal Reserve member banks, by creating a federal corporation to provide insurance on deposits (the F.D.I.C.). More than this, it prevented Federal Reserve Banks from engaging in stock-market speculation either directly or through affiliated banks. The second act (1935) tried to increase federal control of monetary affairs by giving the Federal Reserve Board (through its Open Market Committee described in an earlier chapter) some supervisory authority over the credit policy of member banks, the right to vary their reserve requirements within certain limits, and the right to check their chief staff appointments. On the other hand, nothing was done to give the board authority over all commercial banks, including nonmembers, and this dichotomy remained the chief weakness in United States banking structure, especially in times of crisis.

But the most important device for pushing up prices was neither currency nor banking reforms, but pump priming—federal government lending and spending. After the apparent failure of the NRA, the administration came to depend increasingly on the policy of deficit financing. The notion that a cyclical fall in production and prices could be impeded by the deliberate use of deficit financing (government expenditure in excess of revenue) was thoroughly Keynesian. It was believed that the additional money being pumped into the economy (and into circulation) by such financing would increase consumption, thereby encourage investment, and thus lead to renewed economic growth.

What happened in practice? The theory—like most economic theories—was neither proved nor disproved by the facts. In the first place not all the money pumped into the economy by deficit spending was pumped thereby into circulation. This initial setback left the theory more or less intact. The question is: What were the effects of the money that did manage to get into circulation? This query must be preceded by another: Which federal expenditures did and which did not get into circulation?

Government spending for the relief of debtors took two forms: that which operated through the strengthened RFC and that which was administered by newly created agencies. RFC loans to bankers and industrialists were mainly used to pay off old debts, and as creditors remained wary to redeploy their repaid resources, which, like manna from Heaven, they had scarcely dared hope for, the money did not add directly to circulation or employment. Not all RFC loans went in this way, and those used for investment did of course add to the total of money in circulation and to employment. The finances administered by special agencies, such as the Federal Farm Mortgage Corporation and the Home Owners Loan Corporation, did not add directly to employment or circulation either. The Home Owners Loan Corporation, set up in 1933, was an extension of a scheme that originated in the Home Loan Bank Act (1932) of the Hoover regime. The 1932 act established federal banks to lend on real-estate mortgages to building and loan associations; the New Deal corporation (assimilated three years later by the Federal Housing Administration) was empowered to issue bonds up to $2,000 million to refinance first mortgages on moderate and small-sized homes.

Money spent on the relief of debtors, however necessary and justifiable from other economic and social viewpoints, did not perform the functions hoped of it by the disciples of Keynes in Roosevelt's "brain trust." Some federal expenditures did add to circulation: direct relief payments, such as those to farmers, the unemployed, and war veterans, and expenditures on public works (which also added directly to employment). Farm and unemployment relief will be considered later; here we can take as an example of direct payments those to veterans. An Adjusted Compensation Act of 1924 gave every veteran an endowment and insurance policy valued according to length of service, with higher rates for service abroad, and averaging about $1,000 per policy.[17] When the depression struck, many veterans demanded immediate payment of the face value of these endowment policies, to be made in greenbacks. In 1931 Congress passed a bill over President Hoover's veto allowing men to borrow up to one-half of the face value. This was not enough, and in June, 1932, a "Bonus Expeditionary Force" of impoverished veterans, about 20,000 in number, marched to Washington to present a "petition on boots," and camped in hastily constructed ramshackle slum huts, on Anacostia Flats, in view of the Capitol itself. Hoover ordered General Douglas MacArthur to use the National Guard to drive them out and burn their shelters— a blunder that earned him much unpopularity. Under the New Deal in 1935 Roosevelt vetoed the Patman bill for the payment of bonus certificates through currency inflation, but in January, 1936, a new Bonus Act was forced through over his veto, by which the federal government had to pay out $1,500 million.

Such relief payments, augmented by later old-age pensions, subsidies, grants-in-aid, and other devices, had a stimulating effect on the economy, as did public-works schemes. The latter included shipbuilding, slum clearance, construction of public buildings and roads, reafforestation and conservation, flood control, dam construction, and even cultural projects.

Now we can revert to the original question: How effective was the money that did add to circulation? In 1930, with a balanced budget, federal expenditures totaled about $3,600 million; six years later there was a deficit of $5 billion, and a total expenditure of about $9 billion. The national debt rose from $16 billion to over $33 billion, a per capita increase of from $131 to $263, and by 1939 it totaled over $40 billion—or a figure per head of population of $309. After 1939 these figures are dwarfed by wartime finances, but they represent nevertheless a considerable increase in their day.

The results were in general not very startling. Consumption did increase slowly. Personal expenditures of consumers began to creep up from the low level of $46 billion (1933) to a high of $67 billion (1937), but there was another fall in 1938, and the level of consumer buying of 1929 was not equaled until as late as 1941. Unemployment fell from about 13 million to slightly under 8 million (1933–1937) but jumped back to 10, 9, and 8 million respectively in the years 1938, 1939, and 1940. GNP increased from $74 billion to $109 billion, 1933–1937 (at 1929 prices)—a fair achievement. The wholesale price index climbed from its 1932 low of 64.8, to 86.3 in

1937 (1929 = 100). Having fallen more steeply than the general price trend, farm prices rose more steeply (48.2 to 86.4). But private investment remained sluggish.

So pump priming was neither a shattering failure nor a brilliant success—a verdict that could be passed perhaps on the New Deal economic policies as a whole. Especially disappointing was the continued high rate of unemployment and the all too visible outward signs of national poverty and degradation it brought.

Labor and the New Deal

Despite the tragedy of secular unemployment, the New Deal represents a revolutionary break with the past in United States labor history. Besides those provisions of the NRA that survived Supreme Court scrutiny, the Roosevelt administration introduced legislation like the National Labor Relations Act (1935) and the Fair Labor Standards Act (1938). The first (known as the Wagner-Connery Act) came after a growing number of violent industrial conflicts had caused Congress to pass a Labor Disputes Joint Resolution (1934) which authorized the President to establish permanent machinery to handle disputes. (Stoppages averaged 2,000 a year in 1934, 1935, and 1936.) The Wagner Act created a standing, independent National Labor Relations Board[18] to investigate complaints and proclaim "cease and desist" orders against "unfair practices" such as the coercion of workers in the exercise of their collective bargaining rights, discrimination against union members on the part of employers taking on men, and outright refusal of employers to bargain collectively.

The Fair Labor Standards Act of 1938 came as the logical conclusion of a legislative movement that included the National Employment Service Act (1933) establishing a network of national employment exchanges, the Railroad Retirement Act (1934) whereby federal control was extended over the administration of pension schemes for railroad workers (judicially nullified May 6, 1935), and the Walsh-Healey (Government Contracts) Act, 1936, which prohibited the offering of contracts for public work to any employer who did not meet certain minimum conditions regarding the hours and pay of his workers—the 8-hour day and 40-hour week, for instance, and no employment of lads under 16 years old, or girls under 18. The 1938 Act itself was first introduced by Senator Hugo Black of Alabama in the middle of 1937, a year of nearly 5,000 strikes involving about 2 million workers. Senator Black, who was soon to resign from the Senate to become a Supreme Court Justice, had introduced a radical bill in 1933 demanding a national 6-hour day and 30-hour week to spread employment, wanted to place "a ceiling over hours and a floor under wages." While his Fair Labor Standards Act was probably not quite so momentous as the President described it ("the most far-sighted program for the benefit of workers ever adopted in this or any other country"), it was nevertheless an important measure, ultimately giving protection to about 13 million workers. It established, for all labor engaged in interstate commerce or the production of goods for such commerce, a maximum working week of 40 hours and a minimum wage of 40 cents an hour, the time limit to be enforced after two years and the wage level after seven years. Furthermore, the act prohibited child labor in all industries connected with interstate commerce. The Supreme Court upheld the new law in a case in 1941 (overruling the case of 1918 which had invalidated the Keating-Owen Child Labor Act).

Meanwhile, the impact of the New Deal on the labor movement was very marked. The long decline in trade-union influence and membership since 1920 was abruptly reversed. Section 7(a) of the NIRA forbade employers' regulations forcing workers to join "company unions," or to promise not to join a union at all, as a condition of being given work. A spate of enthusiastic labor organization ensued, also protected by the Norris–La Guardia Act passed in 1932 under Hoover, which built safeguards against the misuse of the injunction in labor disputes. Out of the resurgence of labor activity emerged one very important development: the CIO.

The drive to expand trade-union membership after 1933 led to the acquiescence of the AFL in the organization of so-called "federal unions" on a basis of industry rather than craft. These unions, whose members were less experienced, more energetic and more radical than the staid AFL leadership, forced through at the annual convention of 1934 a motion to promote industrial unionism in the mass-production industries—such as the automobile, steel, rubber, radio, aluminum—and in addition the textile industries and public utilities.

The conservative leadership could not bring itself to execute this mandate, and newer radical elements coalesced under John L. Lewis (president of United Mineworkers) and formed a "Committee for Industrial Organization." Very soon the unions supporting Lewis were suspended from AFL membership. What has been called "Labor's Civil War" was on.

The CIO (its name altered to Congress of Industrial Organizations in 1938, when it also adopted a constitution and a more permanent form) aimed at uniting the skilled, unskilled, and white-collar workers alike in the previously nonunionized industries. It represented a formidable resurrection of the industrial unionism of the 1880's and the Knights of Labor, but in a changed society dominated by huge oligopoly firms. These concerns, with their "yellow dog" contracts (forbidding unionization) and "company unions," their huge armories of tear and sickening gas, grenades, shells, submachine guns, rifles, revolvers, their industrial "detectives" and spies,[19] had no intention of giving way easily. But on the other hand, many unions followed the lead of Lewis and left the AFL for the CIO, and at first the latter body had much public sympathy, professional affiliated groups being formed by teachers, liberal journalists, and administrative workers. By mid-1937 the CIO had captured 32 unions and almost 4 million members, while the AFL, with 100 affiliated unions, had under 3 million members.

Lewis therefore determined to pursue a forceful strike policy, chiefly to assert CIO hegemony, and began a new method: the "sit-down" strike in which workers refused to give up company machinery and property until they received satisfaction. The result was both highly successful and tragic. Many firms gave way—much to the surprise of everyone concerned—and the CIO won several spectacular triumphs, culminating in the submission of United States Steel in March, 1937. The last of the automobile firms to hold out against the CIO, Ford, acceded in 1941. But there was much violence. Firms like Republic Steel and General Motors denied the legality of the sit-down and went to court; when the courts issued injunctions that the unions flatly disobeyed, there was fighting. Perhaps the worst example was the "Memorial Day Massacre" in South Chicago in June, 1937. Police fought the strikers of the Republic Steel Corporation, killing ten. Similarly, labor leaders were beaten up during a strike at Ford's River Rouge plant near Detroit. Although the report of a Senate committee on violence was not unfavorable to labor, public opinion turned against the CIO and the sit-down technique.

CIO membership reached the 5 million mark in 1941, although the dynamic John L. Lewis resigned the previous year. By the end of World War II both AFL and CIO had over 6 million members each, and had become highly developed bureaucratic institutions —blocs of what J. K. Galbraith has called "countervailing power" in modern American society.

Toward "welfare capitalism"

In the meantime the New Deal had developed a more generalized form of social insurance to cover all United States citizens inside and outside the ranks of labor.

The central measure was the Social Security Act of August, 1935 (judicially validated 1937, amended 1939). This act made more general the miscellaneous local provisions for unemployment and old-age pensions. In 1929 old-age pensions existed in only 29 of the 48 states; unemployment-insurance schemes had been introduced in only one state (Wisconsin) by 1932. The federal system provided pensions for the needy, over 65 years old, the individual states who cooperated paying half the cost. Furthermore, an old-age insurance scheme gave benefits to members according to a complex structure of graduated premiums, paid by employer and worker. For unemployment insurance the plan was to tax employers (on the size of their payroll) and then give 90 percent of this federal impost to those individual states whose unemployment schemes came up to the standards demanded by the Social Security Board. The federal government also gave the states $25 million for relief to dependent children, and started annual appropriations of the same size to be used for maternal and child health, crippled children, the blind, and vocational rehabilitation. The scope of American social security remains far behind that of the United Kingdom, or indeed of several European nations, but the Social Security Act was the first national attempt to insure the underprivileged in the United States.

Of the attempts to provide work, as opposed to federal charity, for the needy, the outstanding agencies and schemes worth mentioning here included the CCC, the PWA, the WPA, and the USHA. The first, the Civilian Conservation Corps, providing work-relief to young men, will be considered later with agriculture; the Public Works Administration was set up under the Recovery Act of 1933 with a capital of $3,300 million to promote construction in the public interest, and spent over $7,000 million during its existence; the Works Progress Administration was established by executive order in 1935 after large appropriations for a second public-works program had been sanctioned by Congress, because the PWA's efforts had not appreciably reduced unemployment. The WPA (later styled the Works Projects Administration) had the job of coordinating all public-works schemes. Thus it was an important agency in the pump-priming operations. Given a capital of $4,880 million for relief, loans and grants to nonfederal projects, roads, conservation, flood control, slum clearance, education, health and cultural work, it soon needed extra appropriations, and spent altogether about $10,500 million and a further $2,700 million donated by state and local authorities, between 1935 and 1942, when it was dissolved. There was no doubt much waste and plenty of incompetence, but at the height of its career the WPA found jobs for 3,800,000. It constructed 122,000 public buildings, 77,000 bridges, 285 airports, 664,000 miles of road, 24,000 miles of sewers, countless parks, playgrounds, reservoirs, and power plants—truly a gigantic prospectus, fit to bring tears to the eyes of a Louis Blanc.

The USHA—United States Housing Authority[20]—served the dual purpose of providing low-cost housing and finding employment for workers. Although the housing boom had petered out after 1928, there still remained, as there still remains in many parts of the United States, an urgent demand for cheap housing. This demand was increased by depression conditions. The function of the USHA was to assist local communities in slum clearance and the building of low-cost homes, for which it was given a capital of $500 million (later trebled). Private real-estate interests fought this idea bitterly and managed to hold up the program so that by 1941 only 120,000 housing units had been actually completed.

New hope for the farmer

FDR's great undertaking encompassed industry, finance, economic growth, the needs of labor and general welfare.[21] What did the New Deal offer to the farmer? The last we heard of American

agriculture was in 1929, the year not only of the Crash but also of a
Hoover Agricultural Marketing Act, principally concerned with surpluses and farm credit. The same subjects were dominant in New
Deal agricultural policy. As with industry, Roosevelt introduced a
master measure, which did not live very long because it was
judicially quashed and had to be replaced by several new acts.

The master plan was the first Agricultural Adjustment Act (May,
1933, otherwise known as the Farm Relief and Inflation Act). Its
broad aim was to raise the status of agriculture within the economy
by stimulating the prices of farm goods and lightening the burden
of debts and mortgages. An Agricultural Adjustment Administration (AAA) was set up to supervise a system of agreements with
farmers whereby production of the basic staples (cotton, wheat,
corn, hogs, and tobacco) was restricted deliberately, in return for
government subsidies. In the following year the list of staples was
enlarged to include beef and dairy cattle, rye, flax, barley, peanuts,
sugar beet and cane, and other products. Taxes on the processing of
the goods concerned were to pay for the subsidies.

This recourse to "planned scarcity" involved what Professor
Broadus Mitchell has called the "plow-up" and the "kill": the plowing back into the soil of 10 million acres of cotton and 12,000 acres
of tobacco; the slaughter of over 6 million pigs; the abandonment of
California fruit crops, left to rot on the trees and bushes. This incredible step, in a country where countless people were on the
verge of starvation or at least utter destitution, seemed at the time
the logical conclusion pushed to its extreme of a free-enterprise,
profit-motive economy in which individual financial gain meant
more than social production. It could be taken to illustrate the conservative nature of the New Deal, because this maneuver, supported
by farmers and industrialists, was hated by the general public.

For reducing the cotton crop by about 4 million bales, the planters received $200 million from a grateful government; the average
price of cotton almost doubled. Wheat farmers received $100 million
for taking about 8 million acres of land out of production; the price
of wheat was doubled. Corn and pig producers received about $300
million for presenting a bewildered nation with the smallest corn
crop since 1881 and tons of fertilizer instead of pork. But national
farm income did increase from $3 billion to $7 billion (1932–1937).[22]

The Supreme Court declared the Agricultural Adjustment Act
unconstitutional in January, 1936, and Congress thereupon passed a

conservation measure the underlying aim of which was in fact to curtail production but which also proved helpful in the general progress of conservation. This was the Soil Conservation Act (1936). It proposed to spend $500 million for the improvement and preservation of soil fertility and to ensure safeguards against bad farming practices that lead to soil erosion and the depletion of its natural values. In his second term, however, Roosevelt had a more sympathetic Court, and the result was the second Agricultural Adjustment Act (February, 1938), which authorized the limitation of acreage to be planted; established control over the marketing of surplus crops; began the system of "parity price" payments to farmers who agreed to limit production; gave subsidies to those who planned production according to already approved soil-conservation practices; took over storage facilities for surpluses (the limited production of which was approved) in order to maintain an "ever-normal granary" in case of drought or emergency; and introduced federal insurance for wheat.

Meanwhile, what of farm credit? The Hoover Marketing Act established the Federal Farm Board to make loans to agricultural cooperatives. The board was abolished by order of President Roosevelt in May, 1933, but its legislative authorization and remaining assets were useful in the creation of the Farm Credit Administration—a consolidation of the varied federal agricultural credit agencies, regularized by the Farm Credit Act (June, 1933). In May (technically as Part II of the first Agricultural Adjustment Act), Congress had passed an emergency Farm Mortgage Act, which empowered the Federal Land Banks (set up by the Act of 1916) to issue $2,000 million in 4 percent bonds to refinance the thousands of farm mortgages that were being called by private lenders. Within three years more than 760,000 farms had been so saved. In January, 1934, the government also created the Federal Farm Mortgage Corporation, authorized to exchange private agricultural long-term paper for public guaranteed paper. It could issue fully guaranteed bonds up to a total of $2,000 million. Five months later Congress approved the Frazier-Lemke Amendment to the Federal Bankruptcy Act of 1898, allowing bankrupt farmers a five-year abeyance in which they could continue to inhabit their farms at a moderate rent; but in 1935 the amendment was declared to violate the Fifth Amendment to the Constitution, and was accordingly revised as the Farm Mortgage Moratorium Act which gave farmers a respite of three, instead of five, years before seizure. The new version was upheld by the Supreme Court in March, 1937, and continued in operation down to 1947.

Finally, no treatment of the New Deal for farmers would be adequate if it omitted to mention the tenancy laws. The Bankhead-Jones Farm Tenant Act (July, 1937), besides providing for the retirement of submarginal lands, gave loans to tenant farmers and sharecroppers who wanted to own their farms. In September of the same year the Farm Security Administration was formed to advance small loans for agricultural rehabilitation, to maintain camps for migratory farm workers, and to administer generally to the needs of the poorest and least protected members of rural society.

New hope for the land

Closely connected with agricultural policy was the revived concern for conservation, which constituted in fact the second Conservation Movement. During the depression years the physical results of overexploitation of natural resources became increasingly visible, especially in the dreaded "Dust Bowl" of the southern Plains area of 1934-1935. The immediate causes of the Dust Bowl were severe drought that withered the crops and dried to dust the exposed soil, and strong winds that gathered the dust up into immense, dark clouds. Its long-term causes were overcropping and overgrazing in parcels of land that were too small for the geographical conditions of the area but were determined by the homestead legislation. The result was that Kansas farms were literally blown away, 9 million acres of land being destroyed by wind erosion and many humans and animals killed by dust pneumonia.

The predominant steps in New Deal conservation policy were: the relevant parts of the NIRA (public-works provisions); the institution of the Civilian Conservation Corps; the Tennessee Valley scheme; the formation of the Federal Power Commission and the National Resources Board; the Taylor Grazing Act; the Soil Erosion Act and its later amendments; and, of course, the conservation work of the WPA already discussed. The CCC was created in March, 1933. In the years 1933 to 1941 it employed almost 3 million young men, supervised by army officers and foresters. Their main functions were to fight forest fires, investigate and check animal diseases and pests, gather tons of fish in hatcheries, add about 17 million acres of forest land to the nation's diminished reserves, build bridges and dams, prevent soil erosion by assuring water supplies, and lay or suspend miles of telephone lines. The Federal Power Commission was set up by the Wheeler-Rayburn Act of August, 1935, to regulate the public-utility companies who provided electricity, but also was authorized to make a survey of national waterpower resources; the National Resources Board (existing under various titles between June, 1934, and June, 1943) was expected to present the President with an overall scheme for the utilization of land, water, and other natural resources. About 142 million acres of western grazing land were to be kept free of homesteaders by the Taylor Grazing Act of June, 1934 (as we have seen).

But the most spectacular and internationally famous of all the conservation measures of Roosevelt was the Tennessee Valley Development Act (May 18, 1933). The idea was, in simple terms, to dam the river and its tributaries, thus providing flood regulation, navigable reaches, and an important source of power. The plan covered an area of about 40,000 square miles in seven states. Before long the TVA assumed second place among American electrical supply systems. Working hand in hand with state governments, the National Park Service, the National Resources Board, the Public Roads Administration, the United States Bureau of Fisheries (the largest fish hatchery in the world was established in the area), and the Biological Survey, the Authority not only embarked on a large-scale scheme of land reclamation but also opened huge sections to the tourist trade as recreational grounds and laid out five demonstration parks. The TVA carried out to the full its broad mandate to develop "the economic and social well-being of the people living in the river basin"; it was a successful and courageous experiment in the rehabilitation of an area as a geographical entity, and it became a great showpiece of American capitalism, new-style.

The New Deal in substance: capitalism refurbished

In 1938 Roosevelt made the following observation:

As a nation we have rejected any radical revolutionary program. For a permanent correction of grave weaknesses in our economic system we have relied on *new applications of old democratic processes.*

Much of the "revolutionary" appearance of the New Deal was derived from its breathtaking rapidity and the vast scope and detail
of its countless provisions. But this can be readily accounted for by
two facts: the severity of the Great Depression and the great back-
log of essential reforms created by the political stagnation since
World War I. The war cut across all lines of social development
and put an abrupt end to the legislative reform movement that had
been gathering speed since the 1880's. The sterility of the twenties
left a long-accumulated miscellany of abuses, anachronisms, and
malpractices—cracks in the body politic and economic—in need of
urgent therapy. Roosevelt therefore faced a double challenge: relief
and recovery from the economic depression, and long-term reform
to give America the chance to catch up on time lost through war
and "normalcy." While it is still extremely difficult to judge the true
effects of his relief and recovery measures, the "reform New Deal"
did introduce certain "structural" changes in the United States economy that have proved to be of enormous value in extending the life,
strengthening the fabric, and enriching the spirit of American
capitalism.

A new recession in 1937–1938 brought the recovery and growth
aspects of New Deal policy to the verge of disaster. Deficit spending under the second New Deal (the Social Security Act of 1935
and the Veterans' Bonus bill forced through in January, 1936) and
the economic stimulus afforded by the Spanish Civil War helped to
create a small-scale commodity boom (a "boomlet" in Broadus
Mitchell's phrase) in 1936–1937. The year 1937 was, as we have
seen, an economic peak, with unemployment at its lowest for the
thirties and growth indices at their highest (though still below pre-
Crash achievements). Unfortunately, the boomlet lacked taproots.
Bonus payments, for instance, are fairly shortlived. Unemployment
was still too heavy and purchasing power still too depressed. Durable goods could not recoup adequately. Genuine recovery waited
upon the restoration of long-term investment. The so-called "Roosevelt Depression" of 1937–1938 was the outcome of these weaknesses
and of other unfavorable influences, noticeably federal policy
changes. Trying to restrain the rising level of prices, the administration took two unfortunate steps: deficit spending was reduced and
a credit squeeze was initiated. The Federal Reserve System raised

its reserve requirements twice (March 1 and May 1, 1937). The
economy reacted badly to these maneuvers. Here was concrete evidence for the Keynesians. Roosevelt quickly reverted to a policy of
government spending and the Federal Reserve System lowered its
requirements once more (April 16, 1938).[23] Business spokesmen
blamed the recession on FDR's "alienation" of the business community (as they were later to blame the stock-market collapse of
1962 on President Kennedy's action against big steel). More significant than this doubtful notion were the economic losses caused in
the farm sector by bad drought and in the labor sector by renewed
friction. Apart from the Memorial Day Massacre itself, 1937 was
after all a year of over 5,000 labor stoppages.

The indices of 1937–1938 sagged painfully. About 3 million
Americans were added to the ranks of the unemployed. Total personal consumer expenditure fell by $3 billion. GNP (at 1929 prices)
was cut by about $6 billion.[24] Roosevelt's reversion to pump priming
helped to stem the tide in the later months of 1938. WPA expenditures were 50 percent higher than in the last half of the previous
year; "triple-A" expenditures were four times as high. Despite the
President's greater willingness to adopt pump priming in the late
1930's, it seems unlikely that deficit spending alone could have
solved America's long-run growth problems. What "saved" the
economy and perhaps the administration was the outbreak of
Hitler's War.

In Europe armaments orders were already pouring in by 1938.
The United States economy faltered in 1939, but in the following
spring the European war began to make itself felt across the Atlantic; from now on there would be little fear of economic contraction. For Franklin Delano Roosevelt the greatest challenges were
yet to come. For his New Deal the judgment on its capacity to sim-
ulate the recovery and future long-term expansion of America's
consumer economy must rest on the evidence of the years before
1939. That evidence we have seen to be inconclusive. Nevertheless
the economic indicators of 1939 were unrecognizably healthier than
those of 1933. The President had led the nation through the valley
of stagnation, though he had not yet gained the high ground from
which can be viewed that misty plateau economists are wont to call
"balanced economic growth."

The economy of the 1950's and 1960's, sustained by the unexpected renewal of population growth and boosted by "local" hot wars, cold war, and immense military expenditures in the public sector, is in no position to slight the New Deal's achievement in the field of economic growth. The pump-priming outlay of the 1930's was dwarfed by government expenditures in the Second World War and since. And in the field of reform the New Deal era is equaled only by the 1830's and 1840's and Progressivism. Europeans might regard the New Deal as a rather mild affair,[25] and recent United States historians might seem to emphasize the conservative nature of Roosevelt's personal background, while the President himself wished only to make "new applications of old democratic processes" —but the reforms of the thirties modified American capitalism in both style and structure.

Modulations in the style of economic life are not readily discerned or explained. The NRA's "self-policing" code authorities for business and the idealism of public-works bodies like the CCC and National Youth Administration injected a greater sense of responsibility and social conscience into the nation; yet the roots of this "responsible capitalism" go back at least to the reform spirit of the "Social Gospel" period. Even between the world wars this spirit did not entirely perish, and credit should be given to autonomous changes within the business system itself in deference to public opinion and shifts in the national mood. While the New Deal undoubtedly hastened the process of business self-education, of greater moment was an altered balance of prestige within the American culture. Harding, Coolidge, and Hoover brought little respect or authority to the presidential office or to the federal government in an age mesmerized by the glittering figures of business. Total collapse of the business empire in the years 1929–1933, followed by the election of a dynamic President and a federal government determined to fulfill its constitutional role to "promote the general welfare," produced a swing in favor of public authority. This cultural swing or change in style has much to do with the later acquiescence of nearly all Americans in the "mixed economy" with its enlarged public sector.

Any list of modifications made to the structure of American capitalism by the New Deal must include the two securities acts. In

May, 1933, an act compelled the registration of all new issues of stocks and bonds with the Federal Trade Commission and demanded a full descriptive prospectus on each issue to keep investors informed about the stock. The act of June, 1934, created the Securities and Exchange Commission (SEC) to license stock exchanges and regulate their operation, and empowered the Federal Reserve Board to prescribe margin requirements. Business hostility to these measures was intense at the time, but the SEC is fully accepted, even welcomed, by responsible Wall Street men today. (Like other regulatory bodies, the SEC soon became identified to some extent with the sector it was intended to superintend.) Another move to strengthen the financial fabric was the creation of the Federal Deposit Insurance Corporation by the Banking Act of 1933 to guarantee individual bank deposits. In 1935 a Revenue Act raised surtax rates on individual incomes over $50,000, grading them much more steeply. Similarly, large corporations were taxed more heavily and small firms given tax relief. A tax measure of this kind, besides its obvious redistributive effects, added to the power of government to guide the economy in times of crisis; the progressive income tax is in fact one of the so-called "built-in stabilizers" that operate automatically to mitigate the effects of fluctuations in the modern mixed economy.

The New Deal's farm-support program and social-security payments form two additional examples of structural change and sources of stabilization, largely because they call for continued and steady government expenditure even in times of depression, and so stimulate consumption. Other federal and locally supported welfare programs—rural electrification, housing projects, credit and insurance operations and the like—perform a similar stabilizing function. Meanwhile, by encouraging trade unions the New Deal gave official support to the emergence of valuable "countervailing power" inside the economy, power that could be exercised democratically through the NLRB under the Wagner Act.

Business expansion in the war years and the resurgence of the consumer economy in the late 1940's reconciled the business community and the nation to the transformations wrought by the New Deal. The 1950's produced no reversions to old-style capitalism, however different the climate became.

3. WAR AND BOOM

The attitude of Americans to the Second World War (once the United States had joined) contrasted strongly with the attitude of the men of 1917. Roosevelt's war message to Congress of December 9, 1941, set the tone:

The true goal we seek is far above and beyond the ugly field of battle. ... We Americans are not destroyers—we are builders. ... We are going to win the war and we are going to win the peace that follows.

Here was no zealous "war to end wars." Yet the peace that followed produced not blind isolationism but the generosity, wisdom, and leadership of the Marshall Plan.

Arsenal of democracy

The Second World War was a "global" land, sea, and air war, affecting every facet of national life. In the United States in particular it implied: rapid changeover from peacetime to wartime production; raising, equipping, and maintaining armed services totaling about 15 million men; transporting men and materials to five continents and scores of sea islands; maintenance of home production to safeguard the domestic population and supply the Allies; and continuance of normal trade relations with Latin America and neutral nations. A more complete mobilization the American people had never known. On the speed and efficiency of the industrial transformation of the United States depended the ultimate outcome of the war against the Nazis. The President promised that his country would become the "arsenal of democracy"; this promise was entirely fulfilled.

The United States possessed many advantages over her Allies in the matter of mobilization, not the least of which were immunity from air raids, blackouts, and food restrictions. Her huge industrial plant and labor force could work unhampered. Moreover, American industry was already on a partial war basis before she entered the battle, owing to Lend-Lease (sanctioned by Congress in March, 1941) and the large defense commitments of 1940-1941. Peacetime conscription through the Selective Service Act of 1940 laid the basis for the larger drafting of manpower that followed closely after the Japanese surprise attack on Pearl Harbor (December 7, 1941). Already more than 6 million workers had been added to the labor force, the index of manufacturing production almost doubled (1938–1941), and GNP increased 30 percent.

Nevertheless, general lack of urgency before Pearl Harbor, and constant failure to understand how near America was to being forced into the international crisis, accounted for many serious shortages. The automobile industry long remained reluctant to turn over to military production; the steel industry's increase of 16 million tons was plainly insufficient; the armed services placed too few orders in the fear that rapid development in the technique of warfare would render the goods obsolete before delivery. There were critical shortages of machine tools and of medical products such as quinine, and inadequate stocks of copper, chrome, rubber, and aluminum. Leading businessmen refused to cooperate with the New Deal government until they received heavy guarantees that the nation would take the financial risk; but this "sit-down strike" of capital did not last long, as all the assurances were given.

Once the United States had entered the conflict and everyone knew exactly where he stood, production underwent an immense expansion. In 1942 the President set a target of 60,000 aircraft, 45,000 tanks, and 8 million tons of merchant shipping—a target thought to be impossible by the War Production Board. To unify and coordinate the war machine on the domestic front, the Office of War Mobilization was set up, under former Supreme Court Justice James F. Byrnes (May, 1943). The OWM was meant to supervise the work of the War Production Board, the Oil Administration, the Office of Economic Stabilization, the War Labor Board and War Manpower Commission, and the Food Administration. The shock of Pearl Harbor effectively rid Americans of the idea that war production could continue alongside an unaltered or ever-increasing production of consumer goods; the latter was checked, and in 1943 and 1944 the "impossible" target of 60,000 military aircraft a year was surpassed by the totals 85,405 and 95,237. The fear of a shipping shortage was reduced in 1943 by production figures of a million tons a month. There was a need for more rubber, however, and Japanese victories cut off American imports; domestic production did not bridge the gap until 1944–1945, and even then its total was

97,000 tons below the Baruch Committee's target of 1,037,000 tons, set in 1942. The steel industry did not expand phenomenally either, and was a constant headache to those concerned.

Contracts for increased wartime production went mainly to the largest corporations, both out of habit and for the sake of speed and efficiency. Ten corporations received one-third of all war orders, and General Motors itself accepted about $14 billion of work. Despite the great deal of subcontracting to smaller firms, one result of war production was thus the steady elimination of some 500,000 smaller businesses. During the war total industrial output almost doubled; but total productivity did not increase so rapidly because gains in such fields as shipbuilding and aircraft manufacture were offset by lower productivity elsewhere. Greater use of existing means and lengthened working hours probably accounted for much of the enlarged output rather than increase of productivity per manhour. Whatever the causes, American industry produced enough for domestic and Allied needs; it equipped the French and Chinese armies; it built airfields and harbors the world over; it supplied Iran, Russia, and Great Britain among others; it built highways in Burma and Alaska; and but twelve months after Pearl Harbor, outstripped the total production of the Axis powers combined.

The labor shortage during the war was indeed a new experience, not known for many decades. To meet the need there was an increase in young labor, and over 5 million women went to work. Key workers were exempt, and retired men returned to their former jobs or new ones. By 1945 the total labor force (including the forces) totaled 65 million as compared with 56 million (employed and unemployed) in 1940. The average working week had been extended from 40 to 48 hours, though the extra hours were normally counted as overtime. The trade unions made considerable progress in the war years (as in World War I), total membership rising to 14,796,000 (1945).

The more or less normal migration of population from country to town was accentuated by increased labor mobility, causing great urban housing, police, transportation, and schooling problems. Urban population rose by almost 9 millions, and there was a noticeable tendency to move west and southwest with the shift of industry that was gradually taking place. Despite the growth of urban population, there was an increase of farm output, perhaps to some extent the belated result of New Deal price subsidies, conservation, and electrification schemes. The productivity of farm labor increased by 25 percent, and farm incomes doubled. There were large increases in the production of cereals, eggs, and dairy goods, and meanwhile the Price Stabilization Act (1942) assured "parity prices" for the farmer until at least two years after the war's end. Agriculture profited even more than the large industrial corporations from the war.

The greatest fear was of inflation. To avoid the tragedy of a price spiral the government took several steps. Price-regulation machinery was introduced in April, 1941 (the Office of Price Administration—OPA), but no general controls were exerted until January, 1942, when prices had already risen 25 percent. The Emergency Price Control Act of that month was soon supplemented by the "general maximum price regulation" of the OPA, in April, and the stabilization act of October. The latter extended price and rent control to wages, and the law was stiffened again in April, 1943. In addition, restrictions were imposed by the mild rationing of goods and the prohibition of installment buying. Assimilation of surplus income (which might have otherwise stimulated the black market or immediate postwar inflationary buying) was achieved by the sale of war bonds, and by a heavy taxation of the middle- and upper-income ranges through corporate, income, excise, and inheritance taxes. In addition, there was a universal 5 percent "Victory Tax." Taxation covered only 47 percent of government expenditure in 1944, to select one year. The Second World War was financed in the United States like its predecessors: by borrowing. The national debt increased at the rate of $50 billion yearly after 1941. In 1945 it totaled $258 billion. The tax burden of the American citizen thus never approached that of Great Britain.

Obviously "total" war as experienced in Europe remains fortunately unknown on the American continent. The phenomenal all-out American economic effort was achieved without any definite control of manpower or direction of labor, for instance. It did not imply stringent rationing below normal food-consumption levels: meats, fats, sugar, coffee, and canned goods were restricted to some extent; automobiles remained on the roads in thousands despite the rationing of gasoline and tires and the pressing rubber shortage. American living standards remained, as ever, generally high.

But the Second World War cost the United States eleven or twelve times as much as World War I—$360 billion. This sum exceeded the combined total expended by Great Britain and the Soviet Union. Furthermore, it was American natural resources, wealth, and engineering skill that enabled large-scale experimentation in atomic energy to be undertaken (the Manhattan Project), a development that was to prove of such moment after 1945.

How did the war affect United States economic growth? Given the poor health of the economy in 1939, it is impossible to disregard the positive stimulus the war's outbreak gave to American economic activity. What is more, United States population growth was not retarded by this particular war but spurred. (The birth rate rose from 18.8 per 1,000 population to 22.7 by 1943, declining to 20.4 in 1945.) GNP climbed from its 1938 low of $103 billion to a wartime high of almost $184 billion in 1944 (at 1929 prices). Some of this gain was lost when war production ceased in 1945, but the GNP of the late 1940's remained 60 or 70 percent above that of the late 1930's. The GNP of 1950 surpassed forever the level of 1944, and opened an amazing decade of high mass consumption.

Continuing amendments to capitalism: the Fair Deal

America emerged from World War II as the political and military leader of the Western Hemisphere and as the world's richest, most advanced, and most powerful nation. The war, even more than its predecessor, had revealed flexibility, responsiveness, and enormous hidden reserves of productive power within the United States economy. Some of this power continued to be absorbed by military expenditures in the postwar years; the international situation dictated that the economy remain on a quasi-war footing. Many resources, however, were diverted into a gigantic consumer boom, an upsurge that invites comparison with the twenties. Meanwhile, the social climate (unlike that of the New Era) remained affirmative and Progressive for some years.

One man, President Harry Truman, had much to do with the maintenance of the New Deal spirit against any possible postwar hysteria or reaction. An unknown quantity as Vice-President, and bowled over at his sudden elevation to the nation's leadership by

FDR's death in April, 1945 (". . . last night the moon, the stars and all the planets fell on me!" he told reporters), Truman grew with the job and was at all times determined to uphold the principle of a strong Presidency. "I could do nothing else and still be President of the United States," he explained after the famous recall from Korea of General MacArthur. Truman maintained this position of positive leadership throughout seven years of upheaval (1945–1952) which involved the presidential office in decisions of appalling magnitude: Hiroshima and Nagasaki, the formation of the UN, the "Truman Doctrine" (foreign aid to nations under pressure from Communist expansion), the Marshall Plan, the creation of NATO, and the Berlin airlift of 1948–1949 that helped to cement it, and the tremendous decision to intervene militarily in Korea in June, 1950. Bipartisanship in foreign policy and deliberate consultation with the Republican opposition helped the President over these hurdles. Home economic policy was more divisive.

Resolved to continue and amplify the New Deal, Truman stepped directly into the lion's mouth with his first important message to Congress on domestic affairs. He demanded (September 6, 1945) higher minimum wages, national health insurance, greater slum clearance, extended social-security benefits, new regional development plans like TVA and, most important, a full-employment act.

The Employment Act of 1946 is the most important single piece of economic legislation of the entire postwar period. It created a clear legal obligation on the part of the federal government to use all practicable means "to promote maximum employment, production, and purchasing power," and it created the basic core of machinery for such economic planning—the Council of Economic Advisers working directly for the President, and the Joint Committee on the Economic Report in Congress.[26] Under the Employment Act swift measures by the administration and the Federal Reserve authorities have held in check four recessions: 1948–1949, 1953–1954, 1957–1958 and 1960–1961. (Most recently the act seems to have had less success in the area of unemployment.)

Elsewhere the Truman program met concerted opposition from a conservative coalition of Republicans and southern Democrats, the latter being alienated by the President's pressure for civil-rights legislation. Despite his achievements—the Employment Act, the Atomic Energy Authority Act, a Rent Control Act, a Displaced Persons Act (to admit 200,000 outside the quota system), the National Security Act (creating a unified Department of Defense) and lesser measures—Truman's political position looked very poor in 1948. The congressional elections of 1946 had given the Republicans control of both Houses for the first time since 1930, and in the 1948 campaign both right and left wings of the Democrats revolted, the Southerners forming a "Dixiecrat" faction and Henry Wallace running as an independent. As for labor, Truman had vetoed the hostile Taft-Hartley Act (1947) but could not prevent its ultimate passage, and although his administration generally favored rising wages and full employment the President had been forced to the point of taking over the coalmines during the strike of 1946 (John L. Lewis receiving a $10,000 contempt of court fine, and the United Mineworkers paying a $700,000 fine for defying the federal government injunction). Surprisingly, Truman overcame all this, and by dint of an aggressive personal campaign in which he excoriated the "do-nothing" Eightieth Congress and proposed a "Fair Deal" for the American people, the President was reelected with a sweeping victory and the Democrats recaptured both Houses.

From the 1948 election to that of Eisenhower in 1952, the Fair Deal managed to achieve extensions of social security (a new act added about ten million beneficiaries), a Fair Labor Standards Act that established a 75-cent-an-hour minimum wage, an Agricultural Act (1949) maintaining price supports at 90 percent of parity, an important Housing Act (1949) to provide for federal aid to local authorities in low-cost housing and urban renewal projects, and a doubling of the admissions numbers for displaced persons to 400,000 (1950). Truman failed to repeal the Taft-Hartley Act and could not implement either his scheme for a "Missouri Valley Authority" or the international St. Lawrence Seaway and Power Project. For agriculture the Brannan Plan was rejected, and in medicine the hope of a national health-insurance scheme was blighted by a massive political campaign organized by the American Medical Association at considerable expense. The last issue, reminiscent of the techniques used by the private utility corporations between the wars, was destined to recur in the 1960's with President Kennedy's "Medicare" plan.

All in all, however, the Fair Deal represents an important further adaptation of "New Deal capitalism" to fit the needs of the present day. If this were not so, one would expect a deep reaction to reformed capitalism by the Republican opposition once Eisenhower came to the helm in 1952. This revulsion did not take place: "welfare capitalism" was maintained intact.

The Eisenhower years, 1952–1960

The first Republican President in twenty years came to the White House with a political platform that promised to curb inflation, cut government expenditures, and balance the budget. President Eisenhower roundly declared his opposition to "creeping socialism." For the most part the negative campaign note was not belied by the policies that actually followed. The evolution of American reform capitalism did in some ways slow down. History was against the Eisenhower platform, however, and faced with the realities of economic life in the recession of 1953 the President made no bones about his intentions to act vigorously and use all his constitutional powers to prevent a catastrophe.

Although his legislative program was meager compared with those of his predecessor and successor, Eisenhower resisted the extreme right wing and accepted the concept of federal responsibility for full employment, social security, education, health, housing, and civil rights. The only modification he made to the New and Fair Deal farm program was the sensible replacement of rigid price supports by flexible supports (1954). In April, 1953, the Department of Health, Education, and Welfare was created, and in 1958 the National Defense Education Act gave about $600 million for student loans, grants to state schools, and fellowships. Other Eisenhower measures were various Housing Acts (1954–1960) to liberalize mortgage requirements, rehouse families displaced by extensive slum clearances and accelerate urban renewal; a regional development program for the upper Colorado River (1956); the Wiley-Dondero Act (1954), which established the St. Lawrence Seaway Development Corporation and brought about the final completion of that remarkable project in 1959 after years of frustration; and a huge roadbuilding program (under the Federal-Aid Highway Acts of 1956 and 1958), which planned to construct over 40,000 miles of road and was to spend up to $40 billion of federal money—a new "highway revolution" greater than that which flourished under the 1916 act.[27]

An irreversible revolution

The lesson is obvious: the difference between Republicans and Democrats, "conservatives" and "liberals" in modern America was one of degree and not of kind. Republican acceptance of reformed capitalism as their own was paralleled in the same period by Tory attempts to claim credit for the Welfare State in Britain. The Western world had moved a step forward since the thirties, and there was no going back. Naturally, Republicans still prefer federal "intervention" in the economy by a Republican government to federal "interference" by a Democratic administration; and naturally Democrats have short memories for constructive economic legislation by Republican administrations. But both parties operate when in power under the high-pressure economics that have prevailed since the war—the sustained high level of aggregate demand, the vast military and scientific expenditures of government, the constant nagging of inflation, and what Kuznets calls the "high secular propensity to consume."

A fresh breeze blew through the Democratic party and the nation in 1960 when John F. Kennedy was elected to the Presidency to open his "New Frontier." It seemed that the breeze might fill the sails of reform and bring further modifications to American consumer capitalism. Meanwhile, the winds of change were blowing elsewhere, for instance in Western Europe where negotiations were taking place to create a Common Market. The proposed free-trade market loomed large in the minds of American businessmen, economists, and statesmen. Not only did the new administration face the old problems, but more than ever before the major issues in American economic life were subject to developments in the world economy and society.

Abundance and Responsibility

Extraordinary prosperity and ebullience have characterized consumer capitalism since the Second World War,[1] under a regime of
high wages, high mass consumption, and high government disburse-
ments. On occasions, as in 1953 and 1957, steam has escaped from
the great American pressure cooker, and strange inner bubblings are
sometimes heard. But post–New Deal administrations—even though
expert advice is conflicting about the relative rôle of "built-in" as
against "discretionary" stabilizers—know what can be done generally to prevent a blowout of the safety valve. On occasions, too,
misgivings are reasserted about the adequacy of America's economic
safeguards and controls (as for example during the stock-market
slide of 1962). Here there is no final test except events themselves,
but at least Americans of the sixties are reasonably sure that, whatever party is in power, serious economic malfunctioning will bring
serious federal therapy.

The Age of Abundance is also an age of increased responsibility.
At home the responsibility is vigilance—the protection of those conditions of social democracy, mobility, and opportunity that this book
has tried to prove are the ultimate historical foundations for the
growth of America's wealth.[2] Abroad the responsibility is to speed
the emergence of "developing" nations out of the dangerous and

susceptible stage of poverty and deprivation and to prevent the recurrence of massive global war that would destroy or maim us all, rich nations and poor nations alike. In the years after World War II, morbid traits did appear at home—the loyalty hysteria, for instance—but the general health of society was good. The contrast was sharp and unreal between the success story of internal affairs and the complexities and frustrations of foreign relations. Superabundance at home served to underline the incredible nature of the external threats.

The rich nation's burden

The burden of leadership that was thrust upon the United States by history was explored by the distinguished neo-orthodox theologian Reinhold Niebuhr in *The Irony of American History* (1952). Besides America's celebrated "loss of innocence" and her "vast involvement" in the guilt and responsibility that go with leadership, especially poignant for Niebuhr was her apparent impotency, at the hour of her greatest strength, to change things. Fortunately, some American statesmen were still prepared to try, and even in the international field had already experienced more than a modest degree of success in the Marshall Plan.

The wave of Nazi nihilism and barbarism that swept over Europe left her helpless economically, though it never entirely sapped her moral resources. Food production was halved, great cities and towns were laid waste, transportation facilities dislocated and gratuitously destroyed, mines flooded, ports and harbors choked with debris, money reduced to worthless paper. Ten or twelve million uprooted refugees wandered hopelessly or inhabited shanty camps over the face of the continent. The average nourishment of a European was 1,500 calories a day—often less. The American average was more than twice that amount (3,500 calories). Starvation, disease, and anarchy typified the condition of the ancient centers of Western civilization.

The heaviest burden of responsibility for relief devolved upon the United States in view of her economic and military position. The New World was to redress the balance of the Old. As early as

December, 1942, Roosevelt had established an Office of Foreign Relief inside the State Department, mainly for North Africa. In June, 1943, the United States proposed an international relief organization that eventually formed the basis for UNRRA—the United Nations Relief and Rehabilitation Administration. Forty-eight nations collaborated in this body to provide direct relief in the form of food, clothing, livestock, seed, fertilizer, machinery, and medical supplies. UNRRA spent $4 billion, of which the United States gave almost $3 billion. Furthermore, the United States Army helped to feed much of occupied Europe.

Despite its scale this program was inadequate and well within the means of a nation that continued to feed cereals to cattle and had no postwar rationing. Lend-Lease was cut short rather abruptly in August, 1945, and UNRRA was allowed to expire in 1947; congressmen complained that American supplies were being used to build up the strength of Communist areas, and there was a general feeling that the major crisis in Europe was over. On the other side, the reciprocal trade agreements of the thirties were renewed in 1945, and two years later about forty nations agreed to lower tariffs on leading staples. Although American imports rose to over $7 billion, there was a persistent "dollar gap" of about $8 billion. This problem had never been really solved after 1919, but after 1945 it was much worse. Nothing could be sold by the United States to a bankrupt Europe. If trade were to flow, this gap must be closed.

Meanwhile, the Treasury had begun plans in 1943 for currency stabilization, and in the summer days of 1944 the Bretton Woods Conference took place in New Hampshire. It was agreed to create two agencies: the International Monetary Fund (IMF), to maintain stable exchange rates and ease the international transfer of funds, and the World Bank, to lend and borrow money and to underwrite private loans for productive uses. But the story of international aid had scarcely begun.

Remaining Lend-Lease orders were delivered during 1946. Total Lend-Lease grants amounted to about $50 billion, and reverse Lend-Lease about $8 billion. After the war the settlement of Lend-Lease accounts by Britain, France, China, and other nations was prompt and much less acrimonious than the settlement of debts after 1919. For Britain, however worthy the settlement might seem from the international viewpoint, the financial effort precipitated a severe economic crisis.

Before the war the trade deficit of the United Kingdom was filled by "invisible exports"—foreign investments, shipping, banking, and insurance services. These assets were badly affected by the conflict: Britain lost investments abroad and incurred heavy debts in addition; she lost a third of her shipping and many foreign markets; she had a great part of her industrial plant at home destroyed by Nazi action. She could neither recapture her export markets nor pay for imports with accumulated capital. Moreover, she had large foreign commitments, such as occupation costs in Germany and Austria, military expenses in Palestine, Greece, and the Far East, colonial expenses, contributions to UNRRA, the IMF, and the World Bank. Sir Stafford Cripps negotiated a loan of $3,750 million from the United States (having asked for $5,000 million), to run for 50 years at 2 percent. Canada lent the Mother Country about $1,750 million as well. For her part the United Kingdom had to abolish her exchange controls and blocked credits, and scale down her obligations to other countries.

Within two years the loans were used up in spite of the strict maintenance of wartime rationing and a fierce struggle to recapture export markets abroad. Great Britain approached a new crisis in 1947. This fresh disaster, coming as it did with poor economic conditions in Italy, France, and elsewhere, and the growing fear of Communism, led the United States to draw up a more adequate plan for European aid. On June 5, 1947, Secretary of State Marshall made a crucial speech at Harvard; Marshall's plan had as its motif the idea that America would help those who helped themselves. Almost immediately the British and French governments invited twenty-two nations, including the Soviet Union, to a Paris meeting to implement the idea. Molotov soon dissociated himself and his satellites from the plan, and the final total of cooperating nations was sixteen. With Sir Oliver Franks in the chair, an elaborate European Recovery Program was drafted. New production targets were fixed, the restoration of West German industries was advocated, and measures were initiated for greater monetary stability and free trade. The total cost of the plan was settled at $22 billion, of which the United States would pay the most, with help from Canada, Latin America, the IMF, and the World Bank.

In Congress opposition to the Marshall Plan was led by Senator Taft, who dubbed it "Operation Rathole"; support came from Senator Vandenberg (an internationally-minded Republican), and from liberals and labor groups. The Marshall Plan Act was pushed through in April, 1948—with encouragement from the Communist coup in Czechoslovakia. A special agency was established to administer the scheme in Washington—the Economic Cooperation Administration—under Paul Hoffman. To ensure the very closest cooperation between the nations concerned, it was necessary also to create a permanent Organization for European Economic Cooperation (OEEC) in April, 1948, barely two weeks after the passage of the act. The work of OEEC in Paris involved annual discussions on the economic progress of member nations, recommendations to the ECA in Washington on how best to distribute the aid, submission by all members of long-term development plans, and particular concentration on certain specific problems such as manpower, intra-European payments, free trade, and colonial development.

Underlying all these arrangements was the principle that Western Europe would make an all-out effort to restore its own trade and production. The effects of United States aid were manifold: to make good the war losses in food, raw materials, and machinery; to enable Europe's factories, mines, and farms to increase output; and to stimulate a trade revival between OEEC nations. All over the face of Europe new steel plants, oil refineries, and power stations were constructed. For every United States dollar that went into Europe there was, up to 1950, an increase in production worth six or seven dollars. Under the Marshall Plan the United States supplied Europe with $621 million worth of oil products, $607 million of cotton goods, $287 million of machinery, $273 million of coal, $117 million of motor vehicles, $150 million of iron and steel, $185 million of copper, and huge amounts of lead, zinc, aluminum, leather, and other essential materials. Industrial production in Europe rose 30 percent in two years and by 1949 was already a remarkable 15 percent higher than in 1938.

Marshall Aid was planned to end in 1952; but United States foreign aid under other programs has continued to flow ever since, and has remained true to the spirit and magnanimity of Secretary of State George C. Marshall's plan,[3] in his own noble words, directed "not against any country or doctrine but against hunger, poverty, desperation and chaos." Surely no nation and no economy was ever better equipped to fight these evils.

Responsibilities at home: some issues of the 1950's

Though the fifties were an age of abundance generally, the decade did inherit some of the unsolved problems left over from before the war. Twenty or thirty years from now we may be able to understand more clearly what these problems were and how they responded to public policy. From our present too close viewpoint we lack perspective and cannot see the forest for the trees; but it is tempting nevertheless to glance at one or two issues of the decade, those that were linked to previous themes of this book, such as what happened to the American farmer, the exciting new St. Lawrence Seaway, and natural resources, the emerging South, the status of labor, and the concept of the American corporation.

Farming remained a weak economic sector, especially noticeable when the Korean War boom began to peter out and farm prices fell after 1952 in conjunction with a rise in farming costs. Technical change did not relent. Though his real purchasing power and standard of living declined or was barely maintained in the fifties, the American farmer's output went up and up. While agricultural production was an embarrassing failure in most Communist nations, it continued to be an embarrassing success in the United States. Reviving the methods of FDR's "triple-A," the Eisenhower administration introduced the "Soil Bank" Act in May, 1956.[4] Surpluses still piled up, and with the steady decrease in numbers of the farm population it has been suggested that redundant farm land be taken back into the public domain from whence it came. However, no radical change in the United States farm-support program or the surplus question seems likely to occur in the near future.

An allied issue, the constant depletion of natural resources, still received less attention than it deserved. The development of nuclear power did not progress so swiftly as in Britain (where the problem of fuel shortage with the failing of coal supplies was more pressing); but in the 1960's a campaign to purify America's poisoned water supplies and rivers got under way, and a great leap forward was made by the completion of the St. Lawrence Seaway and Power Project.

The project was finally opened in June, 1959, after years of delay. Envisaged at least as long ago as the Canadian–United States treaty of 1932 (rejected by the Senate), the scheme was revived in 1941 and won approval by the act of 1954. A continuous waterway 2,500 miles long, built by cooperative international planning and navigable for oceangoing vessels of deep draft (up to 27 feet) now leads deep into the inland heart of the North American continent. It stretches from the Atlantic Ocean to the pulp and lumber mills, iron-ore docks and grain elevators of Duluth, Minnesota (or, on the Canadian side, to similar facilities at Port Arthur, Ontario). In the United States the Seaway was opposed by time-honored sectional rivalries little different in character from those of the 1840's a century earlier. Eastern coastal ports and cities of transshipment like Buffalo on Lake Erie (whose rise was described earlier) feared that improvement of St. Lawrence navigation could cause their decline; the railroads of the East, which bore, then as now, high operating costs and could afford no extra competition, knew they would suffer severely as oceangoing vessels cut them out of the carrying trade to the midcontinent. What finally "clinched" the great cooperative venture between the two nations was the winning over of the huge United States steel corporations, whose Midwest plants were becoming increasingly dependent on iron-ore supplies from the newly opened Labrador-Quebec mines a couple of thousand miles away to the East. The long-term prosperity of states like Ohio, Indiana, Illinois, and Michigan seemed threatened by a predicted future ore shortage and the need to import huge quantities. For this the Seaway would be essential.[5] Only the later twentieth century will show how far this imaginative and bold plan will fulfill its promise, and what changes it will wreak on the United States market economy.

Another promise for the future lay in the economic transformation of the South. The Industrial Revolution hit the southern states in the 1880's with the migration of the textile industry, the exploitation of the southern Appalachian mineral deposits, and the later migration of the oil industry. As noted, post-Reconstruction Dixie was economically in a quasi-colonial status to the Northeast. The so-called "New South" with its plantation-type, paternalistic textile factories in rural settings, its "Jim Crow" laws, and its revived Bourbon rule, was but slightly further along the road to regional economic growth and equality with the rest of the nation. Extreme income inequalities, lack of social mobility, race discrimination, a consequent duplication of already limited public resources, and an artificial limitation of the potential Negro consumer market (10 or 11 million by 1920) helped to delay the South's emergence. Strong reluctance to invest in public education resulted from the uneven social stratification and economic inequality (since the tax burden could not be widely spread, and the benefits of public education would make little difference to the children of the upper groups). The fate of the Negro was wrapped up in the fate of the South as a section, and a large part of the South's regional misery was agricultural. The New South did not become genuinely "New" until the farm aid and TVA programs initiated by Franklin D. Roosevelt. A distinguished Texan historian, Walter Prescott Webb, has spoken of the "enormous material progress" of the South under the New Deal; many stumbling blocks still refused to dissolve. Lack of capital, lack of what has been called "an unintimidated middle class," and lack of skilled artisans impeded southern industry; tenancy, sharecropping, and the financial domination of the country-merchant class crippled southern agriculture, which failed to free itself from the grip of staple production. The southern "style" and modern industrialism simply did not harmonize.[6]

Alvin Hansen has pointed out that two-thirds of the worst-educated and poorest-paid rural families live in the South today. Yet the catalyst of World War II and rising farm prices did achieve great things south of Mason and Dixon's line, and the boom in that region has not relapsed. As southern authorities involve themselves in social-overhead capital investments like new schools, new airports, and (federally aided) highways, and as large industrial corporations decide to decentralize and build plants in southern cities like Atlanta and Memphis, and as the Negro assumes first-class citizenship and realizes his full productive and consumption potential,[7] the regional economy of Dixie will thrive and the southern states will pull themselves out of one hundred years of poverty and backwardness. If all goes well, the South should be a prime factor of future growth in the history of America's wealth during the years ahead.

The continuing out-migration of Negroes from the South to
northern, midwestern, and Californian cities, together with the in-
cessant flow from country to city all over the nation, brought a shift
in occupational trends and changes in the structure of the United
States labor force. In 1920, for example, 27 percent of the labor
force still worked on farms; by 1960 only 7.1 percent were farmers,
92.9 percent being nonfarm workers. In the total labor force of 1960,
over 22 million women compared with over 48 million men; in 1920
a mere 8 million women workers compared with 33 million men.
Other statistics could be used to illustrate the dramatic expansion
in the number of Americans involved in service, leisure, and "white
collar" jobs and the steady elimination that is taking place of manual
labor and human drudgery.

What happened to the labor movement during these years of
high wages and high mass consumption? In brief, the pressure of
prosperity made the movement even more middle-class and respectable in outlook, and bureaucratic in structure. In 1949 the CIO
purged itself of suspected Communists and expelled both the United
Electrical Workers and Harry Bridges' West-coast longshoremen.
Toward the mid-fifties the AFL and the CIO began to come together
and finally formed a loose affiliation in 1955, the AFL-CIO, which
went on to expel the Teamsters in 1957 after a congressional investigation of union corruption. "Collective bargaining" had by
now become a complex and expensive affair conducted by skilled
specialist lawyers on both sides, who had to interpret an elaborate
body of industrial jurisprudence. With higher living standards all
round, differentials and "fringe benefits" often became more significant than overall wage levels. Encouraged by the brilliant Walter
Reuther, the gigantic labor unions of the 1960's were losing interest
in mere dollar income and seeking wider cultural and "status" goals,
such as greater participation in the sacred realm of management
itself. Already the United Automobile Workers had won a guaranteed annual wage for some classes of worker (1955)—a radical
move toward quasi-professional ("salary" rather than "wage") status.
In truth the United States economy had been so successful in producing money income that other values had risen in relative importance—dollars alone, apparently, have a declining marginal utility.[8]
(What European critics have been wont to call "worship of the
Almighty Dollar" is perhaps a function of poorer rather than richer
societies.)

The labor unions, with their huge financial resources and welfare funds, their investments, and their astronomically priced professional officers had been hit by the "managerial revolution." How had this continuing revolution affected the corporations themselves? First, the long-standing separation between ownership and control became a practical divorce. The large corporation of the postwar world was a wholly professionalized affair managed by career-conscious trained business executives. The evolution from the proprietory business form of early Victorian capitalism was complete. In the later stages of economic development it appears that the need for "captains of industry" declines rapidly with changing technology and mass urban markets. Expensive market research programs designed by college-trained statisticians replace the intuitive "hunches" of a presiding genius. Business management by board and committee replaces the individual entrepreneur, at least in established areas of enterprise; vast corporation research departments replace the Duryeas and Edisons.

Within the intricate hive of corporate management the motives that guide the executive hierarchy could not readily be equated with the familiar and handy "profit maximization" drive of classical economics. Large organizational structures have a momentum of their own, and the qualities that make a good "organization man" are not necessarily those associated with a relentless pursuit of the profit motive.[9] Elsewhere in the economy, however, the profit motive was to be seen more clearly, and several writers have shown that *small* business still thrives and that "competition" (defined in various ways) survives in America. J. K. Galbraith and Adolf Berle, Jr., argue, each in his own style, that size did not destroy competition (Galbraith arguing that the antitrust laws are in fact effective). Despite the apparent immortality of large corporations, some form of competition was to be found. And while mergers continued heavily in the 1940's and 1950's, encouraged by tax laws and capital-gains regulations, the number of small businesses also increased. Professor Cochran has concluded that only a cessation of technical progress can ever eliminate the small business. The Eisenhower administration, which finally abolished Hoover's RFC in 1954, replaced it with the Small Business Administration to encourage small-scale enterprise by offering federal loans. Meanwhile, the large firms seek to perfect a structural form to avoid the bleak impersonality, conformist pressures, and frustration of individual talent allegedly involved in existing corporations. Their task is the harder.

The economy of abundance

The one outstanding characteristic of the fifties, however, was abounding prosperity. The "extension of the market" upon which this boom built itself was the product of renewed population growth (the decisions of countless Americans to have more children and have them earlier in life), large government expenditures for scientific and military purposes, and extraordinarily high family incomes. Greater social depth was given to the consumer market by the expansion of the middle-income-range group in the United States social structure, and by improved marketing techniques.

The editors of *Fortune* magazine have projected a population of 210 million by 1970 supported by a GNP of $750 billion.[10] The official United States population estimate at the opening of 1960 was 179 million; GNP for 1959 was about $480 billion.[11] Over 60 percent of GNP went into consumer goods and services in the late fifties. Total personal consumer income in the United States more than tripled between 1929 and 1959. During the eight years 1950-1958, total personal income increased 58 percent, with very remarkable growth in the South and the Mountain States. Florida's total personal income rose 129 percent, Louisiana 67 percent, Alabama and Texas 64 percent; in the mountains Colorado's personal income expanded 82 percent, New Mexico's 94 percent, Nevada's 118 percent, and Arizona's—the boom state of the fifties—125 percent.

At the close of the war in Europe (1945), 20 percent of all "spending units" (families and unattached individuals) in the United States received under $1,000 a year, and only 3 percent received $7,500 or more. By 1958 the situation was almost reversed: 20 percent received over $7,500 and only 7 percent under $1,000. The average number of people per family in 1959 was 3.42; the *average* income of the American family in 1959 was $6,250.

The demands of the insatiable consumer market supported by this purchasing power were met (and magnified) by the adoption of specialized marketing techniques, stepped-up advertising, and consumer credit. Total advertising expenses of 1959 surpassed $11 billion (under $3 billion in 1945). Most characteristic of the continuing "retail revolution" of the decade was the self-service *supermarket*. Set in the semi-rural "exurbs" near fast highways, or else deep in the suburbs, these large stores handled a wide range of consumer goods from durables to frozen foods and vegetables. The family automobile and the refrigerator-freezer made their growth possible, since the housewife could now buy all her staples for two weeks or more at one time.[12] The established city department stores soon found it necessary to build branches in these exurban shopping complexes, and fears were expressed lest the city centers should die. (In fact, the local "quality" shops seemed to survive—especially in cities like New York and Chicago where a local delivery service and the individual touch means far more than greater range and lower price.) With these changes came a magnification of consumer credit—diners', gasoline, and department-store cards for short-term credit, and bank, mortgage, and personal loans for longer-term real estate, consumer durables, and other purchases. Even vacations could now be paid for by installments. Total outstanding consumer credit rose from under $6 billion to over $52 billion (1945–1959).

These dramatic circumstances make the 1950's seem not unlike the twenties writ large. Yet the *differences* between the two decades mark the distance traveled by American economic institutions in their evolution toward a "responsible capitalism." The idea of federal intervention in and responsibility for the national economy was by the fifties widely respected. In the working machinery of United States economic life, the New and Fair Deals had made structural alterations that changed its character. In addition, the prosperity of the fifties was constructed upon a more democratic, a broader, and therefore a more stable income base—the growing American middle class. Above all, there had been a change in the culture itself; the style of the 1950's was not simply economically aggressive but socially affirmative too, and founded on a population explosion.

The future of America's wealth

The wealth-producing machinery of the American people—"consumer capitalism" we have chosen to call it here—seems unlikely to undergo any drastic political overhaul in the near future. No doubt the influence of government may be extended into areas of public need more readily than in the past—to rationalize public transportation, to reduce expensive medical costs for the needy through social insurance, to eliminate as painlessly as possible submarginal farms, to preserve America's beautiful and rich landed heritage from commercial abuse and pollution, to clear urban slums, and to speed investment in the future through aid to education. No doubt the element of public control may be strengthened where necessary in the fields of fiscal, monetary, wage, and investment policy for fuller employment and economic growth without too much inflation. Government military outlays will not diminish in light of the intransigent foreign situation. Only the outbreak of war (or of peace) threatens to disturb this set of conditions.

Future federal policy therefore appears fairly predictable. But economic evolution will not cease. The impact of unbroken technological change and rising national wealth is somewhat less predictable. How long will population continue to expand? Can the United States improve her rate of economic growth, which has been too low in recent years, to make adequate use of existing human and physical capacity? Will automation bring technological displacement of labor and raise once more the specter of "secular stagnation" through sheer lack of work? Or (what seems more likely) will the working, spending, and leisure patterns of the American populace be accommodated to yet higher, undreamed-of levels?

A twentieth century United States redefinition of "poverty" that would astonish the rest of the world is already in the making. Robert Hunter's study of 1904 already quoted considered an urban income of $460 essential to sustain life at the turn of the century. Leon H. Keyserling, former chairman of the Council of Economic Advisers for President Truman, has directed a report[13] that considers a *family* income of $4,000 or under a year as "poverty"—and goes on to define the lesser ordeal of "deprivation" as a family income of under $6,000.

Few Earthlings are so fortunately "deprived" at the present point in world economic history. But within the framework of American expectations for the future, these levels are not so ludicrous. The threat of massive external military pressure is always constant, of course; but as far as conditions at home are concerned, it seems likely that consumer capitalism will clearly exceed even the hopes of the early sixties, provided the essential social circumstances that have encouraged the growth of America's wealth throughout its history are not subjected to sudden or radical change. Such change could be brought about through internal negligence and a relaxation of political vigilance. For instance, the complacency and conformity that are said to accompany economic abundance might permit a retardation or even, at the worst, a halt of the movement toward greater social equality through civil rights. And many Americans are concerned about the possibility of political extravagance from the Radical Right. In contrast, the Radical Left seems to have been virtually wiped out by modern prosperity and the identification of Communism with Soviet expansion.

If any one "conclusion" may be drawn from a study of the economic history of the United States, it is that America's wealth will not cease to grow so long as the American people preserve the open society that is their finest heritage.

Notes

Chapter One

1. We owe the Principle of Comparative Advantage (or Cost) to David Ricardo. It states that profitable trade can exist between two nations even if the seller cannot produce the article any cheaper than the buyer could, in absolute terms. England might be able to produce grain more cheaply than a colony but might be able to make more profit by producing steel instead. In that case England would produce steel and buy its grain from the colony, and still have profits left over. An absolute productive advantage is not necessary. In the New World the southern colonies had great comparative advantage with regard to agricultural staples—the advantage of bountiful virgin soil—and consequently remained the richest part of the nation for 250 years.

2. One would suppose that with modern American bulldozing and other equipment, in some cases this period of initial hard labor could be considerably reduced. (Simply watch, for ten minutes or so, the construction of a modern federal highway.) The young economy would remain highly labor-intensive, however, for many years. In nations where labor is *not* scarce (so-called "over-populated" areas), it would seem more logical, in fact, to encourage the trend toward labor-intensive production, in order to provide fuller employment and raise consumption levels in the swiftest way.

3. We owe to Ricardo the Principle of Comparative Advantage, and to his master, Adam Smith, the concept that increasing division of labor depends (in his quaint phrase) on "the extent of the market." As we consider further the growth of American wealth, we shall need to enlarge Smith's concept of the "extent" of the market, to include the idea of the *social depth* of the market. But more of this later (Adam Smith, *Wealth of Nations*, 1776; any edition, Bk. I, Chap. 3).

4. Today, for instance, we realize that general practitioners need a certain number of patients to support them and that they must calculate area needs before taking up a medical practice. The number of clients needed will depend on the type of service offered, area health standards, public policy, and general income levels. In the colonial period Boston and Philadelphia could support specialized silversmiths and engravers like the Revere family, along with many other trades and professions denied to rural or village communities. The growth of cities was therefore a key element in the economic emergence of the United States itself.

5. Harvard University Press, Cambridge, Mass., 1956.

6. The Molasses Act of 1733 could have ruined Yankee distillers, but it was more or less evaded.

7. Concluding with scholarly caution on the significance of the West Indies trade, Richard Pares said: "We must be satisfied with the knowledge that more North American shipping was employed in this trade than in any other, that every North American port and nearly every North American merchant had something to do with it" (*op. cit.*, p. 163).

8. The first permanent working of 1646 is still to be seen in the historical reconstruction at Saugus, Massachusetts, completed by the American Iron and Steel Institute. The town of Lynn has claim to a working three years earlier, but is better known for the shoe industry that began there in 1635.

9. The Iron Act of 1750 prohibited the manufacture of iron products by the colonists, beyond the pig-iron stage. There was no way of strictly enforcing this measure. One can only suppose that the colonies continued to have a net import of iron goods because of market conditions.

10. New York University Press, 1950.

11. Tocqueville, in his brilliant and wayward manner, was especially impressed by the public-education provisions of the Massachusetts School Law of 1647, which he thought placed "in the clearest light" the "original character of American civilization."

12. An interesting example of the misunderstanding that arises from the application of European categories to American history is in the use of the phrase "private property." A doctrine mistrusted and despised for decades by European workingmen and liberals, private property deserves its hatred when caste or other barriers limit its benefits to a small minority of pedigreed or well-placed individuals. But private property when widely spread gains wide support. The constant association of "property" with "liberty" in the United States, where this association has had more meaning, has only seemed hypocritical and time-serving to many Europeans, or to the underprivileged masses of Latin America. This is *not* to say that private property has been used wisely or with social justice at all times in the United States. On the contrary, wide opportunity and the impermanence of poverty for any one individual or group can breed callousness and unconcern for the needs of the less fortunate and unprotected in a buoyant society. Irresponsible use of private empires of economic power was to some extent protected by the liberty-property dogma in later Victorian days. Colonial America was not entirely free from this danger either, as progressive-minded historians of the twentieth century, like Charles Beard, were quick to uncover.

13. Jacksonian democracy brought a widened franchise and a greater degree of public education. In this connection it is interesting to remember that the urban worker in Britain received the right to vote in 1867 and the right to elementary public education three years later in 1870. The one follows closely upon the other.

14. Tocqueville had New England chiefly in mind perhaps when he described the genesis "in full size and panoply from the midst of an ancient feudal society" of "a democracy more perfect than any which antiquity had dreamed of." This description would hardly fit the South. In any case, he eulogized New England. "The civilization of New England," he wrote, "has been like a beacon lit upon a hill, which, after it has diffused its warmth around, tinges the distant horizon with its glow."

15. Perhaps one should note that much of the legendary southern way of

life came into being before the Civil War (or was invented afterwards). Colonial farmers had little time for dueling and the charms of European chivalry.

16. The oft-quoted Virginia quitrent roll of 1704 reveals a society of small farmers, two-thirds of whom did not own slaves or use indentured labor. But this is not the myth by which the South lived.

17. Traces of this image of America have persisted in Europe down to the present day. It is ironic that the French regarded the British (of all people) in this way in the seventeenth century; the British have in turn thought the French to be unfit for orderly government ever since the fall of the Bastille; and modern Americans have the same image of their neighbors to the south in Latin America.

18. "Bacon's Castle," the only surviving American example of high-Jacobean architecture, is to be seen today in Surry County. Bacon captured the house during his rebellion. (The building is shown in Oliver Larkin's *Art and Life in America*, rev. ed., 1960, p. 16.)

19. A long historical debate about the nature of the Revolution has been in progress since the 1830's, when the Jacksonian Democrat George Bancroft began his monumental ten-volume *History of the United States*. Bancroft painted a black-and-white picture of royal tyranny and colonial democratic faith. Much has been written after him to change that picture very drastically. But the overwhelming fact remains that Americans decided to cut loose from the historical roots they loved, to reject colonial dependency, and to risk all in a war against one of the world's greatest powers. Nothing short of independence will ever satisfy colonial peoples for long. As early as 1754, in his Albany Congress plan, Ben Franklin himself looked forward to a system of autonomous legislatures, federated within the Empire, joined by allegiance to a common monarch: the root concept of what is now called the British Commonwealth of Nations.

Chapter Two

1. The loss of British imports brought a demand for larger native American production of cloths. This was possible only with an accelerated decline of usufacture and the emergence of merchant employers (or entrepreneurs) to supply the home commercial market. That is, demand was met either through small "manufactories" or through the *putting-out system*: the production of cloth for the market by people working at home, its collection and sale being organized by large merchants.

2. A deeply humane approach to criminal law in America can be traced back to the extraordinary "Body of Liberties" drawn up by the Reverend Nathaniel Ward and adopted by the Massachusetts General Court in 1641. This advanced code prohibited "inhumane, barbarous or cruel" bodily punishments, and its exacting provisions protected the rights of women, children, servants, "forreiners and strangers," and even cattle—"No man shall exercise any Tiranny or Crueltie towards any bruite Creature which are usuallie kept for man's use."

3. Bureau of the Census, *Historical Statistics of the United States* (Washington, D.C., 1960), Series A 45 and 46: There were 3,172,000 white and 757,-000 nonwhite.

4. These figures are rather striking to the modern reader who is aware of the extreme distaste of Americans today for the very word "confiscation," especially when used (in not entirely dissimilar revolutionary circumstances) to describe the policy of some Latin American governments toward foreign corporations. What is more, some Loyalists were lucky to escape with mere loss of property

—others were tarred, feathered, and driven out of town on rails. The facts about such events are hard to evaluate, however (especially the data on migration of Loyalists to Canada).

5. The Act of 1787 created the "Territorial" system: an area with a population of at least 5,000 free male adults could be organized under a federal governor, a legislative council, a house of representatives, and a judiciary staffed by federal judges. Such a "Territory" could enter the Union as a state once its population reached the total of 60,000 free residents. Slavery was banned in the Northwest. In 1790 the Old Southwest was organized in precisely the same way, except that slavery was fully accepted as an institution.

6. Massachusetts minted the "pine-tree shilling" between 1652 and 1684. All kinds of commodity were used as circulating money in colonial times, whenever barter proved to be impossible: tobacco, grain, wampum, skins, cattle.

7. It is too easy to apply the categories "conservative" and "radical" to this situation. The Treaty of 1783 stated that no legal obstacle was to be placed in the way of collecting prewar debts. Is this stipulation truly as "conservative" as it has been called? Is there any more moral justification for the windfall profits gained by debtors through currency depreciation than there is for the profits made by creditors in years of high interest rates and capital shortage? Our sympathy is often with the debtor western farmer; but in truth backwoodsmen sometimes controlled state legislatures, imposed "stay" laws to postpone debt collection and "tender" laws to make land or goods at a fixed price a legal discharge of previous debts. In Rhode Island they forced creditors by law to accept worthless paper as legal repayment of loans given in good faith.

8. The vexatious problem of state issues of paper money was not solved permanently: later, by giving charters to state banks with note-issuing powers, local legislatures once more presented the nation with a currency controversy.

9. Beard permitted himself certain lapses of technique that have been heavily criticized by later writers—notably R. E. Brown and, even more thoroughly and less personally, Forrest McDonald. In justice to the memory of Charles Beard, however, one should read the Preface to his *Economic Interpretation*, his American Historical Association presidency acceptance speech of 1933 ("Written History as an Act of Faith"), and his article of 1935 ("That Noble Dream") defending the position of the economic historian against loose charges of "determinism" and partiality. It has often been unjustifiably assumed that "economic interpretation" is more open to subjective bias than "political interpretation" or "intellectual interpretation."

Chapter Three

1. The situation is admirably explained in Professor D. C. North's *Economic Growth of the United States: 1790–1860* (Prentice-Hall, Inc., Englewood Cliffs, N.J., 1961), to which I am greatly indebted, here and elsewhere.

2. *Observations on the Commerce of the American States* (London, 1783). Sheffield argued that "no treaty can be made with the American States that can be binding on the whole of them." His view was greatly weakened by the later ratification of the federal Constitution.

3. In the Seminole War of 1816–1818, he went on to eliminate the Florida Indians too, and in 1819 the whole of Spanish Florida was ceded to the United States.

4. In the 1780's Britain had purchased over half its cotton imports from the

West Indies, and about one-quarter from Turkey. Only twenty years later the southern states had captured three-fifths of the British market, and that market had increased through continuing application of mechanized spinning and weaving processes in Lancashire.

5. One might justifiably ask, What is an "economy"? The mere existence of international trade between two countries does not usually in itself justify the application of the concept. Presumably, there should be some mobility of the factors of production within the trading area, before it can be called an "economy." Within the Atlantic Economy, especially from the 1840's onward, large-scale labor migration and capital movements did take place.

6. Richard Henry Dana's famous voyage on the square-rigger *Pilgrim* in 1835–1836 had taken 150 days from Boston to Santa Barbara. His *Two Years Before the Mast* (1840), which describes the journey and the way of life of American seamen in the 1830's, is a brilliant social document. Especially revealing to the student of economic life is his additional chapter ("Twenty-four Years After") based on a return trip to California on the "superb steamship" *Golden Gate* in 1859. San Francisco—one adobe house in 1836—was now "a solid city of brick and stone, of nearly 100,000 inhabitants," and its harbor, "the great centre of a world-wide commerce," was crowded with great clipper ships.

7. In 1845 Texas was annexed to the United States, and in 1846 the Oregon Treaty with Britain gave the Pacific Northwest south of the 49th parallel to the United States. Meanwhile, American settlement of the Mexican province of California had increased since the colonization of the San Joaquin Valley in 1843; the discovery of gold at Sutter's sawmill in 1846 brought a gold rush, and the Mexican War conquests of 1846–1848 opened the way clear through to the Pacific.

8. Storekeepers would replenish their stocks by regular visits to a local town. The French traveler Michel Chevalier wrote of this in his famous *Letters on North America* (Paris, 1836): "The country trader who sells a little of everything is sure to find almost anything he wants in Cincinnati. Therefore he goes there before any other place in order to lay in his stock of goods."

9. *Domestic Manners of the Americans* (London, 1832), the famous satirical commentary by Mrs. Frances Trollope (mother of the British novelist Anthony Trollope), owes much to Cincinnati. She sailed for the United States in 1827 to start her department store or "Bazaar," as she called it, in Cincinnati. An outrageous snob but a witty writer, Mrs. Trollope declared: "I am sure I should have liked Cincinnati much better if the people had not dealt so very largely in hogs. . . . our feet, that on leaving the city had expected to press the flowery sod, literally got entangled in pigs' tails and jawbones." But Michel Chevalier defended Cincinnati against her implication that the city was a mere slaughterhouse. "The fact is," he published in 1836, "that Cincinnati is a large and beautiful town, charmingly situated in one of those bends which the Ohio makes. . . . There is not in the whole course of the river a single spot which offers such attractions."

10. At least, this was obvious to Albert Gallatin, the brilliant Secretary of Treasury (1801–1814) under Jefferson and Madison. His justly renowned and penetrating *Report on Roads and Canals* said in 1808 that the chief impediments to American economic growth ("new undertakings") were capital shortage and the land-man ratio ("the extent of territory compared with the population"). His position was quite clear: "The General Government can alone remove these obstacles." He advocated federal aid to road and canal construction through land grants from the public domain, and drew up a detailed $16 million

plan for internal improvements. Gallatin was born in Switzerland, and his references to the European experience suggests he understood that older, more heavily populated nations (like Britain), having already built up at least a minimum social overhead capital (colleges and schools, labor and professional skills, roads, canals, banking institutions, and the like), had much less of a problem than a new, previously colonial country like the United States. Private businessmen alone could hardly be expected to provide for America in a few years the social capital of several centuries' growth in Europe.

Chapter Four

1. The 1950 figure of 51 people per square mile was a stark contrast with Britain's 535 or even with France's 200.

2. Already discussed on p. 25 n. 5.

3. Preemption: the right of any squatter then on the public domain to buy the land he occupied at a minimum price. The Act of 1841 said that any adult male could "pre-empt" 160 acres of surveyed land simply by erecting a "dwelling" and making certain minimum improvements.

4. The American prairies strongly resemble other open grassland areas of the world—the Manchurian plains, Argentina's pampas, the former *puszta* of Hungary and Russia's vast steppe lands that reach from the Ukraine to the interior heart of Kazakstan. (Rather less similar are the savanna-type grasslands of Africa and Australia.) *Prairie*, from the French, means literally "meadowland," and in this chapter refers to the tall grassland of the Central Lowlands, not to be confused with the short grassland farther west between the twenty-inch rainfall line and the Rockies—the Great Plains—once inscribed "the Great American Desert" by mapmakers, but later the seat of the Cattle Kingdom.

5. In most of North America and all of Latin America the earliest domestic horses were Spanish, and even the smaller number of New England horses imported in the early years from Europe came to have Spanish blood intermingled. America's first horses since the Ice Age were brought to Mexico in February, 1519, by Cortés. They were described in detail by the historian Bernal Díaz (*True History of the Conquest of New Spain*, not published until 1632), who was a foot soldier in the campaigns of the conquistadores. Horse lovers will find much enjoyment in Professor G. G. Simpson's excellent paperback, *Horses* (Doubleday Anchor, Garden City, N.Y., 1961).

6. In Massachusetts today, for instance, about three-quarters of the cultivated area is under hay (to support beef and dairy cattle); eggs and poultry account for much of the state's total farm dollar income; cranberries, a perfect example of specialization, are grown in the famous Cape Cod and South Shore bogs (up to two-thirds of the world's output); in the Connecticut Valley, revivified by immigrant Polish farmers, acres of tobacco—a highly-specialized coarser leaf for the outsides of cigars—are cultivated with enormous care under great sheets of cheesecloth; and there are, of course, the maple trees to be tapped to make maple syrup and sugar.

7. The Creek and Cherokee Indians were moved to more western reservations, and Spain was ejected from Florida and Texas.

8. On this whole problem the most recent study is Stanley M. Elkins' *Slavery: A Problem in American Institutional and Intellectual Life* (University of Chi-

cago Press, 1959). Appendix B is an excellent short review of the literature on the economics of slavery.

9. *Hominy grits* consists of maize, coarsely ground and boiled; it is commonly eaten nowadays at breakfast time throughout the South. Another maize dish with a characteristically southern name, in essence a fried ball of cornmeal dough, is called a "hush puppy"—being originally thrown to keep hunting dogs quiet and still their hunger pangs.

10. In 1831 and 1832, when the British antislavery movement was at its height, the Virginia Legislature debated the notion of abolishing slavery but were deterred from doing so by the cost of compensation and transporting the freedmen out of the state. Some individuals freed their own slaves, like John Randolph of Roanoke who released 400 in 1833 at considerable financial loss.

11. We must assume that these figures for kitchen stoves have special philosophical significance in American history, since not a few European thinkers have apparently been profoundly disturbed by the interior temperature of private homes and hotels. Benjamin Franklin's ventilated open stove (invented 1742) was for many years a chief source of comfort in cold weather to all who could afford one. From about 1830 the American stove took a more modern shape, burned coal as well as timber, and could be used both as a cooking range and heater. The open fireplace still used in most British homes today began to vanish from the American scene, and pipes from the stove would carry hot air to upper rooms. More sophisticated forms of central heating—hot-air furnaces and even steam or hot-water radiators—could be enjoyed for a price before the Civil War. The hotel industry took the lead in such comfortable innovations. It seems likely that the average American of the later nineteenth century, with his stove, was about twice as warm as the average Englishman of today with his open coal fire. Is this progress?

Chapter Five

1. The sale and transfer of these marketable shares soon became a specialized profession controlled by stock "brokers" (agents working on a commission basis), organized in "exchange houses." In colonial America business had been small and adequately handled by unspecialized merchants meeting in coffeeshops. This was no way to trade a growing flood of bank stock, corporation shares, and —above all—United States Government securities. Accordingly the businessmen of Philadelphia and of New York each established a "stock exchange" in 1791 and 1792, respectively, agreeing to a fixed commission charge. New York's exchange began to overtake Philadelphia's in volume of trading during the 1820's when New York State placed bonds on the market to pay for its building of the Erie Canal.

2. The loss of federal funds deposited for keeping in state banks had caused Congress to establish the Independent Treasury system in 1840 (repealed by the Whigs in 1841, reestablished by the Democrats in 1846). This system of subtreasuries in various cities (New York, Washington, Boston, Philadelphia, St. Louis, New Orleans, Charleston) made it easier to move funds around the country, and left the government in complete control of its own resources. Together with the National Bank Act of 1863, the Independent Treasury remained the foundation of the United States fiscal system down to the creation of the Federal Reserve structure in 1913.

3. Contemporary writers in 1857 blamed the invention of the telegraph for the spread of the panic, since it enabled bad news to travel fast and made it impossible to localize liquidation. It was invented by Samuel Morse in 1832, followed by the Morse Code, 1838.

4. Though one American argument could have been that given the unique opportunities available, the cobblers had no business striking; if they did not like the trade they should get out. Equality of opportunity does not always breed respect for the grievances of the underprivileged.

5. While the statistics are extremely poor for this period and subject, Hansen's conclusions are supported in a general way by the Federal Reserve Bank of New York's cost-of-living index (1938) and by the findings of other scholars, like J. Kuczinsky (1943) and H. G. Moulton (1949). Compared with Hansen, Kuczinsky's work would indicate *less* of an overall increase in real wages between 1820 and 1860; Moulton's would indicate *more*.

6. The epidemics hit Memphis in 1873, 1878, and 1879, killing 8,000 people, and in the last two years the city was practically closed off from the outside world for months at a stretch. In January, 1879, the Tennessee Legislature repealed the city charter, and since Memphis was bankrupt turned the area into a taxing district governed by a legislative council. (Today a city of half a million, Memphis is the world's largest hardwood lumber market, and its Cotton Exchange handles half the total United States cotton crop.)

7. *American Notes* (1842). Normally hostile, Dickens wrote of Lowell: "I am now going to state three facts, which will startle a large class of readers on this side of the Atlantic [Britain] very much.

"Firstly, there is a joint-stock piano in a great many of the boarding-houses. Secondly, nearly all these young ladies subscribe to circulating libraries. Thirdly, they have got up among themselves a periodical called *The Lowell Offering*, 'a repository of original articles, written exclusively by females actively employed in the mills.'

". . . The large class of English readers, startled by these facts, will exclaim with one voice, 'How very preposterous! . . . These things are above their station.' In reply to that objection, I would beg to ask what their station is.

"It is their station to work. And they *do* work. They labor in these mills, upon an average, twelve hours a day. . . ."

8. It is an obvious conviction of the author that beyond a given stage of economic development a wide distribution of benefits goes hand-in-hand with overall economic growth and that the artificial division of the market into a hierarchy of consumption levels based on social class has been a fundamental block to economic progress in class-conscious nations like Britain and France. The flows set in motion by the European Common Market may wash away many class distinctions within member nations, diversifying and deepening consumer markets.

9. There is even a "conspiratorial" view: namely, that the war could have been avoided but was precipitated by the agitation of ruthless, fanatical minority pressure groups, strategically well placed—Southern "fire-eaters" and Northern abolitionists. An excellent review of these interpretations for the general reader and student alike is David Potter's chapter in *Interpreting and Teaching American History* (31st Yearbook, National Council for the Social Studies, N.E.A., Washington, D.C., 1961).

10. In fact, states' rights was more than a southern stratagem in the sectional struggle for power. The rigid adherence of many Southerners to the principle of localism, and their extreme distrust even of the Confederate gov-

ernment during the war were serious impediments to the South's war effort.

11. Sectional area names include the same states as for the Preemption bill of 1841.

Chapter Six

1. Later the income-tax clauses attached to the Wilson-Gorman Tariff Act of 1894 were invalidated by Supreme Court decision (*Pollock* v. *Farmers' Loan and Trust Company*, 1895), and the Sixteenth Amendment was needed (1913) to establish the right of Congress to tax incomes directly for federal purposes.

2. Runaway inflation drove up prices of all necessities. For instance, salt which had cost about 80 cents a bushel in 1861 cost about 30 Confederate dollars a bushel only a year or so later. In Virginia's capital city of Richmond a local editor demanded, "For God's sake tax us." (Whiskey, after all, was rising to $5 or more a jigger.)

3. These figures, like others used throughout the book, can readily be checked in United States Census publications, as indicated in the bibliography. The peak year of railroad mileage in operation was 1930 (429,883 miles).

4. To be precise, 7,342 miles were constructed and 23,661 miles were abandoned between 1920 and 1940.

5. Meanwhile, in Germany, Karl Benz (1878) and Gottlieb Daimler (1883) had independently built internal-combustion engines for motor vehicles. Selden had applied for his patent as early as 1879; but the automobile was basically a European invention.

6. According to the Census Bureau, the United States possessed only 154,000 miles of surfaced roads in 1904, a total that doubled by the time she plunged into World War I (1917) and doubled again (to 700,000 miles) by 1930. Total mileage, surfaced and "rural," in 1957 was just under 3½ million miles, of which about 2⅓ million miles were classified as surfaced. There were in 1957 about 780,000 miles of federal highways.

7. Phenomenal growth of this sort did not satisfy the demographers. Toward the end of the period and on into the 1920's and 1930's, they argued that the rate of population growth was slowing down (in the United States as in other Western nations) and that as a result the American population was aging. The future held out economic contraction and decay. A hundred years before, especially in Britain, they had been arguing exactly the opposite: that population was increasing too much, quicker, in fact, than food supplies and that the future held out starvation and decay. In both cases the experts were wrong. The "Malthusians" who feared population growth ignored the productivity potential of mechanized labor; the later demographers who feared population contraction miscalculated the long-run effects of rising living standards on the birth rate and family size. The population expert is a professional pessimist, and the (rather ineptly styled) population "explosion" since the 1940's has brought us a crop of neo-Malthusians, scared and stimulated by the specter of dwindling world food supplies. We would be foolish not to listen to them, but unimaginative not to look around for some factor they might have again ignored.

8. One writer claimed early in the century that only "the very rich and the anarchists" favored unrestricted immigration (Robert Hunter, *Poverty*, New York, 1904).

9. Schlitz, for one instance, began advertising "The Beer That Made Milwaukee Famous" in 1898.

10. Massachusetts, and indeed much of New England, is dotted with North-of-England place names.

11. Henry George's *Progress and Poverty* (1879), perhaps the most famous radical book of the century (the central concern of which was to tax landownership out of existence), grew out of his combined experience on the Far West mining frontier in California and as an unemployed printer on the edge of starvation in New York City.

12. The most recent, W. P. Webb of Texas, produced a book in 1952, *The Great Frontier,* which applies Turner's ideas broadly to world history, with Europe as the "Metropolis" and all the areas discovered in the fifteenth, sixteenth, and seventeenth centuries as the "Frontier."

13. Established by Congress in September, 1850, this Territory included the whole of modern Utah and Nevada together with parts of Wyoming and Colorado. Utah State proper was admitted in 1896.

14. In particular the "Chivington Massacre" (November 29, 1864) when 450 Indians, including women and children, were butchered in the early hours of the morning (Sand Creek, Colorado).

15. Cattle were first introduced into southern Texas by the Spaniards in the eighteenth century. The climate and vegetation were so ideal that a great cattle range already existed in the Nueces Valley when Americans first invaded Texas.

16. The White-Jones Act (1928) went on to give better-paid, mail-carrying contracts and offered cheap loans to shipbuilders. The first provision created a public financial scandal and the second was ignored; so Franklin Roosevelt's Merchant Marine Act (1936) established the United States Maritime Commission to administer a comprehensive plan of building and operational subsidies. At this time United States tonnage was 15 percent of the world total; by 1946, after a second global war, it was over 60 percent.

17. One should add that despite the harsh and degrading terms of the Platt Amendment, one excellent result followed from United States Army intervention. In 1900 a great army surgeon, Dr. Walter Reed, was won over to the epoch-making discovery by the Cuban scientist, Dr. Carlos Finlay, that yellow fever was carried by mosquitoes. Experiments with soldier volunteers proved Dr. Finlay's theory conclusively, and the American Army helped to wipe out this dreadful scourge by pouring oil on breeding grounds and draining swampland (1900). Later, another army surgeon, Dr. W. C. Gorgas, eliminated the mosquitoes of Panama.

18. Guam is an island with a very badly balanced economy, its chief importance being as an air-passenger transit station (Pan-American Airways) and naval base. The naval commander acts as governor, and has a Congress that is purely advisory.

Chapter Seven

1. In 1901 the American Can Company emerged as a "100 percent trust," and began to force up can prices; the major rival, Continental Can, broke into the field in 1904. Cans (habitually misnamed "tins" in Britain) are made up of 99 percent steel with the barest coating of tin.

2. People can claim that the distress of the American farmer—described so well in the writings of Wilia Cather, Hamlin Garland, and Ole Rölvaag—would

have been even greater *without* the advent of industrial change. The classic object lesson in the contrasting perils of social immobility is the Latin American model of a highly stratified society dominated by a landed elite, with a persistent pattern of family-unit subsistence peasant farming, starved of entrepreneurial experience or capital, and operating at a low level of technology, health, and human welfare. This knowledge would have been little comfort to the North American farmer, however; many of his ills were unnecessary, and could have been removed.

3. Organization brought hope of greater returns for the urban factory worker than for the farmer, some of whose problems would always remain insoluble. Each harvest was subject to "the hand of God," and no pressure from public opinion or trade unions could stay a duststorm or produce a bountiful crop. (Frank Norris's mixed-up "realist" novel of 1901, *The Octopus*, which tried to investigate the war between California farmers and the railroad corporations, ends on a purely mystical note of homage to "that mighty world-force, that nourisher of nations"—the Wheat.)

4. As we have seen, *Montgomery Ward* survived.

5. Six silver-mining states were admitted to the Union in 1889–1890 under an "Omnibus bill": the Dakotas, Washington, Montana, Idaho, and Wyoming.

6. The manufacturer can create a kind of monopoly market for himself by "product differentiation"—use of brand names, advertising, and artificially created differences. With most bulk farm products such differentiation is impossible; competition is more open between wheat farmers or between cotton planters.

7. Occasionally farmers did attempt to fix output and prices, like the Kentucky tobacco planters of 1907–1908 whose "night riders" pillaged the countryside, burning villages and murdering recalcitrant farmers who were slow to join them. (Depicted in Robert Penn Warren's novel *Night Rider*.)

8. The incremental capital-output ratio (I.C.O.R.) is the relationship between additional units of capital investment and additional units of output resulting. (An important concept for economic growth, especially in capital-scarce nations.)

9. That is to say, as prices fall or consumer incomes rise, few additional supplies of farm products are demanded. According to the nineteenth century statistical investigations of the German scholar Ernst Engel, as incomes rise above the poverty level people eat more and superior-quality food; but beyond a certain income level food demand levels off, and money is spent in other ways. "Engel's Law" spells trouble for farmers when per capita incomes are rising.

10. Quite understandably, the occupational disease of American economic historians is elephantiasis of the epithet.

11. In 1924 Pittsburgh Plus was abandoned in favor of a multiple-basing-point system in which Birmingham was itself made a basing point, along with Chicago and other centers.

12. Apart from the years of World War II, United States copper production seemed to be declining (600,000 tons, 1946); but the nation still maintained its world position, with Chile a poor second (398,000 tons) and Rhodesia a rising third. However, since 1946 American copper output has risen once more and in 1956 (1,104,000 tons) reached its highest point in history. One reason for this success is the use of very large-scale mining operations, giant steam shovels, and new techniques like "flotation" to separate low-yield ores. (The unseparated heavy ores are finely ground and, mixed with oil, are forced to rise to the surface

of a mass of water through which air is driven.) At Bingham, Utah, near the
Great Salt Lake, thirty gigantic terraces have been cut into a steep mountain
face, and low-grade ore reserves are being made to yield up their copper.

13. Alloys are basic metals like steel to which fractional amounts of rarer
substances have been added, or they are combinations of the newer metals
which have emerged since the 1880's in response to growing demands for metals
to withstand enormous heat and stress, and for machine-tool steels. Today's
superalloys use rarer metals like tungsten, molybdenum, chromium, nickel, vanadium, titanium, and manganese. Sheffield, England, pioneered in the alloy steels
—high-speed carbon crucible steels, stainless steel, and so forth. The world's
largest and oldest sawmakers, Spear and Jackson, Ltd., today produce in their
Sheffield factory such wonders as the nickel-chrome strip bandsaw and the
tungsten-carbide tipped circular saw. My own *Story of the Saw* (Manchester,
1961, with E. N. Simons) describes this evolution.

Many different steels are used in the modern automobile—in fact the famous
Model T owed much of its durability to vanadium steel, manufactured under
the supervision of an English technician introduced by Ford for the purpose
(1905–1906). The aircraft and missile industries rest on alloy steels, but the
United States is dependent on foreign sources for several of the strategic metals
involved, especially nickel, chromium, and magnesium. (Vanadium and molybdenum are less scarce; small amounts of the latter are even exported.)

14. Besides the states mentioned, even vaster bituminous strata can be
found in Michigan, southern Indiana, and much of Illinois; in a north-south
belt crossing Iowa, Missouri, Kansas, and Oklahoma; and in the Rockies (Utah,
Colorado, Wyoming, and Montana).

15. In Scotland, James Young had already been experimenting with the
production of shale oil, but it was upon the accessible, richer, and more easily
converted mineral oil that the modern industry was built.

16. *Fractional distillation* depends on the convenient fact that the compo-
nents of petroleum evaporate at different temperature ranges ("fractions") and
can therefore be separated by heating. Distillation itself produces a host of by-
products—asphalt, coke, paraffin wax, lubricating and fuel oils, hydrocarbon
gases (on which countless products depend, especially synthetics and plastics),
naphthas, and various gasolines. *Cracking plants* actually break down the molec-
ular structure of the oil, to create the lighter molecules that compose gasoline
or by "polymerization" (the rearrangement of lighter molecules in chains not
found in nature) to create entirely new physical properties. Chief by-products
of the modern refining process are basic chemicals like glycerol, alcohol, and
ammonia, synthetic rubber and fibers (nylon, dacron, etc.), and the latest plastics with their increasingly familiar polysyllabic names.

17. Standards are relative, of course: the more recent automated factories
represent a still greater advance in the same direction, which seems to be to
make factories more like offices every day.

18. The first successful United States gasoline-engined car, made by the
Duryea brothers (Springfield, Mass.), went on the road in 1893, two years
after the Panhard Company had begun commercial automobile production in
France; in 1896 another Duryea model won European honors by coming in
first in the London-Brighton race.

19. Finally, the spread of installment buying, changes in style and public
taste, and heavy competition from the cheap secondhand car market cut into
Ford sales, and the obstinate millionaire was obliged to take account of the
success of his dominant rivals—GM, Dodge, and the rising Chrysler Corpora-

tion (created in 1925) which acquired Dodge Brothers' holdings in 1928. Quite unprepared by its leader, the Ford Company went out of production altogether for a year before coming up with the Model A.

20. Charlie Chaplin's *Modern Times* (1936) gave a terrifying picture of the modern American, driven insane by hours of endless, brainless, routinized labor at the conveyor belt.

21. Producing for a mass national market, it was essential for the industry to become concentrated, but modern "location theory" does not fit the centralization of automobile production in southeastern Michigan, since the area had no previous reservoir of labor skills, no steel, no glass, no rubber, or other raw-material resources, and little to recommend it except that some of the early automotive entrepreneurs happened to live there, and the Great Lakes provided transportation. As the industry developed, it naturally created its own "external economies": labor migration (much of it foreign) built up Detroit's population, and various servicing industries sprang up in the region to support the automobile. More recently decentralization has occurred: large corporations have located assembling plants in other parts of the country (for instance, the South), in part to avoid delivery costs from Detroit to distant customers.

22. A word recently coined in Britain, "ergonomics," describes the science and art of shaping tools to the hand.

Chapter Eight

1. Simon Kuznets' brilliant statistical research work is a principal source for post–Civil War United States economic development (see Bibliography); an interesting essay by Alfred H. Conrad could provide a useful analytical introduction ("Income Growth and Structural Change," in *American Economic History*, ed. Seymour E. Harris, New York, 1961).

2. Beecher's sermonizing brought him in a presumably adequate salary of $20,000 a year.

3. As for the judicial branch, the Supreme Court was in no mood to relax its "tough" attitude to labor of earlier decades. Rather, encouraged by Justice Stephen J. Field, the Court went on to make strong statements about the government's role in economic life, and began to extend the Fourteenth Amendment to protect corporations from any form of public regulation, claiming them as legal "persons" under the Amendment. In later years the great Justice Oliver Wendell Holmes dissented strongly from this concept. "The Fourteenth Amendment does not enact Mr. Herbert Spencer's *Social Statics*," he declared bluntly in 1905 (*Lochner* v. *New York*).

4. The "Tariff Board" made some investigation into comparative production costs but was suspected by Congress of being a tool to increase presidential power. A Democratic Congress dissolved the board in 1912 by refusing to appropriate its funds.

The corporate income tax was given the ambiguous name of an "excise," because the Supreme Court had previously invalidated a congressional attempt to impose an income tax under the Wilson-Gorman Act. President Taft meanwhile suggested a constitutional amendment empowering Congress to tax incomes directly. This Sixteenth Amendment passed both chambers, many conservatives failing to oppose the bill because they thought it would never be ratified. In February, 1913, it became law.

5. These included state commercial banks, state savings banks, and state

trust companies. State bank notes were driven from circulation by the tax, but the banks remained, and devised other methods of creating credit.

6. The use of checks also expanded in England during the nineteenth century. Although the background to the two cases is very different, in some respects they are similar. In England the trouble arose out of Peel's Bank Charter Act (1844), the provisions of which were also inelastic. In both cases this expansion of "credit currency" for long remained insufficient to meet the needs of crisis periods. Eventually the money "created" by commercial banks through the demand deposit and check system greatly exceeded in importance the use of currency notes within the economy. By the late 1880's the Comptroller estimated that under 10 percent of United States business was transacted in currency.

7. Member banks' reserves are reduced by the amount of the bond sale because the buyer's check, drawn on his own bank, is made payable to a Federal Reserve District Bank. Moreover, the reduction in the reserves deposited at the District Bank by the bond buyer's bank may cause still greater economic contraction, since its reserves are the foundation for its bank deposits. The total reduction in the nation's demand deposits depends upon the average level of required reserves; given an average rate of 20%, the contraction may be 5 times the amount of the bond sale. If the member bank seeks to recoup its reserves by borrowing from the System, the discount rate can be raised to check this maneuver. Thus, when the Federal Reserve sells bonds in the open market the nation's total money supply is likely to fall disproportionately, and the economy is curbed.

8. The $5 and $10 notes in general use by all Americans today are Federal Reserve notes (as a quick glance will reveal). The $1 bills, however, are really silver certificates, though few of us would try to cash them in.

9. A writing-machine patent was taken out in London as early as 1714, but the first marketable typewriter was produced (though not invented) by E. Remington & Sons, gunmakers of Ilion, New York, in 1874. The cash register was invented by James Ritter of Ohio in 1879. A practicable recording adding machine was produced by W. S. Burroughs in 1888. (Calculating devices go back to the abacus, however, the first genuine machine being that of the great French scientist and mystic, Blaise Pascal (1642).

10. The parallel here is with United States military might since World War II.

11. In the same year "General" Jacob Coxey, a Populist from Ohio, led an "army" of unemployed from the Midwest to Washington to petition for federal relief action. He was arrested for walking on the White House lawns, and nothing was done by the administration to help the unemployed.

12. Three which failed to survive were: the Knights of St. Crispin (a shoemakers' organization established in 1867), the Industrial Brotherhood (a loose federation of about thirty national trade unions), and the Sovereigns of Industry (a consumers' cooperative organization established in Massachusetts in 1874 and finally dissolved in 1880).

13. A body set up in 1881 modeled on the British T.U.C., which later became the more famous American Federation of Labor.

14. Of the remaining four, one young man committed suicide in prison in a particularly ghastly, bungling way, and the rest were pardoned by Governor Altgeld in 1893.

15. Employers' associations were formed—such as the Stove Founders' National Defense Association (1886), the National Association of Manufacturers (1895), and the National Metal Trades Association (1899)—to assist members

to fight strikes and unions. For instance, they enlisted strikebreakers and armed private "detectives," hired lawyers to fight court cases, and lobbied Congress to pass bills favorable to their interests.

16. There are several kinds of injunction: mandatory (commanding the performance of a specific act), preventive (a restraining order), interlocutory (to prevent a danger immediately threatened, whilst the court decides the pros and cons), and permanent (the final decree of the court). Labor injunctions were first used in England in 1868, but the decision was criticized and the precedent not followed, though the Trade Disputes Act of 1927 did empower the Attorney General to use the injunction against the application of trade union funds for "illegal" strikes. In the United States, however, the labor injunction took firm root. It was used successfully by federal courts against engineers on strike against the Chicago, Burlington and Quincy Railroad in 1888, and against railway strikers in the early 1890's, and was justified by reference to the Interstate Commerce Act (1887) and, ironically, the Sherman Antitrust Act (1890).

17. Not to mention the British economist William Jevons, the great Italian social scientist Vilfredo Pareto and the Frenchman, Léon Walras.

18. In his principal works, *Theory of the Leisure Class* (1899), *Theory of Business Enterprise* (1904), Veblen appears to the reader as a Voltaire (or rather a Bernard Shaw) of Progressivism. In later years his desire to replace the "price system" with something he thought better, and his idealization of the engineers betrayed a constructive urge that foreshadowed "technocracy." By far the most sensitive essay on Veblen is that of the late C. Wright Mills—an understandable achievement since the two men seem so similar in spirit. (See his brilliant introduction to Veblen's *Theory of the Leisure Class* for a paperback edition, Mentor Books, New York, 1953).

19. Roosevelt's true achievement was in conservation. He took advantage of the Forest Reserve Act of 1891 to speed up the setting aside of timbered areas in the public domain, reserving three times as much as the previous three Presidents put together. (Since 1907 when the act was repealed, additions of forest lands to the public reserve have been by purchase, under the Weeks Act of 1911.) Later, in 1907 and 1908, T.R. established the Inland Waterways Commission to investigate problems of water and river resources and related forest and soil conditions, and the National Conservation Commission, led by his remarkable naturalist friend Gifford Pinchot, America's first official forester; many acres of coal and phosphate lands and water-site areas were reserved from private development in the public domain. Despite Roosevelt's crusade, however, conservation of America's depleting natural wealth failed to keep up with the rate of its exploitation. (One average Sunday edition of a newspaper in the 1920's cost 50 acres of timber.) It took a world slump to bring about the second conservation movement of the New Deal, and a Second World War followed by cold war to dispel from the American mind the dangerous assumption that all exploitation adds to national wealth.

20. By the midcentury the government and courts alike had reversed many former attitudes about giant combinations, and economists were emphasizing the "stabilizing" influence of large corporations on the United States economy because of the long-term nature of their production planning.

21. About 2 million children under the age of 14 were employed in mines, quarries, and factories in the peak year of 1910, many of them in tough and unwholesome jobs.

22. In 1956 life expectancy at birth was about 67 years for men and 73 years for women.

23. Of this, the sum of $9,400 million was loans to the Allies under the four

Liberty Loan Acts (April, 1917–July, 1918) and spent on American goods in the United States.

24. Growth loss to the population (1910–1920) owing to the war has been estimated at over 3 million people (compared with C. W. Wright's calculated loss of 1¼ million owing to the Civil War, already noted). Much of this loss was caused by the abrupt cessation of immigration from Europe in the war years rather than by enemy action.

Chapter Nine

1. Among the rights won by American women must be listed the vote (Nineteenth Amendment, 1920), continuing dress reform (the skirt had reached the knees by 1927), the spread of cosmetics and smoking for women, greater legal influence (the divorce rate had probably doubled since 1900 and over 70 percent of the decrees of 1929 were granted to wives; the rate was fairly steady in the 1920's, its real increase coming in the late 1940's), and the enormous rise of feminine journalism.

2. The cocktail was not invented at this time; it dates back at least to a French drink (*coquetel*) of the early nineteenth century. But the vile quality of much prohibition liquor made the addition of some fruit juice or mixer essential, and the cocktail's great popularity in the United States was certainly built up in the 1920's.

3. Some exceptions were made for refugees after the Second World War. In the 1950's the largest group of immigrants came from Germany (448,000), followed by Canada and Mexico. Italy and Britain came next, with 172,000 and 145,000, respectively.

4. These statistics can be checked in Series A219, F9, F 3-4 of *Historical Statistics of the US* (Census Bureau, Washington, D.C., 1960).

5. The title for this section is in fact taken from Ramsay Muir's modest but shrewd *America the Golden: An Englishman's Notes and Comparisons* (London, 1927), a little book worthy of greater notice.

6. Coming from abroad, Ramsay Muir saw evidence of deeper insecurity: inherited suspicion between labor and capital, dating back to the "Industrial Revolution" of the 1840's, and stodgy conservatism on the part of the employer class many of whom had inherited family businesses. "Perhaps New England and Old England are not wholly dissimilar in this regard," he concluded.

7. In the 1920's, 1½ million farmers abandoned the countryside (*net* loss). During the depressed 1930's the shift to the towns was temporarily reversed as thousands of workless Americans tried to find rural jobs or return to their home farms.

8. Modifications after 1900 had included the Kirkaid Act (1904), the Forest Homestead Act (1906), the Enlarged Homestead Act (1909: allowing half-section homesteads), the Three-Year Homestead Act (1912), and the Stock-Raising Homestead Act (1916). The last allowed whole-section grants to be taken up. After World War I much large-scale homesteading was attempted by wholly inexperienced men (e.g., war veterans) entirely unused to conditions in the semiarid zones. Eventually the New Deal's Taylor Grazing Act (1934) had to reserve 142 million acres in order to preserve natural grass coverage. This land was leased out only under strict regulations.

9. Several large cooperatives became prominent in the 1920's in the wheat, livestock, cotton, and fruit production areas, and in dairying.

10. As Professor Benedict has pointed out, the "socialism" of the league did not extend to farming; the notion was to socialize other businesses but run North Dakota in the interests of farmers.

11. The figures can be examined in *Historical Statistics of the United States,* Series D 47, D 685–690, and E 13.

12. All figures derived from *Historical Statistics of the United States,* Series X 351–354, X 366, and X 373.

13. Among the leading historians, Richard Hofstadter views the patrician Roosevelt as a truly "conservative" man, and sees the New Deal as a kind of holding operation that sought to conserve the essential framework of American capitalism by making as few structural alterations as possible to stress-points within the system. But Hofstadter's overall affirmation of the New Deal is scarcely less than that of Arthur Schlesinger Jr., for whom FDR was a true liberal figure. Frank Freidel's six-volume biography of Roosevelt (of which three are already published) is judicious, temperate, and analytical—wholly in tune with this modern scholarly approach to the thirties.

14. In other nations the masses fared as badly and sometimes worse; but the leading European countries all had considerable unemployment-compensation laws and central poor relief administrations, institutions that had gained decades of experience. In the United States, where relief of poverty was a purely local matter, no state took decisive action until September, 1931, when FDR as governor created the Emergency Relief Administration in New York. In 1932 the Wisconsin Legislature passed the first unemployment-insurance act in United States history.

15. Although in 1936 the Robinson-Patman Act aimed against chain stores tried to check price discrimination and undercutting in the retail trades, and in 1937 the Miller-Tydings Act legalized retail price maintenance in interstate commerce by public agreement between producer and retailer, in a similar attempt to prevent excessive price competition.

16. A Silver Purchase Act was also passed in 1934, after agitation from the silver bloc, which remained influential in Congress. This purely national policy adopted by Roosevelt forced him to wreck the World Economic Conference of 1933 by refusing point-blank to cooperate in any way. (The conference aimed at currency stabilization on the basis of the gold standard and general tariff reductions.)

17. This idea of a bonus is not to be confused with disability compensation, which was on the whole liberal and about which there was little complaint.

18. A board of the same name did in fact already exist, having replaced in June, 1934, the National Labor Board set up in August, 1933. Although the judicial invalidation of the NIRA did not specifically include its labor provisions, it was felt necessary to create a more permanent body under a new act in 1935. The act was accepted by the Supreme Court on April 12, 1937.

19. The Senate Committee on Education and Labor (1936–1940) found that the Republic Steel Corporation was the largest purchaser of tear and sickening gas in the United States. The arsenals of the Republic and the Youngstown Sheet and Tube Co. would equip a small war, and Republic Steel in particular had an army of 400 armed "police."

20. Established by the Wagner-Steagall Housing Act (1937), and not to be confused with the Federal Housing Administration, set up in 1934 (which assimilated the financial work of the Home Owners Loan Corporation).

21. In the international field the New Deal established the Export-Import Bank to regulate American trade, and passed the Trade Agreements Act (May,

1934), amending the highly protectionist Hawley-Smoot Tariff of 1930 by allowing reciprocal trade agreements to be made with foreign nations. Twenty-six agreements were made up to 1941, but their effects on trade are not measurable in a period of such abnormal international conditions.

22. Figures are at current prices and include forestry and fisheries (*Historical Statistics of the United States*, Series F 23).

23. For details see *Historical Statistics of the United States*, Series X 262.

24. *Ibid.*, Series D 46, F 3, and G 191.

25. The editors of the London *Economist* in their well-known treatment (*The New Deal: An Analysis and Appraisal*, New York, Knopf, 1937), characterized Roosevelt's policies as "very moderate Liberalism" put forth in occasionally strong language.

26. As Alvin Hansen points out, the reports of these bodies not only serve to keep congressmen on their toes but have helped to "educate" the American people in the workings of their national economy. Newspapers today abound with the jargon of "economic growth," and the GNP is almost as familiar as the breakfast cereal on television. East-West rivalry and the "emerging" nations also play their part in this growth of economic intelligence.

27. See pp. 142-143 and Chapter Six, Footnote 6.

Chapter Ten

1. One indicator of the growth of wealth in this age of patios and barbecue pits, outboard motors, and swimming pools is available in *Historical Statistics of the United States*, Series H 500—total personal consumer expenditures for recreation. Such outlays rose from $6 billion to $16 billion, 1945–1957. The recreation expenditure of 1957 was four or five times that of the late twenties.

2. From the author's point of view the problem of a closed society is to pry it open; the problem of an open society is the less dramatic but equally difficult task of keeping it open.

3. The UK government now commemorates the Plan with a scheme of "Marshall Scholarships" for United States students to study in Britain. (General Marshall himself was awarded the Nobel Peace Prize in 1953, and died in 1959.)

4. The act gave federal compensation to farmers who reduced their basic farmed acreage allotment. Unfortunately, with the help of fertilization, modern chemical products, and irrigation some farmers managed to maintain their normal output on reduced acreage and receive the federal payment too.

5. As for the Canadians themselves, the rapidly expanding industries of southern Ontario and Quebec were equally in need of Labrador ores, and the nickel, copper, and aluminum industries were desperately short of cheap power (to supplement the costly steam-generated electric plants of Toronto and Windsor), which would be provided by the hydroelectric part of the project. The Seaway area was estimated to be able to produce more energy in relation to installed capacity than any other in the world, because the water flow is dependable and backed by the huge natural storage reservoirs of the Great Lakes.

6. Twelve leading southern intellectuals banded together to defend the so-called "agrarian tradition" and to reject flatly modern industry and economic development in a book of essays, *I'll Take My Stand*, published in 1930. (Now available in a paperback reprint by Harper Torchbooks, New York, 1962.) The group was centered on Vanderbilt University in Nashville, Tennessee. Professor W. H. Nicholls, a Vanderbilt economist of the present day, took quite a differ-

ent view in his spirited presidential address to the Southern Economic Association (November 20, 1959), "Southern Tradition and Regional Economic Progress." Professor Nicholls asked the pointed question: Is the South poor because it is traditional, or traditional because it is poor?

7. The United States population of 1960 (170 million) included about 20 million colored Americans. The median income—and therefore the purchasing power—of nonwhite families was about half that of white families ($5,300 whites; $2,711 nonwhites in 1958). See Bureau of the Census, *Statistical Abstract of 1960, op. cit.*, p. 322). Obviously the United States must take heed of the "underdeveloped areas" within her own borders as well as abroad if she is to maintain her leadership and her capacity, both economic and spiritual, to uphold the parliamentary and democratic way of life.

8. The sociologist George C. Homans is interesting on this question. See *Social Behavior: Its Elementary Forms* (Harcourt, Brace & World, New York, 1961), especially pp. 392–394.

9. See, for instance, Professor T. C. Cochran's *The American Business System* (Harvard University Press, Cambridge, 1957), pp. 180-182, and of course W. H. Whyte's *The Organization Man* (Doubleday, New York, 1957 in the paperback edition; first published in 1956).

10. *America in the Sixties* (Harper Torchbook, New York, 1960).

11. These and following figures are from Bureau of the Census, *Statistical Abstract of the United States, 1960* (81st ed., Washington, D.C., 1960).

12. Some of the largest supermarkets were of the "drive-in" variety, adding considerably to the cult of informality that typified the age of abundance. "Drive-in" service spread from movies and markets to other areas, including laundries and banks. Helicopter shopping has not yet arrived.

13. Conference on Economic Progress, *Poverty and Deprivation in the United States* (Washington, D.C., April, 1962).

Selected Bibliography

A SHORT GUIDE TO THE LITERATURE OF
AMERICAN ECONOMIC LIFE

For the scholars of United States economic development, good bibliographical guides already exist, and it would seem pointless to reproduce here the long lists of books and articles on each of the special areas we have covered. My debt to several scholars is mentioned in the body of the book, and the aim of this very selective list is to help the student who is seeking a basis of background knowledge upon which to build for himself later; as well as to provide for the general reader, and for the nonspecialist who is interested in the economic and social life of the American people, some possible readings of various kinds—economic, narrative, and fictional.

The economics background

Among the available economics textbooks by Paul A. Samuelson, George Bach, Kenneth Boulding, and the rest, I would recommend a reading of *The Social Framework of the American Economy,* by Hicks, Hart, and Ford (2nd edition, Oxford University Press, New York, 1955). This is an Americanized version of a famous British textbook by the Oxford economist J. R. Hicks. Though elementary, its main advantage is that Hicks has emphasized down-to-earth description and explanation of such things as national-income analysis, the process of production and exchange, and the economics of labor and population, rather than plunging the nonspecialist reader into neomarginal theory.

A standard text on developmental economics is that of Benjamin Higgins (University of Texas): *Economic Development* (W. W. Norton and Co., New York, 1959). Walt Whitman Rostow presents his own historical theory of growth in *The Stages of Economic Growth* (Cambridge University Press, New York, 1960; also in paperback), referred to several times in this book for its concept of "Take-off." Bert F. Hoselitz's *Sociological Aspects of Economic Growth* (The Free Press of Glencoe, New York, 1960) is a collection of that author's stimulating and far-ranging articles in the field. Simon Kuznets has given us the benefit of some of his thoughts in several books, including *Economic Change* (W. W. Norton and Co., New York, 1953) and *Six Lectures on Economic Growth* (The Free

Press of Glencoe, New York, 1959). The great classic is Joseph A. Schumpeter's *Theory of Economic Development*, first written in 1911 and now happily available in paperback (as a Galaxy Book of Oxford University Press, New York, 1961). A good introduction to Schumpeter's work is R. V. Clemence and F. S. Doody, *The Schumpeterian System* (Addison-Wesley Publishing Co., Cambridge, Mass., 1950).

The United States Bureau of the Census is a major source for the statistics of United States history, supplemented by the work of private scholars and institutions, particularly by Simon Kuznets and the National Bureau of Economic Research. Kuznets' latest investigations have produced an important book, *Capital in the American Economy: Its Formation and Financing* (Simon Kuznets, assisted by Elizabeth Jenks; National Bureau of Economic Research, Princeton University Press, Princeton, N.J., 1961). The Census Bureau, apart from its annual *Statistical Abstract of the United States*, has produced a historical volume, recently revised as *Historical Statistics of the United States: Colonial Times to 1957* (Washington, D.C., 1960), referred to many times in this book.

The history background

A reliable and lively general history is that by Hofstadter, Aaron, and Miller, *The American Republic* (2 vols., Prentice-Hall, Englewood Cliffs, N.J., 1959). Nine volumes of a general *Economic History of the United States* are already published by Holt, Rinehart and Winston of New York, with individual volumes by C. P. Nettels, Paul W. Gates, G. R. Taylor, Fred A. Shannon, Edward C. Kirkland, Harold U. Faulkner, George Soule, and Broadus Mitchell. Each volume has a detailed bibliography adequate for all normal needs and sufficient to start off the research student. When complete, the ten-volume set will be the standard narrative economic history.

Of the countless single-volume textbooks, Chester W. Wright's *Economic History of the United States* (McGraw-Hill, New York, 1949) is very thorough and solid, although it is beginning to date a little. *The Growth of the American Economy*, edited by Harold F. Williamson (2nd edition, Prentice-Hall, Englewood Cliffs, N.J., 1951), holds its own as the best cooperative single-volume text, despite recent newcomers to the field like Seymour E. Harris, ed., *American Economic History* (McGraw-Hill, New York, 1961).

A well-known and very readable social history, recently revised for paperback publication, is *The Age of Enterprise*, by Thomas C. Cochran and William Miller (Harper Torchbooks, New York, 1961, originally published by The Macmillan Company, 1942). A good collection of readings culled from the specialist journals is *Economic Change in America*, edited by J. T. Lambie and R. V. Clemence (Stackpole Co., Harrisburg, Pa., 1954), and a forthcoming paperback anthology is *The American Eco-*

nomic System: An Anthology of Writings Concerning the American Economy (Liberal Arts Press, Bobbs-Merrill Co., New York, 1963), by Massimo Salvadori.

The novel as source

All novels reveal something of their age; but some novelists have taken a more deliberate interest in economic and social affairs. Occasionally, as with *The Grapes of Wrath*, the social novel is also great literature—a happy combination for the historian. The following list represents a handful of American novels that help to bring to life for the reader certain aspects of United States economic and social history. Some are considered by the literary critics to be major works, and some are not.

Richard Henry Dana, *Two Years Before the Mast* (1840).
Herman Melville, *Moby-Dick* (1851).
Mark Twain, *The Adventures of Huckleberry Finn* (1885) and *Life on the Mississippi* (1883). *The Gilded Age* (1873) gave a title to a whole era of American political and economic life.
William Dean Howells, *The Rise of Silas Lapham* (1885), *A Hazard of New Fortunes* (1889).
Hamlin Garland, *Main-Travelled Roads* (1891).
Stephen Crane, *Maggie: A Girl of the Streets* (1892).
Sarah Orne Jewett, *The Country of the Pointed Firs* (1896).
Theodore Dreiser, *Sister Carrie* (1900).
Frank Norris, *McTeague* (1899), *The Octopus* (1901).
Upton Sinclair, *The Jungle* (1906).
Jack London, *The Iron Heel* (1907), and his many tales of Alaska.
Willa Cather, *O Pioneers!* (1913), *My Antonia* (1918).
Sinclair Lewis, *Main Street* (1920), *Babbitt* (1922).
Ole Rölvaag, *Giants in the Earth* (1927).
F. Scott Fitzgerald, *This Side of Paradise* (1920), *The Great Gatsby* (1925).
John Dos Passos, *Manhattan Transfer* (1925) and the trilogy, *U S A* (1937).
John Steinbeck, *The Grapes of Wrath* (1939).
Robert Penn Warren, *All the King's Men* (1946).

Note: These novels are all to be bought in paperback editions. Two paperbacks on art and architecture are J. T. Flexner's *Pocket History of American Painting* (Pocket Books, New York, 1950), and *American Skyline*, by C. Tunnard and H. H. Reed (Mentor Books, New York, 1956). Though both these books relate their subjects to the social context, they are very brief. The standard work is Oliver Larkin's *Art and Life in America* (rev. ed. Holt, Rinehart and Winston, New York, 1960).

358   SELECTED BIBLIOGRAPHY

A shelf of recent books about modern American capitalism

The 1950's and 1960's have been prolific in the production of critical works on various aspects of American life and society, some more lasting than others. The following is a brief list, again highly selective, that might make up a useful bookshelf. Many of these books are now in paperback.

Thomas C. Cochran, *The American Business System: A Historical Perspective, 1900-1955* (Harvard University Press, 1957; now available in a paperback edition by Harper Torchbooks, New York, 1962).

A. A. Berle, Jr., *The Twentieth Century Capitalist Revolution* (Harcourt, Brace, New York, 1954).

Peter Drucker, *The Concept of the Corporation* (John Day Co., New York, 1946).

Kenneth E. Boulding, *The Organizational Revolution* (Harper & Brothers, New York, 1953).

John Kenneth Galbraith, *American Capitalism* (Houghton Mifflin paperback edition, Cambridge, Mass., 1962 [1952]).

———, *The Affluent Society* (Houghton Mifflin, Cambridge, Mass., 1958).

Sumner H. Slichter, *Economic Growth in the United States* (ed. by John T. Dunlop, Louisiana State University Press, 1961).

Calvin B. Hoover, *The Economy, Liberty and the State* (Twentieth Century Fund, New York, 1959; also available in paperback).

Alvin H. Hansen, *The American Economy* (McGraw-Hill, New York, 1957).

———, *Economic Issues of the 1960's* (McGraw-Hill, New York, 1960).

Vance Packard, *The Hidden Persuaders* (David McKay Co., New York, 1957; also in paperback).

———, *The Status Seekers* (David McKay Co., New York, 1959; also in paperback).

Martin Mayer, *Madison Avenue, U.S.A.* (Harper & Brothers, New York, 1958; paperback, Pocket Books, New York, 1959).

William H. Whyte, Jr., *The Organization Man* (Simon and Schuster, New York, 1956; Anchor paperback by Doubleday, New York, 1957).

C. Wright Mills, *White Collar: The American Middle Classes* (Oxford University Press, New York, 1951; Galaxy paperback, New York, 1956).

———, *The Power Elite* (Oxford University Press, New York, 1956).

President's Commission on National Goals, *Goals For Americans* (Spectrum paperback, Prentice-Hall and The American Assembly, Columbia University, New York, 1960).

Massimo Salvadori, *The Economics of Freedom* (Doubleday, New York, 1959).

The Editors of Fortune, *America in the Sixties: The Economy and the Society* (Harper Torchbooks, New York, 1960).

Index

Dock Strike (1889, in Britain), 242
Dodge automobile, 346 f.
"Dollar diplomacy," 168
"Dollar gap," 322 f.
Domestic Manners of the Americans,
339
Dow, Neal, 110
Drake, Col. Edwin, 196
Dreiser, Theodore, 248
Dress reform, 350
"Drive-in" services, 353
Dry farming, 155 f., 278
Duluth, 189, 326
Duryea Brothers, 142, 346
"Dust Bowl," 305
Dynamo, 197

Economic Cooperation Administration
(ECA), 324 f.
Economic Stabilization, Office of, 312
Economic thought and policy, 86 f.,
246 f., 331 f.
Economist, 352
Edison, Thomas, 197
Education, public, 14, 65, 118, 144,
177 f., 206, 253, 318, 327, 336
Eight-hour day, 234, 253, 259, 298 f.
Eisenhower, Dwight D., 317 f., 325,
329
Elections, 126 f. (1860); 213 f., 225,
232 (1896).
Electrical industry, 191, 197, 220,
275 f., 288
Electrical Workers, United (UEW),
328
Electrolytic process, 193
Elevator, 175, 326
Elkins, Prof. Stanley M., 73, 340 f.
Ely, Prof. R. T., 246 f.
Embargo Act, 36 f., 88
Emergency Banking Act, 295
Emergency Credit Acts, 281
Emergency Fleet Corporation, 162
Emerson, H., 202
Employment Act, 298, 313, 316, 318
Employers' associations, 348 f.
Engel, Ernst, 279, 345
Erdman Act, 241
"Ergonomics," 347
Erie Canal, 41, 125, 228, 341
European Recovery Program, 323 f.

Evans, G. H., 110
Evans, Oliver, 85, 198
"Ever-normal granary," 304
Export-Import Bank, 351 f.
"External economies," 347
"Ex-urbs," 149, 331

Fabian socialism, 186, 246
"Factors of production," 4 f., 33, 59
Fair Deal, 315 f.
Fair Labor Standards Act, 298 f., 317
Farm Bloc, 280 f.
Farm Bureau Federation, 280
Farm Credit Administration, 304
Farm Mortgage Moratorium Act, 305
"Farm problem," 178 f.
Farm Security Administration, 305
Farmer-Labor Party, 280, 282
Farmers' Alliances, 180 f., 279
Farmers' National War Council, 280
Farmers' Nonpartisan Political League,
280 f.
Farmers' Union, 280; in Louisiana, 183
Federal-Aid Highways Acts, 318
Federal Bankruptcy Act, 304 f.
Federal Deposit Insurance Corpora-
tion (FDIC), 285, 295, 308
Federal Farm Board, 281, 291, 304
Federal Farm Mortgage Corporation,
296, 304 f.
Federal Housing Administration
(FHA), 296, 351
Federal Power Commission, 275, 306
Federal Reserve System, 214, 217 f.,
251, 285 f., 295, 310, 316, 341, 348
Federal Trade Commission (FTC),
190, 250, 292, 307
Federal Warehouse Act, 251
Federation of Organized Trades and
Labor Unions, 236
Fencing. *See* Barbed wire
Field, S. D., 142
Field, Justice S. J., 347
Film industry, 149, 157, 266
Finlay, Dr. Carlos, 344
First National Bank of New York, 226
Fisher, Prof. I., 287
Fisheries, U.S. Bureau of, 309
Fishing industry, 8 f., 166
Fitch, J., 54